SEVENTH EDITION

MARKETING
MISTAKES
AND
SUCCESSES

Robert F. Hartley
Cleveland State University

JOHN WILEY & SONS, INC.

New York • Chichester • Weinheim • Brisbane
Singapore • Toronto

ACQUISITIONS EDITOR Ellen Ford
MARKETING MANAGER Karen Allman
PRODUCTION EDITOR Tony VenGraitis
DESIGNER Laura Boucher
ILLUSTRATION COORDINATOR Anna Melhorn
This book was set in Palatino by V & M Graphics and printed and bound by Courier/Westford.
The cover was printed by Phoenix Color.

Recognizing the importance of preserving what has been written, it is a policy of John Wiley & Sons, Inc. to have books of enduring value published in the United States printed on acid-free paper, and we exert our best efforts to that end.

Library of Congress Cataloging in Publication Data

Hartley, Robert F., 1927–
    Marketing mistakes and successes / Robert F. Hartley.— 7th ed.
        p.   cm.
    Rev. ed. of: Marketing mistakes / Robert F. Hartley. 6th ed.
    c 1995.
        Includes bibliographical references.
        ISBN 0–471–15905–0 (pbk. : alk. paper)
        1. Marketing—United States—Case studies.   I. Hartley, Robert
    F., 1927–   Marketing mistakes.   II. Title.
    HF5415.1.H37   1998
    658.8'00973—dc21   97–14092
                                                                        CIP

Printed in the United States of America

10 9 8 7 6 5 4 3 2

Preface

Once again, I would like to welcome back past users of *Marketing Mistakes*. I hope you will find this new edition and format, with its many new and very current cases, a worthwhile change from the earlier editions. It is always difficult to abandon interesting cases that have stimulated student discussions and provided good learning experiences. But newer case possibilities are always competing for inclusion. Examples of good and bad handling of problems and opportunities are always emerging.

For new users, I hope the book will meet your full expectations and be an effective instructional tool. Although case books abound, you and your students may find this somewhat unique, very readable and, hopefully, able to transform dry and rather remote concepts into practical reality, and in so doing, lead to lively class discussions, and even debates.

NEW TO THIS EDITION

In contrast to the early editions, which examined only notable mistakes, and based on your favorable comments about the last edition, I have again included a number of well-known successes. The hypothesis is that as we can learn from mistakes, we can also learn from successes. We especially can learn by comparing the unsuccessful with the successful.

I have again included several cases dealing with the challenges but great satisfaction that can come from entrepreneurship. From polls of my students, interest in entrepreneurship has never been greater.

A number of you have asked that I identify which cases would be most appropriate for the traditional coverage of marketing topics as organized in most marketing texts. With many cases it is not possible to truly compartmentalize the mistake or success strictly according to each topic. The patterns of success or failure tend to be more pervasive. Still, I think you will find the following classification of cases by their subject matter to be helpful. I thank those of you for this and other suggestions.

Table 1   Classification of Cases by Major Marketing Topics

Topics	Most Relevant Cases
Marketing research and consumer analysis	Maytag, Euro Disney, Coca-Cola, McDonald's, Pepsi
Product	Nike, Harley, Borden, Coca-Cola, Euro Disney, Snapple, Microsoft, Southwest Air, Saturn, Parma Pierogies, Boston Beer, Tobacco
Distribution	Food Lion, Sears, Elizabeth Taylor, Coca-Cola, Snapple, Pepsi, Boston Beer, Saturn
Promotion	Nike, Harley, Maytag, Liz Taylor, Snapple, Southwest Air, Saturn, McDonald's, Parma Pierogies, Boston Beer, Met Life
Price	IBM, Borden, Euro Disney, Southwest Air, Saturn, Maytag, McDonald's, Boston Beer
Total Marketing Strategy	Nike, IBM, Sears, Harley, McDonald's, Borden, Euro Disney, Microsoft, Southwest Air, Saturn, Parma Pierogies, Boston Beer, Tobacco
International	Nike, Harley, Maytag, Euro Disney, Pepsi, McDonald's, Tobacco, ADM
Non-Profit/Non-Product	United Way, Euro Disney
Social and Ethical	United Way, Food Lion, Tobacco, Met Life, ADM

TARGETED COURSES

As a supplemental text, this book can be used in a great variety of courses, both undergraduate and graduate, ranging from introduction to marketing to marketing management or strategic marketing. Even retailing, entrepreneurship, and ethics courses could well use a number of these cases and their learning insights.

TEACHING AIDS

As in the previous editions, this edition presents a number of teaching aids within and at the end of each chapter. Some of these will be common to several cases, and illustrate that certain successful and unsuccessful practices tend to cross company lines.

This edition includes even more pedagogical features than previous editions did. Updated Information Boxes and Issue Boxes are included within every chapter to highlight relevant marketing concepts and issues. Learning insights help students see how certain practices—both errors and

successes—are not all that unusual and are prone to be either traps for the
unwary or success modes. Discussion Questions and Hands-On Exercises
encourage and stimulate student involvement. An additional pedagogical
feature of this new edition is the Team Debate Exercises, in which formal
sides and options can be debated regarding various decisions and issues
within the respective cases. Invitation to Research suggestions allow students to take the cases a step further, to investigate what has happened since
the case was written. In the final chapter, the various learning insights are
summarized and classified into general conclusions.

An Instructor's Manual accompanies this text to provide possible
answers and considerations for the pedagogical material within and at the
ends of chapters.

ACKNOWLEDGMENTS

A number of persons have provided encouragement, information, advice,
and constructive criticism. I thank in particular Sanford Jacobs, my colleague
at CSU.

To the many reviewers of previous editions, whose input has been so
valuable in continuing this work, a special thank you for your ongoing comments and suggestions. In particular, I wish to thank the reviewers of this
edition, Peter Schneider, Seton Hall University; Glenna Dod, Wesleyan
College; Paula Saunders, Wright State University; Anthony F. McGann,
University of Wyoming; Curt Dommeyer, California State University/
Northridge for their efforts in guiding the development of the seventh
edition.

Finally, I express my appreciation to Ellen Ford, acquisitions editor at
Wiley, for her kind assistance and support.

I really welcome your suggestions, criticisms, and other comments. In
particular I would like to hear how you have used this book in your classes,
perhaps successes and less-than-successes. Please feel free to contact me.

Robert F. Hartley
James J. Nance College of Business
Administration
Cleveland State University
Cleveland, Ohio 44115

Table of Contents

CHAPTER 1

Introduction

In this seventh edition, we have added eight new cases, with the rest revamped and updated, and in some instances, reclassified. Many of these cases are as recent as today's headlines; some have still not come to complete resolution.

In accordance with your expressed preferences, we have continued the format of the sixth edition by examining not only notable mistakes but also notable successes. We continue to seek what can be learned—insights that are transferable to other firms, other times, and other situations. What key factors brought monumental mistakes for some firms and resounding successes for others? Through such evaluations and studies of contrasts, we may learn to improve the "batting average" in the intriguing, ever-challenging art of decision making.

We will encounter examples of the phenomenon of organizational life cycles, with an organization growing and prospering, then failing (just as humans do), but occasionally resurging. Success rarely lasts forever, but even the most serious mistakes can be (but are not always) overcome.

As in previous editions, a variety of firms, industries, mistakes, and successes are presented. You will be familiar with most of the organizations, although probably not with the details of their situations.

We are always on the alert for particular cases that bring out certain points or caveats in the art of marketing decision making, and that give a balanced view of the spectrum of marketing problems. We have sought to present examples that provide somewhat different learning experiences, where at least some aspect of the mistake or success is unique. Still, we see similar mistakes occurring time and again. The prevalence of some of these mistakes makes us wonder how much decision making has really improved over the decades.

Let us then consider what learning insights we should gain, with the benefit of hindsight, from examining these examples of successful and unsuccessful marketing practices.

LEARNING INSIGHTS

Analyzing Mistakes

In looking at sick companies, or even healthy ones that have experienced difficulties with certain parts of their operations, we are tempted to be unduly critical. It is easy to criticize with the benefit of hindsight. Mistakes are inevitable, given the present state of decision making and the dynamic environment facing organizations.

Mistakes can be categorized as errors of omission and of commission. *Mistakes of omission* are those in which no action was taken and the status quo was contentedly embraced amid a changing environment. Such errors, which often characterize conservative or stodgy management, are not as obvious as the other category of mistakes. They seldom involve tumultuous upheaval; rather, the company's fortunes and competitive position slowly fade, until management at last realizes that mistakes having monumental impact have been allowed to happen. The firm's fortunes often never regain their former luster. But sometimes they do, and this leads us to the intriguing cases described in Part II, Great Turnarounds, which shows how IBM, Sears, and Harley Davidson fought back successfully from adverse positions.

Mistakes of commission are more spectacular. They involve bad decisions, wrong actions taken, misspent or misdirected expansion, and the like. Although the costs of the erosion of competitive position coming from errors of omission are difficult to calculate precisely, the costs of errors of commission are often fully evident. For example, the costs associated with the misdirected efforts of Met Life in fines and restitution totalled nearly a hundred million dollars. With Euro Disney, in 1993 alone the loss was $960 million; it improved in 1994 with only a $366 million loss. With Maytag's overseas Hoover Division, the costs of an incredibly bungled sales promotion were more than $70 million.

Although they may make mistakes, organizations with alert and aggressive management are characterized by certain actions or reactions when reviewing their own problem situations:

1. Looming problems or present mistakes are quickly recognized.
2. The causes of the problem(s) are carefully determined.

3. Alternative corrective actions are evaluated in view of the company's resources and constraints.
4. Corrective action is prompt. Sometimes this requires a ruthless axing of the product, the division, or whatever is at fault.
5. Mistakes provide learning experiences. The same mistakes are not repeated, and future operations are consequently strengthened.

Slowness to recognize emerging problems leads us to think that management is lethargic and incompetent or that controls have not been established to provide prompt feedback at strategic control points. For example, a declining competitive position in one or a few geographical areas should be a red flag to management that something is amiss. To wait months before investigating or taking action may mean a permanent loss of business. Admittedly, signals sometimes get mixed, and complete information may be lacking, but procrastination cannot be easily defended.

Just as problems should be quickly recognized, the causes of these problems—the "why" of the unexpected results—must be determined as quickly as possible. It is premature, and rash, to take action before knowing where the problems really lie. To go back to the previous example, the loss of competitive position in one or a few areas may occur because of circumstances beyond the firm's immediate control, such as an aggressive new competitor who is drastically cutting prices to "buy sales." In such a situation, all competing firms in that area will likely lose market share, and little can be done except to remain as competitive as possible with prices and servicing. However, closer investigation may disclose that the erosion of business is due to unreliable deliveries, poor quality control, uncompetitive prices, or incompetent sales staff.

With the cause(s) of the problem defined, various alternatives for dealing with it should be identified and evaluated. This may require further research, such as obtaining feedback from customers or from field personnel. Finally the decision to correct the situation should be made as objectively and prudently as possible. If drastic action is needed, there usually is little rationale for procrastination. Serious problems do not go away by themselves: They tend to fester and become worse.

Finally, some learning experience should result from the misadventure. A vice president of one successful firm said,

> I try to give my subordinates as much decision-making experience as possible. Perhaps I err on the side of delegating too much. In any case, I expect some mistakes to be made, some decisions that were not for the best. I don't come down too hard usually. This is part of the learning experience. But God help them if they make the same mistake again. There has been no learning experience, and I question their competence for higher executive positions.

Analyzing Successes

Successes deserve as much analysis as mistakes, although admittedly the urgency is less than with an emerging problem that requires remedial action lest it spread.

Any analysis of success should seek answers to at least the following questions:

Why were such actions successful?

Was it because of the nature of the environment, and if so, how?

Was it because of particular research, and if so, how?

Was it because of particular engineering and/or production efforts, and if so, can these be adapted to other aspects of our operations?

Was it because of any particular element of the strategy—such as service, promotional activities, or distribution methods—and if so, how?

Was it because of the specific elements of the strategy meshing well together, and if so, how was this achieved?

Was the situation unique and unlikely to be encountered again?

If not, how can we use these successful techniques in the future or in other operations at present?

ORGANIZATION OF BOOK

In this seventh edition we have modified the classification of cases somewhat from earlier editions by introducing a new Part called Question Marks, which has two cases describing a firm and an industry that may be approaching crossroads, despite decades of growth during which they warded off all threats. We have kept a change introduced in the sixth edition, Great Turnarounds. The learning insights from experiences in which great adversity is finally turned to success seem fertile enough to deserve a position in the book. Another section first introduced in the sixth edition, Entrepreneurial Adventures, is continued with popular support, giving us two intriguing and perhaps inspirational cases. Finally, of course, we can hardly ignore social and ethical concerns in today's environment of closer scrutiny of business practices than ever before.

Again, as in earlier editions, I have chosen to place public image cases in the most prominent position. So often I have found that students as well as executives gloss over the importance of an organization's public image or reputation. Yet, in studying mistakes and successes for almost three decades, I have become more and more convinced that the public perception of an organization and its products or services can play a crucial role in success or failure.

The Power of the Public Image

Three very current cases illustrate the power of public image, either for good or bad. The image of Nike's products and brand logo, through its association with admired athletes, developed by paying millions for endorsements by such big names as Michael Jordan and more recently Tiger Woods, has been a powerful impetus to the success of this footwear and athletic equipment and apparel marketer.

On the other hand, Food Lion was devastated by national publicity from investigative reporters as to its food handling and labor practices. Although such practices as repackaging outdated food were unacceptable, they were not uncommon in this industry. But the media, egged on by a militant union, blew the short-sighted blunder far out of proportion. A growing company was brought to its knees.

In the last case in this part, we have the image problems of United Way of America, a not-for-profit organization. The man who led it to prominence as the nation's largest charity came to perceive himself as virtually beyond authority. His exorbitant spending, favoritism, and conflicts of interest were unchallenged until investigative reporters for the *Washington Post* publicized the scandalous conduct. Amid the hue and cry, charitable contributions nationwide fell drastically.

Great Turnarounds

In the previous edition, I classified IBM as a prime example of a giant firm that had failed to cope with changing technology. Along with almost all other analysts, I thought the behemoth could never rouse itself enough to again be a major player. But we were wrong, and IBM deserves the premier spot in this section.

Sears was another huge bureaucracy that seemed destined for the scrap heap. For well over half a century, it had been the country's largest retailer, only to become supplanted by Kmart and then Wal-Mart in recent years. Sears found itself in danger of losing much more than first place as it struggled to even survive in a rapidly changing industry, harnessed as it was with bureaucratic bloat and outmoded policies. But, somehow, today it is stubbornly coming back, although it will probably never again achieve first place in the industry.

In the early 1960s, Harley Davidson dominated a static motorcycle industry. Suddenly Honda burst on the scene and Harley's market share dropped from 70 percent to 5 percent in only a few years. It took nearly three decades for Harley to revive, but now it has created a mystique for its heavy motorcycles.

Marketing Mistakes

Borden, with its enduring symbol, Elsie the Cow, was the country's largest producer of dairy products. In the 1980s, through a host of acquisitions, it became a diversified food processor and marketer and a $7 billion company. But Borden allowed consumer acceptance of its many brands to deteriorate through unrealistic pricing and ineffective advertising.

The problems of Maytag's Hoover subsidiary in Great Britain almost defy reason and logic. The subsidiary planned a promotional campaign so generous that the company was overwhelmed with takers; it was unable either to supply the products or to grant the prizes. In a marketing miscue of multimillion-dollar consequences, Maytag had to foot the bill while trying to appease irate customers.

In April 1992 just outside Paris, Disney opened its first theme park in Europe. It had high expectations and supreme self-confidence (critics would say this confidence bordered on arrogance). The earlier Disney parks in California, Florida, and, more recently, Japan were all spectacular successes. But the rosy expectations soon became a delusion as a variety of marketing strategy miscues finally showed Disney that Europeans, and particularly the French, were not necessarily carbon copies of visitors elsewhere.

The miscalculation of Coca-Cola in changing the flavor of its traditional and major product shows planning flaws even with the use of extensive evaluation and reveals the limitations of marketing research. Although the situation eventually worked out, embarrassed executives had to make a major improvisation.

The Elizabeth Taylor case focuses on her endorsement of Black Pearls, a new prestige perfume launched by Elizabeth Arden in 1995. Because of Arden's bungled dealings with major department stores, most refused to carry the brand. To her dismay, Liz Taylor found only less glamorous retailers stocking her signature scent.

Snapple, a marketer of noncarbonated fruit-flavored and iced tea drinks, was acquired by Quaker Oats in late 1994 for $1.7 billion. As sales declined and losses mounted, it soon became apparent to all but the president of Quaker that far too much had been paid for this acquisition. No amount of marketing manipulations was able to turn Snapple around. Yet, Gatorade had been similarly acquired for a big price eleven years before, and turned out to be a billion-dollar brand.

The travails of PepsiCo in South America is the last case in this section. In 1994 it began an ambitious assault on the soft-drink market in Brazil, the third-largest soft-drink market in the world. Despite new facilities and a flashy marketing campaign, things went sour. And soon, Pepsi's troubles involved more than Brazil.

Marketing Successes

The first case in this section describes the breakthrough of Microsoft with its software and its continuing innovation and aggressiveness. This spirit propelled it to surpass for a time even the once-mighty IBM in stock market valuation and profits. Bill Gates, its young founder, was the richest man in America by 1992, with a net worth of over $7 billion. At that time he was 36 years old and still a bachelor.

Southwest Air found a strategic window of opportunity as the lowest cost and lowest price carrier between certain cities. And how it milked this opportunity! Now it threatens major airlines in all their domestic routes.

General Motors' Saturn seemed to represent a new tomorrow in U.S. automaking. Relying on a motivated work force, Saturn had been able to produce cars matching Japanese cars in quality, often priced better, and achieved the greatest customer satisfaction ratings of any U.S. car. But profits mostly eluded it to the discontent of GM management, and some union officials remained critical of the progressive labor-management relationship. But the promise is intriguing.

Question Marks

In this section we examine a firm and an industry that may be reaching a crossroads. It may seem surprising to find McDonald's here (and most McDonald's executives would be shocked), but there are some troubling signs on the domestic horizon, despite the exuberance of overseas expansion.

The tobacco industry seems to be constantly under fire. Yet, allied with special political and economic interests it had been able to beat off all attacks. Now its problems are intensifying, as are its critics, while its supporters on Capitol Hill are fading away. Still, the tobacco industry continues to pursue its profit-maximizing strategy and until recently denied all harmful effects of smoking. Rather than assume a defensive stance, tobacco firms aggressively attacked their critics. But recent developments suggest vulnerability.

Entrepreneurial Adventures

This was a new section in the last edition, and the many favorable comments led us to continue it. Certainly, interest in entrepreneurship is growing. My surveys of students' career expectations today show this: for example, whereas 5 percent of students 20 years ago expressed such an interest, 50 percent and more in some classes today claim a strong desire for self-employment.

The first case in this section concerns a young woman who has a natural flair for public relations. She found investors for her Parma Pierogies Polish-style restaurant in a truly ingenious way. Even President Clinton was impressed, became a customer, and extolled her as an example of "Faces of Hope," Americans who have succeeded despite major obstacles.

Boston Beer burst upon the microbrewery scene with Samuel Adams beers, higher priced even than most imports. Notwithstanding that, Boston Beer has become the largest microbrewer, and recently floated its first public stock issue to overwhelming demand. Boston Beer has shown that a small entrepreneur can compete successfully against the giants in the industry, and do this on a national scale.

Ethical and Social Pressures

ADM presents a paradox: It is a highly successful firm, but its success is tarnished by admissions of price fixing, the cronyism of its board of directors, and its aggressive seeking of political favoritism. We address the question of whether the CEO should be permitted to act dictatorially and unilaterally in such matters.

Met Life, the huge insurance firm, whether through loose controls or tacit approval, permitted an agent to use deceptive selling tactics on a grand scale, and enrich himself in the process, of course. When the ax fell from investigations of several state attorneys general, the company was forced to cough up almost a hundred million dollars in fines and restitutions.

GENERAL WRAP-UP

When possible, we have depicted the major personalities involved in these cases. Imagine yourself in their positions, confronting the problems and decisions they faced at their points of crisis or just-recognized opportunities. What would you have done differently and why? We invite you to participate in the discussion questions, the hands-on exercises, and, yes, the debates appearing at the ends of chapters. In addition there are discussion questions in the various boxes within chapters. We urge you to consider the pros and cons of alternative actions in your thoughts and discussions.

In so doing you may gain a feel for the excitement of decision making under conditions of uncertainty and see the great challenge of this. And could it be that you may even become better future executives and decision makers as a result?

QUESTIONS

1. Do you agree that it is impossible for a firm to avoid mistakes? Why or why not?
2. How can a firm speed up its awareness of emerging problems so that it can take responsive action? Be as specific as you can.
3. Large firms tend to err on the side of conservatism and are slower to take corrective action than smaller ones. Why do you suppose this is so?
4. Which do you think is likely to be more costly to a firm, errors of omission or errors of commission? Why?
5. So often we see the successful firm eventually losing its pattern of success. Why cannot success have more durability?

PART I

THE POWER OF THE PUBLIC IMAGE

CHAPTER 2

Nike: Riding High With a Great Image

On August 27, 1996, the sports world was intrigued at what was in store for Tiger Woods, the 20-year-old golfer who had just won his third consecutive U.S. Amateur championship. He decided to begin his professional career and dropped out of Stanford in what would have been his junior year.

His pro-golf career started with a contract with Nike worth $40 million. After the signing he was flown in a Gulfstream IV owned by the founder of Nike, Phil Knight, to play in the Greater Milwaukee Open. All this for a young man who had always flown coach class and had to count his meal money. He had played amateur golf for the last time. Before the year was over he was to win two tournaments and be named by *Sports Illustrated,* "Sportsman of the Year." This was only the beginning, as he won the prestigious Masters on April 13, 1997 by the biggest margin ever achieved, in the most watched golf finale in the history of television.

With what some thought was a commodity product, one that could command little brand uniqueness, and one that many others saw as only a short-term fad phenomenon, Phil Knight has fashioned for Nike a marketing strategy and image that put it in the forefront of growth firms and brought it to become one of the world's great brand names. Among the 1,200 U.S. brands tracked by Young & Rubicam, Nike ranks among the top ten, alongside Coke, Disney and Hallmark.[1] In the process, Knight has become one of the richest Americans, worth $5.3 billion, behind only Bill Gates of Microsoft; Warren Buffett, the investor supreme; and three others.

---

[1]Randall Lane, "You Are What You Wear," *Forbes* (October 14, 1996): 42.

PHIL KNIGHT

The founder of the great Nike running machine was himself only a mediocre runner, a miler of modest accomplishments. His best time was a 4:13, hardly in the same league as the below-4:00 world-class runners. But he had trained under the renowned coach Bill Bowerman at the University of Oregon. In the late 1950s, Bowerman had put Eugene, Oregon, on the map when year after year he turned out world-record-setting long-distance runners.

In the process of completing his MBA at Stanford University, Phil wrote a research paper based on the theory that the Japanese could do for athletic shoes what they were doing for cameras, that is, make a cheaper, better product. After receiving his degree in 1960, Knight went to Japan to seek an American distributorship from the Onitsuka Company for Tiger shoes. Returning home, he took samples of the shoes to Bowerman.

In 1964, Knight and Bowerman went into business. They each put up $500 and formed the Blue Ribbon Shoe Company, sole distributor in the United States for Tiger running shoes. They put the inventory in Knight's father-in-law's basement, and they sold $8,000 worth of these imported shoes that first year. Knight worked by days as a Cooper & Lybrand accountant, while at night and on weekends he peddled these shoes mostly to high school athletic teams.

But Knight and Bowerman worried that Tiger would find a more established distributor, and so they developed their own shoe and the brand name, Nike, after the Greek winged goddess of victory. At the same time

---

INFORMATION BOX

THE NIKE "SWOOSH" LOGO

The Nike "swoosh" is one of the world's best-recognized logos. In the very early days of Nike, a local design student at Portland State University was paid $35 for creating it. The curvy, speedy-looking blur turned out to be highly distinctive and has from then on been placed on all Nike products. Phil Knight even has the swoosh logo tattooed on his left calf. Because it has become so familiar, Nike no longer has to add the name Nike to the logo. (Tiger Woods wears a cap and other clothing with the swoosh logo discretely visible.)

The power of such a well-known logo makes Nike's sponsorship of famous athletes unusually effective as they wear shoes and other products displaying it in their sports exploits.

In your judgment, do you think Nike could have achieved its present success without this unique but simple logo? In other words, how important is a good logo to a firm?

they introduced the "swoosh" logo, described in the preceding information box. The Nike shoe's first appearance in competition came during the 1972 Olympic trials in Eugene, Oregon. Marathon runners persuaded to wear the new shoes placed fourth through seventh, whereas Adidas, the number one running footwear-maker in the world, had wearers finishing first, second, and third in these trials.

On a Sunday morning in 1975, Bowerman began tinkering with his wife's waffle iron and some urethane rubber, and he fashioned a new type of sole, a "waffle" sole whose tiny rubber studs made it more springy than those of other shoes currently on the market. This product improvement— seemingly so simple—gave Knight and Bowerman an initial impetus.

THE INITIAL CHARGE OF NIKE

The new "waffle sole" developed by Bowerman proved popular with runners, and this, along with the favorable market, brought 1976 sales to $14 million, up from $8.3 million the year before, and from only $2 million in 1972.

Nike stayed in the forefront of the industry with its careful research and development of new models. By the end of the decade Nike was employing almost 100 people in the research and development section of the company. Over 140 different models were offered in the product line, some of these the most innovative and technologically advanced on the market. This diversity came from models designed for different foot types, body weights, running speeds, training schedules, sexes, and different levels of skills.

By the late 1970s and early 1980s, demand for Nikes was so great that 60 percent of its 8,000 department store, sporting goods, and shoe store dealers gave advance orders, often waiting six months for delivery. This gave Nike a big advantage in production scheduling and inventory costs. Table 2.1 shows the phenomenal growth of Nike, with sales rising from $14 million in 1976 to $694 million only 6 years later. Table 2.2 shows the market shares in the U.S. market for the beginning of 1979. By then Nike was the market

Table 2.1   Nike Sales Growth, 1976–1981

Year	Sales $ (in millions)	Percent Change from Previous Year
1976	$14	—
1977	29	107
1978	71	145
1979	200	182
1980	370	35
1981	458	70
1982	694	34

Source: Company annual reports.

Table 2.2   U.S. Running-Shoe Market Shares, 1978

	Percentage of Total U.S. Market
Nike	33
Adidas	20
Brooks	11
New Balance	10
Converse	5
Puma	5

Source: Compiled from various published material, including "The Jogging-Shoe Race Heats Up," *Business Week* (April 9, 1979): 125.

leader with 33 percent of the market; within 2 years it had taken an even more commanding lead, with approximately 50 percent of the total market.[2] Adidas's share was falling, well below that of Nike, and it also had U.S. firms such as Brooks and New Balance to worry about.

In 1980 Nike went public, and Knight became an instant multimillionaire, reaching the coveted *Forbes* Richest Four Hundred Americans with a net worth estimated at just under $300 million.[3] Bowerman, at 70, had sold most of his stock earlier and owned only 2 percent of the company, worth a mere $9.5 million.

In the January 4, 1982, edition of *Forbes* in the "Annual Report on American Industry," Nike was rated number one in profitability over the previous 5 years, ahead of all other firms in all other industries.[4]

A LETDOWN AND THEN REJUVENATION

By the latter 1980s, however, Reebok had emerged as Nike's greatest competitor, and threatened its dynasty. A good part of the reason for this was Nike's underestimation of an opportunity. Consequently, it came late into the fast-growing market for shoes worn for the aerobic dancing that was sweeping the country, fueled by best-selling books by Jane Fonda and others. But Reebok was there with the first athletic shoe designed especially for women to use for this exercise. Between 1986 and 1987, Nike's sales dropped 18 percent, with profits sinking over 40 percent.

The recharge of Nike, after letting its guard down to the wildly charging Reebok, was impressive. Usually when a front runner loses momentum, the trend is difficult to reverse. But Phil Knight and Nike were not to be denied.

---

[2]"Joggings' Fade Fails to Push Nike Off Track," *The Wall Street Journal* (March 5, 1981): 25.
[3]"The Richest People in America—The *Forbes* Four Hundred," *Forbes* (Fall 1983): 104.
[4]*Forbes* (January 4, 1982): 246.

Still, even in 1993, Nike did not look very much a winner though it had wrested market dominance from Reebok. From the high 80s in February of that year, share prices plummeted to the mid-50s. The reason? Nike's sales were up only 15 percent and earnings just 11 percent, nothing outstanding for what investors considered a growth stock. So Wall Street began questioning: How many pairs of sneakers does the world need? (Critics had once assailed McDonald's under the same rationale: How many hamburgers can the world eat?)

Knight's response was that the Nike mystique could sell other kinds of goods: outdoor footwear from sandals to hiking boots; apparel lines, such as uniforms, for top-ranked college football and basketball teams—from pants and jerseys to warm-up jackets; even practice gear such as soccer balls. Would not such products associated with athletes be eagerly sought by the general public? Could an athletic shoe company still be a growth company? Apparently so, through wise diversification within the larger athletic goods industry.

In his quest to remain the dominant player, Knight recalled what he learned from his old coach and Nike cofounder, Bill Bowerman: "Play by the rules, but be ferocious."[5]

THE CREATION OF AN IMAGE

Knight had come to the realization that shoes were becoming a disposable consumer good, almost a commodity, with little difference in quality among shoemakers. The challenge for success would come from the ability to transform shoes into status symbols, with a new model for every season. Then if you can combine a fashion image, of being "in" or being "cool," with an aura of entertainment, this can be a powerful appeal to impressionable consumers, especially those under 30.

Now Nike introduces new models for every season, new baseball shoes in the spring, new tennis shoes in the summer, hiking shoes in the fall. Basketball and running shoes are revamped quarterly. Nike, on average, now puts out more than one new shoe style every day.

The natural tie-in of Nike products with entertainment combined with personal accomplishment in sports suggested a new advertising theme, one not geared to promoting shoes, as such, but to what they represented. Knight reasoned that people rooted for a favorite team or courageous athlete, and so Nike would sell not shoes but the athletic ideals of determination, individuality, self-sacrifice, and winning.[6]

---

[5]Fleming Meeks, "Be Ferocious," *Forbes* (August 2, 1993): 41.
[6]Lane, "You Are What You Wear," 44.

Nike had always sponsored athletes, but now it increased that sponsorship by paying $100 million a year to get athletes to use and pitch Nike products. All this started in 1973 when Nike paid star runner Steve Prefontaine to wear Nike shoes. Brilliant, fiercely competitive, and a nonconformist, he had the model athlete persona Knight was seeking. Unfortunately, Prefontaine died in a car crash in 1975. Eventually Michael Jordan took his place in Nike promotions, and the Chicago Bulls star became recognized as the best basketball player in history and perhaps the most popular athlete in the country.

As Nike sought to rejuvenate itself, Knight recruited other top athletes: John McEnroe, then Andre Agassi in tennis; Nolan Ryan in baseball; Deion Sanders in football; Carl Lewis and Alberto Salazar in track; football/baseball star Bo Jackson; as well as such basketball players as Charles Barkley and Scottie Pippen. And now Tiger Woods. Nike headquarters in Beaverton, Oregon, is today a shrine to athletes, with hundreds of bronze plaques and giant banners.

The use of athletes from different sports enables Nike to segment the market, but all under the umbrella of a single brand. The average American teenager now buys ten pairs of athletic shoes a year, six for specific sports, four for fashion; this results in 6 million teenagers buying more than $1 billion worth of Nike shoes.[7]

"You don't win silver, you lose gold," was the theme of Nike TV spots and billboards throughout Atlanta during the summer Olympics in 1996. Rather than being a sponsor firm and paying up to $40 million to the Olympic committee, Nike furthered its visibility by having hundreds of individual athletes and teams endorse the brand by wearing the swoosh on their uniforms and shoes.

Knight is taking the company in three new directions as he seeks to make Nike a $12 billion company by the end of the decade (it was $6.5 billion in the fiscal year ending May 31, 1996). These are women's sports, foreign markets, and Nike Town stores.

Dozens of top women athletes have been signed up and are being promoted with heavy spending. In nonconformist advertising, little girls are depicted imploring their parents to give them a ball instead of a doll.

While Nike has certainly been marketing internationally, its results so far have been far below what might be reasonably expected. For example, in the U.S. the average consumer spends $12 a year on Nike products; in Germany only $2. Now Nike is signing up the best athletes in each country: e.g., baseball player Hideo Nomo in Japan, the Boca Juniors soccer team in Argentina, Germany's Formula 1 race car champion, Michael Schumacher.

---

[7]Lane, "You Are What You Wear," 45.

In 1993, Nike opened a Nike Town superstore in Chicago. Now it ranks with the Navy Pier and the Lincoln Park Zoo as one of the city's top tourist attractions. The seventh Nike Town, a 90,000-square-foot store opened on 57th Street in New York in November 1996. The landlord is Donald Trump and he says the rent for the store is about $10 million a year.[8] Three more Nike Towns are scheduled to open in 1997.

These huge sports stores feature the broad range of Nike products, as Nike has expanded into in-line skates, swimwear, hockey equipment, even sports sunglasses. All kinds of sports apparel is offered, even for toddlers. And of course, there are hundreds of different shoes. Each sport has its own room in the store.

But the stores not only display merchandise but also invite hands-on experiencing, such as basketball courts that allow customers to try out various shoes. The stores are also part sports shrines with odes to Nike athletes as well as featuring their autographed goods. The overwhelming displays and commercials channeled to multiscreen TVs give a subtle (or perhaps not so subtle) commercial touch. Some customers wind up buying three and four pairs of shoes, and other paraphernalia, at a single visit.

Threats to the Image

In the summer of 1996, critical publicity surfaced about a number of U.S. manufacturers, including Nike, operating sweatshops primarily in Asia. Indeed, all Nike's footwear, except the Cole Haan label, is produced primarily in Asia by independent subcontractors according to Nike specifications.

In the onslaught of criticisms, even Kathie Lee Gifford was forced to confess tearfully on her television show that she didn't know that her line of outfits, sold by Wal-Mart, were made by Honduran girls paid 31 cents an hour.

Hundreds of multinational corporations in almost every industry have gone overseas in recent years to reduce manufacturing costs, but footwear and apparel makers now faced the strongest public-relations problems.

Nike became the newest target of Made in the U.S.A. Foundation, an organization funded in part by organized labor with the goal of bringing jobs back home. After failing to get a Gifford-like reaction from Michael Jordan, the premier Nike symbol, Made in U.S.A. shifted attention to Phil Knight.

Such initial negative publicity was further fueled by other prominent exposés: of Asian child labor in *Life* magazine; then by the "Foul Ball" campaign of Labor Secretary Robert Reich who was leading an effort to ban soccer balls, including Nike's, stitched by boys and girls in Pakistan; as well as

---

[8]Lane, "You Are What You Wear," 46.

by efforts of several members of Congress to ban imports of all goods made with child labor. Even the enormously popular Jordan was being criticized for his professing ignorance of the matter by *New York Times* columnist, Ira Berkow.[9] On the night of October 17, 1996, Dan Rather and "Forty-eight Hours" criticized Nike on primetime network TV.

Criticisms of Nike continued into 1997. Activists charged that not only were factory workers in Vietnam paid low wages, but that some were even limited to one trip to the bathroom and two drinks of water per shift, as well as being subjected to verbal abuse, sexual harassment and corporal punishment, such as being forced to stand for long periods in the hot sun. A Nike company executive promised to work to improve working conditions overseas: "Bring us information we can use, and we'll do our damnedest to correct any situations that are wrong."[10]

In early April 1997, another tarnish on Nike's image burst on the scene. Thirty-nine members of the Heaven's Gate cult committed suicide in a California mansion. All were wearing new black Nike's, with the swoosh logo readily visible on TV and pictures in the print media. The "Just Do It" slogan of Nike was trumpeted as being entirely apt, and some even spoofed that Nike's slogan should be changed to "Just Did It."

Countercharge

The criticisms had little impact on sales. Most customers were not upset with working conditions in the Far East. The association of Nike with the sordid cult suicides, while misplaced brand loyalty, attested to the pervasiveness of the logo and the slogan.

Early in April 1997, a presidential task force reached an agreement to banish clothing sweatshops world-wide. The eight-month-old White House task force comprised labor unions, human-rights groups, and such apparel and footwear firms as Nike, Reebok, and Liz Claiborne, with other U.S. companies urged to join the crusade. An independent monitoring association will oversee compliance.[11] This should remove the onus of profiteering at the expense of the underprivileged that critics hung on Nike, although prices may rise somewhat.

[9]As reported in Mark O'Keefe and Jeff Manning, "Firms Find Ways to Share the Guilt," *Cleveland Plain Dealer* (July 28, 1996): 1-I and 3-I.

[10]"Nike Workers in Vietnam Suffer Abuse, Group Says," *The Wall Street Journal* (March 28, 1997) B15.

[11]Wendy Bounds and Hilary Stout, "Sweatshop Pact: Good Fit or Threadbare?" *The Wall Street Journal* (April 10, 1997) A2.

The greatest boost to the image of Nike had to be young Tiger Woods. His winning of the Masters Tournament before a vast worldwide TV audience and, in the process, breaking or tying nine records including those of being the youngest winner and the first minority to win this most prestigious of all golf tournaments, all while wearing the conspicuous swoosh, had focused attention on Nike as perhaps not even Michael Jordan had been able to do. The day after the Masters, ABC News reported that Nike's sales of golf clothing had risen 100 percent since the signing of Tiger.

ANALYSIS

Going back to its beginnings, undoubtedly Nike faced an extraordinarily favorable primary demand in the 1970s. It was positioned to take advantage of this, and indeed most of the running-shoe manufacturers had impressive gains during those years. But Nike's success went far beyond simple coasting with favorable primary demand. Nike outstripped all its competitors, including the heretofore dominant Adidas. Nike was able to overcome whatever mystique such foreign producers as Adidas, Puma, and Tiger had had. And this at a time when foreign brands—for all kinds of products—had an aura of somehow being better, in fashion and quality and dependability, than American brands.

Nike, as it began to reach for its potential, offered an even broader product line than Adidas, the pioneer of the strategy of having many shoe styles. A broad product line can have its problems: It can be overdone and hurt efficiency, create consumer confusion, and greatly add to costs. Most firms are better advised to pare their product lines, to prune their weak products so that adequate attention and resources can be directed to the winners. Here we see the disavowal of such a policy.

Although Nike may have violated some product-mix concepts, we should recognize what it accomplished and at what cost. By offering a great variety of styles, prices, and uses, Nike was able to appeal to all kinds of runners. It was able to convey the image of the most complete running-shoe manufacturer of all. In a rapidly evolving industry in which millions of runners of all kinds and abilities were embracing the idea, such an image became very attractive. Furthermore, in a rapidly expanding market, Nike found that it could tap the widest possible distribution with its breadth of products. It could sell its shoes to conventional retailers, such as department stores and shoe stores, and it could continue to do business with the specialized running-shoe stores. It could even offer some models to discounters since there were certainly enough styles to go around—different models for different types of retail outlets, and everyone could be happy.

Short production runs and many styles generally add to production costs, but in Nike's case this was less of a factor. As we have seen, most of the production was contracted out, with up to 95 percent to foreign, mostly Far East factories. Short production runs were less of an economic deterrent where many foreign plants were contracted for part of the production.

Early on Nike placed a heavy emphasis on research and technological improvement. It sought ever more flexible and lighter weight running shoes that would be protective but would also give the athlete—world-class or slowest amateur—the utmost advantage that technology could provide. Nike's commitment to research and development was evident in its employees working in this area, many of whom held degrees in biomechanics, exercise physiology, engineering, industrial design, chemistry, and related fields. The firm also engaged research committees and advisory boards, including coaches, athletes, athletic trainers, equipment managers, podiatrists, and orthopedists who met periodically to review designs, materials, and concepts for improved athletic shoes. Activities included high-speed photographic analyses of the human body in motion, the use of athletes on force plates and treadmills, wear testing using over 300 athletes in an organized program, and continual testing and study of new and modified shoes and materials. Even back in 1981, the budget was about $4 million, a major commitment to research and development for such an apparently simple thing as a shoe.

Nike at first attempted no major deviation from the accepted marketing strategy norm of the industry. This norm was established several decades earlier by Adidas. It primarily involved testing and development of better running shoes, a broad product line to appeal to all segments of the market, a readily identifiable trademark or logo prominently displayed on all products, and the use of well-known athletes at prestigious athletic events to show off the products in use. Even the contracting out of much of the production to low-cost foreign factories was not unique to Nike. But Nike used these proven techniques far, far better than any of its competitors.

This was particularly true in the development of its public image. The great identification of Nike with athleticism, "Just Do It," and its association with the greatest names in sports, maximized the appeal of Nike products. Particularly with a younger customer segment, such identification of its name, logo, and products with those athletes who were most looked up to and emulated had to be powerfully effective.

Diversifying to non-shoe products, while still staying in the athletic realm, was a natural evolution for growth. It permitted a positive and effective transference of image. And such expanding of the basic product idea opened great growth possibilities.

The Ethics Controversy of Using Foreign Child Labor

Was Nike—and other U.S. manufacturers as well—guilty of violating accepted moral and ethical standards in farming out production to foreign subcontractors in Third World countries using child labor at very low wages? The critics would maintain this violates corporate ethics with American companies exploiting underpaid workers to maximize profits back home. But while long hours in a smelly shoe or garment factory may be less than idyllic, others would suggest it was preferable to subsistence farming or laboring in even harsher workplaces.

Knight is convinced that Nike is a force for positive change in Asia: ".... good corporations are the ones that lead these countries out of poverty. When we started in Japan, factory labor there was making $4 a day, which is basically what is being paid in Indonesia and being so strongly criticized today. Nobody today is saying, `The poor old Japanese.' We watched it happen all over again in Taiwan and Korea, and now it's going on in Southeast Asia."[12]

Many of the 120,000 Indonesian workers who produce Nike shoes come from impoverished rural backgrounds. These factories provide a chance not only to earn but to save money and to send the extra cash back to families. The workers are daughters of rural farmers, village schoolteachers and shop clerks. They live together in factory towns, a dozen to a dormitory room, sleeping on bunk beds. Would they be better off without these jobs? Would some of them be homeless or have to turn to prostitution otherwise? Indeed, should we try to impose our value system on other peoples and other nations?

WHAT CAN BE LEARNED?

The right image can bring great psychological product differentiation. Granted that the technological differences in running shoes have narrowed so that any tangible advantages of a brand are practically imperceptible, what makes Nike stand out? Of course it is the image and the "swoosh" that identifies the brand. For something like running shoes and athletic equipment and apparel, the visibility of products in athletic and normal use readily stands out. For many youth, the sight of famous and admired athletes actively using this brand is an irresistible lure, and brings the desire to emulate them even in only that they use the same brand . . . and maybe to dream a little. This is known as reference group influence, and is described in the following information box.

---

[12]"Nike's Indonesian Operations Facing Scrutiny and Criticism," *Cleveland Plain Dealer* (August 27, 1996): 10.

INFORMATION BOX

REFERENCE GROUP INFLUENCE

Reference groups are those individuals and groups with whom an individual identifies. These become a standard or point of reference for forming one's lifestyle and aspirations. Such groups can be ones that a person would like to belong to but does not. They can be ones to which a person does belong to. Regardless of whether aspirational or membership, these groups influence product and brand purchases, and even store patronage, under certain circumstances. Nike with its sponsoring of famous athletes provided a very potent reference group for many of its customers, people they admired and would like to emulate. And with their peers also wearing Nike products, the buying influence was doubly strong.

Two things are necessary for a product or brand to be susceptible to reference group influence. First, the product must be visible so that other people can see it being worn or used. And second, the product must be conspicuous, that is, it must stand out and not be so common that practically everybody has it. Of course, the Nike logo provides both visibility and conspicuousness, and the identification with athletes is unmistakable.

Would you expect a car to be susceptible to reference group influence? A brand of beer? A TV set? Why or why not?

Nike has fostered this image of celebrity users more than any other firm. With its financial resources it can afford the enormous sponsorships and publicity demanded by the best of these celebrities.

Now then, for many people—especially youth—the popularity of the brand becomes a further attraction. Wearing Nike products is seen as being "cool," belonging to the "in" crowd.

How long is this attraction to athletes and athletics likely to last? To the end of time? Or will the ever increasing huge compensations demanded by professional athletes and the selfishness and arrogance of some eventually sour the general public, who after all support sports through attendance and products both?

Is Nike's success in building its image transferable to other firms whose products cannot be identified with use by the famous? Do such firms have any possibilities for developing image-enhancing qualities for their brands? They certainly do.

Nike's use of reference group influence represents one way to use image to great advantage. But there are other approaches that can be very effective. Consider the long-advertised lonesome Maytag repairman. Maytag has been highly successful in building a reputation, an image, for dependability and assured quality. In so doing it has been able to sustain a higher price advantage over its competitors. For many firms, an image carefully nurtured of good quality, dependability, reliable service, being in the forefront of technology or fashion can bring the firm great success in its particular industry.

No one is immune from mistakes; success does not guarantee continued success. Many executives delude themselves into thinking success begets continued success. It is not so! No firm, market leader or otherwise, can afford to rest on its laurels, to disregard a changing environment and aggressive but smaller competitors. In the mid-1970s, Adidas had as commanding a lead in its industry as IBM once had in computers. But it was overtaken and surpassed by Nike, a rank newcomer, and a domestic firm with few resources in an era when foreign brands (of beer, watches, cars, electronics, and cameras, for example) had a mystique and attraction for affluent Americans that few domestic brands could achieve. But Adidas let down its guard at a critical point. A decade later, Nike then lagged before the aggressive Reebok because of its underestimation or unawareness of the growing interest in aerobic dancing.

It is possible to regain market leadership. We examine this learning insight in more detail in Part II, Great Turnarounds. For now, it is worth pondering how Adidas could never regain its lost leadership, while Nike was able to do so with gusto. Examples abound of firms that once faltering could never regain their former luster: Kmart, for example, is unlikely ever to regain its lead lost to Wal-Mart; nor are Sears and IBM likely to again be the dominant forces in their industries, even though they have made remarkable comebacks. There are few examples of firms that have been able to bounce back as Nike has done. But they are there, and the possibility remains for others.

Growth can be maintained in a saturated industry. Apparently Nike has been able to do this, to continue and even increase its growth trend, while facing the reality of how many running shoes can a market absorb year after year and still be a growth industry. Nike has done this by expanding its horizons from running shoes to all kinds of athletic and outdoor footwear, to athletic apparel and uniforms, to women's and children's wear. A greater penetration of international markets offers opportunity, as well as the Nike Town superstores.

This is a unique growth plan for Nike; it would not work for every firm. The key element, however, is that diversification into related areas complementing the already strong image of a firm have a higher probability of successful growth. On the other hand, diversification that has little relationship to the strengths and image of the firm are far more questionable, and often unwise. We will see examples of unwise diversifications—in the quest for growth—in other cases to come, particularly Maytag and Borden. Often such unwise diversifications come in buyouts in which an unreasonable price is paid along with overreliance on the management resources of the acquired firm. In Nike's case, the diversifications came internally.

Beware of blemishes on the public image; some may not be serious, but others may truly be. The criticisms surfacing in the summer of 1996 and even into 1997 about the labor practices in Third World factories seemingly had little impact on Nike's fortunes or its image. Partly this was due to Nike being only one of many firms who subcontract production to foreign factories. It also reflected that the typical Nike customer was hardly concerned with underpaid foreign workers who probably would be worse off without Nike's business, and was more interested in getting the best value for his or her money.

However, such attacks on a firm's reputation or public image usually bring far worse consequences. As we will see in the next several cases, such attacks can often be devastating.

CONSIDER

Can you think of any other insights coming from this case that have transferability to other firms and other situations?

QUESTIONS

1. "The success of Nike was strictly fortuitous and had little to do with great decision making." Evaluate this statement.
2. In recent years Nike has moved strongly to develop markets for running shoes in the Far East, particularly in China. Discuss how Nike might go about stimulating such underdeveloped markets.
3. Do you think the athletic goods industry is still a growth industry? Or does it have more limited potential? Give your opinions and rationale.
4. "A great image is very transitory. It can go anytime." Evaluate this statement.
5. Do you really think Nike can continue to be a growth stock, or is the end in sight?
6. Can celebrity advertising be overdone? How would you attempt to ascertain whether you are getting your money's worth from paying some athlete millions to wear your products?

7. Should Nike be concerned that some ghetto youths have such an attachment to the Nike image that they will strongarm and even kill to get an Air Jordan shoe, for example? If so, how can Nike combat this overzealousness?
8. Donald Trump has claimed that Nike is paying $10 million in rent for its Manhattan store on his premises. Do you think Nike made a mistake with this? Why or why not?

HANDS-ON EXERCISES

1. Phil Knight has charged you with developing a marketing plan to more fully tap the female market for shoes and athletic equipment. Be as specific as you can in your recommendations and defend them as well as you can.

TEAM DEBATE EXERCISES

1. Debate the issue of endorsements of athletes. How much is too much? Where do we draw the line? Should we go only for the few famous? Or should we gamble on lesser stars eventually making it big and offer them long-term contracts? Argue the two sides of the issue: aggressive and conservative.
2. Debate the contentious issue of Nike's use of overseas sweatshop labor in its production.

INVITATION TO RESEARCH

Is the popularity of running and jogging waning today? Has the "sweatshop" issue died out or has it become stronger and more compelling? Are the Nike superstores achieving the success expected?

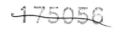

CHAPTER 3

Food Lion: Bad Publicity Throttles Success

For 10 years, Food Lion, a regional supermarket giant, had seen its sales and profits steadily rise. It had a 10-year compounded growth rate of 22.5 percent. From 1983 to 1992 sales had risen from $1.172 billion to $7.196 billion. Net income had risen from $27.718 million to $178.005 million during this time. Such performance had made Food Lion the nation's fastest growing supermarket chain. Its customer appeal rested on everyday low prices.

On the night of November 5, 1992, however, an event occurred that was to seriously affect sales for the peak months of November and December and subdue the total 1992 figures. The impact of negative publicity was both immediate and profound. It was to sabotage the growth momentum of the company and test the mettle of Tom E. Smith, president and CEO.

NOVEMBER 5, 1992

On the evening of November 5, 1992, before a nationwide audience, the ABC television news program "Primetime Live" severely and graphically criticized Food Lion's sanitation and food-handling procedures in its meat and deli departments. ABC backed up the charges with hidden camera videotape of employees forced to cut corners on food safety and sanitation by the company's stringent demands for operational results. Spoiled and outdated food was shown being repackaged for sale to unsuspecting customers. Overnight, Food Lion's public image was devastated. See the following information box for a discussion of public image.

INFORMATION BOX

WHAT IS THE PUBLIC IMAGE?

The public image of an organization is its reputation, how it and its output (products, services, or both) are viewed by its various publics: customers, suppliers, employees, stockholders, financial institutions, the communities in which it dwells, and the various governments, both local and federal. And to these groups must be added the press, which is influenced by the subject's reputation and cannot always be relied upon to deliver objective and unbiased reporting.

Two other terms, *publicity* and *public relations,* are related to public image development. Publicity is communication about the firm, sometimes but not always initiated by the firm, which is disseminated by the media without charge and with little or no control by the firm. Public relations involves a broad set of planned communications about the company, including publicity releases designed to promote goodwill and a favorable image.

Publicity, then, is part of public relations when it is initiated by the firm. When it comes about through no planned efforts of the firm, it is often adverse and detrimental, as was the "Primetime Live" exposé. Such revealing of misdeeds, real or alleged, enhances audience appeal. Because public relations involves communications with stockholders, financial analysts, government officials, and other noncustomer groups, it is usually placed outside the marketing function, perhaps as a staff department or as the responsibility of an outside consultant who reports to top management.

What do you think is the effectiveness of advertising in enhancing the public image?

Immediately after the program aired, Tom Smith, Food Lion's president, called it "lies" and "fabrication." He blamed the United Food and Commercial Workers Union (UFCW) for originating the idea and working closely with ABC in developing the charges. The enmity of the union toward Food Lion was well known. The union had failed in its efforts to organize Food Lion employees and allegedly was committed to "economically damaging the company." As Smith charged in the company's annual report,

> By its own admission, the UFCW plans to continue its "corporate campaign," which is designed to eliminate the competitive pressure Food Lion has caused unionized chains because of their inefficiencies and additional costs. The stakes are high for the UFCW. It is our belief that the UFCW will go to great lengths to harass, pressure and cause trouble for the Company so that it can accomplish its stated objective of economically damaging the Company.[1]

---

[1] Tom E. Smith, "Letter to Shareholders," *Food Lion 1993 Annual Report,* 3.

LABOR DEPARTMENT PROBLEMS

The UFCW had been instrumental in initiating a 1991 Labor Department investigation, contending that Food Lion had saved $65 million each year by not paying employees' overtime. In its subsequent investigation, the U.S. Department of Labor charged the chain with both widespread overtime violations and child labor law violations. The charges were first aired in a Congressional hearing in September 1992.

In early August 1993, Food Lion agreed to pay a record $16.2 million to settle the charges, this being the largest settlement ever reached with a private employer over federal wage and hour violations. Tom Smith said the settlement allowed Food Lion to avoid spending "considerable resources and years in litigation," thus allowing the chain to "turn a page" and move forward. Food Lion admitted no wrongdoing in this agreement.[2]

The union was not pleased. Al Zack, assistant director for organizing, claimed the settlement fell far short of compensating workers for lost wages: "You still have the problem of . . . management physically and verbally abusing workers who ask for overtime. A supervisor will say, 'If you can't do your job, then I have 10 people out on the street who will.'"[3]

THE COMPANY

Food Lion operates a chain of retail food supermarkets in 14 states, principally in the southeast states. As of January 2, 1993, it operated 1,012 stores, with 353 located in North Carolina, 98 in South Carolina, 196 in Virginia, 69 in Tennessee, 50 in Georgia, 110 in Florida, 14 in Maryland, 6 in Delaware, 12 in Kentucky, 8 in West Virginia, 3 in Pennsylvania, 70 in Texas, 18 in Oklahoma, and 5 in Louisiana.

Ralph Ketner, together with his brother Brown Ketner and Wilson Smith, founded Food Lion in 1957. In 1967, when it had only seven stores, Food Lion lowered 3,000 items' prices. In an interview with the Salisbury, North Carolina *Post*, Ralph Ketner took credit for introducing everyday low pricing, forward buying, and centralized buying to the food industry.[4]

The company has grown vigorously. Table 3.1 shows the growth in sales for the 10 years from 1983 to 1993. Table 3.2 gives the growth in net income, and Table 3.3 shows the growth in number of stores opened during this period.

[2] Joanne Ramey, "Food Lion to Pay Record Labor Settlement Sum," *Supermarket News* (August 9, 1993): 1.

[3] Ramey, "Food Lion to Pay Record Labor Settlement Sum," 2.

[4] "Disputes Prompt Ketner to Quit Food Lion Board," *Supermarket News* (May 3, 1993): 6.

Table 3.1   Food Lion's Sales Growth, 1983–1992

	Sales (000)	*Percent Change*
1983	$1,172,459	—
1984	1,469,564	25.3%
1985	1,865,632	30.0
1986	2,406,582	29.0
1987	2,953,807	22.7
1988	3,815,426	29.2
1989	4,717,066	23.6
1990	5,584,410	18.4
1991	6,438,507	15.3
1992	7,195,923	11.8

Source: Company public records.
Commentary: The company showed a strong growth pattern during these years, but the sales in later years were increasing at a decreasing rate. This, of course, reflects the difficulty of maintaining the same growth rate as a firm becomes larger.

CONSEQUENCES

In October 1992, before the "Primetime Live" broadcast, same-store sales were 1 percent higher than October 1991 sales. But for November, after broadcast, sales plummeted to 9.5 percent below the previous November's sales. Sales were slow in coming back, showing the lasting impact of the bad publicity: For the entire fourth quarter of 1992, same-store sales were down 4.6 percent compared with 1991 sales. They fell to a negative 6 percent below previous year's sales in the first quarter of 1993, climbed

Table 3.2   Food Lion's Net Income Growth, 1983–1992

	Net Income (000)	*Percent Change*
1983	$ 27,718	—
1984	37,305	34.6%
1985	47,585	27.6
1986	61,823	30.0
1987	85,802	38.8
1988	112,541	31.2
1989	139,775	24.2
1990	172,571	23.5
1991	205,171	18.9
1992	178,005	(13.2)

Source: Company public records.
Commentary: Note the decline in net income in 1992, reflecting the November 5 broadcast.

Table 3.3   Food Lion's Growth in Number of Stores, 1983–1992

	Number of Stores Opened	Total Number of Stores	Percentage Increase
1983	44	226	
1984	25	251	11.1%
1985	66	317	26.3
1986	71	388	22.4
1987	87	475	22.4
1988	92	567	19.4
1989	96	663	16.9
1990	115	778	17.3
1991	103	881	13.2
1992	131	1,012	14.9

Source: Company public records.

to a negative 4.8 percent in the second quarter, and moved up to a negative 4 percent by the third quarter. Earnings for the first three quarters of 1993 fell 48.7 percent, although overall sales rose 5.8 percent owing to new store openings. Food Lion's stock slipped from $18 to $6 per share between early 1992 and early 1994. Experts were quick to cast a pall over the company:

> "Food Lion won't ever go back to being the kind of growth company it once was. Like an automobile that goes in for an overhaul, it will never be the same again."
>
> "The company suffered a mass exodus of customers at the end of 1992, and it's working to rebuild things gradually. But there's been a permanent crack in Food Lion's fundamentals."
>
> "Food Lion customers have always been very loyal, but maybe some of them tried an alternative and in some cases didn't come back."[5]

The consequences of the damaged public image of Food Lion thus were more enduring than might have been expected. Part of the reason for this may have been the union. The UFCW continued its unrelenting efforts to undermine nonunion Food Lion. It refused to let the "PrimeTime Live" story die: Food Lion officials claimed it mailed more than a million brochures to consumers to remind them of the exposé.[6] And early in 1994, a labor-backed consumer coalition, of which the UFCW was a member, accused Food Lion of repeatedly selling outdated infant formula in violation of state and federal

---

[5] Elliot Zwiebach, "Food Lion Struggles Back," *Supermarket News* (November 8, 1993).
[6] James Ketelsen, "Lionized No More," *Forbes* (January 17, 1994): 16.

regulations. The group presented its findings to the Food and Drug Administration, which planned an investigation.[7]

See the following box for a general discussion of the importance of the public image.

Food Lion reluctantly found it prudent to tone down its expansion plans. In mid-1991, before the broadcast, the company, in its role of America's fastest growing supermarket chain, had planned to open 145 to 150 stores in 1993 and as many as 165 in 1994. It continued some of its expansion after the crisis, primarily because of real estate commitments made prior to the broadcast, but the company now expected to open only about 100 new stores in 1993 and possibly 40 to 50 in 1994.[8] It was going ahead with plans to complete 60 to 70 renovations in 1994 as a partial substitute for new store openings.

In May 1993 Ralph W. Ketner, one of the founders of Food Lion, resigned from the company's board. In an interview with the Salisbury, North Carolina, *Post*, Ketner said he was "in disagreement with too many decisions of the management and board." In particular, he disagreed with the company's reaction to the "PrimeTime" broadcast. In addition, he cited his disagreement with management's growth philosophy. He thought Food Lion should have "enlarged the circle" of existing stores rather than jumping over several states to expand, as the chain did in moving into Texas.[9]

DEFENSE OF FOOD LION

The company bitterly condemned the actions of ABC's "PrimeTime Live" in its attack. It filed a lawsuit charging that ABC had illegally entered Food Lion facilities and had broadcast a knowingly biased report using unreliable sources. Food Lion vice president Vince Watkins claimed ABC had chosen not to use evidence it had gathered disproving some of its allegations regarding the meat-handling practices and employee management. The company was able to obtain the complete unedited videotape, which had been taken surreptitiously by ABC's undercover reporters during the investigation. "If you look at all the raw videotape, ABC could very well have put together a show showing what a fine company Food Lion is," said Watkins.[10]

Watkins also objected that Food Lion was the only company investigated, maintaining that a more thorough look at food safety in supermarkets

---

[7] Frank Swoboda, "Food Lion Accused of Selling Outdated Infant Formula," *The Wall Street Journal* (February 4, 1994): B5.

[8] Mark Tosh, "Expansion Plans Cut Back by Food Lion," *Supermarket News* (August 9, 1993): 34.

[9] Reported in "Disputes Prompt Ketner to Quit Food Lion Board," *Supermarket News* (May 3, 1993): 6.

[10] Michael Garry, "The Lion Talks," *Progressive Grocer* (June 1993): 19.

INFORMATION BOX

IMPORTANCE OF THE PUBLIC IMAGE

A firm's public image plays a vital role in the attractiveness of the firm and its products. In some situations it is impossible to satisfy all the diverse publics: for example, a new, highly automated plant may meet the approval of creditors and stockholders, but it will undoubtedly find resistance from employees who see jobs threatened. On the other hand, high-quality products and service standards should bring almost complete approval and pride of association—given that operating costs are competitive—while shoddy products and false claims would be widely decried.

A firm's public image, if it is good, should be cherished and protected. It is a valuable asset built up from a long and satisfying relationship with the various publics. If a firm has developed a quality image, this image is not easily countered or imitated by competitors. Such an image may enable a firm to charge higher prices, to woo the best distributors and dealers, to attract the best employees, and to expect the most favorable creditor relationships and the lowest borrowing costs. It should enable a firm's stock to command a higher price-to-earnings ratio than other firms in the same industry that lack such a good reputation and public image. All these factors can give a competitive advantage.

Of course, as we see from the Food Lion example, a bad image hurts a firm with all the different publics with which it deals. All can turn critical and even litigious, depending on the source and extent of the bad image. At best, present and potential customers may simply seek alternative sources for goods and services and switch to competitors' products whenever possible.

How long would you estimate it normally should take for a damaged public image, such as Food Lion's, to be forgotten by the interested publics? What factors might influence this length of time?

---

would have included other companies. The company adamantly maintained a major union connection in the ABC exposé:

> We believe that UFCW officials approached ABC to do a show on Food Lion, supplied ABC with the names of disgruntled former and current employees of the Company to assist in creating a story, provided ABC's undercover reporters with phony references in order to gain employment with the Company, and even provided training to the undercover reporters. "PrimeTime Live" chose to ignore independent evidence, such as state health inspection reports and, instead, chose to rely upon the information and assistance of the UFCW—an organization with the stated purpose of economically damaging the Company.[11]

[11]The President's Message to Stockholders," *Food Lion 1993 Annual Report*, 3.

RECOVERY EFFORTS

The damage to the public image of Food Lion, as evidenced by the diminished sales of existing stores, naturally was of great concern to company executives, who sought to counter the damage and bolster the image. In the days following the broadcast, Food Lion gave store tours to shoppers, media, and members of Congress. In a rather unique attempt to allay customer concerns, it put windows in new stores so that shoppers could see inside the meat-cutting room; in renovated stores, it installed glass doors. The company changed its policy regarding the sale of meat after its expiration date. In the past, if the meat was still good, it remained on sale for one day at a reduced price. The new policy mandated that nothing could be sold after the expiration date, at any price. And management made a major commitment to clean and renovate all the stores, improve lighting, and buy new uniforms for employees.

In perhaps the most significant action, Food Lion hired Webb Technical Group of Raleigh, North Carolina, as consultants to thoroughly investigate Food Lion products and implement a quality control program. "We're going to inspect at every point, including when we get [products] from the manufacturer. We could have done a better job in the past, when it was inspected at random."[12]

The company also aired TV commercials emphasizing its efforts to improve quality control and citing the hiring of outside consultants to ensure quality. In a major departure from its strict everyday-low-pricing policy, it began offering hot promotional specials and double coupons in some markets. These efforts, in addition to the legal efforts, were, not surprisingly, a drain on profits as Food Lion committed time, money, and resources to counteract the accusations. Some analysts saw such efforts as mere window dressing, creating an illusion of better service, but others saw these as positive steps.

The United Food and Commercial Workers Union was quick to criticize Food Lion efforts: "Consumer wariness about Food Lion's denials prompted the hiring of consultants to fix a problem Food Lion said didn't exist. Shoppers shouldn't have to accept conclusions about nonexistent problems made by handpicked, paid consultants who now appear in Food Lion's paid television ads." It called for Food Lion to submit the findings of a 100-store safety survey of the Webb consultants to an independent panel of public health experts: "A review by public health experts, whose credentials and credibility speak louder than any commercial, would assure the public that this is not another public relations gimmick."[13]

---

[12] As reported in "Food Lion Hires Consulting Firm," *Supermarket News* (Oct. 18, 1993): 16.

[13] "Independent Experts Should Review Safety Survey Conducted by Food Lion's Consultants, UFCW Says," *PR Newswire* (Nov. 4, 1993): 1104.

Other Problems

Not all of Food Lion's problems could be attributed directly to the TV exposé or to UFCW machinations. Some of the company's expansion efforts had been less than noteworthy. The stores in Texas and, to a lesser degree, Florida remained significant problem areas. Although the Food Lion marketing strategy had been strong in the southeast, customers were not so quick to embrace low prices and minimum amenities elsewhere. In its marginal markets of Texas and Florida, the impact of the TV report may have been greater because the company had not been able to build up a loyal customer base. Winn-Dixie in particular posed a strong challenge. It offered prices similar to Food Lion's, but in addition it had newer, larger stores with more service departments and other amenities. With the handicap of a wounded public image and the presence of a strong and aggressive competitor in some markets, the wavering comeback of Food Lion was perhaps not surprising.

ANALYSIS

We have in this case a dilemma of sorts. Who should carry the burden of blame: Food Lion, ABC and "PrimeTime Live," the union? Was Food Lion truly guilty of the charges of blatantly and unethically cutting corners on food safety and sanitation as well as abusive employment practices? Or was it the innocent victim of a vengeful union and a TV network interested only in sensationalizing alleged wrongdoings with no desire to uncover facts that might not match the charges? Most likely, all three parties were culpable. Whether Food Lion's guilt was related to carelessness or deliberate company policy may never be fully known. Perhaps Food Lion's fault was one of corporate insistence on profit goals that in turn led to less-than-desirable conduct by some employees.

What we do know is that an attack on a firm's reputation or public image is not to be taken lightly. It can have immediate repercussions on sales and profitability. It can waylay a growth trend of years. And the damage to the public image may be enduring. Especially is this likely when aggressive competitors are given the opportunity to gain market share they could not easily have gained otherwise; this loss of market share may never be recovered.

Could Food Lion have done a better job of trying to recover its reputation? Perhaps. The founder of the company and chairman emeritus, Ralph Ketner, apparently thought more could have been done and resigned from the board in disagreement. Yet the company seemed aggressive in trying to recover and to assure consumers that problems were not widespread and that strong efforts were being made to ensure no further repetition. These efforts, however, produced no immediate positive results. The following box shows the various factors that contribute to the public image mix, as well as the outputs or consequences of such a public image.

INFORMATION BOX

THE PUBLIC IMAGE MIX

Figure 3.1 shows the major inputs in creating an image, as well as the outputs or consequences of the resulting image on the various publics. Notice that some of the factors are both inputs and outputs—employees, for example. Employees can help foster a negative or a positive image, but they are also affected by their firm's image, with better employees attracted only to the firm with a good reputation. And price can be both an input and an output, in the sense that a favorable image may enable a firm to charge higher prices than a less regarded competitor, one without the reputation for quality and service.

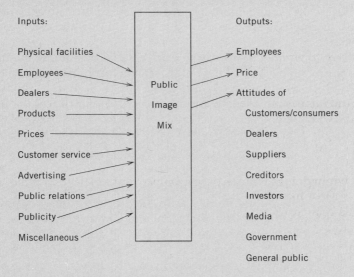

Figure 3.1. Major inputs and outputs of the public image mix.

The very negative publicity of "PrimeTime Live" of course also involved products and employees and raised concerns about health. Perhaps more damaging was the raising of doubts about the company as a responsible citizen. Could the company be trusted not to shortchange its publics in other ways? Was Food Lion's primary motivation to "[take] the bottom line as [its] guiding beacon and the low road as [its] route"?[14]

You can see that most of the inputs or factors that affect the public image are controllable to a considerable extent. A firm can determine its facilities, products,

---

[14]This is a quote of a federal judge concerning another firm and another product, the Dalkon Shield: Miles W. Lord, "A Plea for Corporate Conscience," as reprinted in *Harpers* (June 1984): 13–14.

advertising, customer service, and prices relative to competing products and can develop public relation and publicity efforts to favorably affect the image. But the firm can hardly escape blame for poor customer service, poor quality control, or the bad publicity about product safety or pollution or employee abuses. In such serious matters, public relations efforts may do little to salvage the image.

Given the bad publicity about Food Lion, do you think any public relations efforts could have erased the problem? Why or why not?

Perhaps the company was guilty of overemphasizing its growth commitment. Increasing the number of stores—adding close to 10 percent every year—dilutes top management attention from existing stores and operations; most attention has to be devoted to the planning and establishment of the new stores.

We have to wonder at the extreme adversarial position of the union. Its attempts at unionizing Food Lion failed, but such animosity seems extreme. Maybe Food Lion could have handled the situation more diplomatically, possibly more fairly, and not incurred such enmity, which was to come back to haunt the company.

UPDATE

By 1996, it would seem that Food Lion had recovered from the November 5, 1992, scarring of its public image. True, the growth rate of opening new stores had slowed far below the 10 percent annual rate achieved before 1992, but still the firm had continued to grow to 1,073 stores by the end of 1995, from 1,012 three years before. Sales had climbed steadily each year, as shown below, but the percent change from year to year was far less than previously achieved, as can be seen in comparing with Table 3.1:

Year	Sales (000,000)	Percent Change
1992	$7,196	11.8%
1993	7,610	5.8
1994	7,933	4.2
1995	8,211	3.5

In a November -December issue of the prestigious *Harvard Business Review*, Norman Augustine, president of Lockheed Martin Corporation, extolled the efforts of Food Lion in resolving the crisis the company had faced. He praised the quickness to act, "offering public tours of stores, putting large windows in meat-preparation areas, improving lighting, putting workers in new uniforms, expanding employee training, and offering large discounts to draw customers back into stores.[15]

Despite such heroic efforts and praise, the acid test of the public devastation of an image still showed enduring effects—on profitability. As the following statistics show, Food Lion has not yet regained the profitability it had achieved before the episode.

Year	Net Income (000,000)
1990	$173
1991	205
1992	178
1993	4
1994	153
1995	172

(*Source:* Company annual reports)

Does this suggest the enduring stigma of a bad reputation?

In breaking news in late December 1996, a significant court victory for Food Lion was announced. A federal jury ruled that ABC and members of its news staff committed fraud and trespassing in sending reporters to go undercover as Food Lion employees for the "PrimeTime Live" expose.

Food Lion had contended that the 1992 broadcast report was false, and that this cost it $1.7 billion to $2.5 billion in lost sales and stock value. But it chose not to fight the network with a conventional suit alleging libel; instead it attacked ABC on the legality of its news-gathering techniques. While the judge ruled that it could not recover damages for lost business, it could seek punitive damages, to be determined later.

This ruling is expected to seriously jeopardize undercover reporting, a practice that has spread with the rise of tabloid TV shows such as "Hard Copy," network newsmagazines and local newspapers eager for high-profile stories. ABC's "PrimeTime Live" had been one of the most prolific producers of such investigations.[16]

[15] Norman R. Augustine, "Managing the Crisis You Tried to Prevent," *Harvard Business Review* (November–December 1995): 156.

[16] Estes Thompson, "Jury Says ABC Committed Fraud," *Cleveland Plain Dealer*, December 21, 1996, p. 8-A; and Elizabeth Jensen, "ABC News Is Dealt Another Legal Blow," *The Wall Street Journal* (December 23, 1996): B2.

WHAT CAN BE LEARNED?

The Food Lion experience should be sobering for many firms. It should raise some real concerns about the possibility of damage to the public image, damage that can be difficult to rebuild. Specifically, these are major points to be learned from this experience:

The vulnerability of the public image. A reputable image, or at least one that is neutral and not negative, can be quickly besmirched. A firm should not underestimate the danger of a looseness in the operation and a willingness to tread the thin line between scrupulously honest dealings and something less so. It must be wary of sacrificing a good reputation as it walks the edge in the quest for more profits. Once the public image has been denigrated, it is not easily or quickly recovered.

The power of a hostile media. In its quest for newsworthy items, the media—print, broadcast or both—is quick to pounce on alleged instances of misdeeds, especially by well-known organizations. No firm can anticipate that the media will be objective and unbiased in its reporting. Rather, the media tends to be eager to find a "fault object," and when this is a large and rather impersonal target, such as a firm, the media will likely emphasize the negatives of a particular situation far more than any positive side of the issue. And, as Food Lion found, the media may even ignore information supportive of the firm in seeking sensational and inflammatory news.

The longevity of a besmirched reputation. One would think that negative publicity would soon be forgotten in an environment in which critical disclosures are more the rule than the exception. Perhaps this may be the case in many scenarios. But when another party—in the case of Food Lion, a militant and unforgiving union denied acceptance by the company's employees—continually seeks to keep the allegations of misdeeds in the limelight, disclosure of misdeeds may not be allowed to sleep.

Public relations deficiencies. Public relations is not the answer when certain aspects of a firm's operation are the focal point of criticism. The act must be cleaned up first, but even then, public relations efforts may be negatively labeled as mere "posturing." Tom Smith tried to correct the situation and introduce highly visible measures to ensure compliance with highly ethical standards, but the critics were not appeased.

The power of a militant and hostile union. The UFCW union played a major role in initiating the bad publicity and in maintaining it. A hostile union allied with an eager media is a dangerous combination for any organization. It is easy for an organization to say that it will never leave itself vulnerable to critical public scrutiny; but probers intent on uncovering misconduct may still find something to trumpet. It is better to avoid severe confrontations with any group—be it unions, environmentalists, social activists, or another group—by either bowing to some of the demands or seeking a compromise solution.

The potential of marketing efforts to affect the public image. Marketing inputs have the greatest potential for affecting the public image, positively or negatively. A firm's marketing efforts are the most visible aspects of the operation. This visibility can be a curse sometimes, as it was with Food Lion, when marketing efforts regarding product quality and packaging were compromised in some instances in the quest for higher profits. The caveat is to consider marketing efforts part of the public image mix, one of the aspects of the operation most vulnerable to critical scrutiny, and to be guided accordingly.

CONSIDER

Do you see any other learning insights coming from this case?

QUESTIONS

1. "Good customer service doesn't do you much good, but poor customer service can kill you." Evaluate this statement.
2. Can a firm guarantee complete product safety and sanitation?
3. Give some specific examples of how a firm's public image both affects and is affected by the other components of the marketing mix (i.e., products, price, promotion, and place).
4. Discuss the pros and cons of placing the public relations function under the control of the marketing department.
5. Do you think Food Lion was unfairly picked on? Why or why not?
6. Given the exceedingly adversarial stance of the UFCW, would you recommend that Food Lion's top managers try to do anything to lessen it? If so, what? How successful do you think such efforts would likely be?
7. How could the public relations efforts of Food Lion have been used more effectively?

HANDS-ON EXERCISES

1. Several years have gone by since the negative "PrimeTime Live" broadcast, and same-store sales have still not achieved their pre-broadcast levels. CEO Tom Smith has asked you to design a program to restore the public image. What specifics can you suggest? How successful do you think such remedial efforts could be?

2. Sales and profits of the 70 stores in Texas are still far below expectations and are a drain on the rest of the company. The board has asked you for your recommendations about the Texas situation. Present your recommendations as persuasively as you can. (If you need to make some assumptions, keep them reasonable and specific.)

TEAM DEBATE EXERCISES

1. Debate whether a firm believing its conduct to be reasonable according to industry standards should bow to a hostile press or labor union, or should it steadfastly maintain its innocence of any wrongdoing.

INVITATION TO RESEARCH

What is Food Lion's current situation? Has it been able to resume its growth pattern in sales and profits? Has it still been able to escape unionization?

CHAPTER 4

United Way: A Not-for-Profit Destroys Its Image

The United Way, the preeminent charitable organization in the United States, celebrated its 100-year anniversary in 1987. It had evolved from local community chests, and its strategy for fund raising had proven highly effective: funding local charities through payroll deductions. The good it did seemed unassailable.

Abruptly in 1992, the image that United Way had created was jolted by revelations from investigative reporters of free spending and other questionable deeds of its greatest builder and president, William Aramony. A major point of public concern was Aramony's salary and uncontrolled perks in a lifestyle that seemed inappropriate for the head of a charitable organization that depended mostly on contributions from working people.

We are left to question the callousness and lack of concern with the public image of such a major charitable and not-for-profit entity. After all, unlike business firms that offer products or services to potential customers, charitable organizations depend on contributions that people give freely out of a desire to help society, with no tangible personal benefits. An image of high integrity and honest dealings without any semblance of corruption or privilege would seem essential for such organizations.

THE STATURE AND ACCOMPLISHMENTS OF THE UNITED WAY

For its 100-year anniversary, then President Ronald Reagan summed up what the United Way stood for:

December 10, 1986

United Way Centennial, 1887–1987
By The President Of The United States Of America
A Proclamation

Since earliest times, we Americans have joined together to help each other and to strengthen our communities. Our deep-roots spirit of caring, of neighbor helping neighbor, has become an American trademark—and an American way of life. Over the years, our generous and inventive people have created an ingenious network of voluntary organizations to help give help where help is needed.

United Way gives that help very well indeed, and truly exemplifies our spirit of voluntarism. United Way has been a helping force in America right from the first community-wide fund-raising campaign in Denver, Colorado, in 1887. Today, more than 2,200 local United Ways across the land raise funds for more than 37,000 voluntary groups that assist millions of people.

The United Way of caring allows volunteers from all walks of life to effectively meet critical needs and solve community problems. At the centennial of the founding of this indispensable voluntary group, it is most fitting that we Americans recognize and commend all the good United Way has done and continues to do.

The congress, by Public Law 99-612, has expressed gratitude to United Way, congratulated it, and applauded and encouraged its fine work and its goals.

NOW, THEREFORE, I, RONALD REAGAN, President of the United States of America, by virtue of the authority vested in me by the Constitution and laws of the United States, do hereby proclaim heartfelt thanks to a century of Americans who have shaped and supported United Way, and encourage the continuation of its efforts.

IN WITNESS WHEREOF, I have hereunto set my hand this tenth day of December, in the year of our Lord nineteen hundred and eighty-six, and of the independence of the United States of America the two hundred and eleventh.

Ronald Reagan

Organizing the United Way as the umbrella charity to fund other local charities through payroll deductions established a most effective means of fund-raising. As a not-for-profit marketer, the United Way became the recipient of 90 percent of all charitable donations. Employers sometimes used extreme pressure to achieve 100 percent participation of employees, which qualified companies for organizational bonuses. Business organizations achieved further cooperation by involving their executives as leaders of annual campaigns, amid widespread publicity. It would consequently cause such an executive acute loss of face if his or her own organization did not go "over the top" in meeting campaign goals. A local United Way executive admitted that "if participation is 100 percent, it means someone has been coerced."[1]

For many years, except for some tight-lipped gripes of corporate employees, the organization moved smoothly along, generally increasing local contributions every year, although the needs for charitable contributions invariably increased all the more.

The national organization, United Way of America (UWA), is a separate corporation and has no direct control over the approximately 2,100 local United Ways. But most of the locals voluntarily contributed 1 cent on the dollar of all funds they collected. In return the national organization provided training and promoted local United Way agencies through advertising and other marketing efforts.

Much of the success of the United Way movement in becoming the largest and most respected charity in the United States was due to the 22 years of William Aramony's leadership of the national organization. When he first took over, the United Ways were not operating under a common name. He built a nationwide network of agencies, all operating under the same name and all using the same logo of outstretched hands, which became nationally recognized as the symbol of charitable giving. Unfortunately, in 1992 an expose of Aramony's lavish lifestyle, as well as other questionable dealings, led to his downfall and burdened local United Ways with serious difficulties in fund-raising.

WILLIAM ARAMONY

During Aramony's tenure, United Way contributions increased from $787 million in 1970 to $3 billion in 1990. He increased his headquarters budget from less than $3 million to $29 million in 1991. Of this, $24 million came from the local United Ways, with the rest coming from corporate grants, investment income, and consulting.[2] He built up the headquarters staff to 275 employees. Figure 4.1 shows the organizational chart as of 1987.

Aramony moved comfortably among the most influential people in our society. He attracted a prestigious board of governors, many of these top executives from America's largest corporations, with only 3 of the 37 from

[1] Susan Garland, "Keeping a Sharper Eye on Those Who Pass the Hat," *Business Week* (March 16, 1992): 39.

[2] Charles E. Shepard, "Perks, Privileges and Power in a Nonprofit World," *The Washington Post* (February 16, 1992): A38.

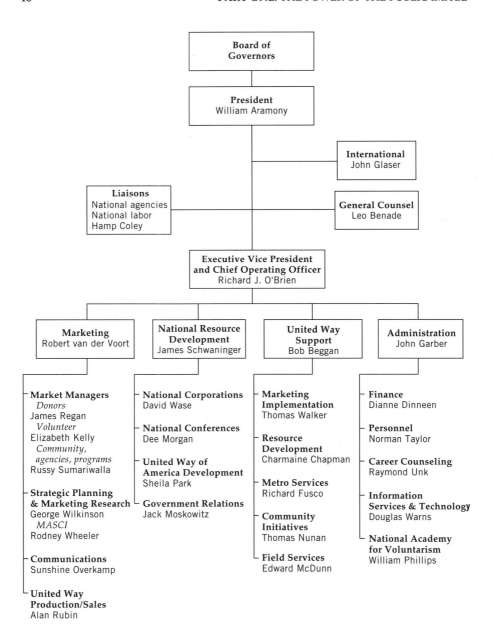

Figure 4.1. Organizational chart, United Way of America, 1987.
Source: E.L. Brilliant, "Appendix B," *United Way: Dilemmas of Organized Charity* (New York: Columbia University Press, 1990): 272.

not-for-profit organizations. The board was chaired by John Akers, chairman and CEO of IBM. Other board members included Edward A. Brennan, CEO of Sears; James D. Robinson III, CEO of American Express; and Paul J. Tagliabue, commissioner of the National Football League. The presence on the board of such top executives brought prestige to United Way and spurred contributions from some of the largest and most visible organizations in the United States.

Aramony was the highest paid executive in the charity field. In 1992 his compensation package was $463,000—nearly double that of the next highest paid executive in the industry, Dudley H. Hafner of the American Heart Association.[3] The board fully supported Aramony, regularly giving him 6 percent annual raises.[4]

Investigative Disclosures

The *Washington Post* began investigating Aramony's tenure as president of United Way of America in 1991, raising questions about his high salary, travel habits, possible cronyism, and dubious relations with five spinoff companies. In February 1992 it released the following information of Aramony's expense charges:[5]

- Aramony had charged $92,265 in limousine expenses to the charity during the previous five years.
- He had charged $40,762 on airfare for the supersonic Concorde.
- He had charged more than $72,000 on international airfare, which included first class flights for himself, his wife, and others.
- He had charged thousands more for personal trips, gifts, and luxuries.
- He had made 29 trips to Las Vegas between 1988 and 1991.
- He had expensed 49 journeys to Gainesville, Florida, the home of his daughter and a woman with whom he had had a relationship.
- He had allegedly approved a $2 million loan to a firm run by his chief financial officer.
- He had approved the diversion of donors' money to questionable spin-off organizations run by long-time aides and had provided benefits to family members as well.
- He had passed tens of thousands of dollars in consulting contracts from the UWA to friends and associates.

[3]Shepard, "Perks, Privileges, and Power," A38; and Charles E. Shepard, "United Way of America President is Urged to Resign," *The Washington Post* (February 27, 1992): A1.
[4]Joseph Finder, "Charity Case," *The New Republic* (May 4, 1992): 11.
[5]Shepard, "Perks, Privileges and Power"; Shepard, "Urged to Resign"; Kathleen Teltsch, "United Way Awaits Inquiry on its President's Practices," *The New York Times* (February 24, 1992): A12 (L); Charles E. Shepard, "United Way Report Criticizes Ex-Leader's Lavish Lifestyle," *The Washington Post* (April 4, 1992): A1.

United Way of America's corporate policy prohibited the hiring of family members within the actual organization, but Aramony skirted the direct violation by hiring friends and relatives as consultants within the spin-off companies. The United Way paid hundreds of thousands of dollars in consulting fees, for example, to two aides in vaguely documented and even undocumented business transactions.

The use of spin-off companies provided flexible maneuvering. One of the spin-off companies Aramony created to provide travel and bulk purchasing for United Way chapters purchased a $430,000 condominium in Manhattan and a $125,000 apartment in Coral Gables, Florida, for use by Aramony. Another of the spin-off companies hired Aramony's son, Robert Aramony, as its president. Loans and money transfers between the spin-off companies and the national organization raised questions. No records showed that the board members had been given the opportunity to approve such loans and transfers.[6]

CONSEQUENCES

When the information about Aramony's salary and expenses became public, reaction was severe. Stanley C. Gault, CEO of Goodyear Tire & Rubber Co., asked, "Where was the board? The outside auditors?"[7] Robert O. Bothwell, executive director of the National Committee for Responsive Philanthropy, said, "I think it is obscene that he is making that kind of salary and asking people who are making $10,000 a year to give 5 percent of their income."[8] At this point, let us examine the issue of executive compensation: Are many executives overpaid? See the following issue box.

ISSUE BOX

EXECUTIVE COMPENSATION: IS IT TOO MUCH?

A controversy is mounting over multimillion-dollar annual compensations of corporate executives. For example, in 1992 the average annual pay of CEOs was $3,842,247; the 20 highest paid ranged from over $11 million to a mind-boggling $127 million (for Thomas F. Frist, Jr., of Hospital Corporation of America).[9]

Activist shareholders, including some large mutual and pension funds, began protesting pay practices, especially for top executives of those firms that

---

[6]Shepard, "Perks, Privileges and Power," A38.

[7]Susan Garland, "Keeping a Sharper Eye," 39.

[8]Felicity Barringer, "United Way Head Is Forced Out In a Furor Over His Lavish Style," *The New York Times* (February 28, 1992): A1.

[9]John A. Byrne, "Executive Pay: The Party Ain't Over Yet," *Business Week* (April 26, 1993): 56–64.

were not even doing well. New disclosure rules imposed in 1993 by the Securities & Exchange Commission (SEC) spotlighted questionable executive-pay practices. In the past complacent boards, themselves well paid and often closely aligned with the top executives of the organizations, condoned liberal compensations. Now this may be changing. Still, the major argument supporting high executive compensations is that compared to some entertainers' and athletes', their salaries are modest. And are not their responsibilities far greater than those of any entertainer or athlete?

In light of the for-profit executive compensations, Aramony's salary was modest. And results were on his side: He made $369,000 in basic salary while raising $3 billion; Lee Iacocca, on the other hand, made $3 million while Chrysler lost $795 million. Where is the justice?

Undoubtedly as head of a large for-profit corporation Aramony could have earned several zeros more in compensation and perks, with no raised eyebrows. But is the situation different for a not-for-profit organization? Especially when revenues are derived from donations of millions of people of modest means? This is a real controversy. On one side, shouldn't a charity be willing to pay for the professional competence to run the organization as effectively as possible? But how do revelations of high compensation affect the public image and fund-raising marketing of such not-for-profit organizations?

What is your position regarding Aramony's compensation and perks, relative to the many times greater compensations of for-profit executives?

As a major consequence of the scandal, some United Way locals withheld their funds, at least pending a thorough investigation of the allegations. John Akers, chairman of the board, noted that by March 7, 1992, dues payments were running 20 percent behind those of the previous year, and he admitted, "I don't think this process that the United Way of America is going through, or Mr. Aramony is going through, is a process that's bestowing a lot of honor."[10]

In addition to the decrease in dues payments, UWA was in danger of having its not-for-profit status revoked by the Internal Revenue Service due to the relationship of loans made to the spin-off companies. For example, it loaned $2 million to a spin-off corporation of which UWA's chief financial officer was a director—a violation of not-for-profit corporate law. UWA also guaranteed a bank loan taken out by one of the spin-offs, another violation of not-for-profit corporate law.[11]

[10]Felicity Barringer, "United Way Head Tries to Restore Trust," *The New York Times* (March 7, 1992): 8L.

[11]Shepard, "Perks, Privileges and Power," A38; Charles E. Shepard, "United Way Chief Says He Will Retire," *The Washington Post* (February 28, 1992): A1.

The adverse publicity benefitted competing charities, such as Earth Share, an environmental group. United Way, at one time the only major organization to receive contributions through payroll deductions, now found itself losing market share to other charities able to garner contributions in the same manner. All the building that William Aramony had done for the United Way as the primary player in the American charitable industry was now in danger of disintegration owing to his uncontrolled excesses.

On February 28, amid mounting pressure from local chapters threatening to withhold their annual dues, Aramony resigned. In August 1992 the United Way board of directors hired Elaine Chao, Peace Corps director, to replace Aramony.

ELAINE CHAO

Chao's story is one of great achievement for one only 39 years old. She is the oldest of six daughters in a family that came to California from Taiwan when Elaine was 8 years old. She did not then know a word of English. Through hard work, the family prospered. "Despite the difficulties . . . we had tremendous optimism in the basic goodness of this country, that people are decent here, that we would be given a fair opportunity to demonstrate our abilities," she told an interviewer.[12] Chao's parents instilled in their six daughters the conviction that they could do anything they set their minds to, and the daughters all went to prestigious universities.

Elaine Chao earned an economics degree from Mount Holyoke in 1975, then went on for a Harvard MBA. She was a White House fellow, an international banker, chair of the Federal Maritime Commission, deputy secretary of the U.S. Transportation Department, and director of the Peace Corps before accepting the presidency of the United Way of America.

Chao's salary was $195,000, less than one-half that of Aramony. She cut budgets and staffs: no transatlantic flights on the Concorde, no limousine service, no plush condominiums. She expanded the board of governors to include more local representatives, and she established committees on ethics and finance. Still, she had no illusions about her job: "Trust and confidence once damaged will take a great deal of effort and time to heal."[13] The following box discusses the particular importance of the public image for not-for-profit agencies.

[12]"United Way Chief Dedicated," *Cleveland Plain Dealer* (March 28, 1993): 24-A.f.
[13]"United Way Chief Dedicated," 24-A.f.

INFORMATION BOX

PUBLIC IMAGE FOR NOT-FOR-PROFIT ORGANIZATIONS

Product-oriented firms ought to be concerned and protective of their public image; even more so not-for-profit organizations such as schools, police departments, hospitals, politicians, and most of all, charitable organizations, should be concerned. Let us consider here the importance of public image for representative not-for-profits.

Large city police departments often have a poor image among important segments of the population. The need to improve this image is hardly less important than for a manufacturer faced with a deteriorating brand image. A police department can develop a "marketing" campaign to win friends; examples of possible activities aimed at creating a better image are promoting tours and open houses of police stations, crime laboratories, police lineups, and cells; speaking at schools; and sponsoring recreation projects, such as a day at the ballpark for youngsters.

Public school systems, faced with taxpayers' revolts against mounting costs and image damage owing to teacher strikes, need conscious effort to improve their image in order to obtain more public support and funds.

Many nonbusiness organizations and institutions, such as hospitals, governmental bodies, even labor unions, have grown self-serving, dominated by a bureaucratic mentality so that perfunctory and callous treatment is the rule and the image is in the pits. Improvement of the image can come only through a greater emphasis on satisfying the public's needs.

Not-for-profits are particularly vulnerable to public image problems because they may depend solely on voluntary support. The need to be untainted by any scandal becomes crucial. In particular, great care should be exerted that contributions are being spent wisely and equitably, that overhead costs are kept reasonable, and that no opportunities exist for fraud and other misdeeds. The threat of investigative reporting must be feared and guarded against.

How can a not-for-profit organization be absolutely assured that moneys are not being misspent and that there are no ripoffs?

A Local United Way's Concerns

In April 1993, for the second time in a year, United Way of Greater Lorain County (Ohio) withdrew from the United Way of America. The board of the local chapter was still concerned about the financial stability and accountability of the national agency. In particular, it was concerned about the retirement settlement for Aramony. A significant "golden parachute" retirement package was being negotiated by the national board and Aramony; it was in the neighborhood of $4 million. Learning of this triggered the decision to again withdraw from UWA.

There were other reasons as well for this decision. The national agency was falling far short of its projected budget, as only 890 of the 1,400 affiliates that had paid membership dues two years before were still paying. Roy Church, president of the Lorain Agency, explained their decision: "Since February . . . it has become clear that United Way of America's financial stability and ability to assist locals has been put in question. The benefit of being a United Way of America member isn't there at this time for Lorain's United Way."[14]

Elaine Chao's task of resurrecting United Way of America would not be easy.

Chao's Remedial Efforts

As it turned out, Elaine Chao did a fine job. She was hired to restore public faith and confidence in the United Way. And this she did. She oversaw formation of new oversight committees and established policies that would insure "that United Way of America will be accountable and responsive to local United Ways."[15] The board of governors was expanded from 30 to 45 members and included more local representatives.

On May 20, 1996, she announced her resignation effective September 1. "My job is complete," she said.[16] Her plans were to lecture, join a Washington think tank, volunteer for Bob Dole's presidential campaign and work for the re-election of her husband, Sen. Mitch McConnell (R., Ky.).

Still, had United Way recovered completely from the scandal? The enduring aftereffects say not completely. For the nation's leading chapter, Cleveland, donations have slipped considerably from the 1989–90 campaign that raised $52 million. Total contributions in 1995 were only $40 million, and more than $1 million below the goal set at the beginning of the campaign.[17]

The stigma of an abuse to the public image can be enduring. This may especially be true of public service organizations that derive their revenues from voluntary contributions.

---

[14] Karen Henderson, "Lorain Agency Cuts Ties with National United Way," *Cleveland Plain Dealer* (April 16, 1993): 7C.

[15] Matthew Tungate, "United Way Chief Hails Local Efforts," *Cleveland Plain Dealer* (May 25, 1996): 2-B.

[16] "Head of United Way to Leave Her Post Saying Job Is Done," *The Wall Street Journal* (May 20, 1996): B8.

[17] Michael K. McIntyre, "United Way Changing Fund Drive Strategies," *Cleveland Plain Dealer* (September 1, 1996): 4-B.

See the following box for a discussion of a related example of nonprofit callousness to its parties.

INFORMATION BOX

ANOTHER CONTROVERSY: GIRL SCOUTS AND THEIR COOKIES

The main funding source for the nation's 2.6 million Girl Scouts is the annual cookie sale, estimated to generate $400 million in revenue. The practice goes back some 70 years, although in the 1920s the girls sold homemade cookies. Now each regional council negotiates with one or two bakeries that produce the cookies; sets the price per box, which ranges from $2 to $3; and divides the proceeds as it sees fit. Typically, the Girl Scout troops get 10 to 15 percent, the council takes more than 50 percent, and the rest goes to the manufacturer.[18]

Criticisms have emerged and received public attention regarding the dictatorial handling of these funds by the councils. There are 332 regional councils in the United States, each having an office and a paid staff overseen by a volunteer board. Some councils have dozens of employees, with most serving mainly as policy enforcers and supervisors. At the troop level, volunteer leaders, often women with daughters in the troop, guide their units in the true tradition of scouting, giving their time tirelessly. For the cookie drives, the girls are an unpaid sales force—child labor, as critics assail—that supports a huge bureaucratic structure. Little of the cookie revenue comes back to the local troops.

The bureaucracy does not tolerate dissent well. *The Wall Street Journal* cites the case of a West Haven, Connecticut, troop leader, Beth Denton, who protested both the way the Connecticut Trails council apportioned revenue and the $1.6 million in salaries and benefits paid to 42 council employees. After she complained to the state attorney general, the council dismissed her as leader.[19]

Admittedly, the individual salaries in the bureaucracy were not high by corporate standards or even by not-for-profit standards. Council administrators' salaries ranged up to about $90,000. Perhaps more disturbing was that volunteer leaders saw no annual financial statements of their councils' expenditures and activities.[20]

Evaluate the council's position that annual financial records of their council's activities should be entirely confidential and limited to full-time staff.

---

[18] Ellen Graham, "Sprawling Bureaucracy Eats Up Most Profits of Girl Scout Cookies," *The Wall Street Journal* (May 13, 1992): A1.

[19] Graham, "Sprawling Bureaucracy Eats Up Most Profits," A4.

[20] *Ibid.*

ANALYSIS

The lack of accountability to the donating public was a major contributor to UWA's problems. Such a loosely run operation, with no one to approve or halt administrators' actions, encouraged questionable practices. It also opened the way for great shock and criticism, come the revelation. The fact that voluntary donations were the principal source of revenues made the lack of accountability all the more crucial. The situation was similar for the Girl Scouts. In a for-profit organization, lack of accountability primarily affects stockholders; for a major charitable organization, it affects millions of contributors, who see their money and commitment being squandered.

ISSUE BOX

WHAT SHOULD BE THE ROLE OF THE BOARD OF DIRECTORS?

In the past, most boards of directors have tended to be rubber stamps, closely allied with top executives and even composed mostly of corporate officials. In some organizations today this is changing, mostly in response to criticism of board tendencies always to support the status quo and to perpetuate the "establishment."

More and more, opinion is shifting to the idea that boards must assume a more activist role:

> The board can no longer play a passive role in corporate governance. Today, more than ever, the board must assume . . . a role that is protective of shareholder rights, sensitive to communities in which the company operates, responsive to the needs of company vendors and customers, and fair to its employees.[21]

Incentives for more active boards have been the increasing risks of liability for board decisions, as well as liability insurance costs. Although the board of directors has long been seen as responsible for establishing corporate objectives, developing broad policies, and selecting top executives, this is no longer viewed as sufficient. Boards must also review management's performance to ensure that the company is well run and that stockholders' interests are furthered. And, today, they must ensure that society's best interests are not disregarded. All of this translates into an active concern for the organization's public image or reputation.

But the issue remains: To whom should the board owe its greatest allegiance—the entrenched bureaucracy or the external publics? Without having board members representative of the many special interests affected by the organization, board members may be inclined to support the interests of the establishment.

Do you think a more representative and active board will prevent a similar scenario for United Way in the future? Why or why not?

---

[21]Lester B. Korn and Richard M. Ferry, *Board of Directors Thirteenth Annual Study* (New York: Korn/Ferry International, February 1986): 1–2.

Where full disclosure and a system of checks and balances is lacking, two consequences tend to prevail, neither one desirable nor totally acceptable. The worst case scenario is outright "white-collar theft," when the unscrupulous see it as an opportunity for personal gain. The absence of sufficient controls and accountability can make even normally honest persons succumb to temptation. Second, insufficient controls tend to promote a mindset of arrogance and allow people to play fast and loose with the system. Aramony seemed to fall into this mindset, with his spending extravagances, cronyism, and other conflict-of-interest activities. (At least some of the Girl Scout Councils, too, perceived themselves as aloof from the dedicated volunteer troop leaders, tolerating no criticism or questioning, dictating and enforcing all policies without consultation or participation, and allowing no scrutiny of their own operation.)

The UWA theoretically had an overseer: the board, similar to the board of directors of business corporations. But when such boards act as rubber stamps, where they are solidly in the camp of the chief executives, they are not really exercising control. This appeared to be the case with United Way of America during the "reign" of Aramony; similarly with the regional councils of the Girl Scouts, many of the volunteer boards appear to have exercised little or no oversight.

Certainly such a situation of a board's failure to fulfill its responsibility is not unique to not-for-profits. Corporate boards have often been notorious for promoting the interests of the incumbent executives. Although this situation is changing today, it still prevails. See the preceding issue box for a discussion of the role of boards of directors.

WHAT CAN BE LEARNED?

Beware the arrogant mindset. A leader's mindset that he or she is so superior to subordinates—and even to concerned outsiders—that other opinions are unacceptable is a formula for disaster, both for an organization and for a society. It promotes dictatorship, intolerance of contrary opinions, and an attitude that "we need answer to no one." The consequences are such as we have seen with William Aramony: moving over the edge of what is deemed by most as acceptable and ethical conduct, assuming the role of the final judge who brooks no questions or criticisms. The absence of real or imagined controls or reviews seems to bring out the worst in humans. We seem to need periodic scrutiny to avoid the trap of arrogant decision making devoid of responsiveness to other concerns. The Girl Scout bureaucracy's dealings with its volunteers corroborates the inclination toward arrogance and dictatorship in the absence of objective oversight.

Checks and balances are even more important in not-for-profit and govern-mental bodies than in corporate entities. For-profit organizations have "bottom-line" performance (i.e., profit and loss statistics) as the ultimate control and standard. Not-for-profit and governmental organizations do not have this control, so they have no ultimate measure of their effectiveness.

Consequently, not-for-profit organizations should be subject to the utmost scrutiny of objective outsiders. Otherwise, abuses seem to be encouraged and perpetuated. Often these not-for-profit organizations are sheltered from com-petition, which protects them from demands for greater efficiency. Thus, with-out objective scrutiny, not-for-profits have a tendency to get out of hand, to be run as little dynasties unencumbered by the constraints that face most busi-nesses. Fortunately, investigative reports and increased litigation by allegedly abused parties today act as needed controls for such organizations. In view of the revelations of investigative reporters, we are left to wonder how many other abusive and reprehensible activities have not yet been detected.

Marketing of not-for-profits depends on trust and is particularly vulnerable to bad press. Not-for-profits depend on donations for the bulk of their revenues. They depend on people to give without receiving anything tangible in return (unlike most businesses). And the givers must have trust in the par-ticular organization, trust that the contributions will be well spent, that ben-eficiaries will receive the maximum benefit, that administrative costs will be held low. Consequently, when publicity surfaces that causes such trust to be questioned, the impact can be devastating. Contributions can quickly dry up or be shunted to other charities.

With governmental bodies, of course, their perpetuation is hardly at stake with bad publicity. However, administrators can be recalled, impeached, or not reelected.

CONSIDER

Can you add to these learning insights?

QUESTIONS

1. How do you feel, as a potential or actual giver to United Way cam-paigns, about Aramony's "high living"? Would these allegations affect your gift giving? Why or why not?
2. What prescriptions do you have for thwarting arrogance in not-for-profit and/or governmental organizations? Be as specific as you can, and support your recommendations.
3. How do you personally feel about the coercion that some organiza-tions exert for their employees to contribute substantially to the

United Way? What implications, if any, emerge from your attitudes about this?

4. Given the information supplied about the dictatorial relationships between Girl Scout councils and the local volunteers—and recognizing that such anecdotal information may not be truly representative—what do you see as the pros and cons of Girl Scout cookie drives? On balance, is this marketing fund-raising effort still desirable, or might other alternatives be better?

5. "Since there is no bottom-line evaluation for performance, not-for-profits have no incentives to control costs and prudently evaluate expenditures." Discuss.

6. How would you feel, as a large contributor to a charity, if you learned that it spent $10 million for advertising? Discuss your rationale for this attitude.

7. Do you think the UWA's action after Aramony left was the best way to salvage the public image? Why or why not? What else might have been done?

HANDS-ON EXERCISES

1. You are an advisor to Elaine Chao, who has taken over the scandal-ridden United Way. What advice do you give her for as quickly as possible restoring the confidence of the American public in the integrity and worthiness of this preeminent national charity organization?

2. You are a member of the board of governors of United Way. Allegations have surfaced about the lavish lifestyle of the highly regarded Aramony. Most of the board members, being corporate executives, see nothing at all wrong with his perks and privileges. You, however, feel otherwise. How do you convince the other board members of the error of condoning Aramony's activities? Be as persuasive as you can in supporting your position.

3. You are the parent of a Girl Scout, who has assiduously worked to sell hundreds of boxes of cookies. You now realize that her efforts and that of thousands of other girls are primarily supporting a bloated central and regional bureaucracy, and not the local troops. You feel strongly that this situation is an unacceptable use of child labor. Describe your proposed efforts to institute change.

TEAM DEBATE EXERCISE

Debate this issue: no not-for-profit organization can ever attain the efficiency of a business firm that always has the bottom line to be concerned about.

INVITATION TO RESEARCH

What is the situation with the United Way today? Are local agencies contributing to the national? Have donations matched or exceeded previous levels? Has Elaine Chao restored public confidence? Did William Aramony receive his multimillion dollar severance package?

PART II

GREAT TURNAROUNDS

CHAPTER 5

IBM's Rejuvenation

IBM had for decades dominated the computer industry. But this was to change, and violently, by the early 1990s. Doomsayers now were even predicting the demise of this icon as it found itself seemingly unable to cope with a changed technological environment, aggressive new competitors, and its own inadequacies as a clumsy behemoth.

Somehow, a new CEO brought IBM to an improbable resurrection. The case of a great firm brought to its knees, and then regaining its balance, can provide intriguing learning insights.

THE FLAWED ILLUSION

On January 19, 1993, International Business Machines Corporation (IBM) reported a record $5.46 billion loss for the fourth quarter of 1992 and a deficit for the entire year of $4.97 billion, the biggest annual loss in American corporate history. (General Motors recorded a 1991 loss of $4.45 billion, after huge charges for cutbacks and plant closings. And Ford Motor Company reported a net loss of more than $6 billion for 1992, but that was a noncash charge to account for the future costs of retiree benefits.) The cost in human lives, as far as employment was concerned, was also consequential, because some 42,900 had been laid off during 1992, with an additional 25,000 planned to go in 1993. In its fifth restructuring, seemingly endless rounds of job cuts and firings had eliminated 100,000 jobs since 1985. Not surprisingly, IBM's share price, which was above $100 in the summer of 1992, closed at $48.375, an 11-year low. And yet IBM had long been the ultimate blue-chip company, reigning supreme in the computer industry. How could its problems have surfaced so suddenly and so violently?

THE ROAD TO INDUSTRY DOMINANCE

"They hired my father to make a go of this company in 1914, the year I was born," said Thomas J. Watson, Jr. "To some degree I've been a part of IBM ever since."[1] Watson took over his father's medium-sized company in 1956 and built it into a technological giant. Retired for almost 19 years by 1992, he was witnessing in that year the company in the throes of its greatest adversity.

IBM had become the largest computer maker in the world. With its ever-growing revenues, since 1946 it had become the bluest of blue-chip companies. It had 350,000 employees worldwide and was one of the largest U.S.-based employers. Its 1991 revenues had approached $67 billion, and while profits had dropped some from the peak of $6.5 billion in 1984, its common stock still commanded a price-to-earnings ratio of over 100, making it a darling of investors. In 1989, it ranked first among all U.S. firms in market value (the total capitalization of common stock, based on the stock price and the number of shares outstanding), fourth in total sales, and fourth in net profits.[2]

During the days of Watson, IBM was known for its centralized decision making. Decisions affecting product lines were made at the highest levels of management. Even IBM's culture was centralized and standardized, with strict behavioral and dress codes. For example, a blue suit, white shirt, and dark tie was the public uniform, and IBM became widely known as "Big Blue."

One of IBM's greatest assets was its research labs, by far the largest and costliest of their kind in the world, with staffs that included three Nobel Prize winners. IBM treated its research and development (R & D) function with tender, loving care, regularly budgeting 10 percent of sales for this forward-looking activity: For example, in 1991, the R & D budget was $6.6 billion.

The past success of IBM and the future expectations for the company with a seeming stranglehold over the technology of the future made it a favorite of consultants, analysts, and market researchers. Management theorists from Peter Drucker to Tom Peters (of *In Search of Excellence* fame) lined up to analyze what made IBM so good. The business press regularly produced articles of praise and awe for IBM.

Alas, the adulation was to abruptly change by 1992. Somehow, insidiously, IBM had gotten fat and complacent over the years, and now the devil had to be paid. (In a later case in this book, that of motorcycle maker Harley Davidson, we encounter a similar situation of complacency coming with

[1]Michael W. Miller, "IBM's Watson Offers Personal View of the Company's Recent Difficulties," *The Wall Street Journal* (December 21, 1992): A3.

[2]"Ranking the Forbes 500s," *Forbes* (April 30, 1990): 306.

longstanding market dominance.) IBM's problems, however, went deeper, as we will explore in the next section.

CHANGING FORTUNES

Perhaps the causes of the great IBM debacle of 1992 started in the early 1980s with a questionable management decision. The problems may have been more deep-rooted than any single decision; perhaps they were more a consequence of the bureaucracy that often typifies behemoth organizations (Sears and General Motors faced somewhat similar worsening problems), in the growing layers of policies, and entrenched interests.

In the early 1980s, two little firms, Intel and Microsoft, were upstarts, just emerging in the industry dominated by IBM. Their success by the 1990s can be largely attributed to their nurturing by IBM. Each got a major break when it was "anointed" as a key supplier for IBM's new personal computer (PC). Intel was signed on to make the chips, and Microsoft, the software. The aggressive youngsters proceeded to set standards for successive PC generations, and in the process wrested from IBM control over the PC's future. The PC was to become the product of the future, shouldering aside the giant mainframe that was IBM's strength.

As IBM began losing ground in one market after another, Intel and Microsoft were gaining dominance. Ten years before, in 1982, the market value of stock of Intel and Microsoft combined had amounted to about one-tenth of IBM's. By October 1992, their combined stock value had surpassed IBM's; by the end of the year, they had topped IBM's market value by almost 50%. See Table 5.1 for comparative operating statistics of IBM, Intel, and Microsoft. Table 5.2 shows the market valuation of IBM, Intel, and Microsoft from 1989 to 1992, the years before and during the collapse of investor esteem.

Defensive Reactions of IBM

As the problems of IBM became more visible to the entire investment community, Chairman John Akers sought to institute reforms to turn the behemoth around. His problem—and need—was to uproot a corporate structure and culture that had developed when IBM had no serious competition.

A cumbersome bureaucracy stymied the company from being innovative in a fast-moving industry. Major commitments still went to high-margin mainframes, but these mainframes were no longer necessary in many situations, given the computing power of desktop PCs. IBM had problems in getting to market quickly with the technological innovations that were revolutionizing the industry. In 1991 Akers warned of the coming difficulties before an unbelieving group of IBM managers: "The business is in crisis."[3]

[3]David Kirkpatrick, "Breaking Up IBM," *Fortune* (July 27, 1992): 44.

Table 5.1   Growth of IBM and the Upstarts, Microsoft and Intel, 1983–1992 (in $ millions)

	1983	1985	1987	1989	1991	1992
IBM:						
Revenues	$40,180	$50,056	$54,217	$62,710	$64,792	$67,045
Net Income	5,485	6,555	5,258	3,758	(2,827)	(4,970)
% of Revenue	13.6%	13.1%	9.7%	6.0%	—	—
Microsoft:						
Revenues	$ 50	$ 140	$ 346	$ 804	$ 1,843	$ 2,759
Net Income	6	24	72	171	463	708
% of Revenue	12.0%	17.1%	20.8%	21.3%	25.1%	25.7%
Intel:						
Revenues	$ 1,122	$ 1,365	$ 1,907	$ 3,127	$ 4,779	$ 5,192
Net Income	116	2	176	391	819	827
% of Revenue	10.3%	0.1%	9.2%	12.5%	17.1%	15.9%

Sources: Company annual statements: most 1992 figures are from "Annual Report of American Industry," *Forbes* (January 4, 1993): 115–16.

Commentary: Note the great growth of the "upstarts," both in revenues and in profits, compared with IBM. Also note the great performance of Microsoft and Intel in profit as a percent of revenues.

He attempted to push power downward, to decentralize some of the decision making that for decades had resided at the top. His more radical proposal was to break up IBM—to divide it into 13 divisions and to give each more autonomy. He sought to expand the services business and make the company more responsive to customer needs. Perhaps most important, he saw a crucial need to pare costs by cutting the fat from the organization.

The need for cost cutting was evident to all but the entrenched bureaucracy. IBM's total costs grew 12 percent a year in the mid-1980s, but revenues were not keeping up with this growth.[4] Part of the plan for reducing costs involved cutting employees, which violated a cherished tradition dating back to Thomas Watson's father and the beginning of IBM: a promise never to lay off IBM workers for economic reasons.[5] (Most of the downsizing was indeed accomplished by voluntary retirements and attractive severance packages, but eventually outright layoffs became necessary.)

The changes decreed by Akers would leave the unified sales division untouched. But each of the new product group divisions would act as a separate operating unit, with financial reports broken down accordingly. Particularly troubling to Akers was the recent performance of the personal computer (PC) business. At a time when demand, as well as competition, was burgeoning for PCs, this division was languishing. Early in 1992 Akers

[4] Kirkpatrick, "Breaking Up IBM," 53.
[5] Miller, "Watson Offers Personal View," A4.

Table 5.2   Market Value and Rank of IBM, Microsoft, and Intel among All U.S. Companies, 1989 and 1992

| | *Rank* | | *Market Value* | *($ millions)* |
	1989	*1992*	*1989*	*1992*
IBM	1	13	$60,345	$30,715
Microsoft	92	25	6,018	23,608
Intel	65	22	7,842	24,735

Source: "The *Forbes* Market Value 500," *Forbes* Annual Directory Issue (April 13, 1990): 258–59; and *Forbes* (April 26, 1993): 242. The market value is the per share price multiplied by the number of shares outstanding for all classes of common stock.

Commentary: The market valuation reflects the stature of the firms in the eyes of investors. Obviously, IBM has lost badly during this period, while Microsoft and Intel have more than tripled their market valuation, almost approaching that of IBM. Yet, IBM's sales were $65.5 billion in 1992, against Microsoft sales of $3.3 billion and Intel sales of $5.8 billion.

tapped James Cannavino to be head of the $11 billion Personal Systems Division, which also included workstations and software.

IBM PCs

PCs had been the rising star of the company, despite the fact that mainframes still accounted for about $20 billion in revenues. But in 1990, market share dropped drastically as new competitors offered PCs at much lower prices than IBM; many experts even maintained that these clones were at least equal in quality. Throughout 1992, IBM had been losing market share in an industry price war. Even after it had attempted to counter Compaq's price cuts in June, IBM's prices still remained as much as one-third higher. Even worse, IBM had announced new fall models, and this curbed sales of current models. At the upper end of the PC market, firms such as Sun Microsystems and Hewlett-Packard were bringing out more powerful workstations that tied PCs together with minicomputers and mainframe computers. James Cannavino faced a major challenge in bringing back the PC to a powerful competitive entity.

Cannavino planned to streamline operations by slicing off a new unit to focus exclusively on developing and manufacturing PC hardware. By so doing, he would cut PCs loose from the rest of Personal Systems and the workstations and software. This, he believed, would create a streamlined organization that could cut prices often, roll out new products several times a year, sell through any kind of store, and provide customers with whatever software they wanted, even if it was not IBM's.[6] Such autonomy was deemed necessary in order to respond quickly to competitors and opportunities, without having to deal with the IBM bureaucracy.

[6]"Stand Back, Big Blue—And Wish Me Luck," *Business Week* (August 17, 1992): 99.

THE CRISIS

On January 25, 1993, John Akers announced that he was stepping down as IBM's chairman and chief executive. He had lost the confidence of the board of directors. Until mid-January, Akers had seemed determined to see IBM through its crisis, at least until he would reach IBM's customary retirement age of 60, which would be December 1994. But the horrendous $4.97 billion loss in 1992 changed that, and investor and public pressure mounted for a top management change. The fourth quarter of 1992 was particularly shocking, brought on by weak European sales and a steep decline in sales of minicomputers and mainframes. Now IBM's stock sank to a 17-year low, below $46 per share.

Other aspects of the operation were also emerging to accentuate IBM's fall from grace: most notably, the jewel of its operation, its mainframe processors and storage systems.

For 25 years IBM had dominated the $50 billion worldwide mainframe industry. In 1992 overall sales of such equipment grew at only 2 percent, but IBM experienced a 10 percent to 15 percent drop in revenue. At the same time, its major mainframe rivals—Amdahl and Unisys—had sales gains of 48 percent and 10 percent, respectively.[7]

The fact was becoming clear that IBM was seriously lagging behind in developing new computers that could outperform the old ones—such as IBM's old System/390. Competitors' products exceeded IBM's not only in absolute power but in prices—as much as a tenth or less per unit of computing. For example, with IBM's mainframe computers, customers paid approximately $100,000 for each MIPS, or the capacity to execute 1 million instructions per second, the rough gauge of computing power. Hewlett-Packard offered similar capability at a cost of only $12,000 per MIPS. Similarly, AT&T's NCR unit could sell for $12.5 million a machine that outperformed IBM's $20 million ES/9000 processor complex.[8]

In a series of full-page advertisements appearing in such business publications as *The Wall Street Journal*, IBM defended the mainframe and attacked the MIPS measure of computing power:

> One issue surrounding mainframes is their cost. It's often compared using dollars per MIPS with the cost of microprocessor systems, and on that basis mainframes lose. But . . . dollars per MIPS alone is a superficial measurement. The real issue is function. Today's appetite for information demands serious network and systems management, around-the-clock availability, efficient mass storage, and genuine data security. MIPS alone provides none of these, but IBM mainframes have them built in, and more fully developed than anything available on microprocessors.[9]

[7] John Verity, "Guess What: IBM Is Losing Out in Mainframes, Too," *Business Week* (February 8, 1993): 106.
[8] Verity, "Guess What," 106.
[9] Taken from advertisement, *The Wall Street Journal* (March 5, 1993): B8.

On March 24, 1993, 51-year-old Louis V. Gerstner, Jr., was named the new chief executive of IBM. The 2-month search for a replacement for Akers had captivated the media, with speculation ranging widely. The choice of an outsider caught many by surprise: Gerstner had been CEO of RJR Nabisco, a food and tobacco giant, but this was a far cry from a computer company. And IBM had always prided itself on promoting from within—for example, John Akers—and most IBM executives were lifelong IBM employees. Not all analysts supported the selection of such an outsider. While most did not criticize the board for going outside IBM to find a replacement for Akers, some questioned going outside the computer industry or other high-tech industries. Geoff Lewis, senior editor of *Business Week,* fully supported the choice. He had suggested the desirability of bringing in some outside managers to Akers in 1988:

> Akers seemed shocked—maybe even offended—by my question. After a moment, he answered: "IBM has the best recruitment system anywhere and spends more than anybody on training. Sometimes it might help to seek outsiders with unusual skills, but the company already has the best people in the world."[10]

See the following box for a discussion of promotion from within.

ISSUE BOX

SHOULD WE PROMOTE FROM WITHIN?

A heavy commitment to promoting from within, as had long characterized IBM and other firms as well, is sometimes derisively called "inbreeding." The traditional argument against it maintains that an "inbred" organization is not alert to needed changes and that it is enamored with the status quo, "the way we have always done it." Proponents of promotion from within talk about the motivation and great loyalty it engenders, with every employee knowing that he or she has a chance of becoming a high-level executive.

However, the opposite course of action—that is, heavy commitment to filling important executive positions with outsiders—plays havoc with morale of trainees and lower level executives and destroys the sense of continuity and loyalty. A middle ground seems preferable: filling many executive positions from within, promoting this idea to encourage both the achievement of present executives and the recruiting of trainees, and at the same time bringing strong outsiders into the organization where their strengths and experiences can be most valuable.

Do you think there are particular circumstances where one or the other extreme regarding promotion from within might be best? Discuss.

---

[10]Geoff Lewis, "One Fresh Face at IBM May Not Be Enough," *Business Week* (April 12, 1993): 33.

ANALYSIS

In examining the major contributors to IBM's fall from grace, we will break down the analysis into predisposing or underlying factors, results, and controversies.

Predisposing Factors

Cumbersome Organization. As IBM grew with its success, it became more and more bureaucratic. One author described it as "big and bloated." Another used the phrase "inward-looking culture that kept them from waking up on time."[11] Regardless of phraseology, the facts were that by the late 1980s the IBM organization could not bring new machines quickly into the market and was unable to make the fast pricing and other strategic decisions of its smaller competitors. Too many layers of management, too many vested interests, a tradition-ridden mentality, and a gradually emerging contentment with the status quo shackled it in an industry that some thought to be mature, but which in reality had important sectors still gripped by burgeoning change. As a huge ship requires a considerable time and distance to turn or to stop, so the IBM behemoth found itself at a competitive disadvantage to smaller, hungrier, more aggressive, and above all, more nimble firms. And impeding all efforts to effect major changes was the typical burden facing all large and mature organizations: resistance to change. See the following information box for a discussion of this phenomenon.

Overly Centralized Management Structure. Often related to a cumbersome bureaucratic organization is rigid centralization of authority and decision making. Certain negatives may result when all major decisions have to be made at corporate headquarters rather than down the line. Decision making is necessarily slowed, because headquarters executives feel they must investigate fully all aspects, and because they are not personally involved with the recommendation, they tend to be not only skeptical but critical. More than this, the typical conservatism of higher management—divorced from the intimacy of the problem or the opportunity—may curb the enthusiasm and creativity of lower-level executives. The motivation and morale needed for a climate of innovative-mindedness and creativity is stifled under a bureaucratic attitude of "don't take a chance" and "don't rock the boat."

---

[11] Jennifer Reese, "The Big and the Bloated: It's Tough Being No. 1," *Fortune* (July 27, 1992): 49.

INFORMATION BOX

RESISTANCE TO CHANGE

People as well as organizations have a natural reluctance to embrace change. Change is disruptive. It can destroy accepted ways of doing things and familiar authority–responsibility relationships. It makes people uneasy, because their routines will likely be disrupted; their interpersonal relationships with subordinates, coworkers, and superiors may well be modified. Positions that were deemed important before the change may be downgraded. And persons who view themselves as highly competent in a particular job may be forced to assume unfamiliar duties.

Resistance to change can be combatted by good communication with participants about forthcoming changes. Without such communication, rumors and fears can assume monumental proportions. Acceptance of change can be facilitated if employees are involved as fully as possible in planning the changes, if their participation is solicited and welcomed, and if assurance can be given that positions will not be impaired, only changed. Gradual rather than abrupt changes also make a transition smoother, as participants can be initially exposed to the changes without drastic upheavals.

In the final analysis, however, needed changes should not be delayed or canceled because of their possible negative repercussions on the organization. If change is necessary, it should be initiated. Individuals and organizations can adapt to change, but it may take some time.

The worst change an employee may face is layoff. When uncertainty exists as to when the next layoff will occur, and to whom, total morale may sink to the pits, devastating productivity. Discuss how the necessity of upcoming layoffs might best be handled.

The Three *C*'s Mindset of Vulnerability. Firms that have been well entrenched in their industry and that have dominated it for years tend to fall into a particular mindset that leaves them vulnerable to aggressive and innovative competitors. (We will also encounter this syndrome in a later case, Harley Davidson, the motorcycle maker.)

The following "three *C*'s" are detrimental to a front-runner's continued success:

Complacency

Conservatism

Conceit

Complacency is smugness: A self-satisfied firm, content with the status quo, may no longer be hungry and eager for growth. *Conservatism* characterizes a management that is wedded to the past, to the traditional, to the way things have always been done. Managers see no need to change because nothing is different today (e.g., "Mainframe computers are the models of the industry and will always be"). Finally, *conceit* further reinforces the myopia of the mindset: conceit for present and potential competitors. A belief that "we are the best" and "no one else can touch us" can easily permeate an organization when everything has been going well for years.

With the three C's mindset, there is no incentive to undertake aggressive and innovative actions. There is growing disinterest in such important facets of the business as customer relations, servicing, and even quality control. Furthermore, there is little interest in developing innovative new products that may cannibalize—that is, take business away from—existing products or disrupt entrenched interests. (We will discuss cannibalization in more detail shortly.)

Results

Overdependence on High-Margin Mainframes. The mainframe computers had long been the greatest source of market power and profits for IBM. But the conservative and tradition-minded bureaucracy could not accept the reality that computer power was now becoming a desktop commodity. Although a market still existed for the massive mainframes, it was limited and had little growth potential; the future belonged to desktop computers and workstations. And to these areas, in a lapse of monumental proportions, IBM relinquished its dominance. First the minicomputers opened up a whole new industry, one with scores of hungry competitors. But the cycle of industry creation and decline started anew by the early 1980s as personal computers began to replace minicomputers in defining new markets and fostering new competitors. The mainframe was not replaced, but its markets became more limited, and cannibalization became the fear. See the following information box.

Neglect of Software and Service. At a time when software and service had become ever more important, IBM still had a fixation on hardware. In 1992 services made up only 9 percent of IBM's revenue. Criticisms flowed:

> "Technology is becoming a commodity, and the difference between winning and losing comes in how you deliver that technology. Service will be the differentiator."

> "As a customer, I want a supplier who's going to make all my stuff work together."

"The job is to understand the customer's needs in detail."[12]

The sales force had become reluctant to sell low-margin open systems if it could push proprietary mainframes or minicomputers, regardless of customers' needs.

Bloated Costs. Indicative of the fat that had insidiously grown in the organization, IBM cut some 42,900 jobs in 1992, thankfully all through early retirement programs. An additional 25,000 people were expected to be laid off in 1993, some without the benefit of early retirement packages. Health benefits for employees were also scaled down. Manufacturing capacity was reduced 25 percent, and two of three mainframe development labs were closed. But perhaps the area of greatest bloat was R & D.

INFORMATION BOX

CANNIBALIZATION

Cannibalization occurs when a company's new product takes away some business of its existing product. The new product success consequently does not contribute its full measure to company revenues because some sales will be switched from older products. The amount of cannibalization can range from virtually none to almost total. In this latter case, then, the new product simply replaces the older product, with no real sales gain achieved. If the new product is less profitable than the older, the impact, and the fear, of cannibalization becomes all the greater.

For IBM, the PCs and the other equipment smaller than mainframes would not come close to replacing the bigger units. Still, some cannibalizing was likely. And the profits on the lower priced computers were many times less than those of mainframes.

The argument can justifiably be made that if the company does not bring out such new products, the competitors will, and it is better to compete with one's own products. Still, the threat of cannibalization can cause a hesitation, a blink, in a full-scale effort to rush to market an internally competing product. This reluctance and hesitation needs to be guarded against, lest the firm find itself no longer in the vanguard of innovation.

Assume the role of vocal and critical stockholder at the annual meeting. What arguments would you introduce for a crash program to rush the PC to market, and damn any possible cannibalizing? What contrary arguments would you expect, and how would you counter them?

---

[12] Kirkpatrick, "Breaking Up IBM," 49, 52.

The Diminishing Payoff of Massive R & D Expenditures. As noted earlier, IBM spent heavily on research and development, often as much as 10 percent of sales, as shown in Table 5.3. Its research labs were by far the largest and costliest of their kind in the world.

IBM labs were capable of inventing amazing things. For example, they recently developed the world's smallest transistor, at 1/75,000th the width of a human hair.

Somehow, with all these R & D resources and expenditures, IBM lagged in transferring its innovation to the marketplace. The organization lacked the ability to quickly translate laboratory prototypes into commercial triumphs. Commercial R & D is wasted without this translation.

Controversies

Questionable Decisions. No executive has a perfect batting average of good decisions. Indeed, most executives do well to bat more than 500—that is, to have more good decisions than bad decisions. But, alas, this is all relative. So much depends on the importance and the consequences of these decisions.

IBM made a decision of monumental long-term consequences in the early 1980s. At that time, IBM delegated to two upstart West Coast companies the task of being key suppliers for its new personal computer. Thus, it gave away the chance to control the personal computer industry. Over the next 10 years, each of the two young firms was to develop a near monopoly—Intel in microprocessors and Microsoft in operating-systems software—by setting standards for successive PC generations. Instead of keeping such developments proprietary, that is, within its own organization, in an urge to save developmental time, IBM gave these two small firms a golden opportunity that both grasped to the fullest. By 1992 Intel and Microsoft had emerged as the computer industry's most dominant firms.

Table 5.3   IBM Research and Development Expenditures As a Percent of Revenues, 1987–1991

	1987	1988	1989	1990	1991
Revenues ($ mil)	$54,217	$59,681	$62,710	$64,792	$67,045
Research, Development, and Engineering Costs	5,434	5,925	6,827	6,554	6,644
Percent of Revenues	10.0%	9.9%	10.9%	10.1%	9.9%

Source: Company annual reports.
Commentary: Where has been the significant contribution from such heavy investment in R & D?

And yet the decision is still controversial. It saved IBM badly needed time in bringing its PC to market. And as computer technology becomes ever more complex, not even an IBM can be expected to have the ability and resources to go it alone. Linking up with competitors offers better products and services and a faster flow of technology today, and it seems the wave of the future.

Former IBM CEO Thomas Watson, Jr., has also criticized his successors, Frank Cary and John Opel, for phasing out rentals and selling the massive mainframe computer outright. Originally, purchasers could only lease the machines, thus giving IBM a dependable cushion of cash each year ("my golden goose," Mr. Watson called it).[13] Doing away with this renting left IBM and John Akers a newly volatile business, just as the industry position began worsening. Akers, just installed as CEO, was thus left with a hostile environment without the cushion or support of steady revenues coming from such rentals. So Watson's argument goes. But the counterposition is that selling quickly brought needed cash into company coffers. Furthermore, it is unlikely, given the more competitive climate that was emerging in the late 1980s, that big customers would continue to tolerate the leasing arrangement when they could own their machines, if not from IBM, from another supplier whose machines were just as good, if not better.

Breaking Up IBM. The general consensus of management experts favored the reforms of Akers to break Big Blue up into 13 divisions and give them increasing autonomy—even to the point that shares of some of these new Baby Blues might be distributed to stockholders. The idea is not unlike that of Japan's *keiretsu*, in which groups of companies with common objectives but with substantial independence seek and develop business individually.

The assumption in favor of such a breakup is that the sum of the parts is greater than the whole, that the autonomy and motivation will bring more total revenues and profits. But these hypothesized benefits are not ensured. At issue is whether the good of the whole would be better served by suboptimizing some business units—that is, by limiting profit maximization of some units in order to have the highest degree of coordination and cooperation. Giving disparate units of an organization goals of individual profit maximization lays the seeds for intense intramural competition, with cannibalization and infighting likely. IBM has embarked on a program of decentralization and intramural competition. But will gross profit margins deteriorate even more with such competition? Is the whole better served by a less intensely competitive internal environment? That is the issue.

[13]Miller, "Watson Offers Personal View," A4.

The Comeback Under Gerstner

Louis Gerstner took command in March 1993. The company, as we have seen, was reeling. In a reversal of major proportions, he brought IBM back to record profitability. Table 5.4 shows the statistics of a sensational turnaround. In 1994, the company earned $3 billion, its first profitable year since 1990. Perhaps of greater significance, this represented a profit swing of $11 billion compared with the previous year. Revenues grew for the first time since 1990. Equally important, 1994 finished with financial strength: IBM had more than $10 billion in cash and basic debt was reduced by $3.3 billion.

The winning ways continued. In 1995, record revenues topped $70 billion for the first time. The rate of growth—12 percent over the previous year—was the best in more than a decade. Earnings doubled to $6.3 billion, excluding a one-time charge related to the acquisition of Lotus Development Corporation. Not surprisingly, the stock market value of IBM improved nearly $27 billion from the summer of 1993 through year-end 1995, and continued to improve significantly in 1996.

By all such performance statistics, Gerstner had done an outstanding job of turning the giant around. At first there had been doubters. For the most part, their skepticism was rooted in the notion that Gerstner was not aggressive enough, that he did not tamper mightily with the organizational structure of IBM. For example, a 1994 *Fortune* article questioned, "Is He Too Cautious to Save IBM?" The article went on to say, "After running IBM for more than a year and a half, CEO Lou Gerstner has revealed himself to be something other than the revolutionary whom the directors of this battered and demoralized enterprise once seemed to want . . . he seems to be attempting a conventional turnaround: deep-cleaning and redecorating the house rather than gutting and renovating it."[14]

Before Gerstner took over, IBM was moving toward a breakup into 13 independent units: one for mainframes, one for PCs, one for disk drives, and so on. But he saw IBM's competitive advantage to be offering customers a complete package, a one-stop shopping to all those seeking help in solving technological problems: a unified IBM—somehow, an IBM with a single, efficient team.

The Quiet Revolution. The critics inclined toward revolutionary measures had to be disappointed. "Transforming IBM is not something we can do in one or two years," Gerstner had stated. "The better we are at fixing some of the short-term things, the more time we have to deal with the long-term issues."[15] His efforts were contrasted with those of Albert Dunlap, who

---

[14] Allison Rogers, "Is He Too Cautious to Save IBM?" *Fortune* (October 3, 1994): 78.
[15] Rogers, "Is He Too Cautious," 78.

Table 5.4   IBM's Resurgence Under Gerstner, 1993–1995

	1993	1994	1995
	(millions of dollars)		
Revenue	$62,716	$64,052	$71,940
Net Earnings (loss)	(8,101)	3,021	4,178
Net Earnings (loss) Per Share of Common Stock	(14.22)	5.02	7.23
Working Capital	6,052	12,112	9,043
Total Debt	27,342	22,118	21,629
Number of Employees	256,207	219,839	225,347

Source: Company annual reports.
Commentary: In virtually all measures of performance, IBM has made a significant turnaround from 1993 to 1995. Note in particular the decrease in debt and the great profit turnaround.

overhauled Scott Paper at about the same time. Dunlap replaced 9 of the 11 top executives in the first few days and laid off one-third of the total work force. Gerstner brought in only 8 top executives from outside IBM to sit on the 37-person Worldwide Management Council.

A non-technical man, Gerstner's strengths were in selling: cookies and cigarettes at RJR Nabisco, travel services during an 11-year career at American Express Company. Weeks after taking over, he talked to IBM's top 100 customers at a retreat in Chantilly, Virginia. He asked them what IBM was doing right and wrong. They were surprised and delighted: this was the first time the chairman of the 72-year-old company had ever polled its customers. The input was revealing:

> The customers told him IBM was difficult to work with and unresponsive to customers' needs. For example, customers who needed IBM's famed mainframe computers were being told that the machines were dinosaurs and that the company would have to consider getting out of the business.[16]

Gerstner told these customers that IBM was in mainframes to stay, and would aggressively cut prices and focus on helping them set up, manage, and link the systems. IBM's hardware sales turned around also, rising from $30.6 billion in 1993 to $35.6 billion in 1995.

Perhaps the most obvious change Gerstner instituted was the elimination of a dress code that once kept IBM salespeople in blue suits and white shirts.

By the spring of 1997, *Fortune* magazine highlighted Gerstner on its cover with the feature article, "The Holy Terror Who's Saving IBM."[17] Total company sales for 1996 were $75.947 billion, up 5.6 percent from the previous year, and net profits gained 30% over 1995, to $5.429 billion.

[16]"IBM Focuses on Sales," *Cleveland Plain Dealer* (September 10, 1996): 6C.
[17]Betsy Morris, "He's Saving Big Blue," *Fortune* (April 14, 1997): 68–81.

WHAT CAN BE LEARNED?

Beware of the cannibalization phobia. We have just set the parameters of the issue of cannibalization—that is, how far a firm should go in developing products and encouraging intramural competition that will take sales away from other products and units of the business. The issue is particularly troubling when the part of business that is likely to suffer is the most profitable in the company. Yet cannibalization should not even be an issue. At stake is the forward-leaning of the company, its embracing of innovation and improved technology, and its competitive stance. Unless a firm has an assured monopoly position, it can expect competitors to introduce advances in technology and/or new efficiencies of productivity and customer service.

In general we can conclude that no firm should rest on its laurels. Firms must introduce improvements and change as soon as possible, hopefully ahead of the competition, without regard to any possible impairment of sales and profits of existing products and units.

The need to be "lean and mean" (sometimes called "acting small"). The marketplace is uncertain, especially in high-tech industries. In such environments a large firm needs to be as responsive and flexible as smaller firms. It must avoid layers of management, limiting policies, and a tradition-bound mindset. Otherwise our big firm is like the behemoth vessel, unable to stop or change course without losing precious time and distance. But how can a big firm keep the maneuverability and innovative-mindedness of a smaller firm? How can it remain "lean and mean" with increasing size?

We can identify certain conditions or factors of lean and mean firms:

1. They have simple organizations. Typically, they are decentralized, with decision making moved lower in the organization. This discourages the buildup of cumbersome bureaucracy and staff, which tends to add both increasing overhead expenses and the red tape that stultifies fast reaction time.

   A simple organization is a relatively flat one, with fewer levels of management than complex firms. This also has certain desirable consequences. Overhead is greatly reduced with fewer executives and their expensive staffs. But communication is also improved, since higher executives are more accessible and directions and feedback are less distorted because of more direct communications channels. Even morale is improved because of the better communications and accessibility to leaders of the organization.

2. They encourage new ideas. A major factor in the inertia of large firms is the managers who see their power threatened by new ideas and innovative directions. Consequently, real creativity is stymied by not being appreciated; often it is even discouraged.

   A firm that wishes to be lean and mean must seek new ideas. This implies giving rewards and recognition for creativity but, even more, acting upon the worthwhile ideas. Few things are more thwarting to creativity in an organization than pigeon-holing the good ideas of eager employees.

3. They move participation in planning as low in the organization as possible. Important employees and lower-level managers should be involved in decisions concerning their responsibilities, and their ideas should receive reasonable weight in final decisions. Performance goals and rewards should be moved as low in the organization as possible. Such an organizational climate encourages innovation, improves motivation and morale, and can lead to the fast reaction time that characterizes small organizations.

4. They have minimum frills, even austerity, at the corporate level. This quality does characterize some highly successful and proactive large organizations. Two of our most successful firms today, Wal-Mart and Southwest Airlines, epitomize this philosophy. A no-frills management orientation is the greatest corporate model for curbing frivolous costs throughout an organization.

Beware the "king of the hill" three C's mindset. As a firm gains dominance and maturity, it must guard against conservatism, complacency, and conceit. Usually these three C's set in at the highest levels and eagerly filter down to the rest of the organization. As discussed earlier, this mindset leaves a firm highly vulnerable to smaller and hungrier competitors. And so the "king of the hill" is toppled.

Although top management usually initiates such a mindset, top management can also lead in inhibiting it. The lean and mean organization is anathema to the three C's mindset. If we can curb bureaucratic buildup, then the seeds are thwarted. Perhaps most important in preventing this mindset is encouragement of innovative thinking throughout the organization as well as a policy of bringing in fresh blood from outside the organization to fill some positions. A strict adherence to promotion from within is inhibiting.

The power of greater commitment to customers. One of the bigger contributions Gerstner may have made to the turnaround of IBM was his customer focus: putting the needs of customers first and relying on his in-house experts for the technology. Asking, not merely talking—finding out what customers wanted, and seeing what could be done to best meet these needs as quickly as possible. At the same time, toning down the arrogance of an "elite" staff of sales representatives. Perhaps the style change from blue suits and white shirts was the visible sign of a change in culture and attitudes.

Now many firms profess a great commitment to customers and service. So common are such statements that one wonders how much is mere lip service. It is so easy to say this, and then not really follow up. In so doing, the opportunity to develop a trusting relationship is lost.

We can overcome adversity! Perhaps the most valuable lesson that any organization can embrace is that adversity is not forever. Firms can come back—we will see other examples of this. With the computer technology market broadening and evolving, IBM may never achieve its former dominant position of the 1960s and 1970—all lost ground may not be regained. But it can prosper and again become a strong player in this industry, one to be proud of. Managers should be capable of learning from their mistakes. Mistakes should be valuable learning experiences, leading the way to better performance and decisions in the future.

CONSIDER

What additional learning insights do you see as emerging from the IBM case?

QUESTIONS

1. Assess the pro and con arguments for the 1982 decision to delegate to Microsoft and Intel a foothold in software and operating systems. (Keep your perspective to that of the early 1980s; don't be biased with the benefit of hindsight.)
2. Do you see any way that IBM could have maintained its nimbleness and technological edge as it grew to a $60 billion company? Reflect on this, and be as creative as you can.
3. "Tradition has no place in corporate thinking today." Discuss this statement.
4. Playing devil's advocate (one who takes an opposing position for the sake of argument), can you defend the position that the problems besetting IBM were not its fault, that they were beyond its control?

5. Would you say that the major problems confronting IBM were marketing rather than organizational issues? Why or why not?
6. Which of the three C's do you think was most to blame for IBM's
problems? Why?

HANDS-ON EXERCISES

1. You are a marketing consultant reporting to the CEO in the late
1980s. IBM is still racking up revenue and profit gains. But you detect
serious emerging weaknesses. What do you advise management to
do at this time? (Make any assumptions you feel necessary, but state
them clearly.) Persuasively explain your rationale.
2. You are the executive assistant to Gerstner. It is 1997 and the great
growth in revenues and profits of the last three years has slowed.
The critics are again demanding a drastic overhaul. Gerstner still
stoutly maintains that customer service is the key, and that this has
somehow slipped. He charges you to come up with concrete recommendations for improving the effectiveness of customer service. Be
as specific as you can.

TEAM DEBATE EXERCISE

At issue, whether to break up the company into 10–15 semi-
autonomous units, or to keep basically the same organization. Debate the
opposing views as persuasively as possible.

INVITATION TO RESEARCH

What is the current situation of IBM? Has the great turnaround continued? Is Gerstner still the CEO?

CHAPTER 6

Sears: A Stubborn Comeback

On January 25, 1993, Sears announced that after 107 years, the company would no longer offer its venerable catalog. In its long history, the catalog had become part of the American heritage, at least that of rural and small-town America. It was known as the "wish book," as its well-used pages spurred the dreams of countless children and their parents and stimulated their aspirations for a better life.

At the time of the announcement, the catalog was a $3.3 billion operation. Yet it was a source of recurring losses in its last years, losses that a reeling giant could no longer sustain. The closing would cost 3,400 full-time and 16,500 part-time jobs.[1]

Heavy costs of production and operation at a time of declining demand crippled the catalog's ability to maintain profitability. Perhaps a bigger factor in its demise was the inroads of Wal-Mart stores into rural towns. Consumers could now find a wide variety of goods at lower prices. Yet many other catalogs of all kinds are flourishing. Perhaps the Sears catalog was symptomatic of the problems facing its parent.

The year 1993 proved to be a watershed year, the beginning of a great turnaround in Sears' retail operation. Perhaps the ending of this catalog, a major part of Sears' heritage, symbolized the rejuvenation that was to come.

---

[1]"History Collides With The Bottom Line," *Business Week* (February 8, 1993): 34.

HISTORY

Richard W. Sears founded the R. W. Sears Watch Company in 1886 in Minneapolis. A year later, Alvah C. Roebuck joined the company, and the firm moved to Chicago. The corporate name, Sears, Roebuck and Company, was formalized in 1893.

In the early years, the chief business was selling watches by mail order to people in small towns and rural areas. The assortment of goods rapidly expanded, and by 1896 a first general catalog of over 500 pages was published. It was not until 1925, almost 40 years after the founding, that General Robert E. Wood, then a senior vice president, experimented with a retail store in Chicago. Its success laid the groundwork for the retail expansion to come.

Expansion was rapid. By the end of 1927, Sears had 27 stores in operation, three times the number in the previous years. In 1931 Sears retail stores' sales exceeded mail-order sales for the first time, contributing 53.4 percent of total sales. And the growth continued, slackening only during World War II. See Table 6.1 for the growth in retail stores for selected years.

General Wood formed a major subsidiary in 1931: Allstate Insurance Company. At first it operated only by mail, but in a few years it took sales locations in Sears stores. In his long tenure at the helm of Sears, General Wood also instituted a major store location policy after World War II. Instead of locating additional stores in crowded downtowns, he pioneered the idea of locating in outlying areas with an abundance of free parking. And the expansion

Table 6.1   Number of Retail Stores, 1925–1988

Year	Number of Stores
1925	1
1927	27
1928	192
1933	400
1941	600
1948	632
1970	827
1975	858
1979	864
1985	799
1988	824

Source: Sears annual reports.

Commentary: Note the great growth in the number of stores up until the early 1970s, then a gradual decline, until by the 1980s there were fewer stores than a decade earlier. This reflects that poorly performing stores were being closed. But it also reflects that few new stores were being opened despite the fact that retail space of all retailers doubled during the 1970s and 1980s.

Table 6.2 Sales and Income Statistics for Sears, Ward, and Penney, 1938–1954

	Ward		Sears		Penney	
	Sales	Net Income	Sales	Net Income	Sales	Net Income
Years	(000)	(000)	(000)	(000)	(000)	(000)
1938	$ 414,091	$ 19,210	$ 537,242	$ 30,828	$ 257,971	$ 13,799
1942	632,709	22,353	915,058	29,934	490,356	18,058
1944	595,933	20,677	852,597	33,866	533,374	17,159
1946	654,779	22,932	1,045,359	35,835	676,570	35,495
1948	1,158,675	59,050	1,981,536	107,740	885,195	47,754
1950	1,084,436	47,788	2,168,928	108,207	949,712	44,931
1952	1,106,157	54,342	2,657,408	111,895	1,072,266	37,170
1954	999,123	41,195	2,981,925	117,882	1,107,157	43,617

Source: Moody's and company annual reports for respective years.
Commentary: Note the fading of Ward during this period. This reflects the no-growth policy of Ward chairman, Sewell Avery, after World War II. Ward was never again to be a significant factor, as Sears continued to surge ahead as the biggest retailer.

continued. Table 6.2 shows sales and income statistics for Sears and its two major competitors from 1938 to 1955. By now, Sears was the largest retailer, as it was to remain for over 50 years.

Sears made some important nonretail acquisitions in 1981 by bringing in Coldwell Banker, the nation's largest residential real estate broker, and Dean Witter Reynolds, the fifth biggest U.S. brokerage house. They set up shop in the rich trafficways of Sears stores in the same marketing mode as the highly profitable Allstate Insurance subsidiary. In 1985 Sears celebrated its 100th birthday, and a year later, it introduced the soon-to-be-successful Discover credit card.

But trouble was on the horizon for the huge firm and its key retail sector. Its major competitors now were not Ward and Penney, but two discounters, Wal-Mart and Kmart. By the end of the 1980s, these two would wrest Sears from its long-held position as largest retailer, while Sears struggled to define its identity in a changed environment.

EDWARD A. BRENNAN

The preservation of the traditional greatness of Sears had to loom large in the mind of Edward A. Brennan, chairman and chief executive of the behemoth retail conglomerate, as events unfolded in late 1992. He was a third-generation Sears man and had for more than a decade guided its somehow-faltering destiny. His rise to top position had the flavor of a legend.

Born in Chicago in 1934 to a family wedded to Sears virtually from the company's beginnings—a grandfather had worked beside Richard Sears, the company's founder—Brennan graduated from Marquette University with a degree in business administration in 1955. He left another job to join Sears in 1956, taking a drastic cut in pay of $4,000 to become a salesman in the Madison, Wisconsin, store. Progress was fast. By 1958 he was running the Sears store in Oshkosh, Wisconsin, and by the end of 1959 he was transferred to the Sears headquarters in Chicago. In 1967 he was again made manager of a store, this time in Baltimore's black ghetto, where his performance came to the attention of Edward Telling, the manager of the eastern territory. In 1969 Telling promoted Brennan to one of the biggest stores in the territory, and the following year made him assistant general manager of the New York group of stores. And his star continued to rise.

Invariably in his new positions Brennan distinguished himself by converting losing or mediocre operations to top profit generators. He accepted so many transfers that he once owned homes in three cities. In 1977 he became executive vice president of the southern territory, consisting of 13 groups and 150 stores, and with the promotion also became a member of the company's board of directors. In 1978 the south moved from third to first among territories in profitability, and on March 12, 1980, Telling, then chairman of the company, named Brennan president of Sears and chief operating officer of the merchandising group.

With this achievement, Brennan was viewed as a 46-year-old "boy wonder," who had vaulted over senior executives, putting in 90-hour weeks as he moved from territory to territory, store to store. (The work ethic of the Brennan family also carried over to his younger brother, Bernard, who, after becoming a Sears buyer, eventually wound up as head of Montgomery Ward, Sears' long-time merchandising rival.)

Somehow, Brennan's success pattern, based on hard work and a firm dedication to his company, proved vulnerable in this top corporate job. Perhaps no one could have resurrected the company in the dynamic environment of the 1980s. Or perhaps the task could have been better performed by an outsider, someone not part of the glory days of Sears.

The basic thrust of Sears' merchandising policies had been to provide standard-quality goods at low prices, thereby appealing to low- and middle-income Americans, although several times the company had tried to upgrade and become fashion-oriented for more affluent customers. These attempts had little success; indeed, in the process of such upgrading, Sears risked losing its mainstream customers.

When Brennan took over as president in 1980, his emphasis was on quality, assortment, and service:

We've adopted quality as our number one strategy for the years ahead...The customer also expects to go into a store and find that store fully stocked. The customer wants good service. It's the store that puts all those things together best that will get the best market share.[2]

Brennan continued to centralize major policy decisions in Chicago and began revamping stores with more aisles, lower ceilings, and better displays. He introduced such national apparel brands as Levis, Wrangler, and Wilson to supplement the house brands, such as Craftsman tools, Kenmore appliances, and Diehard batteries, which had strong consumer acceptance. However, the merchandise group continued to slip in profits and market share.

In Brennan's tenure the financial services areas began contributing the bulk of the growth in sales and profits. The company was close to achieving the goal of meeting both the shopping and financial services needs of middle America, a strategy sometimes described as "socks and stocks." Revenues of financial services had grown from $9.5 billion in 1982 to $26 billion in 1991. Even more impressive, the profits of financial services had reached $1.1 billion in 1991, far outstripping the merchandising group profits of $486 million. See Table 6.3 for the trend in relative profits of these two areas. Despite the profitable growth of financial services, the erosion of the core merchandising business had to be troubling.

Brennan, who had been elected chairman and chief executive in 1985, by no means ignored the retailing end of the business. He introduced the first

Table 6.3   Contribution of Total Net Income of Financial Services and Merchandising Group, 1970–1991 (in millions)

Year	Net Income	Financial Amount	%	Merchandising Amount	%
1970	468	125	27	343	73
1975	523	129	25	394	75
1977	838	474	57	364	43
1979	830	549	66	281	34
1982	861	429	50	432	50
1985	1,294	528	41	766	59
1988	1,454	930	64	524	36
1991	1,586	1,100	69	486	31

Source: Sears annual reports.
Commentary: Note the increasingly subordinate role in corporate profits of the merchandising group in recent years, falling to only 31 percent of total in 1991, the lowest ever.

[2]Joseph Winski, "New President Hopes to Strike Balance at Sears," *Chicago Tribune* (March 17, 1980): 10, sec. 5.

"store of the future" in King of Prussia, Pennsylvania, in 1982, shortly after assuming the presidency. By 1989 all Sears stores fit this more modern proto-type. He had tried various programs to promote the clothing end of the business, using supermodel Cheryl Tiegs and tennis star Yvonne Goolagong, to spur apparel sales, but with no apparent success. He even tried "everyday low prices," the strategy used by Wal-Mart and Kmart on customers tired of the "sales" game. This was announced with much fanfare in 1989. Unfor-tunately, it also bombed, as the high overhead structure of Sears did not allow it to give its customers rock-bottom prices. Despite the disappointments of these strategic ventures, let us note a great potential advantage that retail chain organizations have, as described in the following box.

INFORMATION BOX

ADVANTAGES OF CHAINS: OPPORTUNITY FOR EXPERIMENTATION

An organization with numerous similar outlets has an unparalleled opportu-nity for experimenting with new ideas in the quest for what might be most pro-ductive and compelling. Prospective strategy changes can be tested with a few stores, any promising modifications determined, and the success of the strategy ascertained from concrete sales and profits results. All this can be done with rel-atively little risk since only a few outlets of the total chain are involved, and the strategy can be adopted throughout the organization only if results look favor-able. Such experimentation is hardly possible for the firm with few comparable units, which describes most manufacturers, and consequently its risks in making major strategic changes are greater.

How would you design an experiment for a chain organization? Be as spe-cific as you can, and make any assumptions needed.

The great strength of the Sears retail operation had long been its home improvement area—paint, power tools, siding, hardware, tires. These durable goods accounted for almost 70 percent of Sears' revenues from merchandise. But now even this was suffering. Such upstart competitors as Home Depot and Builders Square robustly gained market share at Sears' expense.

SEPTEMBER 30, 1992

In a special meeting, Sears directors approved a program to spin off the Dean Witter Financial Services Group, most of its Coldwell Banker real-estate holdings, and 20 percent of its Allstate insurance unit. The moves would reduce Sears' heavy debt by $3 billion. Essentially, Sears would be taken back to where it was in 1981, when Brennan first assumed the office of president, except that Sears' retail business had lost its dominance in the ensuing years.

The idea of spinning off subsidiaries was nothing new; it had been urged by some shareholders in the past. The assumption behind any such move is that the whole of the company is worth less than the sum of its parts. Therefore, shareholders would benefit. Some estimates were that the breakup of the company could bring $80 to $90 a share, versus the low $40s for the entire firm.[3]

Still, the suddenness and the completeness of the directors' decision was surprising, and Sears became the center of attention in the business press. Besides the slowly deteriorating state of the retail business, several other factors probably led to the abrupt decision. In the previous months, Sears auto centers had received bad publicity about overcharging customers, as we will describe in the next section. In addition, Hurricane Andrew had resulted in huge claims for the Allstate unit. And on September 25, Moody's Investors' Services lowered Sears' credit rating.

The decision was also described in headlines as a "humbling move for Brennan," since he had been the architect of most of the diversification efforts.[4] Despite the plaudits of some Sears investors and a strong $3.375 rise in the stock price the next day, serious concerns could be raised.

Spinning off the healthiest sectors of the business would mean that the underperforming retail sector would no longer be buttressed by financial support. The weaknesses of its operation would be all the more visible to the public and could hardly be hidden in corporate total statistics. With the retail operation unlikely to be quickly—if ever—turned around, Sears was going with its losers and getting rid of its winners.

ACCUSATIONS OF FRAUD AT SEARS AUTO CENTERS

On June 12, 1992, national publications reported that the California Department of Consumer Affairs had accused Sears of systematically overcharging auto-repair customers. The agency even went so far as to propose revoking the company's license to operate its automotive centers in the state.

The year-long undercover investigation had been prompted by a growing number of consumer complaints. For example:

---

[3]Jeff Bailey, "Sears Stock Fails to Show Further Rally," *The Wall Street Journal* (October 1, 1992): A4. Also, Robert A.G. Monks, "Sears and the Shareholder," *The Wall Street Journal* (October 1, 1992): A16.

[4]Gregory A. Patterson and Francine Schwadel, "Sears Suddenly Undoes Years of Diversifying Beyond Retailing Field," *The Wall Street Journal* (September 30, 1992): A1.

Ruth Hernandez of Stockton, California, went to Sears to buy new tires for her 1986 Honda Accord. The Sears mechanic insisted that she also needed new struts at a cost of $419.95. Shocked, she sought a second opinion, and another auto-repair store told her the struts were fine. Hernandez was livid and she returned to Sears where a sheepish mechanic admitted the diagnosis was wrong. "I keep thinking," Hernandez reflected, "how many other people this has happened to."[5]

The Department of Consumer Affairs found that its agents were over-charged at Sears Centers nearly 90 percent of the time by an average of $233. The department said that repairmen were pressured to overcharge by Sears' punitive sales quotas. "This is a flagrant breach of the trust and confidence the people of California have placed in Sears for generations," said Jim Conran, director of the department. "Sears has used trust as a marketing tool, and we don't believe they've lived up to that trust."[6]

The Sears case may be the biggest fraud action ever against an auto-repair firm. Although the investigation was conducted in California, the findings seemingly represented a much more widespread problem, perhaps involving Sears's 850 auto repair centers nationwide.

At first Sears vigorously contested the allegations. It called the accusa-tions by California regulators politically motivated and denied any fraud. It accused regulators of trying to gain support at a time when they were threat-ened by severe budget cuts. Sears' lawyers held this position for several days. But the crisis intensified, especially a few days later when New Jersey regu-lators said that they, too, had found overcharges common in Sears shops.

Sears soon adopted a more conciliatory stance. It took out full-page ads in major newspapers in the form of a letter from Chairman Brennan, who expressed deep concern about the problem and pledged that Sears would satisfy all its customers: "With over two million automotive customers serviced last year in California alone, mistakes may have occurred. However, Sears wants you to know that we would never intentionally vio-late the trust customers have shown in our company for 105 years." But auto service sales dropped 15 percent. And this was a division that had produced 9 percent of Sears' merchandising groups revenues and had been one of the fastest growing and most profitable business units in recent years, servicing 20 million vehicles in 1991.[7]

[5] Example taken from Keven Kelly, "How Did Sears Blow This Gasket?" *Business Week* (June 29, 1992): 38.

[6] Tung Yin, "Sears is Accused of Billing Fraud at Auto Centers," *The Wall Street Journal* (June 12, 1992): B1, B6.

[7] Gregory A. Patterson, "Sears's Brennan Accepts Blame for Auto Flap," *The Wall Street Journal* (June 23, 1992): B1, B12.

To appease the critics and assure the public of its honesty, Sears pledged to stop using the quota and commission system for its auto center employees and to substitute a full salary plan. However, on March 7, 1994, *The Wall Street Journal* disclosed that Sears was quietly reinstating sales incentives in some auto centers. Jim Thornton, Sears automotive vice president, defended the use of commissions and cited safeguards he said should prevent a recurrence of the 1992 problems. "We don't believe all commission is bad," he said.[8]

WHAT WENT WRONG?

Sears merchandising efforts represent a classic example of nonresponse to a changing environment. While Brennan made some efforts to institute change—store of the future, brand-name merchandise, and everyday low prices, for example—these were really only surface gestures of little consequence.

Of much more import, Sears allowed aggressive competitors to capture ever more market share. It ignored sweeping changes in demographics and shopping habits, under the assumption that the Sears way of doing business was unassailable. Yet all the while Sears was losing business: to department stores who offered customers more ambience; to discounters and specialty stores such as Toys R Us, Home Depot, and Circuit City Stores that focused on a single category of goods but offered huge assortments at low prices; and to Wal-Mart and Kmart stores that offered the widest possible variety of goods at prices that Sears simply could not match. See the following box for a discussion of the need for environmental monitoring.

In its many decades of retail dominance, Sears had built up a bureaucratic organizational structure. This seems to be a natural evolution for organizations as they achieve great size and dominance over decades.

The natural consequence of Sears's organization structure was not only that it failed to respond well to a rapidly changing environment, but also that it was burdened with such a high overhead that it was unable to match the prices of its most aggressive competitors. For example, in 1991 Sears spent 29.2 percent of its revenues on salaries, light bills, advertising, and other routine costs. At the same time, Kmart's expenses amounted to 19.6 percent of sales, and Wal-Mart's were even less, at 15.3 percent.[9] So Sears was left somewhere in a sterile middle between department stores and discount stores. By no means did it offer the ambience and fashion atmosphere of good department stores, and it certainly could not profitably match the

[8]Gilbert Fuchsberg, "Sears Reinstates Sales Incentives in Some Centers," *The Wall Street Journal* (March 7, 1994): B1.

[9]Stephanie Strom, "Further Prescriptions for the Convalescent Sears," *The New York Times* (October 1, 1992): D1.

INFORMATION BOX

NEED FOR ENVIRONMENTAL MONITORING

A firm must be alert to changes in the business environment: changes in customer preferences and needs, in competition, in the economy, and even in international events, such as nationalism in Canada, OPEC machinations, and economic and social changes in Eastern Europe. Many of the mistakes in this book are at least partly attributable to a failure to recognize how the business environment was changing and that unchanging policies were no longer appropriate.

How can a firm such as Sears, or IBM for that matter, remain alert to subtle and insidious as well as more obvious changes? A firm must have sensors constantly monitoring the environment. The sensor may reside in a marketing or economic research department, but in many instances such a formal organizational entity is not really necessary to provide primary monitoring. Executive alertness is essential. Few changes occur suddenly and without warning. Companies can get feedback from customers, from sales representatives, from suppliers; can keep abreast of the latest material and projections in business journals; and can observe what is happening in stores, in advertising, in pricing, and in the introduction of new technologies. These sources can provide sufficient information about the environment and how it is changing. Sensors of the environment can be organized and formal, or they can be strictly informal and subjective. But it is surprising and disturbing how many executives overlook, disregard, or are not even aware of important changing environmental factors that presage changes in their present and future business.

How would you go about ensuring that your firm has adequate sensors of the marketplace?

---

prices of its discount competitors. One could wonder whether Sears had become an anachronism, an impotent throwback to an earlier time now sadly out of place and competitively vulnerable.

Perhaps Sears let its attention shift too much away from its core retail business in its quest for diversification into financial services. Brennan was the second Sears chairman to see the stores as a great vehicle for disseminating certain kinds of consumer services in addition to merchandise. Certainly, the logic seemed inescapable. See the following box.

In the last decade at least, the basic business of Sears appears to have been relatively neglected, as attention turned more to services. Perhaps this would also have happened without such diversification. It could well be argued that the lack of substantial change and innovation in the retail operation resulted from a smug and complacent organization (we have certainly encountered this situation before, and we will again). Some telling statistics

---

INFORMATION BOX

SHOULD RETAILERS DIVERSIFY INTO SERVICES?

Although merchandising of services may seem far afield from traditional retailing and its merchandising of goods, in some ways consumer services are natural areas for expansion. This is especially true for the retailer with a reputation for dependability and a sizable body of loyal customers with active charge accounts. Sears led most retailers in such diversifications. Much of the success of Sears in promoting its home repair and appliance servicing, and even its auto service, was due to its image of reliability, honest work, and guaranteed satisfaction. Many customers saw these characteristics sorely needed in repair industries, where honest work and dependability were usually lacking. They trusted Sears. (Unfortunately, such trust received a setback in mid-1992 when publicity, as we have seen, surfaced that Sears auto centers had been overcharging customers— just like the rest of the industry in the thinking of many consumers.)

Financial services—insurance, investments, real estate—are viewed by many middle-class Americans as just as arcane and subject to abuse as repair services. It seemed natural that a trusting relationship regarding Sears' quality and dependability could be transferred also to this area. And indeed there was a mutual compatibility, as the success of financial services in the Sears organization has proven.

Unfortunately, corporate executives from Brennan on down perhaps became too enamored with this end of the total operation. In the process, they let Sears' core business slip, perhaps irretrievably.

On balance, was the diversification of Sears all that wise?

Given that the core business is not neglected in the promotion of services, do you see any other dangers in such diversification?

---

support the conclusion that the retail sector was badly neglected, whatever the reasons might have been.

During the late 1970s and the 1980s, U.S. store space doubled. Yet Sears failed to add retail space in this period. (See Table 6.1 for the trend in number of stores.) Instead, it concentrated on closing unprofitable stores and remodeling others. Naturally, it lost market share. Its share of sales of department-store–type merchandise in the United States dropped to less than 6 percent from more than 8 percent.[10] Sears catalog sales also stagnated, despite a boom in catalogs of all kinds during this period.

The 1980s was also marked as a time of rapid expansion of specialty stores, stores featuring limited lines of merchandise but great depth within

---

[10]Patterson and Schwadel, "Sears Suddenly Undoes Years," A16.

the categories. Some of these were highly successful, such as Limited, Gap, and such discount specialty stores as Toys R Us and Kids R Us. Sears dabbled a bit with specialty stores during this period, opening Business Systems Centers, separate paint and hardware stores, a small chain of eye-care products, and one petite women's clothing chain. And it acquired the Western Auto chain of auto supplies stores. But the efforts seemed too little and too late to capitalize on this specialty store trend.

RENAISSANCE

In 1992, Arthur Martinez came to Sears from Saks Fifth Avenue as head of the retail merchandising division under Brennan. He was the person instrumental in the decision to do away with the catalog. He also closed 113 stores and lopped off 50,000 jobs in a major restructuring. In so doing he was dubbed the man from Saks with the ax by resentful workers. But Martinez seemed to be the elixir needed. One industry analyst said, "I wouldn't call him the Miracle Man, but he comes pretty close. Up until the time Martinez stepped in, I felt that Sears had maybe one or two more years and that would be the end."[11]

In 1995, the last nonretail operations, Allstate Corporation and Homart Development Company, were spun off or divested, leaving only the merchandising group. In that year, Brennan retired and Martinez was named chairman of the company. Martinez said in the *1995 Annual Report*, "We are building on our legacy—which includes a relationship of trust with more than half the households in America, superior store locations and world-class brands like Kenmore, Craftsman and DieHard."[12]

He reported that a five-year, $4 billion store renovation program begun in 1993 was on schedule, and was providing more contemporary environments, better layouts for ease of shopping, and more space for apparel and accessories. He saw other future growth centering around home and auto-related goods and services. These had long been the strength of Sears, and Martinez wanted to build on them. For example, Sears is the leading seller of appliances: Kenmore, found in one out of every two American homes, is a national brand available only at Sears. Other brands, such as Craftsman tools, and Weatherbeater and Easy Living paints give Sears the number one market share in paint, most tool categories, mowers, and tractors.

Furniture departments were being relocated from mall-based stores to new off-the-mall HomeLife stores. Sears had 5.7 million square feet of mall-store space devoted to furniture in 1992, and by 1998 planned to have 5 mil-

---

[11] Quote of Kurt Barnard of Barnard's Retail Marketing Report, reported in *Cleveland Plain Dealer* (July 23, 1996): 2C.

[12] *Sears 1995 Annual Report*, p. 2.

lion in the HomeLife format. Plans were for 500 Sears Hardware stores by the end of the decade; these combined a wide selection with the convenience of a neighborhood hardware store.

In 1995, Sears brought repair services and home improvement products into one operation, called Sears Home Services. This was designed to build on a great strength of Sears, its trust by customers for excellent product repair and installation services. More than 15 million home visits were made in 1995.[13]

By 1995, Sears was even resurrecting the catalog, this time in the form of specialty catalogs. More than 125 million were mailed, including nine million Wish Book catalogs featuring toys for the holiday season. As an example of a select market segment catalog, Workwear was targeted to customers who had purchased Workwear from Sears in the past.

These new emphases, along with streamlining operations and increasing efficiency, brought measurable success to Sears. For example, comparable store sales (the rate of sales increases in stores open for more than one year) increased 8.9 percent in 1993, 8.3 percent in 1994, and 4.7 percent in 1995. During these years, selling, general, and administrative expenses as a percentage of sales declined from 23.3 percent to 21.6 percent. Table 6.4 shows the revenue and operating income statistics from 1992 through 1995.

The favorable performance continued into 1996. For example, for the 3rd period of 1996, Sears beat Wall Street expectations by posting a 22 percent increase in net income. The results were driven by increases in both women's clothing and hardlines.[13]

In late 1996, it was announced that Sears was testing a new format in its Home Stores: ". . . with the population getting older, people who may have

Table 6.4   Sears' Operating Results, 1992–1995 (Not reflecting discontinued financial service affiliates)

	millions of dollars			
	1995	1994	1993	1992
Revenues	$34,925	33,025	30,444	32,943
Operating Income	1,705	1,454	844	(2,980)

Source: Sears annual reports.
Commentary: While the gains in revenues for these four years, which primarily reflects the merchandising group, does not show substantial gains, the gains in profitability are something else and represent a significant turnaround.

[13] Sears 1995 Annual Report, p. 2.
[13] Robert Berner, "Sears Posts 22% Increase in Profit for 3rd Period, Beating Estimates," The Wall Street Journal (October 17, 1996) B4.

formerly been do-it-yourself types, in the future may want to have these services performed for them." As the largest provider of home services, here could be another platform for growth.[14]

WHAT CAN BE LEARNED?

Core business can be the salvation. Unless the prospects for a firm's core business are so bleak that resources and efforts need to be shifted, it is a grave mistake to neglect the core. This is where a company's expertise is; it is the focal point of the heritage of success. The core should not be neglected in the quest for exciting but often unproven new ventures. Sears was guilty of this: It shifted attention from retail goods to financial services. Although these diversifications turned out to be successful, the deemphasis of the flagship part of the business almost brought the company down.

Now we are seeing renewed and effective emphasis on this core. But success depends on rejuvenation, not simply falling back to perhaps outdated policies for the basic core position.

Keys to rejuvenating the core. The turnaround of Sears in its embracing of its core suggests these insights:

1. A must: analyze how the core position can be improved, enhanced, made more competitive. What strengths and weaknesses does it have? How can the strengths be enhanced? Are certain major changes needed, perhaps a different focus or format? Should certain traditional operations be eliminated or modified so that others can be emphasized and given needed resources?

2. What future trends or changes can be seen? How might these impact on the core? What defensive and aggressive actions ought to be considered near-term and further out? We can call these "opportunities" and "threats." These along with the strengths and weaknesses constitute the well-known SWOT analysis discussed in the following box.

Again, beware the "king of the hill" three C's mindset. In the preceding case we encountered the destructive trio that weaken frontrunners: conservatism, complacency, and conceit. As IBM's responsiveness to changing conditions was stymied until recently because of this pervasive orientation, so was Sears. In Chapter 5, we discussed how a large and mature organization can guard against such a mindset. You may want to review this.

---

[14]Phyllis Plitch, "Sears Will Test New Format at Home Stores," *The Wall Street Journal* (September 23, 1996) A15.

INFORMATION BOX

THE SWOT ANALYSIS FOR DECISION MAKING

The SWOT analysis, sometimes called a situation analysis, involves identifying internal strengths and weaknesses (S and W) as well as external opportunities and threats (O and T). It represents a systematic appraisal of the situation, and this is good. However, since the SWOT analysis is primarily dealing with future judgments, it suffers from the dilemma of all forecasting: the future is always uncertain, things can change sometimes in strange ways, or assessments may be flawed. Nevertheless, there is value in systematically considering all the reasonable aspects of a situation and making expert judgments regarding them.

While we do not know how much Martinez may have relied on either formal or informal SWOT analysis in refocusing Sears, we can conjecture. The strengths of Sears were undoubtedly its well-known and accepted national brands, such as DieHard, Craftsman, and Kenmore, and its repair and home improvement products and services. And an image for dependability among many consumers. These Martinez could build on. Profitability figures showed continuing weaknesses in the catalog operation, and he axed this despite many who were shocked. Women's ready-to-wear was another weakness but he thought this could be strengthened. He saw opportunities in non-mall specialty stores, such as neighborhood hardware and furniture stores, in new service formats, and even specialty catalogs. As to threats, no retailer can afford to ignore the competitive threats of department stores, major discounters, and category killer stores such as Builder's Square, Circuit City, and OfficeMax and Office Depot.

How specifically would you evaluate the threat of a category killer store (a store that offers the widest possible variety of one category of goods at very attractive prices)?

Can great size be achieved without becoming a bureaucratic organization? The bureaucratic stage is a natural evolution as a firm becomes larger and more dominant in its industry, but companies can guard against it. A firm can seek an adaptive organizational structure, emphasizing decentralization, minimizing rigid rules and procedures, creating an open and flexible division of labor, having a wide span of control and few layers of management, as well as cultivating a spirit of informality and receptivity to new ideas. So a firm can avoid becoming a ponderous and high overhead organization. But it takes a strong top management commitment, a commitment to minimize the insularity of the executive suite and resist growth in staff positions.

CONSIDER

Do you see some additional learning insights coming from the Sears case?

QUESTIONS

1. Some years ago, Sears attempted to upgrade its fashion image with more emphasis on women's ready-to-wear. The attempt was a costly failure. Do you think Martinez's plans for expanding this are better this time? Why or why not?
2. How would you propose streamlining the Sears bureaucratic organization? Be as specific as you can. If you need to make assumptions, state them clearly.
3. What is your opinion of the Sears auto repair centers? Do you think their overcharging was less than, worse than, or about the same as their competitors? What leads you to this opinion?
4. A common practice of repair people in all areas is to replace some parts that are still workable with new parts. This, of course, raises the price of the repair. But is this really such a bad practice? After all, the new parts should assure longer trouble-free use of the car.
5. Overreliance on promotion from within often is more harmful than desirable in an organization. Evaluate the promotion of Ed Brennan.
6. "We don't believe all commission is bad," said Jim Thornton, the Sears official in charge of its auto centers, in 1994. Evaluate this statement.
7. Do you agree with Martinez's contention that Sears has a great reputation for dependable service? Why or why not?

HANDS-ON EXERCISES

1. It is 1980, and you are the staff assistant to the president of Sears. You sense that major shifts in retailing are emerging and that Sears needs to change if it is to keep its market dominance.
   a. What research do you recommend for tracking competitive threats?
   b. Based on what we know now, what actions should Sears have undertaken in the 1980s? Do you think these efforts would have been successful in preserving market dominance? Why or why not?
2. You are executive assistant to Edward Brennan, CEO of Sears. He wants to institute sweeping reforms in the auto repair operations. What arguments can you give him not to push the panic button, but to institute only very modest changes?

TEAM DEBATE EXERCISES

1. Debate the controversy in the early 1990s of selling off and divesting all the financial services of Sears. After all, they were good money-makers. Which arguments pro and con do you think are most compelling?
2. Martinez has said, ". . . a lot of the growth of the company has to come from formats that are not mall-based because mall-based shopping is a fundamentally mature sector."[15] Debate this contention that Sears expansion efforts should primarily be in non-mall stores.
3. Debate the 1993 decision to drop the Sears catalog. What arguments can you see for keeping it? Be as persuasive as possible in supporting this idea and defending against the contrary position.

INVITATION TO RESEARCH

What is the current situation with Sears? Is Martinez still the CEO? Has the auto repair business had any more negative publicity?

---

[15]"Sears Chairman a Hands-on Guy," *Cleveland Plain Dealer* (July 23, 1996): 2C.

CHAPTER 7

Harley Davidson Fights Back, Finally

In the early 1960s, a staid and unexciting market was shaken up, was rocked to its core, by the most unlikely invader. This intruder was a smallish Japanese firm that had risen out of the ashes of World War II and was now trying to encroach on the territory of a major U.S. firm, a firm that had in the space of 60 years destroyed all of its U.S. competitors and now had a firm 70 percent of the motorcycle market.

Yet, almost inconceivably, in one-half a decade this market share was to fall to 5 percent, and the total market was to expand many times over what it had been for decades. A foreign invader had furnished a textbook example of the awesome effectiveness of carefully crafted marketing efforts. In the process, this confrontation between Honda and Harley Davidson was a harbinger of the Japanese invasion of the auto industry.

Eventually, by the late 1980s, Harley was to make a comeback. But only after more than two decades of travail and mediocrity.

THE INVASION

Sales of motorcycles in the United States were around 50,000 per year during the 1950s: Harley Davidson, Britain's Norton and Triumph, and Germany's BMW accounted for most of the market. By the turn of the decade, Honda had begun to penetrate the U.S. market. In 1960 fewer than 400,000 motorcycles were registered in the United States. While this was an increase of almost 200,000 from the end of World War II 15 years before, it was a rate of increase far below that of other motor vehicles. But by 1964, only 4 years later, the number had risen to 960,000; 2 years later it was 1.4 million; and by 1971 it was almost 4 million.

In expanding the demand for motorcycles, Honda instituted a distinctly different strategy. The major elements of this strategy were lightweight cycles and an advertising approach directed toward a new customer. Few firms have ever experienced such a shattering of market share as did Harley Davidson in the 1960s. (Although its market share declined drastically, its total sales remained nearly constant, indicating that it was getting none of the new customers for motorcycles.)

Reaction of Harley Davidson to the Honda Threat

Faced with an invasion of its staid and static U.S. market, how did Harley react to the intruder? It did not react! At least not until far too late. Harley Davidson considered itself the leader in full-size motorcycles. While the company might shudder at the image tied in with its product's usage by the leather jacket types, it took solace in the fact that almost every U.S. police department used its machines. Perhaps this is what led Harley to stand aside and complacently watch Honda make deep inroads into the American motorcycle market. The management saw no threat in Honda's thrust into the market with lightweight machines. The attitude was exemplified in this statement by William H. Davidson, the president of the company and son of the founder:

> Basically, we don't believe in the lightweight market. We believe that motorcycles are sport vehicles, not transportation vehicles. Even if a man says he bought a motorcycle for transportation, it's generally for leisure-time use. The lightweight motorcycle is only supplemental. Back around World War I, a number of companies came out with lightweight bikes. We came out with one ourselves. They never got anywhere. We've seen what happens to these small sizes.[1]

Eventually Harley recognized that the Honda phenomenon was not an aberration, and that there was a new factor in the market. The company attempted to fight back by offering an Italian-made lightweight in the mid-1960s. But it was far too late; Honda was firmly entrenched. The Italian bikes were regarded in the industry to be of lower quality than the Japanese bikes. Honda, and toward the end of the 1960s other Japanese manufacturers, continued to dominate what had become a much larger market than Harley Davidson had ever dreamed.

---

[1] Tom Rowan, "Harley Sets New Drive to Boost Market Share," *Advertising Age* (January 29, 1973): 34–35.

AFTERMATH OF THE HONDA INVASION: 1965–1981

In 1965 Harley Davidson made its first public stock offering. Soon after, it faced a struggle for control. The contest was primarily between Bangor Punta, an Asian company, and AMF, an American company with strong interests in recreational equipment, including bowling products. In a bidding war, Harley Davidson's stockholders chose AMF over Bangor Punta, even though the bid was $1 less than Bangor's offer of $23 per share. Stockholders were leery of Bangor's reputation of taking over a company, squeezing it dry, and then scrapping it for the remaining assets. AMF's plans for expansion of Harley Davidson seemed more compatible.

But the marriage was troubled: Harley Davidson's old equipment was not capable of the expansion envisioned by AMF. At the very time that Japanese manufacturers—Honda and others—were flooding the market with high-quality motorcycles, Harley was falling down on quality. One company official noted that "quality was going down just as fast as production was going up."[2] Indicative of the depths of the problem at a demoralized Harley Davidson, quality control inspections failed 50 percent to 60 percent of the motorcycles produced. Only 5 percent of Japanese motorcycles failed their quality control checks.

AMF put up with an average $4.8 million operating loss for 11 years. Finally, it called it quits and put the division up for sale in 1981. Vaughan Beals, vice president of motorcycle sales, still had faith in the company: He led a team that used $81.5 million in financing from Citicorp to complete a leveraged buyout. All ties with AMF were severed.

VAUGHAN BEALS

Beals was a middle-aged Ivy Leaguer, a far cry from what one might think of as a heavy motorcycle aficianado. He had graduated from MIT's Aeronautical Engineering School and was considered a production specialist.[4] But he was far more than that. His was a true commitment to motorcycles, personally as well as professionally. Deeply concerned with AMF's declining attention to quality, he achieved the buyout from AMF.

The prognosis for the company was bleak. Its market share, which had dominated the industry before the Honda invasion, now was 3 percent. In 1983 Harley Davidson would celebrate its 80th birthday; some doubted it

---

[2] Peter C. Reid, *Well Made in America—Lessons from Harley Davidson on Being the Best* (New York: McGraw-Hill, 1990), p. 10.

[3] Reid, "Well Made in America," p. 27.

[4] Rod Willis, "Harley Davidson Comes Roaring Back," *Management Review* (March 1986): 20–27.

would still be around by then. Tariff protection seemed Harley's only hope, and massive lobbying paid off. In 1983 Congress passed a huge tariff increase on Japanese motorcycles. Instead of a 4 percent tariff, now Japanese motorcycles would be subject to a 45 percent tariff for the coming 5 years.[5]

The tariff gave the company new hope, and it slowly began to rebuild market share. Key to this was restoring confidence in the quality of its products. Beals took a leading role in this. He drove Harley Davidsons to rallies, where he met Harley owners. There he learned of their concerns and their complaints, and he promised changes. At these rallies a core of loyal Harley Davidson users, called HOGs (for Harley Owners Group), were to be trailblazers for the successful growth to come.

Beals had company on his odyssey: Willie G. Davidson, grandson of the company's founder and the vice president of design. Davidson was an interesting contrast to the more urbane Beals. His was the image of a middle-aged hippie. He wore a Viking helmet over his long, unkempt hair, and a straggly beard hid some of his wind-burned face. With his aged leather jacket, Davidson fit in nicely at the HOG rallies.

THE STRUGGLE BACK

In December 1986 Harley Davidson asked Congress to remove the tariff barriers, more than a year earlier than originally planned. The company's confidence had been restored, and it believed it could now compete with the Japanese head to head.[6]

Production Improvements

Shortly after the buyout, Beals and other managers visited Japanese plants in Japan and Honda's assembly plant in Marysville, Ohio. They were impressed that they were being beaten not by "robotics, or culture, or morning calisthenics and company songs, [but by] professional managers who understood their business and paid attention to detail."[7] As a result, Japanese operating costs were as much as 30 percent lower than Harley's.[8]

Beals and his managers tried to implement some of the Japanese management techniques. They divided each plant into profit centers, assigning managers total responsibility within their particular area. Just-in-time (JIT) inventory and a materials-as-needed (MAN) system sought to control and

---

[5] Robert L. Rose, "Vrooming Back," *The Wall Street Journal* (August 31, 1990): 1.

[6] "Harley Back in High Gear," *Forbes* (April 20, 1987): 8.

[7] Dexter Hutchins, "Having a Hard Time with Just-in-Time," *Fortune* (June 19, 1986): 65.

[8] John A. Saathoff, "Workshop Report: Maintain Excellence through Change," *Target* (Spring 1989): 3.

minimize all inventories both inside and outside the plants. Quality circles (QCs) were formed to increase employee involvement in quality goals and to improve communication between management and workers. See the following box for further discussion of quality circles. Another new program called statistical operator control (SOC) gave employees the responsibility for checking the quality of their own work and making proper correcting adjustments. Efforts were made to improve labor relations by more sensitivity to employees and their problems as well as better employee assistance and benefits. Certain product improvements were also introduced, notably a new engine and mountings on rubber to reduce vibration. A well-accepted equipment innovation was to build stereo systems and intercoms into the motorcycle helmets.

INFORMATION BOX

QUALITY CIRCLES

Quality circles were adopted by Japan in an effort to rid its industries of poor quality control and junkiness after World War II. Quality circles are worker-management committees that meet regularly, usually weekly, to talk about production problems, plan ways to improve productivity and quality, and resolve job-related gripes on both sides. They have been described as "the single most significant explanation for the truly outstanding quality of goods and services produced in Japan."[9] For example, Mazda had 2,147 circles, with more than 16,000 employees involved. They usually consisted of seven to eight volunteer members who met on their own time to discuss and solve the issues that concerned them. In addition to making major contributions to increased productivity and quality, they provided employees an opportunity to participate and gain a sense of accomplishment.[10]

The idea—like so many ideas adopted by the Japanese—did not originate with them: It came from two American personnel consultants. The Japanese refined the idea and ran with it. Now American industry has rediscovered quality circles. Some firms have found them a desirable way to promote teamwork and good feelings and to avoid at least some of the adversarial relations stemming from collective bargaining and union grievances that must be negotiated.

Despite sterling claims for quality circles, they have not always worked out well. Some workers claim they smack of "tokenism" and are more a facade than anything practical. Questions are also raised as to how much lasting benefit such circles have, once the novelty has worn off. Others doubt that the time invested

---

[9] "A Partnership to Build the New Workplace," *Business Week* (June 30, 1980): 101.
[10] As described in a Mazda ad in *Forbes* (May 24, 1982): 5.

in quality circles by management and workers is that productive. And few U.S. workers accept the idea of participating in quality circles on their own time.

How would you feel about devoting an hour or more to quality circle meetings every week or so, on your own time? If your answer is "no way," do you think this is a fair attitude on your part? Why or why not?

The production changes between 1981 and 1988 caused some dramatic results:[11]

Inventory fell by 67 percent.

Productivity increased by 50 percent.

Scrap and rework fell 67 percent.

Defects per unit fell 70 percent.

In the 1970s the joke among industry experts was, "If you're buying a Harley, you'd better buy two—one for spare parts."[12] Now this had obviously changed, but the change still had to be communicated to consumers, and believed.

Marketing Moves

Despite its bad times and its poor quality, Harley had a cadre of loyal customers almost unparalleled. Company research maintained that 92 percent of its customers remained with Harley.[13] Despite such hard-core loyalists, however, the company had always had a serious public image problem. It was linked to an image of the pot-smoking, beer-drinking, woman-chasing, tattoo-covered, leather-clad biker: "When your company's logo is the number one requested in tattoo parlors, it's time to get a licensing program that will return your reputation to the ranks of baseball, hot dogs, and apple pie."[14]

Part of Harley's problem had been with bootleggers, who had helped ruin the name by placing it on unlicensed goods of poor quality. Now the company began to use warrants and federal marshalls to crack down on unauthorized uses of its logo at motorcycle conventions. And it began licensing its name and logo on a wide variety of products, from leather jackets to cologne to jewelry—even to pajamas, sheets, and towels. Suddenly retailers realized that these licensed goods were popular and were even being bought by a new customer segment, undreamed of until now: bankers, doctors, lawyers, and entertainers. These new customers soon expanded their horizons to include the Harley Davidson bikes themselves. They joined the HOGs, only now

[11] Hutchins, "Having a Hard Time," 66.
[12] *Ibid.*
[13] Mark Marvel, "The Gentrified HOG," *Esquire* (July 1989): 25.
[14] "Thunder Road," *Forbes* (July 18, 1983): 32.

they became known as *Rubbies*—the rich urban bikers. High prices for bikes did not bother them in the least.

Beals was quick to capitalize on this new market with an expanded product line with expensive heavyweights. In 1989 the largest motorcycle was introduced, the Fat Boy, with 80 cubic inches of V-twin engine and capable of a top speed of 150 MPH. By 1991 Harley had 20 models, ranging in price from $4,500 to $15,000.

The Rubbies brought Harley back to a leading position in the industry by 1989, with almost 60 percent of the super heavyweight motorcycle market; by the first quarter of 1993, this had become 63 percent. See Figure 7.1. The importance of this customer to Harley could be seen in the demographic statistics supplied by *The Wall Street Journal* in 1990: "One in three of today's Harley Davidson buyers are professionals or managers. About 60 percent have attended college, up from only 45 percent in 1984. Their median age is 35, and their median household income has risen sharply to $45,000 from $36,000 five years earlier."[15]

In 1989 Beals stepped down as CEO, turning the company over to Richard Teerlink, who was chief operating officer of the Motorcycle Division. Beals, however, retained his position as chairman of the board. The legacy of Beals in the renaissance of Harley was particularly notable for his bringing it out of the internal production orientation that had long characterized the firm. See the following information box for a discussion of an internal versus an external (marketing) orientation.

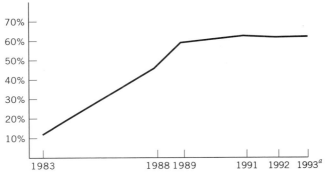

Figure 7.1. Harley Davidson's share of the U.S. heavyweight motorcycle market, selected years, 1983–1993.
(*Sources:* Company reports; R. L. Polk & Company; Gary Slutsker, "Hog Wild," *Forbes* (May 24, 1993): 45–46.)

[a]Data as of first quarter 1993.

[15] Rose, "Vrooming Back," 1.

INFORMATION BOX

INTERNAL VS. EXTERNAL (MARKETING) ORIENTATION

Managers sometimes focus primarily on internal factors, such as technology and cost cutting. They subsequently see the key to attracting customers in improving production and distribution efficiency and lowering costs if possible. Henry Ford pioneered this philosophy in the early 1900s with his Model T. Harley stuck for decades with this orientation in the absence of competition. The internal orientation is most appropriate in three situations (with the third one often of unknown risk):

1. When demand for a product exceeds supply, such as in new technologies and in developing countries.
2. When the product cost is high and the market can be expanded only if costs can be brought down.
3. When there is a present lack of significant competition, and no competitive threat is expected either because of severe entry requirements to the industry or because the market is limited.

Obviously, Harley Davidson in the 1960s had made a major miscalculation with the third situation, assuming that the motorcycle market would be forever limited.

An external, or marketing, orientation recognizes the fallacy of the assumption that products will forever sell themselves "if we maintain our production and technological superiority." Looking outside the firm to the market environment results in giving major priority to determining customers' needs and wants, assessing how these may be changing as evidenced by shifts in buying patterns, and adapting products and services accordingly. The external focus also permits more responsiveness to other external forces that may be influencers, such as major competitive thrusts, changing laws and regulations, economic conditions, and the like. With such an external orientation, attention will more likely be directed to locating new opportunities brought about by changing conditions, rather than focusing on internal production and technology. Such an orientation is more geared to meeting and even anticipating change.

Do all firms need a marketing orientation? Can you think of any that probably do not and will not?

SUCCESS

By 1993 Harley Davidson had a new problem, one born of success. Now it could not even come close to meeting demand. Customers faced empty showrooms, except perhaps for rusty trade-ins or antiques. Waiting time for a new bike could be 6 months or longer, unless the customer was willing to pay a 10 percent or higher premium to some gray marketer advertising in biker magazines.

Some of the 600 independent U.S. dealers worried that these empty showrooms and long waiting lists would induce their customers to turn to foreign imports, much as they had several decades before. But other dealers recognized that somehow Beals and company had engendered a brand loyalty unique in this industry, and perhaps in all industries. Assuaging the lack of big bike business, dealers were finding other sources of revenues. Harley's branded line of merchandise, available only at Harley dealers and promoted through glossy catalogs, had really taken off. Buyers snapped up Harley black leather jackets at $500, fringed leather bras at $65, even shot glasses at $12—all it seemed to take was the Harley name and logo. So substantial was this ancillary business that in 1992 noncycle business generated $155.7 million in sales, up from $130.3 million in 1991.

Production

In one sense, Harley's production situation was enviable: It had far more demand than production capability. More than this, it had such a loyal body of customers that delays were not likely to turn many away to competitors. The problem, of course, was that full potential was not being realized.

Richard Teerlink, the successor of Beals, expressed the corporate philosophy to expanding quantity to meet the demand: "Quantity isn't the issue, quality is the issue. We learned in the early 1980s you do not solve problems by throwing money at them."[16]

The company increased output slowly. In early 1992 it was making 280 bikes a day; by 1993 it was up to 345 a day. With increased capital spending, goals were to produce 420 bikes a day, but not until 1996.

Export Potential

Some contrary concerns with Teerlink's conservative expansion plans surfaced in regard to international operations. The European export market beckoned. Harleys had become very popular in Europe, but the company had promised its domestic dealers that exports would not go beyond 30 percent of total production until the North American market was fully satisfied. Suddenly the European big-bike market grew by an astounding 33 percent between 1990 and 1992. Yet because of its production constraints, Harley could maintain only a 9 percent to 10 percent share of this market. In other words, it was giving away business to foreign competitors.

---

[16]Gary Slutsker, "Hog Wild," *Forbes* (May 24, 1993): 46.

To enhance its presence in Europe, Harley opened a branch office of its HOG club in Frankfurt, Germany, for its European fans.

Specifics of the Resurgence of Harley Davidson

Table 7.1 shows Harley's trend in revenues and net income since 1982. The growth in sales and profits did not go unnoticed by the investment community. In 1990 Harley Davidson stock sold for $7 per share; in January 1993 it hit $39. Its market share of heavyweight motorcycles (751 cubic centimeters displacement and larger) had soared from 12.5 percent in 1983 to 63 percent by 1993. Let the Japanese have the lightweight bike market! Harley would dominate the heavyweights.

Harley acquired Holiday Rambler in 1986. As a wholly owned subsidiary, this manufacturer of recreational and commercial vehicles was judged by Harley management to be compatible with the existing motorcycle business as well as moderating some of the seasonality of the motorcycle business. The diversification proved rather mediocre. In 1992 Rambler accounted for 26 percent of total corporate sales, but only 2 percent of profits.[17]

Table 7.1   Harley Davidson's Growth in Revenue and Income 1983–1992 (in $ Millions)

Year	Revenue	Net Income
1982	$ 210	($25.1)
1983	254	1.0
1984	294	2.9
1985	287	2.6
1986	295	4.3
1987	685	17.7
1988	757	27.2
1989	791	32.6
1990	865	38.3
1991	940	37.0
1992	1100	54.0

Source: Company annual reports.
Commentary: The steady climb in sales and profits, except for a pause in 1985, is noteworthy. The total gain in revenues over these 11 years is 423.8 percent, while income has risen more than 50-fold since 1983.

[17]Company annual reports.

Big motorcycles, made in America by a single U.S. manufacturer, continued the rage. Harley's 90th anniversary was celebrated in Milwaukee on June 12, 1993. As many as 100,000 people, including 18,000 HOGs, were there to celebrate. Hotel rooms were sold out for a 60-mile radius. Harley Davidson was up and running.

ANALYSIS

One of Vaughan Beals's first moves after the 1981 leveraged buyout was to improve production efficiency and quality control. This became the foundation for the strategic regeneration moves to come. In this quest he borrowed heavily from the Japanese, in particular in cultivating employee involvement.

The cultivation of a new customer segment for the big bikes had to be a major factor in the company's resurgence. To some, that more affluent consumers embraced the big, flashy Harley motorcycles was a surprise of no small moment. After all, how could you have two more incompatible groups than the stereotyped black-jacketed cyclists and the Rubbies? Perhaps part of the change was due to high-profile people such as Beals and some of his executives, who frequently participated at motorcycle rallies and charity rides. Technological and comfort improvements in motorcycles and their equipment added to the new attractiveness. Dealers were also coaxed to make their stores more inviting.

Along with this, expanding the product mix not only made such Harley-branded merchandise a windfall for company and dealers alike, but also piqued the interest of upscale customers in motorcycles themselves. The company was commendably aggressive in running with the growing popularity of the ancillary merchandise and making it well over a $100 million revenue booster.

Some questions remain. How durable will be this popularity, both of the big bikes and the complementary merchandise, with this affluent customer segment? Will it prove to be only a passing fad? If such should be the case, then Harley needs to seek diversifications as quickly as possible. But its one major diversification, the Holiday Rambler Corporation, was no notable success. Diversifications often prove to be earnings disappointments compared with a firm's core business.

Another question concerns Harley's slowness in expanding production capability. Faced with a burgeoning demand, should a company go slowly, be carefully protective of quality, and refrain from heavy debt commitments? This has been Harley's most recent strategy. See the following issue box for a discussion of the wisdom of a slow-growth policy.

ISSUE BOX

HOW WISE IS A DELIBERATE SLOW-GROWTH POLICY?

This question could also be described as the issue between being conservative and being aggressive. On the one hand, with a conservative growth approach in a growing market, a firm risks being unable to expand its resources sufficiently to handle the potential, and it may have to abdicate a good share of the growing market to competitors who are willing and able to expand their capability to meet the demands of the market.

On the other hand, an aggressive strategy for growth becomes vulnerable if the growth is a short-term fad rather than a more permanent situation. A firm can easily become overextended in the buoyancy of booming business, only to see the collapse of such business jeopardize its viability.

Harley's conservative decision was undoubtedly influenced by concerns about expanding beyond the limits of good quality control. The decision, right or wrong, was probably also influenced by management's belief that Harley had a loyal body of customers who would not switch despite the wait. We might accept this latter hypothesis, but are customers likely to be less loyal in Europe?

Do you think Harley Davidson made the right decision to expand conservatively? Why or why not? Defend your position.

WHAT CAN BE LEARNED?

Again, a firm can come back from adversity. The resurrection of Harley Davidson almost from the point of extinction proves that adversity can be overcome. It need not be fatal. This should be encouraging to all firms facing difficulties, and to their investors.

What does it take for a turnaround? Above all, it takes a leader who has the vision and the confidence that things can be changed for the better. The change may not necessitate anything particularly innovative; it may involve only a rededication to basics, such as improved quality control or an improved commitment to customer service. But such a return to basics requires that a demoralized or apathetic organization be rejuvenated and remotivated. This is leadership of a high order. If the core business has still been maintained, there is at least a base to work from.

Again, preserve the core business at all costs. Every viable firm has a basic core or distinctive position—sometimes called an "ecological niche"—in its business environment. This unique position may be due to a particular location, or to a certain product. It may come from somewhat different operating methods or from the customers served. In these particular strengths, a firm is better than its competitors. This is the basic core of its survivability. Though it may diversify and expand far beyond this, it should not abandon its final bastion of strength.

Harley almost did this. Its core—and indeed, only—business was its heavyweight bikes sold to a limited and at the time not particularly savory customer segment, but one with surprising loyalty. Harley almost lost this core business by abandoning reasonable quality control to the point that its motorcycles became the butt of jokes. To his credit, Beals acted quickly upon assuming leadership to correct the production and employee motivation problems. With its core preserved, Harley could now pursue other avenues of expansion.

The power of a mystique. We have seen something similar in the earlier Nike case, and this can be a powerful sales stimulus. We might think of a mystique as somewhat greater than a reference group positive influence, something bordering on a cult following. Few products are able to gain such a mystique or cult following. Coors beer did back in the 1960s and early 1970s, when it became the brew of celebrities and the emblem of the purity and freshness of the West. In the cigarette industry, Marlboro rose to become the top seller on a somewhat similar advertising and image thrust: the Marlboro man. Perhaps the Ford Mustang had a mystique at one time. And then, somehow, the big bikes of Harley Davidson developed a mystique. The HOGs expanded to include the Rubbies: two disparate customer segments, but both loyal to their Harleys. The mystique led to "logo magic": Simply put the Harley Davidson name and logo on all kinds of merchandise, and watch the sales take off.

How does a firm develop (or acquire) a mystique? There is no simple answer, no guarantee. Certainly a company's product has to be somewhat different from competitors', even if only psychologically. But this is hardly enough—indeed, many firms strive for this and never achieve a mystique. Image-building advertising, focusing on the type of person the firm is targeting, may help some. Even better is image-building advertising of the persons customers might wish to emulate, such as Nike has done so well with athletes. But the black-leather–jacketed, perhaps bearded, motorcyclist?

Perhaps in the final analysis, acquiring a mystique is more accidental and fortuitous than deliberate. Two lessons, however, can be learned about mystiques. First, do not expect them to last forever (although Phil Knight of Nike might argue that). Second, run with them as long as you can, and try to expand the reach of the name or logo to other goods, even unrelated ones, through licensing.

CONSIDER

What additional learning insights can you see coming from this Harley Davidson resurgence?

QUESTIONS

1. Do you think Beals's rejuvenation strategy for Harley Davidson was the best? Discuss and evaluate other strategies that he might have pursued.
2. How durable do you think the Rubbies' infatuation with the heavy-weight Harleys will be? What leads you to this conclusion?
3. A Harley Davidson stockholder criticizes present management: "It is a mistake of the greatest magnitude that we abdicate a decent share of the European motorcycle market to foreign competitors, simply because we do not gear up our production to meet the demand." Discuss.
4. Given the resurgence of Harley Davidson in the early 1990s, would you invest money in the company? Discuss, considering as many factors bearing on this decision as you can.
5. "Harley Davidson's resurgence is only the purest luck. Who could have predicted, or influenced, the new popularity of big bikes with the affluent?" Discuss.
6. "The tariff increase on Japanese motorcycles in 1983 gave Harley Davidson badly needed breathing room. In the final analysis, politics is more important than marketing in competing with foreign firms." What are your thoughts?

HANDS-ON EXERCISES

1. As a representative of a mutual fund with a major investment in Harley Davidson, you are particularly critical of Vaughan Beals's visible presence at motorcycle rallies and his hobnobbing with black-jacketed cycle gangs. He insists this is a fruitful way to maintain a loyal core of customers. Playing the devil's advocate (a person who opposes a position to establish its merits and validity), argue against Beals's practices.

2. As a staff assistant to Vaughan Beals, you have been charged to design a marketing strategy to bring a mystique to the Harley Davidson name. How do you propose to do this? Be as specific as you can, and defend your reasoning.

TEAM DEBATE EXERCISE

Executives are divided as to whether the recovery efforts should have gone well beyond the heavyweight bikes into lightweights. Debate the two positions.

INVITATION TO RESEARCH

What is the situation with Harley Davidson today? Has the strategy changed? Has penetration of the European market increased? Is the mystique still apparent?

PART III

MARKETING MISTAKES

CHAPTER 8

Borden: Letting Brand Franchises Sour

Elsie the cow has long been the symbol of Borden, the largest producer of dairy products. But Borden grew well beyond dairy products to become a diversified food processor and marketer. Decades of children cherished its Cracker Jacks candied popcorn with a gift in every box; its Creamette pasta was the leading national brand, and it had strong regional brands as well. Lady Borden ice cream, milk, and frozen yogurt were well known, as were other dairy brands, national and regional. Even Elmer's glue belonged to the Borden family. With its well-known brands, Borden experienced solid growth in sales and profits for years and became a $7 billion company. Then in 1991, fortunes took a turn for the worse, and dark days were upon Borden. Top management had somehow allowed its brand franchises—the public recognition and acceptance of its brands—to deteriorate. Regaining lost ground was to prove no easy matter.

PRELUDE TO THE DARK DAYS

Borden was founded in 1857 by Gail Borden, Jr., a former Texas newspaperman. It sold condensed milk during the Civil War and later diversified into chemicals. In the 1960s Borden acquired such food brands as Cracker Jack and ReaLemon. Because of the wide earnings swings of cyclical chemical prices, Eugene J. Sullivan, the CEO, intensified the shift into consumer products in the 1970s.

In November 1991 Anthony S. D'Amato took the helm at Borden. He succeeded Romeo J. Ventres, a good friend, who convinced the board when he retired in 1991 that his protege, D'Amato, was the ideal successor. The two men, however, had sharply different management styles. Ventres was an idea man who had great faith in his top managers and gave them free rein. D'Amato was blunt, profane, and believed in personally becoming deeply involved in operations. D'Amato's different management approach was not well received by some Borden top managers, and the company went downhill fast under D'Amato's chairmanship.

But the seeds of Borden's problems were sowed before D'Amato took the helm. Ventres had dreamed of transforming Borden from a rather unexciting conglomerate into a major food marketer. Between 1986 and 1991, Ventres spent nearly $2 billion on 91 acquisitions. "We were hurriedly buying companies for the sake of buying companies," said one Borden executive. In its rush to move quickly on its acquisition program, the company sometimes spent as little as two weeks researching an acquisition candidate before making a decision.[1]

Some acquisitions turned out to be real losers. For example, in 1987 Borden purchased Laura Scudder potato chips for nearly $100 million. Unfortunately, major union problems led Borden to close all of Laura Scudder's California plants only a year after the purchase. Borden then shifted production to a plant in Salt Lake City, only to encounter high costs and quality control problems it could not correct. In 1993 it sold Laura Scudder for less than $20 million. All told, this fiasco cost Borden nearly $150 million.

Most acquisitions were small and medium-sized regional food and industrial companies. Ventres' strategy was to obtain growth by marketing these regional brands beyond their regular market areas. By consolidating manufacturing and distribution, he thought Borden could become the low-cost producer of a variety of product lines, thereby gaining more clout in the marketplace.

In the late 1980s this strategy seemed to work well. With its acquisitions, company sales grew 54 percent between 1985 and 1988. Earnings climbed even sharper to 61 percent, the most rapid growth in the company's history. (See Table 8.1.) Regional marketing and tailoring products to local tastes seemed a potent strategy.

In 1987, *Fortune* magazine featured Borden as a model of corporate performance. It termed the company "a consumer products brute" and extolled "some 40 acquisitions over two years that have made Borden, already the world's largest dairy company, the nationwide king of pasta and the second-largest seller of snack foods behind PepsiCo's Frito-Lay." The regional brand strategy was praised as motivating regionals to create new products as well as borrow from one another. For example, in just 6 weeks, Snacktime, one of Borden's new regional brands, developed Krunchers!, a kettle-cooked potato

[1] Kathleen Deveny and Suein L. Hwang, "A Defective Strategy of Heated Acquisitions Spoils Borden Name," *The Wall Street Journal* (January 18, 1994): A4.

Table 8.1 Revenues and Net Income, 1983–1989

	Revenues (in $millions)	% Change	Net Income (in $millions)	% Change
1989	7,593	4.8	(61)	
1988	7,244	11.2	312	16.9
1987	6,514	30.2	267	19.7
1986	5,002	6.1	223	14.9
1985	4,716	3.2	194	1.5
1984	4,568	7.1	191	1.1
1983	4,265	—	189	—

Source: Company reports.
Commentary: Growth was steady during most of these years, but it really accelerated in 1987 and 1988. No wonder the 1987 *Fortune* article spoke in glowing terms about Borden.

chip differentiated from those made the conventional way through continuous frying. The chip became an instant success, generating $17 million in annual sales.[2]

In 1987, the milk business was among the most profitable in the industry. Borden, with its Elsie the cow symbol, was able to charge more than competitors could, which was surprising for a commodity such as milk, which is virtually the same product whatever cow it comes from. The company insisted that its high quality and service standards made the "Borden difference." But when asked exactly what that difference was, a veteran dairyman in a succinct quote said, "About a buck a gallon."[3] Perhaps this was a portent of what was to come.

Premonitions

Flaws in the execution of the strategy were beginning to emerge by the end of the 1980s. In the race to expand the food portfolio, the company had ignored some of the well-known and successful brands it already had. For example, it had sold ice cream under the Lady Borden label for decades, but it ignored the golden opportunity in the 1980s to extend the line into super-premium ice cream, which was becoming highly popular. Borden showed the same negligence in not aggressively developing new products for many of its other strongest brand names. (See the following box for a discussion of the effective brand extension strategy.) And one could wonder how much

[2] Bill Saporito, "How Borden Milks Packaged Goods," *Fortune* (December 21, 1987): 139–44.
[3] Saporito, "How Borden Milks Packaged Goods," 142.

INFORMATION BOX

BRAND EXTENSION

Brand extension can be a particularly effective use of branding. It is a strategy of applying an established brand name to new products. As a result, customer acceptance of the new products is more likely because of customer familiarity and satisfaction with the existing products bearing the same name. This reduces the risk of new-product failure. Today about one-half of new consumer products use some form of brand extension, such as the same product in a different form, a companion product, or a different product for the same target market.

The more highly regarded a brand is by customers, the better candidate it is for brand extension—provided that a new product will not hurt its reputation and has some relevance to it. The strong favorable image of the Lady Borden brand made it ideal for such brand extension. A favorable image should be zealously protected from being cheapened or having its perception of good value undermined.

Discuss why brand extension may not always work.

---

longer the price premium charged for milk and Lady Borden ice cream could hold up as the company moved into the skeptical 1990s.

Borden was now finding difficulty in digesting its hodgepodge of acquisitions. (Table 8.2 shows the broad range of food and nonfood products and the business segment contributions to total sales and profits as of 1992.) It continued to operate as a conglomeration of unintegrated businesses and thereby proved to be neither as efficient as major competitors nor as able to amass marketing clout.

By the time D'Amato took over, the company was clearly ailing. By the end of 1991, sales had declined 5 percent from the previous year, and net income had fallen 19 percent. D'Amato quickly tried to consolidate the loosely structured organization, but all his efforts seemed only to make matters worse.

D'AMATO'S FUTILITY

Shortly after becoming CEO, D'Amato tried to better integrate the morass of consumer food businesses. He wanted to tighten up and centralize the widely decentralized company, with its "dozens of independent fiefdoms." Even corporate offices were scattered between New York City and the hub of the company's operations in Columbus, Ohio. Such geographical distance suited the hands-off management style of Ventres, who rarely got involved in day-to-day operations and spent most of his time at Borden's small Park

Table 8.2   Business Segment Contributions to Total Company Sales and
Earnings, 1992

	Sales	*Operating Profits*
Grocery[a]	26%	42%
Snacks and International Consumer[b]	26	18
Dairy[c]	20	5
Packaging and Industrial[d]	28	35

[a]Grocery products include North American pasta and sauces (Creamette, Prince, Dutch Maid, Goodman's, Classico, Aunt Millie's); niche grocery products (Eagle-brand condensed milk, Campfire marshmallows, Cracker Jack candied popcorn); refrigerated products (Borden cheese); and food service operations.
[b]Snacks and International Consumer products include Borden's worldwide sweet and salty snacks (Borden, Wise, Snack Time!); other food products outside the United States and Canada (Weber sweet snacks, KLIM milk powder, Lady Borden ice cream); and films and adhesives in the Far East.
[c]Dairy products, including milk, ice cream, and frozen yogurt, are sold under national and branded labels, which include Borden, Lady Borden, Meadow Gold, Viva, and Eagle.
[d]Packaging and Industrial products include consumer adhesives (Elmer's glue); wallcoverings; plastic films and packaging products (Proponite food packaging film, Resinite and Sealwrap vinyl food-wrap films); and foundry, industrial, and specialty resins.
Source: Company public information.

Avenue offices in New York. D'Amato moved to centralize far-flung operations in Columbus. There he involved himself deeply in day-to-day operations. He increasingly saw the need to eliminate or sell many of Borden's
small regional businesses while focusing most efforts on building national
brands: a reversal of the strategy of Ventres.

Analysts initially applauded D'Amato's strategy for turning Borden
around, but their praise was short-lived. Results failed to meet expectations
and even brought new problems.

D'Amato was especially wedded to the notion that the brand recognition
of certain brands should allow the company to charge a premium price. For
example, Borden's own research had shown that 97 percent of consumers
recognized Borden as a leading milk brand.[4] D'Amato saw this as supporting
such a premium price. Then, in early 1992, raw milk prices dropped by
about one-third. Borden doggedly held its prices while competitors lowered
theirs to reflect the drop in commodity prices. Before long, Borden began
losing customers, who were realizing that milk is milk. Good brand recognition did not insulate a national brand from lower priced competition of other

[4]Elizabeth Lesly, "Why things Are So Sour At Borden," *Business Week* (November 22,
1993): 82.

national brands and private brands. See the following box for a discussion of the battle between national and private brands.

INFORMATION BOX

THE BATTLE OF THE BRANDS: PRIVATE VERSUS NATIONAL

Wholesalers and retailers often use their own brands—commonly referred to as private brands—in place of or in addition to the national brands of manufacturers. Private brands usually are offered at lower selling prices than nationally advertised brands, yet they typically give dealers more per-unit profit since they can be bought on more favorable terms, partly reflecting the promotional savings involved. Some firms, such as Sears and Penney, used to stock mostly their own brands. Thus, they had better control over repeat business since satisfied customers could repurchase the brand only through the particular store or chain.

With private brands directly competing with manufacturers' brands, often at a more attractive price, you may ask why manufacturers sell some of their output to retailers under a private brand. A major reason is to minimize idle plant capacity. Manufacturers can always rationalize that if they refuse private-label business, someone else will not, and competition with private brands will continue. Other manufacturers welcome private-brand business because they lack the resources and know-how to enter the marketplace effectively with their own brands.

By the 1990s, more knowledgeable and frugal consumers were realizing that private brands often offered the best value. National consumer brands were being hurt. Recognizing this new intense competition, some manufacturers of branded goods, led by makers of cigarettes and disposable diapers, in 1993 rolled back the price differentials over private brands of their national labels. Borden management had difficulty accepting the idea that the price premiums of its national brands were no longer sustainable if market share was to be maintained.

How do you personally feel about private brands?

D'Amato opted to tough out the loss of market share, expecting that higher profit margins would offset somewhat lower sales. Only after almost a year of steadily declining sales did he abandon the premium-pricing policy. By then sales had fallen so drastically that the milk division was operating at a loss.

Another marketing mistake involved misuse of advertising. In his strategy to build up Borden's major brands, D'Amato had boosted marketing efforts for Creamette, the leading national pasta brand. With the sizable promotional expenditures, the brand's sales rose 1.6 percent in 1992. This may have seemed like a significant increase but for the fact that, nationally, pasta sales rose 5.5 percent.

How could the promotional efforts have been so ineffective? Unbelievably, most of the advertising featured recipes aimed at increasing pasta consumption, rather than at building selective demand for the Creamette brand.

Making the marketing efforts for Creamette even more misguided, Borden neglected its regional pasta brands, such as Anthony's in the West and Prince in the Northeast. These sales slumped, so that total division sales were down $600 million in the first 9 months of 1993. D'Amato admitted the mistake: "There was a very strong desire to make Creamette the one bigger brand beyond anything else. That's a great objective, [but] when you do it at the expense of your strong regional brands, maybe it doesn't make any sense."[5]

The snack food division also bedeviled D'Amato. He planned to launch a national Borden brand of chips and pretzels in the expectation that this could replace many of the company's regional snack brands. Combining the regionals' manufacturing and distribution costs under a single brand should enable Borden both to cut costs and also gain marketing muscle. The company tested its new snack line in Michigan, but results were only mediocre. Unfortunately, Borden was going up against PepsiCo's Frito-Lay and Anheuser-Busch's Eagle Snacks—major entrenched national brands. It could not wedge its way in. The company finally refocused its efforts to attempt to build up regional brands such as Jay's and Wise. But they were ineffective or too late.

THE CHANGING OF THE GUARD

D'Amato's sweeping strategy to rejuvenate the ailing Borden left the company worse off than before. Two of its four divisions, dairy and snacks, were operating at losses. Its other two divisions, grocery products and chemicals, could not take up the slack. On October 27, 1993, Standard and Poor downgraded much of Borden's debt. Since the beginning of 1993, Borden's share price had plummeted 43 percent.

In June 1993 D'Amato hired Ervin R. Shames, 53, as president and heir apparent. Whereas D'Amato's background had been in chemical engineering for most of his 30 years with Borden, Shames was an experienced food marketer, having spent 22 years in the industry, holding top positions with General Foods USA and Kraft USA. He most recently had been chair, president, and chief executive of Stride Rite Corporation. In making Shames president, D'Amato gave him a compensation package that exceeded those of Borden's other top executives, including himself.

Shames and D'Amato now attempted to correct Borden's problems together. They quickly stopped offering deals to retailers to encourage heavier

[5] Lesly, "Why Things Are So Sour," 84.

end-of-quarter shipments. While these deals temporarily boosted sales, they hurt profits and also stole business from the next quarter.

Shames and D'Amato accelerated the examination of Borden's various businesses. Teams of management consultants and financial advisers helped with the evaluation. As a consequence, morale among managers, who feared drastic changes, plummeted almost to the point of paralysis.

In October 1993 the independent directors of the board considered the possibility of selling the entire company. But the efforts proved futile. Hanson PLC and RJR Nabisco briefly appeared interested, but talks broke down. Several other possible buyers, including Nestle SA, also looked over Borden's portfolio of businesses but declined to negotiate. The weak condition of Borden was proving a major hindrance to any buyout. It likely would have to solve its own problems without outside help.

Shames and D'Amato believed that the biggest problem was the fact that the company was spread too thin in too many mediocre businesses. Although it was unlikely that the entire company could be sold at this time, still certain parts should be salable. They had to decide which should be sold if the company was to be streamlined enough to reverse the consequences of its haphazard and even confused former growth mentality. An early recognized candidate for pruning was the $1.4 billion chemical business. This had little relevance with the core food properties, but still it was a major profit generator, as shown in Table 8.2.

D'Amato was not to see the conclusions of his latest efforts to turn around Borden. On December 9, 1993, the board of directors fired him and left Shames in charge. At the same time, D'Amato's predecessor and former supporter, R. J. Ventres, resigned from his board seat. Operating results through 1993 were a disaster, as shown in Table 8.3.

RECOVERY EFFORTS

Shames announced a $567 million restructuring plan on January 5, 1994. It included the sale of the salty snacks division and other niche grocery lines.

Table 8.3 Operating Performance, 1990–1993

	Revenues (in $millions)	% Change	Net Income (in $millions	% Change
1993	6,600[a]	(7.6)	(593)[a]	
1992	7,143	(1.3)	(253)	
1991	7,235	(5.2)	295	(19.0)
1990	7,633	—	364	—

[a]Estimates.
Source: Borden.

The dividend was also slashed for the second time in 6 months. In a speech to security analysts, Shames identified four reasons for Borden's problems: lack of focus, insufficient emphasis on brand names, absence of first-rate executives and managers, and a tangled bureaucracy. He vowed to purge weak managers and increase advertising with much greater focus on core lines, notably pasta, the namesake dairy products, and industrial businesses such as adhesives and wallcoverings. For example, he planned to increase advertising for pasta from $2 million to $8 million for 1994 and to focus on the company's faded regional brands. The pasta would also be cross-marketed with Classico, the successful premium pasta sauce.

Shames also pledged to bring Borden from last place among food companies to the top 25 percent. See Table 8.4 for a ranking of Borden with other major competitors as of the beginning of 1994. He began bringing in a new management team, many of them his former colleagues. In a major shake-up, three senior managers announced their early retirement: the chief financial officer, the general counsel, and the former executive vice president in charge of the struggling snack food and international consumer products unit.[6]

Some security analysts were encouraged by Shames' speech. They believed that Borden's bringing in an experienced outsider—at the time, Shames had been with the company for only 7 months—showed that the company was truly committed to the drastic changes needed for a turnaround.

Table 8.4   Comparison of Borden and Major Competitors, 5-year Average, 1988–1993

	Return on Equity	Sales Growth	Earnings per Share
General Mills	42.8%	10.0%	10.4%
Kellogg	31.8	10.2	11.6
H. J. Heinz	25.4	5.8	8.6
Quaker Oats	24.6	4.9	12.2
Sara Lee	21.1	6.2	16.1
Hershey Foods	18.4	7.1	8.3
Campbell Soup	16.5	5.3	NM[a]
Dole	11.7	11.7	−5.4
Borden	5.8	1.3	NM

[a]*NM*, Not meaningful.
Source: Industry statistics as reported in *Forbes* (January 3, 1994): 152–54.
Commentary: Borden's poor performance compared with that of its major peers is starkly indicated here, with Borden dead last in 5-year average return on equity, sales growth, and earnings per share.

[6]Suein L. Hwang, "Borden Aides Leaving as Part of Shake-Up," *The Wall Street Journal* (February 15, 1994): A4.

Other people were more skeptical. After all, Borden has been "restructuring" for five years. "Who's to say the latest plan will work any better than previous ones?" Joanna Scharf, an analyst with S. G. Warburg & Co., was among such skeptics: "I found some of [Shames] remarks heartening. However, this is not something that is going to turn around in six months." And she maintained she was not going to change her advice to investors to sell the stock.[7]

With so many brands in its portfolio stable, reflecting nearly 100 recent acquisitions, Borden lost focus. Key brands were often not sufficiently championed. Brand extensions, such as one for Lady Borden Ice cream, were often overlooked or only half-heartedly attempted. One wonders how many opportunities were ignored by a management team whose attention was caught up in a frenzy for acquisitions.

A Sputtering Recovery

The troubles of Borden did not go away. At a $1 million cash salary plus mouth-watering stock options, Shames was unable to turn things around. His initial efforts were to build sales volume, but this adversely affected the bottom line of profitability. For example, with pasta, Borden held firm on prices despite a recent 75 percent increase in durum wheat prices, while competitors raised prices. The result: Borden gained less than a point of market share, but lost on the bottom line. So eager was Borden for volume that in November 1993 it paid an Oklahoma City–based supermarket chain $9.5 million for preferential treatment on grocer shelves.[8]

Shames failed to curb costs. Even though he shed 7,000 employees, payroll costs actually rose. Some of this was hardly Shames' fault. The board approved substantial salaries paid to former top executives. For example, D'Amato was paid $750,000 in cash severance, and $900,000 per year for four years plus $65,000 in secretarial and legal fee reimbursements. Borden still maintained a fleet of company jets to fly board members around the country. Country club memberships of executives hardly attested to a firm on the verge of bankruptcy. Consultant and advisory fees numbered in the millions. The fat could not be trimmed, it seemed.

Efforts to sell off some of the units to ease the crushing burden of creditor demands were also less than successful. For example, H.J. Heinz Company bought Borden's $225 million (sales) food service division for only 31 percent of annual revenues, a miserably low price for assets that should have brought $1 for every $1 in revenues.[9]

---

[7] Vindu P. Goel, "Putting Elsie Back on Track," *Cleveland Plain Dealer* (January 23, 1994): 1-E, 5-E.

[8] Matthew Schifrin, "Last Legs," *Forbes* (September 12, 1994): 150ff.

[9] Schifrin, "Last Legs," 150ff.

In late 1994, Borden was bought for $1.9 billion by Kohlberg Kravis Roberts and Co., a low figure for a $6 billion company but then it had been losing money. Robert Kidder, former top executive of Duracell, became CEO. Borden, once a top 20 public firm became the third largest private firm in the U.S. KKR directed hundreds of millions of dollars for updating plants, installing new systems, and developing new products. In May 1995, Borden underwent a complete restructuring, with all marketing efforts split into 11 business units, each with its own board of directors, capital structure, and operational control, thus assuring 100 percent accountability.[10] Could Borden be on the verge of a turnaround?

ANALYSIS

Acquiring other businesses is a common growth strategy. Through acquisitions a company can quickly achieve a relatively large size, bypassing the time needed to develop such new ventures internally. By acquiring already proven businesses, the buyer can obtain personnel and management experienced to run such businesses effectively.

Several problems, however, can occur in such buyouts: First, a buying firm may pay too much and be saddled with heavy debt and interest overhead. Second, the acquisition may prove incompatible with the buyer's existing resources and strategy. In such a situation, it may find great difficulty in integrating the new enterprise with existing operations and making it a profit contributor.

In the 1980s Ventres, D'Amato's predecessor, took on $1.9 billion in debt to acquire 91 regional food and industrial companies. He had hoped to build these up to be regional powerhouses and to marry efficiencies of scale in manufacturing with the marketing nimbleness of regional operations. By centralizing production in the most efficient plants, costs should be lowered and profits enhanced. And there was always the potential for a regional brand to take off and be worthy of national distribution. This was the theory behind many of Borden's acquisitions in the 1980s.

Unfortunately, theory and practice did not meld well. The businesses were never integrated and continued to operate autonomously with diverse and often competing brands. Production never achieved the efficiency of most of the large competitors, and Borden still lacked their marketing clout. It also encountered great problems in allocating advertising among the diverse brands: Which should be given strong support, and why? And should the other brands be allowed to languish?

---

[10]"A New Life for Borden," *Prepared Foods* (July 1995): 35; and "Borden's CEO Finds Answers to How It's Been Losing Money," *Cleveland Plain Dealer* (February 13, 1996): 5-C.

Compounding its problems with unwise and unassimilated acquisitions, Borden management grievously misjudged the mood of the market. It overestimated consumers' willingness to pay premium prices for its most popular brands. Borden's stubbornness in maintaining high prices for Lady Borden milk at the very time when raw milk prices were collapsing simply invited competitors to increase their market share at Borden's expense. Attempts to raise ice cream prices backfired as well.

The early 1990s, a period of recession and considerable unemployment and fear of layoffs, brought a new consumer recognition that many national brands were not much, if any, better than competing private brands. Many national-brand manufacturers, faced with declining sales in the face of strong private-label competition, began price rollbacks. So it was not surprising that Borden found difficulty with a changed marketing environment. What was surprising was its slowness to adapt to these changing conditions.

WHAT CAN BE LEARNED?

Beware an unfocused strategy. An unfocused strategy often accompanies too much unrelated diversification. A firm has difficulty deciding what it is, other than being a conglomerate. Not many managements cope well with a lot of diversification, although many have tried to. Often such acquisitions become candidates for sale some years later, thus confirming flawed acquisition decisions.

In Borden's case most of the acquisitions were related to its major food business. But there were too many, and they were not integrated into the main corporate structure. Such diffusion of resources and uncoordinated marketing efforts made it difficult indeed to achieve either cost savings or a unified and powerful approach to the marketplace.

How much decentralization? Here we are confronted with the negative consequences of too much decentralization or autonomy. Borden acquisitions' autonomy led to lack of coordination and great inefficiency.

Does this have to be true? Or can decentralization work without causing loss of control and efficiency? Can intrafirm competition among semi-independent units lead to greater performance incentive? The answer is yes, decentralization is often far more desirable than centralization. For example, we saw this in IBM's efforts to move away from its centralized bureaucratic organization toward more decentralization. Still, there are degrees of decentralization. Too much uncontrolled autonomy led to Borden's problems. There has to be some focus and common purpose along with sufficient controls to prevent unpleasant surprises. But in the final analysis, the issue depends on the competence of the managers. If they are highly competent, then an organization will likely thrive under decentralization. If they are incompetent, as appeared to be the case with Borden, then decentralization can be a disaster.

Run with your winners. Although any firm wants to develop new products and bring them to fruition as soon as possible, it must not neglect its older products and brands that are doing well, that are winners. Advertising and other marketing efforts, such as brand extension, should not be curtailed as long as the products are growing and profitable. Marketing commitments should perhaps even be increased for such winners, since favorable growth trends often can continue for a long time. Alas, Borden sometimes exercised the opposite strategy: It cut back on its winners and directed resources to futilely trying to build up weak regional brands.

But we should not completely condemn Borden for ignoring its winners. It threw all its advertising support behind Creamette, the leading national brand of pasta. But Creamette's sales failed to take off. Meantime, Borden's strong regional brands—in particular, Prince in the Northeast and Anthony's in the West—stagnated with no support. D'Amato must have thought "damned if you do and damned if you don't." But there were reasons for the lack of success with the Creamette advertising, as we will examine next.

For mature products, beware using primary-demand advertising. Despite a strong boost in marketing efforts for Creamette in 1992, the brand's sales rose only 1.6 percent. At the same time total U.S. pasta sales rose 5.5 percent.[11] Was this poor showing the fault of the product? Hardly, since it was the leading national pasta brand. Rather, the advertising was at fault. Most of it was built around recipes that did more to promote pasta consumption than to promote the superior qualities of Creamette. In other words, a primary-demand theme was used rather than selective-demand theme stressing the merits of a particular brand. Because primary-demand advertising helps the industry and all competitors, it is best used with new products in a young growth industry. Primary-demand advertising is seldom appropriate in a mature industry. The results of the advertising efforts for Creamette confirm this. Shouldn't Borden managers have been more savvy? They should never have approved such a theme for an advertising campaign.

CONSIDER

Do you see any other learning insights coming from this case?

---

[11] Lesley, "Why Things Are So Sour," 84.

QUESTIONS

1. Do you think the problems in Borden's acquisition strategy stemmed from a flaw in the basic concept or in the execution? Support your position.
2. Is primary-demand advertising ever advisable for a mature product? If so, under what circumstances?
3. Prince is a strong regional pasta brand in the Northeast. What would it take to convert it into a national brand? Should Borden have attempted this?
4. Should Borden have made a strong effort to create a presence in the private brand market? Why or why not?
5. Critics have decried Borden's lack of focus. What does this mean? How can the criticisms best be resolved?
6. "After firing D'Amato, the board one month later adopted virtually the same restructuring plan he had proposed. What an injustice!" Discuss.
7. How much of a price premium do you think national brands ought to command over private brands? Justify your position.

HANDS-ON EXERCISES

1. It is 1984 and you are the assistant to the president. He has asked you to design a growth plan for the next decade. What are your recommendations? Take care to avoid the pitfalls that actually beset the company.
2. It is early 1994. You are the assistant to the new CEO, Erwin Shames. The company is in sorry straits. What do you propose to enable your boss to meet his pledge to boost Borden from the bottom of the food company heap to the top 25 percent?

TEAM DEBATE EXERCISE

Debate the issue of growth by acquisitions versus internal growth. Which of the pros and cons do you think are most compelling?

INVITATION TO RESEARCH

Since Borden is now a private company under the stable of Kohlberg Kravis Roberts & Co., it is difficult to find as much information as if it were publicly held. Still, you may be able to find something about the present fortunes of the firm and its brands.

CHAPTER 9

Maytag:
A Bungled Promotion
in England

The atmosphere at the annual meeting in the little Iowa town of Newton had turned contentious. As Leonard Hadley faced increasingly angry questions from disgruntled shareholders the thought crossed his mind: "I don't deserve this!" After all, he had only been CEO of Maytag Corporation for a few months, and this was his first chairing of an annual meeting. But the earnings of the company had been declining every year since 1988, and in 1992, Maytag had had a $315.4 million loss. No wonder the stockholders in the packed Newton High School auditorium were bitter and critical of their management. But there was more. Just the month before, the company had the public embarrassment and costly atonement resulting from a monumental blunder in the promotional planning of its United Kingdom subsidiary.

Hadley doggedly saw the meeting to its close, and limply concluded: "Hopefully, both sales and earnings will improve this year."[1]

THE FIASCO

In August 1992, Hoover Limited, Maytag's British subsidiary, launched this travel promotion: Anyone in the United Kingdom buying more than 100 U.K. pounds worth of Hoover products (about $150 in American dollars) before the end of January 1993 would get two free round-trip tickets to

[1] Richard Gibson, "Maytag's CEO Goes Through Wringer at Annual Meeting," *The Wall Street Journal* (April 28, 1993): A5.

selected European destinations. For 250 U.K. pounds worth of Hoover products, they would get two free round-trip tickets to New York or Orlando.

A buying frenzy resulted. Consumers had quickly figured out that the value of the tickets easily exceeded the cost of the appliances necessary to be eligible for them. By the tens of thousands, Britishers rushed out to buy just enough Hoover products to qualify. Appliance stores were emptied of vacuum cleaners. The Hoover factory in Cambuslang, Scotland, that had been making vacuum cleaners only three days a week was suddenly placed on a 24-hour, seven days a week production schedule—an overtime bonanza for the workers. What a resounding success for a promotion! Hoover managers, however, were unhappy.

Hoover had never ever expected more than 50,000 people to respond. And of those responding, it expected far less would go through all the steps necessary to qualify for the free trip and really take it. But more than 200,000 not only responded but qualified for the free tickets. The company was overwhelmed. The volume of paperwork created such a bottleneck that by the middle of April only 6,000 people had flown. Thousands of others either never got their tickets, were not able to get the dates requested, or waited for months without hearing the results of their applications. Hoover established a special hot line to process customer complaints, and these were coming in at 2,000 calls a day. But the complaints quickly spread, and the ensuing publicity brought charges of fraud and demands for restitution. This raises the issue of loss leaders—how much should we use loss leaders as a promotional device?—discussed in the following box.

Maytag dispatched a task force to try to resolve the situation without jeopardizing customer relations any further. But it acknowledged that it's "not 100% clear" that all eligible buyers will receive their free flights.[2] The ill-fated promotion was a staggering blow to Maytag financially. It took a $30 million charge in the first quarter of 1993 to cover unexpected additional costs linked to the promotion. Final costs were expected to exceed $50 million, which would be 10 percent of UK Hoover's total revenues. This for a subsidiary acquired only four years before that had yet to produce a profit.

Adding to the costs were problems with the two travel agencies involved. The agencies were to obtain low-cost space available tickets, and would earn commissions selling "packages," including hotels, rental cars, and insurance. If consumers bought a package, Hoover would get a cut. However, despite the overwhelming demand for tickets, most consumers declined to purchase the package, thus greatly reducing support money for the promotional venture. So, Hoover greatly underestimated the likely response, and overestimated the amount it would earn from commission payments.

---

[2]James P. Miller, "Maytag U.K. Unit Find a Promotion Is Too Successful," *The Wall Street Journal* (March 31, 1993): A9.

ISSUE BOX

SHOULD WE USE LOSS LEADERS?

Leader pricing is a type of promotion with certain items advertised at a very low price—sometimes even below cost, in which case they are known as loss leaders—in order to attract more customers. The rationale for this is that such customers are likely to purchase other regular price items as well with the result that total sales and profits will be increased. If customers do not purchase enough other goods at regular prices to more than cover the losses incurred from the attractively priced bargains, then the loss leader promotion is ill advised. Some critics maintain that the whole idea of using loss leaders is absurd: the firm is just "buying sales" with no regard for profits.

While UK Hoover did not think of their promotion as a loss leader, in reality it was: they stood to lose money on every sale if the promotional offer was taken advantage of. Unfortunately for its effectiveness as a loss leader, the likelihood of customers purchasing other Hoover products at regular prices was remote, and the level of acceptance was not capped, so that losses were permitted to multiply. The conclusion has to be that this was an ill-conceived idea from the beginning. It violated these two conditions of loss leaders: they should stimulate sales of other products, and their losses should be limited.

Do you think loss leaders really are desirable under certain circumstances? Why or why not?

If these cost overruns added greatly to Maytag and Hoover's customer relations and public image, the expenditures would have seemed more palatable. But with all the problems, the best that could be expected would be to lessen the worst of the agitation and charges of deception. And this was proving to be impossible. The media, of course, salivated at the problems and were quick to sensationalize them:

> One disgruntled customer, who took aggressive action on his own, received the widest press coverage, and even became a folk hero. Dave Dixon, claiming he was cheated out of a free vacation by Hoover, seized one of the company's repair vans in retaliation. Police were sympathetic: They took him home, and did not charge him, claiming it was a civil matter.[3]

Heads rolled also. Initially, Maytag fired three UK Hoover executives involved, including the president of Hoover Europe. Mr. Hadley, at the annual meeting, also indicated that others might lose their jobs before the

---

[3]"Unhappy Brit Holds Hoover Van Hostage," *Cleveland Plain Dealer* (June 1, 1993): D1; and Simon Reeve and John Harlow, "Hoover Is Sued Over Flights Deal," *London Sunday Times* (June 6, 1993).

cleanup was complete. He likened the promotion to "a bad accident . . . and you can't determine what was in the driver's mind."[4]

The issue receiving somewhat less publicity was why corporate headquarters allowed executives of a subsidiary such wide latitude that they could saddle parent Maytag with tens of millions in unexpected costs. Did not top corporate executives have to approve ambitious plans? A company spokesman said that operating divisions were "primarily responsible" for planning promotional expenses. While the parent may review such outlays, "if they're within parameters, it goes through."[5] This raises the issue, discussed in the following box, of how loose a rein foreign subsidiaries should be allowed.

ISSUE BOX

HOW LOOSE A REIN FOR A FOREIGN SUBSIDIARY?

In a decentralized organization, top management delegates considerable decision-making authority to subordinates. Such decentralization—often called a "loose rein"—tends to be more marked with foreign subsidiaries, such as UK Hoover. Corporate management in the U.S. understandably feels less familiar with the foreign environment and is more willing to let the native executives operate with less constraints than it might with a domestic subsidiary. In the Maytag/Hoover situation, decision-making authority by British executives was evidently extensive, and corporate Maytag exercised little operational control, being content to judge performance by ultimate results achieved. Major deviations from expected performance goals, or widespread traumatic events—all of which happened to UK Hoover—finally gained corporate management attention.

Major advantages of extensive decentralization or a loose rein are: first, top management effectiveness can be improved since time and attention is freed for presumably more important matters; second, subordinates are permitted more self-management, which should improve their competence and motivation; and third, in foreign environments, native managers presumably better understand their unique problems and opportunities than corporate management, located thousands of miles away, possibly can. But the drawbacks are as we have seen: parameters within which subordinate managers operate can be so wide that serious miscalculations may not be stopped in time. Since top management is ultimately responsible for all performance, including actions of subordinates, it faces greater risks with extensive decentralization and giving a free rein.

"Since the manager is ultimately accountable for whatever is delegated to subordinates, then a free rein reflects great confidence in subordinates." Discuss.

---

[4]Gibson, "CEO Goes Through Wringer," A5.
[5]Miller, "Maytag UK Unit," A9.

BACKGROUND ON MAYTAG

Maytag is a century-old company. The original business, formed in 1893, manufactured feeder attachments for threshing machines. In 1907, the company moved to Newton, Iowa, a small town thirty miles east of Des Moines, the capitol. Manufacturing emphasis turned to home-laundry equipment, and wringer-type washers.

A natural expansion of this emphasis occurred with the commercial laundromat business in the 1930s, when coin meters were attached to Maytag washers. Rapid growth of these coin-operated laundries took place in the U.S. during the late 1950s and early 1960s. The 1970s hurt laundromats with increased competition and soaring energy costs. In 1975, Maytag introduced new energy-efficient machines, and "Home Style" stores that rejuvenated the business.

The Lonely Maytag Repairman

For years Maytag reveled in a marketing coup, with its washers and dryers enjoying a top-quality image, thanks to decades-long ads in which a repairman laments his loneliness because of Maytag's trouble-free products. (The actor who portrayed this repairman died in early 1997.) The result of this dependability and quality image was that Maytag could command a price premium: "Their machines cost the same to make, break down as much as ours—but they get $100 more because of the reputation," grumbled a competitor.[6]

During the 1970s and into the 1980s, Maytag continued to capture 15 percent of the washing machine market, and enjoyed profit margins about twice that of competitors. Table 9.1 shows operating results for the

Table 9.1   Maytag Operating Results, 1974–1981 (in millions)

	Net Sales	Net Income	Percent of Sales
1974	$229	$21.1	9.2%
1975	238	25.9	10.9
1976	275	33.1	12.0
1977	299	34.5	11.5
1978	325	36.7	11.3
1979	369	45.3	12.3
1980	346	35.6	10.2
1981	409	37.4	9.1
	Average net income percent of sales: 10.8%		

Source: Company operating statistics.
Commentary: These years show a steady, though not spectacular growth in revenues, and a generally rising net income, except for 1980. Of particular interest is the high net income percentage of sales, with this averaging 10.8% over the 8-year period, with a high of 12.3%.

[6] Brian Bremmer, "Can Maytag Clean Up Around the World?" *Business Week* (January 30, 1989): 89.

period 1974–1981. Whirlpool was the largest factor in the laundry equipment market, with a 45 percent share, but this was largely because of sales to Sears under the Sears' brand.

Acquisitions

For many years, until his retirement on December 31, 1992, Daniel J. Krumm had influenced Maytag's destinies. He had been CEO for eighteen years and chairman since 1986, and his tenure with the company encompassed 40 years. In that time, the home-appliance business encountered some drastic changes. The most ominous occurred in the late 1980s with the merger mania, in which the threat of takeovers by hostile raiders often motivated heretofore conservative executives to greatly increase corporate indebtedness, thereby decreasing the attractiveness of their firms. Daniel Krumm was one of these running-scared executives, as rumors persisted that the company was a takeover candidate.

Largely as a defensive move, Krumm pushed through a deal for a $1 billion buyout of Chicago Pacific Corporation (CPC), a maker of vacuum cleaners and other appliances with $1.4 billion in sales. As a result, Maytag was burdened with $500 million in new debt. Krumm defended the acquisition as giving Maytag a strong foothold in a growing overseas market. CPC was best known for the Hoover vacuums it sold in the U.S. and Europe. Indeed, so dominant was the Hoover brand in England that many people did not vacuum their carpets, but "hoovered the carpet." CPC also made washers, dryers, and other appliances under the Hoover brand, selling them exclusively in Europe and Australia. In addition, it had six furniture companies, but Maytag sold these shortly after the acquisition.

Krumm had been instrumental in transforming Maytag, the Number 4 U.S. appliance manufacturer—behind General Electric, Whirlpool, and Electrolux—from a niche laundry-equipment maker into a full-line manufacturer. He had led an earlier acquisition spree in which Maytag had expanded into microwave ovens, electric ranges, refrigerators, and freezers. Its brands now included Magic Chef, Jenn-Air, Norge, and Admiral. The last years of Krumm's reign, however, were not marked by great operating results. As shown in Table 9.2, revenues showed no gain in the 1989–1992 period, while income steadily declined.

Trouble

Although the rationale for internationalizing seemed inescapable, especially in view of a recent wave of joint ventures between U.S. and European appliance makers, still the Hoover acquisition was troublesome. While it was a

Table 9.2   Maytag Operating Results, 1989–-1992

	Revenue (000,000)	Net Income	% of Revenue
1989	$3,089	131.0	4.3%
1990	3,057	98.9	3.2
1991	2,971	79.0	2.7
1992	3,041	(315.4)	(10.4)

Source: Company annual reports.
Commentary: Note the steady erosion of profitability, while sales remained virtually static. For a comparison with profit performance of earlier years, see Table 9.1 and the net income to sales percentage of this more "golden" period.

major brand in England and in Australia, Hoover had only a small presence in Europe. Yet, this was where the bulk of the market was, with some 320 million potential appliance buyers.

The probabilities of the Hoover subsidiary being able to capture much of the European market were hardly promising. Whirlpool was strong, having ten plants there in contrast to Hoover's two plants. Furthermore, Maytag faced entrenched European competitors such as Sweden's Electrolux, the world's largest appliance maker; Germany's Bosch-Siemens; and Italy's Merloni Group. General Electric had also entered the market with joint ventures. The fierce loyalty of Europeans to domestic brands raised further questions as to the ability of Maytag's Hoover to penetrate the European market without massive promotional expenditures, and maybe not even then.

Australia was something else. Hoover had a good competitive position there, and its refrigerator plant in Melbourne could easily be expanded to include Maytag's washers and dryers. Unfortunately, the small population of Australia limited the market to only about $250 million for major appliances.

Britain accounted for half of Hoover's European sales. But at the time of the acquisition its major appliance business was only marginally profitable. This was to change: after the acquisition it became downright unprofitable, as shown in Table 9.3 for the years 1990 through 1992, as it struggled to expand in a recession-plagued Europe. The results for 1993, of course, will reflect the huge loss for the promotional debacle. Hardly an acquisition made in heaven.

Maytag's earlier acquisitions also were becoming soured. Its acquisitions of Magic Chef and Admiral were diversifications into lower-priced appliances, and these did not meet expectations. But they left Maytag's balance sheet and its cash flow weakened (see Table 9.4). Perhaps more serious, Maytag's reputation as the nation's premier appliance maker became tarnished. Meanwhile, General Electric and Whirlpool were attacking the top end of its product line. As a result, Maytag found itself in the Number 3 or 4 position in most of its brand lines.

Table 9.3 Operating Results of Maytag's Principal Business Components 1990–1992

	Revenue (000,000)	Income[a] (000,000)
1990		
North American Appliances	$2,212	$221,165
Vending	191	25,018
European Sales	497	(22,863)
1991		
North American Appliances	2,183	186,322
Vending	150	4,498
European Sales	486	(865)
1992		
North American Appliances	2,242	129,680
Vending	165	16,311
European Sales	502	(67,061)

[a]This is operating income, that is, income before depreciation and other adjustments.
Source: Company annual reports.
Commentary: While these years had not been particularly good for Maytag in growth of revenues and income, the continuing, and even intensifying, losses in the Hoover European operation had to be troublesome. And this is before the ill-fated early 1993 promotional results.

Table 9.4 Long-Term Debt as a Percent of Capital from Maytag's Balance Sheets, 1986–1991

Year	Long-Term Debt/Capital
1986	7.2%
1987	23.3
1988	48.3
1989	46.8
1990	44.1
1991	42.7

Source: Company annual reports.
Commentary: The effect of acquisitions, in particular that of the Chicago Pacific Corporation, can be clearly seen in the buildup of long-term debt: in 1986, Maytag was virtually free of such commitments; two years later its long-term debt ratio had increased almost seven-fold.

UPDATE

Maytag's invasion of Europe proved a costly failure. In the summer of 1995, Maytag gave up. It sold its European operations to an Italian appliance maker, recording a $135 million loss.

As we come to the end of 1996, the Hoover mess was still not cleaned up. Hoover had spent $72 million flying some 220,000 people and had hoped that ended the matter. But the fight continues four years later with disgruntled customers who never flew taking Hoover to court. "There's about 365,000 people who haven't flown," said Denis Whalley, a Liverpool lawyer. "I hope lots of other people who have been cheated by Hoover will come forward." Hoover declined comment, saying enough has been said about the case that made it a worldwide laughingstock. Even though Hoover had sold this troubled division, it still could not escape emerging lawsuits.[7]

ANALYSIS

Flawed Acquisition Decisions

The long decline in profits after 1989 should have triggered strong concern and corrective action. Perhaps it did, but the action was not effectual as the decline continued, culminating in a large deficit in 1992 and serious problems in 1993. As shown in Table 9.2, the acquisitions brought neither revenue gains nor profitability. One suspects that in the rush to fend off potential raiders in the late 1980s, the company bought businesses it might never have under more sober times, and that it also paid too much for these businesses. Further, they cheapened the proud image of quality for Maytag.

Who Can We Blame in the U.K. Promotional Debacle?

Corporate Maytag management was guilty of a common fault in their acquisitions: it gave newly acquired divisions a loose rein, letting them continue to operate independently with few constraints: "After all, these executives should be more knowledgeable about their operations than corporate headquarters would be." Such confidence is sometimes misguided. In the U.K. promotion, Maytag management would seem as derelict as management in England. Planning guidelines or parameters were far too loose and under-controlled. The idea of subsidiary management being able to burden the parent with $50 million of unexpected charges, and to have such erupt with no warning, borders on the absurd.

Finally, the planning of the U.K. executives for this ill-conceived travel production defies all logic. They vastly underestimated the demand for the promotional offer and they greatly overestimated paybacks from travel

[7]"Hoover Can't Clean Up Mess from Free Flights," *Cleveland Plain Dealer* (December 12, 1996): 1-C; and Dirk Beveridge, "Hoover Loses Two Lawsuits Tied to Promotion," *Gannett Newspapers* (February 21, 1997): 4-F.

agencies on the package deals. Yet, it took no brilliant insight to realize that the value of the travel offer exceeded the price of the appliance—indeed, 200,000 customers rapidly arrived at this conclusion—and that such a sweetheart of a deal would be irresistible to many, and that it could prove to be costly in the extreme to the company. A miscalculation, or complete naivete on the part of executives and their staffs who should have known better?

How Could the Promotion Have Avoided the Problem?

The great problem resulting from an offer too good could have been avoided, and this without scrapping the whole idea. A cost-benefit analysis would have provided at least a perspective as to how much the company should spend to achieve certain benefits, such as increased sales, greater consumer interest, and favorable publicity. See the following information box for a more detailed discussion of the important planning tool of a cost-benefit analysis.

INFORMATION BOX

COST-BENEFIT ANALYSIS

A cost-benefit analysis is a systematic comparison of the costs and benefits of a proposed action. Only if the benefits exceed the costs would we normally have a "go" decision. The normal way to make such an analysis is to assign dollar values to all costs and benefits, thus providing a common basis for comparison.

Cost-benefit analyses have been widely used by the Defense Department in evaluating alternative weapons systems. In recent years, such analyses have been sporadically applied to environmental regulation and even to workplace safety standards. As an example of the former, a cost-benefit analysis can be used to determine if it is socially worthwhile to spend X million dollars to meet a certain standard of clean air or water.

Many business decisions lend themselves to a cost-benefit analysis. It provides a systematic way of analyzing the inputs and the probable outputs of particular major alternatives. While in the business setting some of the costs and benefits can be very quantitative, they often should be tempered by non-quantitative inputs to reach the broadest perspective. Schermerhorn suggests considering the following criteria in evaluating alternatives:[8]

Benefits: What are the "benefits" of using the alternatives to solve a performance deficiency or take advantage of an opportunity?

Costs: What are the "costs" to implement the alternatives, including direct resource investments as well as any potential negative side effects?

---

[8] John R. Schermerhorn, Jr., *Management for Productivity*, 4th ed. (New York: Wiley, 1993), p. 164.

Timeliness: How fast will the benefits occur and a positive impact be achieved?

Acceptability: To what extent will the alternatives be accepted and supported by those who must work with them?

Ethical soundness: How well do the alternatives meet acceptable ethical criteria in the eyes of multiple stakeholders?

What numbers would you assign to a cost-benefit analysis for Maytag Hoover's plan to offer the free airline tickets, under an assumption of 5,000 takers? 20,000 takers? 100,000 takers? 500,000 takers? (Make any assumptions needed as to costs.) What would be your conclusions for these various acceptance rates?

A cost-benefit analysis should certainly have alerted management to the possible consequences of various acceptance levels, and of the significant risks of high acceptance. However, the company could have set limits on the number of eligibles: perhaps the first 1,000, or the first 5,000. Doing this would have held or capped the costs to reasonably defined levels, and avoided the greater risks. Or the company could have made the offer less generous, perhaps by upping the requirements, or by lessening the premiums. Such more moderate alternatives would still have made an attractive promotion, but not the major uncontrolled catastrophe that happened.

WHAT CAN BE LEARNED?

In planning, consider a worst-case scenario. There are those who preach the desirability of positive thinking, of confidence and optimism—whether it be in personal lives, athletics, or business practices. But expecting and preparing for the worst has much to commend it, since a person or a firm is then better able to cope with adversity, not be overwhelmed, and therefore make prudent decisions. And if it is deemed that the risks outweigh probable benefits, then the alternative ought to be scrapped or modified.

Apparently the avid acceptance of the promotional offer was a complete surprise; no one dreamed of such demand. Yet, was it so unreasonable to think that a very attractive offer would meet wild acceptance?

In using loss leaders, put a cap on potential losses. Loss leaders, as we noted earlier, are items promoted at such an attractive price that the firm loses money on every sale. The expectation, of course, is that the customer traffic generated by such attractive promotions will increase sales of other regular profit items so that total profits will be increased.

The risks of uncontrolled or uncapped loss leader promotions is vividly shown in this case. For a retailer who uses loss leaders, the loss is ultimately capped as the inventory is used up. With UK Hoover there was no cap. The moral is clear: attractive loss leader promotions should be capped, such as "the first hundred," or "first thousand," or "one week only." Or else they should be made less attractive.

Beware giving unproven foreign subsidiaries a loose rein. Although moving more authority down into the ranks of the organization is often desirable and stimulates better motivation and management development than centralization, it can be overdone. At the extreme, where divisional and subsidiary executives have almost unlimited decision-making authority and can run their operations as virtual dynasties, then corporate management essentially abdicates its authority. Such looseness in an organization endangers cohesiveness; it tends to obscure common standards and objectives; it can even dilute unified ethical standards.

Such extreme looseness of organizational structure is not uncommon with acquisitions, especially foreign ones, under the assumption that they were operating successfully before the acquisition and have the greater expertise because of their experience. International operations are often given more freedom of scope than domestic operations, simply because such executives are presumed to have more first-hand knowledge of their environment than the parent executives.

Still, there should be limits on how much freedom these divisional and subsidiary executives should be permitted—especially when their operations have not been notably successful. In Maytag's case, the U.K. subsidiary had lost money every year since acquired. One would expect prudent corporate management to have condoned less decentralization and tighter supervision under such circumstances.

The power of a cost-benefit analysis. For major decisions, executives have much to gain from a cost-benefit analysis. It forces them to systematically tabulate and analyze the costs and benefits of particular courses of action. They may find that likely benefits are so uncertain as to not be worth the risk. If so, now is the time to realize this, rather than after substantial commitments have already been made.

Without doubt, regular use of cost-benefit analyses for major decisions improves executives' batting averages for good decisions. Even though some numbers may have to be judgmental, especially as to probable benefits, the process of making this analysis forces a careful look at alternatives and most likely consequences. For more important decisions, input from diverse staff people and executives will bring greater power to the analysis.

CONSIDER

Can you add additional learning insights?

QUESTIONS

1. How could the promotion of UK Hoover have been better planned and designed? Be as specific as you can.
2. Given the fiasco that did occur—in particular, the huge unexpected demand—how do you think Maytag should have responded?
3. "Firing the three top executives of UK Hoover is unconscionable. It smacks of a vendetta against European managers by an American parent. After all, their only `crime' was a promotion that was too successful." Comment on this statement.
4. Do you think Leonard Hadley, the Maytag CEO for only two months, should be soundly criticized for the U.K. situation? Why or why not?
5. Please speculate: Why do you think this UK Hoover fiasco happened in the first place? What went wrong?
6. Evaluate the decision to acquire Chicago Pacific Corporation (CPC). Do this both for the time of the decision, and now—after the fact—as a post mortem. Defend your overall conclusions.
7. Use your creativity: Can you devise a marketing strategy for UK Hoover to become more of a major force in Europe?

HANDS-ON EXERCISES

1. You have been placed in charge of a task force sent by headquarters to England to coordinate the fire-fighting efforts in the aftermath of the ill-fated promotion. There is neither enough productive capacity nor enough airline seats available to handle the demand. How would you propose to handle this situation? Be as specific as you can and defend your recommendations.
2. As a staff vice president at corporate headquarters, you have been charged to develop policies and procedures company-wide that will prevent such a situation from ever occurring again. What would you recommend?

TEAM DEBATE EXERCISE

How tightly should you supervise and control a foreign operation? This Maytag example suggests very tightly. But is this an aberration, unlikely to be encountered again? Debate the issue of very tight controls versus relative freedom for foreign operations.

INVITATION TO RESEARCH

How has Maytag done since this fiasco? How have revenues and profits, as well as the stock market price of Maytag changed since early 1993? Can you find further information on the Hoover operation?

CHAPTER 10

Euro Disney: A Successful Format Stumbles in Europe

With high expectations Euro Disney opened just outside Paris in April 1992. Success seemed ensured. After all, the Disneylands in Florida, California, and, most recently, Japan were all spectacular successes. But somehow all the rosy expectations became a delusion. The opening results cast even the future continuance of Euro Disney into doubt. How could what seemed so right be so wrong? What mistakes were made?

PRELUDE

Optimism

Perhaps a few early omens should have raised some cautions. Between 1987 and 1991, three $150 million amusement parks had opened in France with great fanfare. All had fallen flat, and by 1991 two were in bankruptcy. Now Walt Disney Company was finalizing its plans to open Europe's first Disneyland early in 1992. This would turn out to be a $4.4 billion enterprise sprawling over 5,000 acres 20 miles east of Paris. Initially it would have six hotels and 5,200 rooms, more rooms than the entire city of Cannes, and lodging was expected to triple in a few years as Disney opened a second theme park to keep visitors at the resort longer.

Disney also expected to develop a growing office complex, one only slightly smaller than France's biggest, La Defense, in Paris. Plans also called for shopping malls, apartments, golf courses, and vacation homes. Euro Disney would tightly control all this ancillary development, designing and building nearly everything itself, and eventually selling off the commercial properties at a huge profit.

Disney executives had no qualms about the huge enterprise, which would cover an area one-fifth the size of Paris itself. They were more worried that the park might not be big enough to handle the crowds:

> "My biggest fear is that we will be too successful." "I don't think it can miss. They are masters of marketing. When the place opens it will be perfect. And they know how to make people smile—even the French."[1]

Company executives initially predicted that 11 million Europeans would visit the extravaganza in the first year alone. After all, Europeans accounted for 2.7 million visits to the U.S. Disney parks and spent $1.6 billion on Disney merchandise. Surely a park closer would draw many thousands more. As Disney executives thought more about it, the forecast of 11 million seemed most conservative. They reasoned that since Disney parks in the United States (population of 250 million) attract 41 million visitors a year, then if Euro Disney attracted visitors in the same proportion, attendance could reach 60 million with Western Europe's 370 million people. Table 10.1 shows the 1990 attendance at the two U.S. Disney parks and the newest Japanese Disneyland, as well as the attendance-population ratios.

Adding fuel to the optimism was the fact that Europeans typically have more vacation time than do U.S. workers. For example, five-week vacations

Table 10.1   Attendance and Attendance/Population Ratios, Disney Parks, 1990

| | Visitors | Population | Ratio |
	(millions)		
United States			
Disneyland (Southern California)	12.9	250	5.2%
Disney World/Epcot Center (Florida)	28.5	250	11.4%
Total United States	41.4		16.6%
Japan			
Tokyo Disneyland	16.0	124	13.5%
Euro Disney	?	310[a]	?

[a]Within a two-hour flight.

Source: Euro Disney, Amusement Business Magazine.

Commentary: Even if the attendance/population ratio for Euro Disney is only 10 percent, which is far below that of some other theme parks, still 31 million visitors could be expected. Euro Disney "conservatively" predicted 11 million the first year.

---

[1]Steven Greenhouse, "Playing Disney in the Parisian Fields," *The New York Times* (February 17, 1991): Section 3: 1, 6.

are commonplace for French and German employees, compared with two to three weeks for U.S. workers.

The failure of the three earlier French parks was seen as irrelevant. Robert Fitzpatrick, Euro Disneyland's chairman, stated, "We are spending 22 billion French francs before we open the door, while the other places spent 700 million. This means we can pay infinitely more attention to details—to costumes, hotels, shops, trash baskets—to create a fantastic place. There's just too great a response to Disney for us to fail."[2]

Nonetheless, a few scattered signs indicated that not everyone was happy with the coming of Disney. Leftist demonstrators at Euro Disney's stock offering greeted company executives with eggs, ketchup, and "Mickey Go Home" signs. Some French intellectuals decried the pollution of the country's cultural ambiance with the coming of Mickey Mouse and company: They called the park an American cultural abomination. The mainstream press also seemed contrary, describing every Disney setback "with glee." French officials in negotiating with Disney sought less American and more European culture at France's Magic Kingdom. Still, such protests and bad press seemed contrived, unrepresentative, and certainly not predictive. Company officials dismissed the early criticism as "the ravings of an insignificant elite."[3]

The Location Decision

In the search for a site for Euro Disney, Disney executives examined 200 locations in Europe. The other finalist was Barcelona, Spain. Its major attraction was warmer weather, but its transportation system was not as good as that around Paris, and it lacked level tracts of land of sufficient size. The clincher for the Paris decision was its more central location. Table 10.2 shows the number of people within 2 to 6 hours of the Paris site.

The beet fields of the Marne-la-Vallee area was the choice. Being near Paris seemed a major advantage, since Paris was Europe's biggest tourist draw. And France was eager to win the project to help lower its jobless rate

Table 10.2   Number of People Within 2–6 Hours of the Paris Site

Within a 2-hour drive	17 million people
Within a 4-hour drive	41 million people
Within a 6-hour drive	109 million people
Within a 2-hour flight	310 million people

Source: Euro Disney, Amusement Business Magazine.
Commentary: The much more densely populated and geographically compact European continent makes access to Euro Disney much more convenient that it is in the United States.

[2]Greenhouse, "Playing Disney," 6.
[3]Peter Gumbel and Richard Turner, "Fans Like Euro Disney But Its Parent's Goofs Weigh the Park Down," *The Wall Street Journal* (March 10, 1994): A12.

and also to enhance its role as the center of tourist activity in Europe. The French government expected the project to create at least 30,000 jobs and to contribute $1 billion a year from foreign visitors.

To entice the project, the French government allowed Disney to buy up huge tracts of land at 1971 prices. It provided $750 million in loans at below-market rates, and it spent hundreds of millions of dollars on subway and other capital improvements for the park. For example, Paris's express subway was extended out to the park; a 35-minute ride from downtown cost about $2.50. A new railroad station for the high-speed Train a Grande Vitesse was built only 150 yards from the entrance gate. This enabled visitors from Brussels to arrive in only 90 minutes. Once the English Channel tunnel opened in 1994, even London would be only 3 hours and 10 minutes away. Actually, Euro Disney was the second largest construction project in Europe, second only to construction of the English Channel tunnel.

Financing

Euro Disney cost $4.4 billion. Table 10.3 shows the sources of financing, in percentages. The Disney Company had a 49 percent stake in the project, which was the most that the French government would allow. For this stake it invested $160 million, while other investors contributed $1.2 billion in equity. The rest was financed by loans from the government, banks, and special partnerships formed to buy properties and lease them back.

The payoff for Disney began after the park opened. The company receives 10 percent of Euro Disney's admission fees and 5 percent of the food and merchandise revenues. This is the same arrangement as Disney has with the Japanese park. But in the Tokyo Disneyland, the company took no ownership interest, opting instead only for the licensing fees and a percentage of the revenues. The reason for the conservative position with Tokyo Disneyland was that Disney money was heavily committed to building the Epcot Center in Florida. Furthermore, Disney had some concerns about the Tokyo enterprise.

Table 10.3 Sources of Financing for Euro Disney (percent)

Total to Finance: $4.4 billion	*100%*
Shareholders equity, including $160 million from Walt Disney Company	32
Loan from French government	22
Loan from group of 45 banks	21
Bank loans to Disney hotels	16
Real estate partnerships	9

Source: Euro Disney.
Commentary: The full flavor of the leverage is shown here, with equity comprising only 32 percent of the total expenditure.

This was the first non-American and the first cold-weather Disneyland. It seemed prudent to minimize the risks. But this turned out to be a significant blunder of conservatism, because Tokyo became a huge success, as the following box discusses in more detail.

INFORMATION BOX

THE TOKYO DISNEYLAND SUCCESS

Tokyo Disneyland opened in 1983 on 201 acres in the eastern suburb of Urazasu. It was arranged that an ownership group, Oriental Land, would build, own, and operate the theme park with advice from Disney. The owners borrowed most of the $650 million needed to bring the project to fruition. Disney invested no money but receives 10 percent of the revenues from admission and rides and 5 percent of sales of food, drink, and souvenirs.

Although the start was slow, Japanese soon began flocking to the park in great numbers. By 1990 some 16 million a year passed through the turnstiles, about one-fourth more than visited Disneyland in California. In fiscal year 1990, revenues reached $988 million with profits of $150 million. Indicative of the Japanese preoccupation with things American, the park serves almost no Japanese food, and the live entertainers are mostly American. Japanese management even apologizes for the presence of a single Japanese restaurant inside the park: "A lot of elderly Japanese came here from outlying parts of Japan, and they were not very familiar with hot dogs and hamburgers."[4]

Disney executives were soon to realize the great mistake they made in not taking substantial ownership in Tokyo Disneyland. They did not want to make the same mistake with Euro Disney.

Would you expect the acceptance of the genuine American experience in Tokyo to be indicative of the reaction of the French and Europeans? Why or why not?

Special Modifications

With the experiences of the previous theme parks, and particularly that of the first cold-weather park in Tokyo, Disney construction executives were able to bring state-of-the-art refinements to Euro Disney. Exacting demands were placed on French construction companies, and a higher level of performance and compliance resulted than many thought possible to achieve.

---

[4]James Sterngold, "Cinderella Hits Her Stride in Tokyo," *The New York Times* (February 17, 1991): 6.

The result was a major project on time, if not completely on budget. In contrast, the Channel tunnel was plagued by delays and severe cost overruns.

One of the things learned from the cold-weather project in Japan was that more needed to be done to protect visitors from such weather problems as wind, rain, and cold. Consequently, Euro Disney's ticket booths were protected from the elements, as were the lines waiting for attractions, and even the moving sidewalk from the 12,000-car parking area.

Certain French accents—and British, German, and Italian accents as well—were added to the American flavor. The park has two official languages, English and French, but multilingual guides are available for Dutch, Spanish, German, and Italian visitors. Discoveryland, based on the science fiction of France's Jules Verne, is a new attraction. A theater with a full 360-degree screen acquaints visitors with a sweep of European history. And, not the least modification for cultural diversity, Snow White speaks German, and the Belle Notte Pizzeria and Pasticceria are right next to Pinocchio.

Disney had foreseen that it might encounter some cultural problems. This was one of the reasons for choosing Robert Fitzpatrick as Euro Disney's president. He is American but speaks French, knows Europe well, and has a French wife. However, he was unable to establish the rapport needed and was replaced in 1993 by a French native. Still, some of his admonitions that France should not be approached as if it were Florida fell on deaf ears.

RESULTS

As the April 1992 opening approached, the company launched a massive communications blitz aimed at publicizing the fact that the fabled Disney experience was now accessible to all Europeans. Some 2,500 people from various print and broadcast media were lavishly entertained while being introduced to the new facilities. Most media people were positively impressed with the inauguration and with the enthusiastic spirit of the staffers. These public relations efforts, however, were criticized by some for being heavy-handed and for not providing access to Disney executives.

As 1992 wound down after the opening, it became clear that revenue projections were, unbelievably, not being met. But the opening turned out to be in the middle of a severe recession in Europe. European visitors, perhaps as a consequence, were far more frugal than their American counterparts. Many packed their own lunches and shunned the Disney hotels. For example, a visitor named Corine from southern France typified the "no spend" attitude of many: "It's a bottomless pit," she said as she, her husband, and their three children toured Euro Disney on a 3-day visit. "Every time we turn around, one of the kids wants to buy something."[5] Perhaps investor expectations, despite the logic and rationale, were simply unrealistic.

Indeed, Disney had initially priced the park and the hotels to meet revenue targets and had assumed demand was there at any price. Park admission was $42.25 for adults—higher than at the American parks. A room at the flagship Disneyland Hotel at the park's entrance cost about $340 a night, the equivalent of a top hotel in Paris. It was soon averaging only a 50 percent occupancy. Guests were not staying as long or spending as much on the fairly high-priced food and merchandise. We can label the initial pricing strategy at Euro Disney as *skimming pricing*. The following box discusses skimming and its opposite, penetration pricing.

INFORMATION BOX

SKIMMING AND PENETRATION PRICING

A firm with a new product or service may be in a temporary monopolistic situation. If there is little or no present and potential competition, more latitude in pricing is possible. In such a situation (and, of course, Euro Disney was in this situation), one of two basic and opposite approaches may be taken in the pricing strategy: skimming or penetration.

Skimming is a relatively high-price strategy. It is the most tempting where the product or service is highly differentiated because it yields high per-unit profits. It is compatible with a quality image. But it has limitations. It assumes a rather inelastic demand curve, in which sales will not be appreciably affected by price. And if the product or service is easily imitated (which was hardly the case with Euro Disney), then competitors are encouraged because of the high profit margins.

The penetration strategy of low prices assumes an elastic demand curve, with sales increasing substantially if prices can be lowered. It is compatible with economies of scale, and it discourages competitive entry. The classic example of penetration pricing was the Model T Ford. Henry Ford lowered his prices to make the car within the means of the general public, expanded production into the millions, and in so doing realized new horizons of economies of scale.

Euro Disney correctly saw itself in a monopoly position; it correctly judged that it had a relatively inelastic demand curve with customers flocking to the park regardless of rather high prices. What it did not reckon with was the shrewdness of European visitors: Because of the high prices they shortened their stay, avoided the hotels, brought their own food and drink, and bought only sparingly the Disney merchandise.

What advantages would a lower price penetration strategy have offered Euro Disney? Do you see any drawbacks?

---

[5] "Ailing Euro Disney May Face Closure," *Cleveland Plain Dealer* (January 1, 1994): E1.

Disney executives soon realized they had made a major miscalculation. Whereas visitors to Florida's Disney World often stayed more than 4 days, Euro Disney—with one theme park compared to Florida's three—was proving to be a 2-day experience at best. Many visitors arrived early in the morning, rushed to the park, staying late at night, then checked out of the hotel the next morning before heading back to the park for one final exploration.

The problems of Euro Disney were not public acceptance (despite the earlier critics). Europeans loved the place. Since the opening it attracted just under 1 million visitors a month, thus easily achieving the original projections. Such patronage made it Europe's biggest paid tourist attraction. But the large numbers of frugal patrons did not come close to enabling Disney to meet revenue and profit projections and cover a bloated overhead.

Other operational errors and miscalculations, most of these cultural, hurt the enterprise. A policy of serving no alcohol in the park caused consternation in a country where wine is customary for lunch and dinner. (This policy has since been reversed.) Disney thought Monday would be a light day and Friday a heavy one and allocated staff accordingly, but the reverse was true. It found great peaks and valleys in attendance: The number of visitors per day in the high season could be ten times the number in slack times. The need to lay off employees during quiet periods came up against France's inflexible labor schedules.

One unpleasant surprise concerned breakfast. "We were told that Europeans don't take breakfast, so we downsized the restaurants," recalled one executive. "And guess what? Everybody showed up for breakfast. We were trying to serve 2,500 breakfasts at 350-seat restaurants. The lines were horrendous."[6]

Disney failed to anticipate another demand, this time from tour bus drivers. Restrooms were built for 50 drivers, but on peak days 2,000 drivers were seeking the facilities. "From impatient drivers to grumbling bankers, Disney stepped on toe after European toe."[7]

For the fiscal year ending September 30, 1993, the amusement park had lost $960 million, and the future of the park was in doubt. (As of December 31, 1993, the cumulative loss was 6.04 billion francs, or $1.03 billion). Walt Disney made $175 million available to tide Euro Disney over until the next spring. Adding to the problems of the struggling park were heavy interest costs. As depicted in Table 10.3, against a total cost of $4.4 billion, only 32 percent of the project was financed by equity investment. Some $2.9 billion was borrowed primarily from 60 creditor banks, at interest rates running as high as 11 percent. Thus, the enterprise began heavily leveraged, and the hefty interest

[6]Gumbel and Turner, "Fans Like Euro Disney," A12.
[7]Gumbel and Turner, "Fans Like Euro Disney," A12.

charges greatly increased the overhead to be covered from operations. Serious negotiations began with the banks to restructure and refinance.

ATTEMPTS TO RECOVER

The $921 million lost in the first fiscal year represented a shortfall of more than $2.5 million a day. The situation was not quite as dire as these statistics would seem to indicate. Actually, the park was generating an operating profit, but nonoperating costs were bringing it deeply into the red.

Still, operations were far from satisfactory although they were becoming better. It had taken 20 months to smooth out the wrinkles and adjust to the miscalculations about demand for hotel rooms and the willingness of Europeans to pay substantial prices for lodging, meals, and merchandise. Operational efficiencies were slowly improving.

By the beginning of 1994, Euro Disney had been made more affordable. Prices of some hotel rooms were cut—for example, at the low end, from $76 per night to $51. Expensive jewelry was replaced by $10 T-shirts and $5 crayon sets. Luxury sit-down restaurants were converted to self-service. Off-season admission prices were reduced from $38 to $30. And operating costs were reduced 7 percent by streamlining operations and eliminating over 900 jobs.

Efficiency and *economy* became the new watchwords. Merchandise in stores was pared from 30,000 items to 17,000, with more of the remaining goods being pure U.S. Disney products. (The company had thought that European tastes might prefer more subtle items than the garish Mickey and Minnie souvenirs, but this was found not so.) The number of different food items offered by park services was reduced more than 50 percent. New training programs were designed to remotivate the 9,000 full-time permanent employees, to make them more responsive to customers and more flexible in their job assignments. Employees in contact with the public were given crash courses in German and Spanish.

Still, as we have seen, the problem had not been attendance, although the recession and the high prices had reduced it. Still, some 18 million people passed through the turnstiles in the first 20 months of operation. But they were not spending money as people did in the U.S. parks. Furthermore, Disney had alienated some European tour operators with its high prices, and it diligently sought to win them back.

Management had hoped to reduce the heavy interest overhead by selling the hotels to private investors. But the hotels had an occupancy rate of only 55%, making them unattractive to investors. Although the recession was a factor in such low occupancy rates, a significant part of the problem lay in the calculation of lodging demands. With the park just 35 minutes from the center of Paris, many visitors stayed in town. About the same time as the opening, the real estate market in France collapsed, making the hotels unsalable in the short term. This added to the overhead burden and confounded the business plan forecasts.

While some analysts were relegating Euro Disney to the cemetery, few remembered that Orlando's Disney World showed early symptoms of being a disappointment. Costs were heavier than expected, and attendance was below expectations. But Orlando's Disney World turned out to be one of the most profitable resorts in North America.

ANALYSIS

Euro Disney, as we have seen, fell far short of expectations in the first 20 months of its operation, so far short that its continued existence was even questioned. What went wrong?

External Factors

A serious economic recession that affected all of Europe undoubtedly was a major impediment to meeting expectations. As noted before, it adversely affected attendance—although still not all that much—but drastically affected spending patterns. Frugality was the order of the day for many visitors. The recession also affected real estate demand and prices, thus saddling Disney with hotels it had hoped to sell at profitable prices to eager investors to take the strain off its hefty interest payments.

The company assumed that European visitors would not be greatly different from those visitors, foreign and domestic, of U.S. Disney parks. Yet, at least in the first few years of operation, visitors were much more price conscious. This suggested that those within a 2- to 4-hour drive of Euro Disney were considerably different from the ones who traveled overseas, at least in spending ability and willingness.

Internal Factors

Despite the decades of experience with the U.S. Disney parks and the successful experience with the new Japan park, Disney still made serious blunders in its operational planning, such as the demand for breakfasts, the insistence on wine at meals, the severe peaks and valleys in scheduling, and even such mundane things as sufficient restrooms for tour bus drivers. It had problems in motivating and training its French employees in efficiency and customer orientation. Did all these mistakes reflect an intractable French mindset or a deficiency of Disney management? Perhaps both. But Disney management should have researched all cultural differences more thoroughly. Further, the park needed major streamlining of inventories and operations after the opening. The mistakes suggested an arrogant mind-set by Disney management: "We were arrogant," concedes one executive. "It was like 'We're building the Taj Mahal and people will come—on our terms.'"[8]

The miscalculations in hotel rooms and in pricing of many products, including food services, showed an insensitivity to the harsh economic conditions. But the greatest mistake was taking on too much debt for the park. The highly leveraged situation burdened Euro Disney with such hefty interest payments and overhead that the breakeven point was impossibly high, and it even threatened the viability of the enterprise. See the following box for a discussion of the important inputs and implications affecting breakeven, and how these should play a role in strategic planning.

INFORMATION BOX

THE BREAKEVEN POINT

A breakeven analysis is a vital tool in making go/no go decisions about new ventures and alternative business strategies. This can be shown graphically as follows:

Below the breakeven point, the venture suffers losses; above it, the venture becomes profitable.

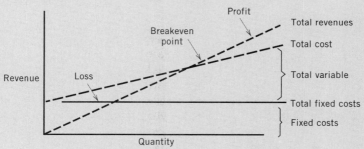

Let us make a hypothetical comparison of Euro Disney with its $1.6 billion in high interest loans (some of these as high as 11 percent) from the banks, and what the situation might be with more equity and less borrowed funds.

For this example, let us assume that other fixed costs are $240 million, that the average interest rate on the debt is 10 percent, and that average profit margin (contribution to overhead) from each visitor is $32. Now let us consider two scenarios: (a) the $1.6 billion of debt, and (b) only $0.5 billion of debt.

---

[8]Gumbel and Turner, "Fans Like Euro Disney," A12.

The number of visitors needed to break even are determined as follows:

$$\text{Breakeven} = \frac{\text{Total fixed costs}}{\text{Contribution to overhead}}$$

Scenario (a):   Interest = 10% ($1,600,000,000) = $160,000,000

Fixed costs = Interest + $240,000,000

= 160,000,000 + 240,000,000

= $400,000,000

Breakeven = $\dfrac{\$400,000,000}{\$32}$ = 12,500,000 visitors needed to break even

Scenario (b):   Interest = 10% (500,000,000) = $50,000,000

Fixed costs = 50,000,000 + 240,000,000

= $290,000,000

Breakeven = $\dfrac{\$290,000,000}{\$32}$ = 9,062,500 visitors needed to break even

Because Euro Disney expected 11 million visitors the first year, it obviously was not going to break even while servicing $1.6 billion in debt with $160 million in interest charges per year. The average visitor would have to be induced to spend more, thereby increasing the average profit or contribution to overhead.

In making go/no go decisions, many costs can be estimated quite closely. What cannot be determined as surely are the sales figures. Certain things can be done to affect the breakeven point. Obviously it can be lowered if the overhead is reduced, as we saw in scenario b. Higher prices also result in a lower breakeven because of greater per-customer profits (but would probably affect total sales quite adversely). Promotion expenses can be either increased or decreased and affect the breakeven point, but they probably also have an impact on sales. Some costs of operation can be reduced, thus lowering the breakeven. But the hefty interest charges act as a lodestone over an enterprise, greatly increasing the overhead and requiring what may be an unattainable breakeven point.

Does a new venture have to break even or make a profit the first year to be worth going into? Why or why not?

Were such mistakes and miscalculations beyond what we would expect of reasonable executives? Probably not, with the probable exception of the crushing burden of debt. Any new venture is susceptible to surprises and the need to streamline and weed out its inefficiencies. While we would have expected such to have been done faster and more effectively from a well-tried Disney operation, European, and particularly French and Parisian, consumers and employees showed different behavior and attitude patterns than expected.

The worst sin that Disney management and investors could make would be to give up on Euro Disney and not to look ahead 2 to 5 years. A hint of the future promise was Christmas week of 1993. Despite the first year's $920 million in red ink, some 35,000 packed the park most days. A week later on a cold January day, some of the rides still had 40-minute waits.

POSTSCRIPT

On March 15, 1994, an agreement was struck aimed at making Euro Disney profitable by September 30, 1995. The European banks would fund another $500 million and make concessions such as forgiving 18 months' interest and deferring all principal payments for 3 years. In return, Walt Disney Company agreed to spend about $750 million to bail out its Euro Disney affiliate.[9] Thus, the debt would be halved, with interest payments greatly reduced. Disney also agreed to eliminate for 5 years the lucrative management fees and royalties it received on the sale of tickets and merchandise.

By 1996, things were definitely looking better. To distance itself from negative media coverage, the name of the park had been changed four times since April 1992, eventually settling on Disneyland Paris for the park, while Euro Disney remained the parent company's name.

Cheaper transportation to the park was a major improvement. For example, a joint promotion with British Airways offered a two-day package at attractive prices. Cross-channel price wars also helped, with increased competition from the channel tunnel Le Shuttle and Eurostar pushing down the costs of traveling to Europe.

Development plans, put on hold during the worst of the financial crisis, were going ahead. These included the opening of a Planet Hollywood restaurant and an eight-screen cinema, in addition to strong expansion of convention facilities. For example, during 1995, more than 1,100 business-related meetings were held at Euro Disney hotels, generating 110,000 hotel nights. Plans for retail and domestic housing development around the park were going ahead: Euro Disney had 4,500 acres of land of which only a third had been developed.

---

[9]Brian Coleman and Thomas R. King, "Euro Disney Rescue Package Wins Approval," *The Wall Street Journal* (March 15, 1994): A3, A5.

For the quarter that ended June 30, 1996, Euro Disney announced a profit of $29.4 million for its theme parks and hotels. Of its 5,700 hotel rooms, each room had been occupied on average every night by three persons.[10] And for all of 1995, 10.7 million people visited the park, up substantially from 8.4 million the previous year.

Still, there were skeptics. "They are not out of trouble," said one French analyst. "They have revamped the marketing and proved to the financial community that the concept is still viable, but the financial improvements are based on internal restructuring and interest holidays."[11]

WHAT CAN BE LEARNED?

Beware the arrogant mindset, especially when dealing with new situations and new cultures. French sensitivities were offended by Disney corporate executives who often turned out to be brash, insensitive, and overbearing. A contentious attitude by Disney personnel alienated people and aggravated planning and operational difficulties. "The answer to doubts or suggestions invariably was, Do as we say, because we know best."[12]

Such a mindset is a natural concomitant with success. It is said that success breeds arrogance, but this inclination must be fought against by those who would spurn the ideas and concerns of others. For a proud and touchy people, the French, this almost contemptuous attitude by the Americans fueled resentment and glee at Disney miscues. It did not foster cooperation, understanding, or the willingness to smooth the process. One might almost speculate that had not the potential economic benefits to France been so great, the Euro Disney project might never have been approved.

Great success may be ephemeral. We often find that great successes are not lasting, that they have no staying power. Somehow the success pattern gets lost or forgotten or is not well rounded. Other times an operation grows beyond the capability of the originators. Hungry competitors are always in the wings, ready to take advantage of any lapse. As we saw with Euro Disney, having a closed mind to new ideas or to needed revisions of an old success pattern—the arrogance of success—makes expansion into different environments more difficult and even risky.

---

[10] Paul Mochaud, "Disneyland Paris Properties Report Third-quarter Growth," *Hotel & Motel Management* (September 2, 1996): 10.

[11] Harriet Marsh, "Variations on a Theme Park," *Marketing* (May 2, 1996): 15.

[12] Gumbel and Turner, "Fans Like Euro Disney," A1.

While corporate Disney has continued to have strong success with its other theme parks and its diversifications, competitors are moving in with their own theme parks in the United States and elsewhere. We may question whether this industry is approaching saturation, and we may wonder whether Disney has learned from its mistakes in Europe.

Highly leveraged situations are extremely vulnerable. During most of the 1980s, many managers, including corporate raiders, pursued a strategy of debt financing in contrast to equity (stock ownership) financing. Funds for such borrowing were usually readily available, heavy debt had income tax advantages, and profits could be distributed among fewer shares so that return on equity was enhanced. During this time a few voices decried the overleveraged situations of many companies. They predicted that when the eventual economic downturn came, such firms would find themselves unable to meet the heavy interest burden. Most lenders paid little heed to such lonesome voices and encouraged greater borrowing.

The widely publicized problems of some of the raiders in the late 1980s, such as Robert Campeau, who had acquired major department store corporations only to find himself overextended and unable to continue, suddenly changed some expansionist lending sentiments. The hard reality dawned that these arrangements were often fragile indeed, especially when they rested on optimistic projections for asset sales, for revenues, and for cost savings to cover the interest payments. An economic slowdown hastened the demise of some of these ill-advised speculations.

Disney was guilty of the same speculative excesses with Euro Disney, relying far too much on borrowed funds and assuming that assets, such as hotels, could be easily sold off at higher prices to other investors. As we saw in the breakeven box, hefty interest charges from such overleveraged conditions can jeopardize the viability of the enterprise if revenue and profit projections fail to meet the rosy expectations.

Be judicious with the skimming price strategy. Euro Disney faced the classical situation favorable for a skimming price strategy. It was in a monopoly position, with no equivalent competitors likely. It faced a somewhat inelastic demand curve, which indicated that people would come almost regardless of price. So why not price to maximize per-unit profits? Unfortunately for Disney, the wily Europeans circumvented the high prices by frugality. Of course, a severe recession exacerbated the situation.

The learning insight from this example is that a skimming price assumes that customers are willing and able to pay the higher prices and have no lower-priced competitive alternatives. It is a faulty strategy when many customers are unable, or else unwilling, to pay the high prices and can find a way to experience the product or service in a modest way.

CONSIDER

Can you think of other learning insights from this case?

QUESTIONS

1. How could the company have erred so badly in its estimates of the spending patterns of European customers?
2. How could a better reading of the impact of cultural differences on revenues have been achieved?
3. What suggestions do you have for fostering a climate of sensitivity and goodwill in corporate dealings with the French?
4. How do you account for the great success of Tokyo Disneyland and the problems of Euro Disney? What are the key contributory differences?
5. Do you believe that Euro Disney might have done better if located elsewhere in Europe rather than just outside Paris? Why or why not?
6. "Mickey Mouse and the Disney park are an American cultural abomination." Evaluate this critical statement.
7. Consider how a strong marketing approach might be made to both European consumers and agents, such as travel agents, tour guides, even bus drivers.

HANDS-ON EXERCISES

Before

1. It is three months before the grand opening. As a staff assistant to the president of Euro Disney, you sense that the plans for high price and luxury accommodations are ill advised. What arguments would you marshall to persuade the company to offer lower prices and more moderate accommodations? Be as persuasive as you can.

After

2. It is six months after opening. Revenues are not meeting target, and a number of problems have surfaced and are being worked on. The major problem remains, however, that the venture needs more visitors and/or higher expenditures per visitor. Develop plans to improve the situation.

TEAM DEBATE EXERCISE

It is two years after the opening. Euro Disney is a monumental mistake, profitwise. Two schools of thought are emerging for improving the situation.

One is to pour money into the project, build one or two more theme parks and really make this another Disney World. The other camp believes more investment would be wasted at this time, that the need is to pare expenses to the bone and wait for an eventual upturn. Debate the two positions.

INVITATION TO RESEARCH

Has the recent profitability of Euro Disney continued? Are expansion plans going ahead? Have other theme parks been announced?

CHAPTER 11

Coca-Cola's Classic Blunder: The Failure of Marketing Research

On April 23, 1985, Roberto C. Goizueta, chairman of Coca-Cola, made a momentous announcement. It was to lead to more discussion, debate, and intense feelings than perhaps ever before resulting from one business decision.

"The best has been made even better," he proclaimed. After 99 years, the Coca-Cola Company had decided to abandon its original formula in favor of a sweeter variation, presumably an improved taste, which was named "New Coke."

Not even 3 months later, public pressure brought the company to admit it had made a mistake, and that it was bringing back the old Coke under the name "Coca-Cola Classic." It was July 11, 1985. Despite $4 million and two years of research, the company had made a major miscalculation. How could this have happened with such an astute marketer? The story is intriguing and provides a number of sobering insights, and it has a happy ending for Coca-Cola.

THE HISTORY OF COCA-COLA

Early Days

Coca-Cola was invented by a pharmacist who rose to cavalry general for the Confederates during the Civil War. John Styth Pemberton settled in Atlanta after the war and began putting out patent medicines such as Triplex Liver Pills and Globe of Flower Cough Syrup. In 1885 he registered a trademark for French Wine Coca, "an Ideal Nerve and Tonic Stimulant." In 1886,

Pemberton unveiled a modification of French Wine Coca that he called Coca-Cola, and began distributing this to soda fountains in used beer bottles. He looked on the concoction less as a refreshment than as a headache cure, especially for people who had overindulged in food or drink. By chance, one druggist discovered that the syrup tasted better when mixed with carbonated water.

When his health failed and Coca-Cola failed to bring sufficient money to meet his financial obligations, Pemberton sold the rights to Coca-Cola to a 39-year-old pharmacist, Asa Griggs Candler, for a paltry $2,300. The destitute Pemberton died in 1888 and was buried in a grave that went unmarked for the next 70 years.

Candler, a small-town Georgia boy born in 1851 (and hence too young to be a hero in the Civil War), had planned to become a physician but he changed his mind after observing that druggists made more money than doctors. He struggled for almost 40 years until he bought Coca-Cola, but then his fortunes changed profoundly. In 1892 he organized the Coca-Cola Company, and a few years later downgraded the therapeutic qualities. At the same time, he developed the bottling system that still exists, and for 25 years he almost singlehandedly guided the drink's destiny.

Robert Woodruff and the Maturing of the Coca-Cola Company

In 1916, Candler left Coca-Cola to run for mayor of Atlanta. The company was left in the hands of his relatives, who, after only 3 years, sold it to a group of Atlanta businessmen for $25 million. Asa was not consulted, and he was deeply distraught. The company was then netting $5 million. By the time of his death in 1929, annual profits were approaching the $25 million sale price. The group who bought Coca-Cola was headed by Ernest Woodruff, an Atlanta banker. Coke today still remains in the hands of the Woodruff family. Under the direction of the son, Robert Winship Woodruff, Coca-Cola became not only a household word within the United States, but one of the most recognized symbols the world over.

Robert Woodruff grew up in affluence but believed in the virtues of personal achievement and effort. As a young man, he ignored his father's orders to return to Emory College to complete the remaining years of his education. He wanted to earn his keep in the real world and not "waste" 3 years in school. Eventually in 1911 he joined one of his father's firms, the newly organized Atlantic Ice & Coal Company, as a salesperson and a buyer. But he and his father violently disagreed again, this time over the purchase by Robert of trucks from White Motors to replace the horse-drawn carts and drays of the day. Ernest fired his son and told him never to return home again. So Robert promptly joined White Motors. At the age of 33, he had become the nation's top truck sales representative and was earning $85,000 a year. But then he heeded the call to come home.

By 1920 the Coca-Cola Company was threatened by bankruptcy. An untimely purchase of sugar just before prices plummeted had resulted in a staggering amount of borrowing to keep the company afloat. Bottler relations were at an all-time low because the company had wanted to raise the price of syrup, thus violating the original franchise contracts in which the price had been permanently fixed. In April of 1923, Robert was named president, and he cemented dealer relationships, stressing his conviction that he wanted everyone connected with Coca-Cola to make money. A quality control program was instituted and distribution was greatly expanded: By 1930, there were 64 bottlers in 28 countries.

During World War II, Coke went with the GIs. Woodruff saw to it that every man in uniform could get a bottle of Coca-Cola for 5 cents whenever he wanted, no matter what the cost to the company. Throughout the 1950s, 1960s, and early 1970s, Coca-Cola ruled the soft-drink market, despite strong challenges by Pepsi. It outsold Pepsi by two to one. But this was to change.

BACKGROUND OF THE DECISION

Inroads of Pepsi, 1970s and 1980s

By the mid-1970s, the Coca-Cola Company was a lumbering giant. Performance reflected this. Between 1976 and 1979, the growth rate of Coca-Cola soft drinks dropped from 13 percent annually to a meager 2 percent. As the giant stumbled, Pepsi Cola was finding heady triumphs. First came the "Pepsi Generation." This advertising campaign captured the imagination of the baby boomers with its idealism and youth. This association with youth and vitality greatly enhanced the image of Pepsi and firmly associated it with the largest consumer market for soft drinks.

Then came another management coup, the "Pepsi Challenge," in which comparative taste tests with consumers showed a clear preference for Pepsi. This campaign led to a rapid increase in Pepsi's market share, from 6 to 14 percent of total U.S. soft-drink sales.

Coca-Cola, in reaction, conducted its own taste tests. Alas, these tests had the same result—people liked the taste of Pepsi better, and market share changes reflected this. As Table 11.1 shows, by 1979 Pepsi had closed the gap on Coca-Cola, having 17.9 percent of the soft-drink market, to Coke's 23.9 percent. By the end of 1984, Coke had only a 2.9 percent lead, while in the grocery store market it was now trailing by 1.7 percent. Further indication of the diminishing position of Coke relative to Pepsi was a study done by

Table 11.1   Coke and Pepsi Shares of Total Soft-Drink Market 1950s–1984

	Mid-1950s Lead	1975 % of Market	Lead	1979 % of Market	Lead	1984 % of Market	Lead
Coke	Better than	24.2	6.8	23.9	6.0	21.7	2.9
Pepsi	2 to 1	17.4		17.9		18.8	

Sources: Thomas Oliver, *The Real Coke, the Real Story* (New York: Random House, 1986), pp. 21, 50; "Two Cokes Really Are Better Than One—For Now," *Business Week* (Sept. 9, 1985): 38.

Coca-Cola's own marketing research department. This showed that in 1972 18 percent of soft-drink users drank Coke exclusively, while only 4 percent drank only Pepsi. In 10 years, the picture had changed greatly: only 12 percent now claimed loyalty to Coke, while the number of exclusive Pepsi drinkers almost matched, with 11 percent. Figure 11.1 shows this graphically.

What made the deteriorating comparative performance of Coke all the more worrisome and frustrating to Coca-Cola was that it was outspending Pepsi in advertising by $100 million. It had twice as many vending machines, dominated fountains, had more shelf space, and was competitively priced. Why was it still losing market share? The advertising undoubtedly was not as effective as that of Pepsi, despite vastly more money spent. And this raises the question: How can we measure the effectiveness of advertising? See the information box for a discussion.

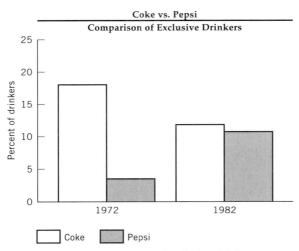

Figure 11.1. Coke versus Pepsi: comparison of exclusive drinkers.

INFORMATION BOX

HOW DO WE MEASURE THE EFFECTIVENESS OF ADVERTISING?

A firm can spend millions of dollars for advertising, and it is only natural to want some feedback of the results of such an expenditure: To what extent did the advertising really pay? Yet, many problems confront the firm trying to measure this.

Most of the methods for measuring effectiveness focus not on sales changes but on how well the communication is remembered, recognized, or recalled. Most evaluative methods simply tell which ad is the best among those being appraised. But even though one ad may be found to be more memorable or to create more attention than another, that fact alone gives no assurance of relationship to sales success. A classic example of the dire consequences that can befall advertising people as a result of the inability to directly measure the impact of ads on sales occurred in December 1970:

> In 1970, the Doyle Dane Bernbach advertising agency created memorable TV commercials for Alka-Seltzer, such as the "spicy meatball man," and the "poached oyster bride." These won professional awards as the best commercials of the year and received high marks for humor and audience recall. But in December the $22 million account was abruptly switched to another agency. The reason? Alka-Seltzer's sales had dropped somewhat. Of course, no one will ever know whether the drop might have been much worse without these notable commercials.

So, how do we measure the value of millions of dollars spent for advertising? Not well. Nor can we determine what is the right amount to spend for advertising, versus what is too much or too little.

Can a business succeed without advertising? Why or why not?

The Changing of the Guard

J. Paul Austin, the chairman of Coca-Cola, was nearing retirement in 1980. Donald Keough, the president for Coca-Cola's American group, was expected to succeed him. But a new name, Roberto Goizueta, suddenly emerged.

Goizueta's background was far different from that of the typical Coca-Cola executive, He was not from Georgia, was not even southern. Rather, he was the son of a wealthy Havana sugar plantation owner. He came to the United States at age 16 to enter an exclusive Connecticut preparatory school, Cheshire Academy. He spoke virtually no English when he arrived, but by using the dictionary and watching movies, he quickly learned the language—and became the class valedictorian.

He graduated from Yale in 1955 with a degree in chemical engineering and returned to Cuba. Spurning his father's business, he went to work in Coke's Cuban research labs.

Goizueta's complacent life was to change in 1959 when Fidel Castro seized power and expropriated foreign facilities. With his wife and their three children, he fled to the United States, arriving with $20. With Coca-Cola he soon became known as a brilliant administrator, and in 1968 he was brought to company headquarters. In 1980 Goizueta and six other executives were made vice chairmen and began battling for top spot in the company.

CEO J. Paul Austin, soon to retire because of Alzheimer's disease, favored an operations man to become the next CEO. But he was overruled by Robert Woodruff, the 90-year-old patriarch. In April 1980, the board of directors approved Woodruff's recommendation of Goizueta for the presidency. When Goizueta became chairman of the board in March 1981, Donald Keough succeeded him as president.

Shortly after, Goizueta called a worldwide managers' conference in which he announced that nothing was sacred to the company anymore, that change was imminent, and that they had to accept that. He also announced ambitious plans to diversify beyond the soft-drink industry.

In a new era of change announced by a new administration, the sacredness of the commitment to the original Coke formula became tenuous, and the ground was laid for the first flavor change in 99 years.

Marketing Research

With the market share erosion of the late 1970s and early 1980s, despite strong advertising and superior distribution, the company began to look at the product itself. Evidence was increasingly suggesting that taste was the single most important cause of Coke's decline. Perhaps the original secret formula needed to be scrapped. And so Project Kansas began.

Under Project Kansas in 1982 some 2,000 interviews in 10 major markets were conducted to investigate customers' willingness to accept a different Coke. People were shown storyboards and comic strip-style mock commercials and were asked series of questions. One storyboard, for example, said that Coke had added a new ingredient and it tasted smoother, while another said the same about Pepsi. Then consumers were asked about their reactions to the "change concept": for example, "Would you be upset?" and "Would you try the new drink?" Researchers estimated from the responses that 10 to 12 percent of Coke drinkers would be upset, and that one-half of these would get over it, but one-half would not.

While interviews showed a willingness to try a new Coke, other tests disclosed the opposite. Small consumer panels or focus groups revealed strong favorable and unfavorable sentiments. But the technical division persisted in trying to develop a new, more pleasing flavor. By September 1984 it thought it had done so. It was a sweeter, less fizzy cola with soft, sticky taste due to a higher sugar content from the exclusive use of corn syrup sweetener that is sweeter than sucrose. This was introduced in blind taste tests, where consumers were not told what brand they were drinking. These tests were highly encouraging. The new flavor substantially beat Pepsi, whereas in previous blind taste tests Pepsi had always beaten Coke.

As a result, researchers estimated that the new formula would boost Coke's share of the soft-drink market by 1 percentage point. This would be worth $200 million in sales.

Before adopting the new flavor, Coca-Cola invested $4 million in the biggest taste test ever. Some 191,000 people in more than 13 cities were asked to participate in a comparison of unmarked various Coke formulations. The use of unmarked colas was intended to eliminate any bias toward brand names. Fifty-five percent of the participants favored New Coke over the original formula, and it also beat out Pepsi. The research results seemed to be conclusive in favor of the new formula.

The Go Decision

While the decision was made to introduce the new flavor, a number of ancillary decisions had to be reconciled. For example, should the new flavor be added to the product line, or should it replace the old Coke? It was felt that bottlers generally would be opposed to adding another cola. After considerable soul-searching, top executives unanimously decided to change the taste of Coke and take the old Coke off the market.

In January 1985, the task of introducing the new Coke was given to McCann-Erickson advertising agency. Bill Cosby was to be the spokesperson for the nationwide introduction of the new Coke scheduled for April. All departments of this company were gearing their efforts for a coordinated introduction.

On April 23, 1985, Goizueta and Keough held a press conference at Lincoln Center in New York City in order to introduce the new Coke. Invitations had been sent to the media from all over the United States, and some 200 newspaper, magazine, and TV reporters attended the press conference. However, many of them came away unconvinced of the merits of the new Coke, and their stories were generally negative. In the days ahead, the news media's skepticism was to exacerbate the public nonacceptance of the new Coke.

The word spread quickly. Within 24 hours, 81 percent of the U.S. population knew of the change, and this was more people than were aware in July 1969 that Neil Armstrong had walked on the moon.[1] Early results looked good; 150 million people tried the new Coke, and this was more people than

---

[1] John S. Demott, "Fiddling with the Real Thing," *Time* (May 6, 1985): 55.

had ever before tried a new product. Most comments were favorable. Shipments to bottlers rose to the highest percent in 5 years. The decision looked unassailable. But not for long.

AFTERMATH OF THE DECISION

The situation changed rapidly. While some protests were expected, these quickly mushroomed. In the first 4 hours, the company received about 650 calls. By mid-May, calls were coming in at a rate of 5,000 a day, in addition to a barrage of angry letters. The company added 83 WATS lines and hired new staff to handle the responses. People were speaking of Coke as an American symbol and as a long-time friend that had suddenly betrayed them. Some threatened to switch to tea or water. Here is a sample of the responses.[2]

> The sorrow I feel knowing not only won't I ever enjoy real Coke, but my children and grandchildren won't either . . . I guess my children will have to take my word for it.

> It is absolutely TERRIBLE! You should be ashamed to put the Coke label on it. . . . This new stuff tastes worse than Pepsi.

> It was nice knowing you. You were a friend for most of my 35 years. Yesterday I had my first taste of new Coke, and to tell the truth, if I would have wanted Pepsi, I would have ordered a Pepsi not a Coke.

In all, more than 40,000 such letters were received that spring and summer. In Seattle, strident loyalists calling themselves Old Coke Drinkers of America laid plans to file a class action suit against Coca-Cola. People began stockpiling the old Coke. Some sold it at scalper's prices. When sales in June did not pick up as the company had expected, bottlers demanded the return of old Coke.

The company's research also confirmed an increasing negative sentiment. Before May 30, 53 percent of consumers said they liked the new Coke. In June, the vote began to change, with more than one-half of all people surveyed saying they did not like the new Coke. By July, only 30 percent of the people surveyed each week said they liked the new Coke.

Anger spread across the country, fueled by media publicity. Fiddling with the formula for the 99-year-old beverage became an affront to patriotic pride. Robert Antonio, a University of Kansas sociologist, stated, "Some felt that a sacred symbol had been tampered with."[3] Even Goizueta's

---

[2] Thomas Oliver, *The Real Coke, the Real Story* (New York: Random House, 1986), 155–156.
[3] John Greenwald, "Coca-Cola's Big Fizzle," *Time* (July 22, 1985): 48.

father spoke out against the switch when it was announced. He told his son the move was a bad one and jokingly threatened to disown him. By now company executives began to worry about a consumer boycott against the product.

Coca-Cola Cries "Uncle"

Company executives now began seriously thinking about how to recoup the fading prospects of Coke. In an executive meeting, the decision was made to take no action until after the Fourth of July weekend, when the sales results for this holiday weekend would be in. Results were unimpressive. The decision was announced to the public on July 11th, when top executives walked onto the stage in front of the Coca-Cola logo to make an apology to the public, without admitting that New Coke had been a total mistake.

Two messages were delivered to the American consumer. First, to those who were drinking the new Coke and enjoying it, the company conveyed its thanks. The message to those who wanted the original Coke was that "we heard you," and the original taste of Coke is back.

The news spread fast. ABC interrupted its soap opera, *General Hospital*, on Wednesday afternoon to break the news. In the kind of saturation coverage normally reserved for disasters or diplomatic crises, the decision to bring back old Coke was prominently reported on every evening network news broadcast. The general feeling of soft-drink fans was joy. Democratic Senator David Pryor of Arkansas expressed his jubilation on the Senate floor: "A very meaningful moment in the history of America, this shows that some national institutions cannot be changed."[4] Even Wall Street was happy. Old Coke's comeback drove Coca-Cola stock to its highest level in 12 years.

On the other hand, Roger Enrico, president of Pepsi-Cola USA, said: "Clearly this is the Edsel of the 80s. This was a terrible mistake. Coke's got a lemon on its hand and now they're trying to make lemonade."[5] Other critics labeled this the "marketing blunder of the decade."[6]

WHAT WENT WRONG?

The most convenient scapegoat, according to the consensus, was the marketing research that preceded the decision. Yet Coca-Cola spent about $4 million and devoted 2 years to the marketing research. About 200,000 consumers were contacted during this time. The error in judgment was surely

[4]Greenwald, "Coca-Cola's Big Fizzle," 48.
[5]Greenwald, "Coca-Cola's Big Fizzle," 49.
[6]"Coke's Man on the Spot," *Business Week* (July 29, 1985): 56.

not from want of trying. But when we dig deeper into the research efforts, some flaws become apparent.

Flawed Marketing Research

The major design of the marketing research involved taste tests by representative consumers. After all, the decision point involved a different-flavored Coke, so what could be more logical than to conduct blind taste tests to determine the acceptability of the new flavor, not only versus the old Coke but also versus Pepsi? And these results were significantly positive for the new formula, even among Pepsi drinkers. A clear "go" signal seemed indicated.

But with the benefit of hindsight some deficiencies in the research design were more apparent—and should have caused concern at the time. The research participants were not told that by picking one cola, they would lose the other. This turned out to be a significant distortion: Any addition to the product line would naturally be far more acceptable to a loyal Coke user than would be a complete substitution, which meant the elimination of the traditional product.

While three to four new tastes were tested with almost 200,000 people, only 30,000 to 40,000 of these tests involved the specific formula for the new Coke. The research was geared more to the idea of a new, sweeter cola than the final formula. In general, a sweeter flavor tends to be preferred in blind taste tests. This is particularly true with youth, the largest drinkers of sugared colas, and the group that had been drinking more Pepsi in recent years. Furthermore, preferences for sweeter tasting products tend to diminish with use.[7]

Consumers were asked whether they favored change as a concept, and whether they would likely drink more, less, or the same amount of Coke if there were a change. But such questions could hardly prove the depth of feelings and emotional ties to the product.

Symbolic Value

The symbolic value of Coke was the sleeper. Perhaps this should have been foreseen. Perhaps the marketing research should have considered this possibility and designed the research to map it and determine the strength and durability of these values—that is, would they have a major effect on any substitution of a new flavor?

---

[7]"New Coke Wins Round 1, but Can It Go the Distance?" *Business Week* (June 24, 1985): 48.

Admittedly, when we get into symbolic value and emotional involvement, any researcher is dealing with vague and nebulous attitudes. But various attitudinal measures have been developed to measure the strength or degree of emotional involvement, such as the *semantic differential*.

INFORMATION BOX

MARKETING TOOL: THE SEMANTIC DIFFERENTIAL

An important tool in attitudinal research, image studies, and positioning decisions is the *semantic differential*. It was originally developed to measure the meaning that a concept—perhaps a political issue, a person, a work of art, or in marketing, a brand, product, or company—might have for people in terms of various dimensions. As first presented, the instrument consisted of pairs of polar adjectives with a seven-interval scale separating the opposite members of each pair. For example:

Good —— —— —— —— —— —— —— Bad

The various intervals from left to right would then represent degrees of feeling or belief ranging from extremely good to neither good nor bad, to extremely bad.

This instrument has been refined to obtain greater sensitivity through the use of descriptive phrases. Examples of such bipolar phrases for determining the image of a particular brand of beer are:

Something —— —— —— —— —— —— —— Just another
special   drink

American —— —— —— —— —— —— —— Foreign
flavor   flavor

Really peps —— —— —— —— —— —— —— Somehow doesn't
you up   pep you up

The number of word pairs varies considerably but may be as many as 50 or more. Flexibility and appropriateness to a particular study are achieved by constructing tailor-made word and phrase lists.

Semantic differential scales have been used in marketing to compare images of particular products, brands, firms, and stores against competing ones. The answers of all respondents can be averaged and then plotted to provide a "profile," as shown below for three competing beers on four scales (actually, a firm would probably use 20 or more scales in such a study).

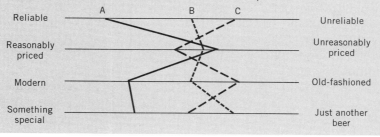

In this profile, brand A shows the dominant image over its competing brands in three of the four categories; however, the negative reaction to its price should alert the company to review pricing practices. Brand C shows a negative image especially regarding the reliability of its product. The old-fashioned image may or may not be desirable, depending on the type of customer being sought; at least the profile indicates that brand C is perceived as being distinctive from the other two brands. Probably the weakest image of all is that of brand B; respondents viewed this brand as having no distinctive image, neither good nor bad. A serious image-building campaign is desperately needed if brand B is to compete successfully; otherwise, the price may have to be dropped to gain some advantages.

Simple, easy to administer and analyze, the semantic differential is useful not only in identifying segments and positions where there might be opportunities because these are currently not well covered by competitors, but it is also useful to a well-established firm—such as Coca-Cola—to determine the strength and the various dimensions of attitudes towards its product. Semantic differential scales are also useful in evaluating the effectiveness of a changed marketing strategy, such as a change in advertising theme. Here the semantic differential could be administered before the campaign and again after the campaign, and any changes in perceptions pinpointed.

Develop eight semantic differential scales for soft drinks, and then profile Coke and Pepsi. What differences do you perceive in the two brands? Are they important? Do you see any untapped soft-drink opportunities?

Herd Instinct

A natural human phenomenon asserted itself in this case—the herd instinct, the tendency of people to follow an idea, a slogan, a concept, to "jump on the bandwagon." At first, acceptance of the new Coke appeared to be reasonably satisfactory. But as more and more outcries were raised— fanned by the press—about the betrayal of the old tradition (somehow this became identified with motherhood, apple pie, and the flag), public attitudes shifted vigorously against this perceived unworthy substitute. And the bandwagon syndrome was fully activated. It is doubtful that by July 1985 Coca-Cola could have done anything to reverse the unfavorable tide. To wait for it to die down was fraught with danger—for who would be brave enough to predict the durability and possible heights of such a protest movement?

Could, or should, such a tide have been predicted? Perhaps not, at least as to the full strength of the movement. Coca-Cola expected some resentment. But perhaps it should have been more cautious, and have considered a "worst case" scenario in addition to what seemed the more probable, and been prepared to react to such a contingency.

WHAT CAN BE LEARNED?

The inconstancy of taste. Taste tests are commonly used in marketing research, but I have always been skeptical of their validity. Take beer, for example. I know of few people—despite their strenuous claims—who can in blind taste tests unerringly identify which is which among three of four disguised brands of beer. We know that people tend to favor the sweeter in taste tests. But does this mean that such a sweeter flavor will always win out in the marketplace? Hardly. Something else is operating with consumer preference other than the fleeting essence of a taste—unless the flavor difference is extreme.

Brand image usually is a more powerful sales stimulant. Advertisers consistently have been more successful in cultivating a desirable image or personality for their brands or the types of people who use them, than by such vague statements as "better tasting."

Don't tamper with tradition. Not many firms have a 100-year-old tradition to be concerned with, or even 25, or even 10. Most products have much shorter life cycles. No other product has been so widely used and so deeply entrenched in societal values and culture as Coke.

The psychological components of the great Coke protest make interesting speculation. Perhaps, in an era of rapid change, many people wish to hang on to the one symbol of security or constancy in their lives—even if this is only the traditional Coke flavor. Perhaps many people found this protest to be an interesting way to escape the humdrum, by "making waves" in a rather harmless fashion, and in the process to see if a big corporation might be forced to cry "uncle."

One is left to wonder how many consumers would even have been aware of any change in flavor had the new formula been quietly introduced without fanfare. But, of course, the advertising siren call of "New!" would have been muted.

So, do we dare tamper with tradition? In Coke's case the answer is probably not, unless done very quietly, but then Coke is unique.

Don't try to fix something that isn't broken. Conventional wisdom may advocate that changes are best made in response to problems, that when things are going smoothly the success pattern or strategy should not be tampered with. Perhaps. But perhaps not.

Actually, things were not going all that well for Coke by early 1985. Market share had steadily been declining to Pepsi for some years. Vigorous promotional efforts by Pepsi featuring star Michael Jackson had increased the market share of regular Pepsi by 1.5 percent in 1984, while regular Coke was dropping 1 percent.[8] Moreover, regular Coke had steadily been losing

---

[8] "Pepsi's High-priced Sell Is Paying Off," *Business Week* (March 4, 1985): 34–35.

market position in supermarkets, dropping almost 4 percent between 1981 and 1985. And foreign business, accounting for 62 percent of total soft-drink volume for Coca-Cola, was showing a disappointing growth rate.[9]

So there was certainly motivation for considering a change. And the obvious change was to introduce a somewhat different flavor, one more congruent with the preference of younger people who were the prime market for soft drinks. I do not subscribe to the philosophy of "don't rock the boat" or "don't change anything until virtually forced to." However, Coca-Cola had another option.

Don't burn your bridges. The obvious alternative was to introduce the new Coke, but still keep the old one. This could be called "don't burn your bridges." Of course, in July, Roberto Goizueta brought back the old Coke after some months of turmoil and considerable corporate embarrassment and competitive glee—which was soon to turn to competitive dismay. The obvious drawback for having two Cokes was dealer resentment at having to stock an additional product in the same limited space, and bottler concern at having a more complicated production run. Furthermore, there was the real possibility that Pepsi would emerge as the number one soft drink due to two competing Cokes—and this would be an acute embarrassment for Coca-Cola.

The ineffectiveness of sheer advertising dollars. Coca-Cola was outspending Pepsi for advertising by $100 million, but its market share in the late 1970s and early 1980s continued to erode to Pepsi. Pepsi's campaigns featured the theme of the "Pepsi Generation" and the "Pepsi Challenge." The use of a superstar such as Michael Jackson also proved to be more effective with the target market of soft drinks than Bill Cosby for Coca-Cola. Any executive has to be left with the sobering realization that the sheer number of dollars spent on advertising does not guarantee competitive success. A smaller firm can still outdo a larger rival.

The power of the media. The press and broadcast media can be powerful influencers of public opinion. With new Coke, the media undoubtedly exacerbated the herd instinct by publicizing the protests to the fullest. After all, this was news. And news seems to be spiciest when an institution or person can be criticized or found wanting. The power of the press should also be sobering to an executive and ought to be one of the factors considered along with certain decisions that may affect the public image of the organization.

Aftermath

Forced by public opinion into a two-cola strategy, the company found the results to be reassuring. By October 1985 estimates were that Coke

---

[9] "Is Coke Fixing a Cola That Isn't Broken?" *Business Week* (May 6, 1985): 47.

Classic was outselling New Coke by better than 2 to 1 nationwide, but by 9 to 1 in some markets; restaurant chains, such as McDonald's, Hardee's, Roy Rogers, and Red Lobster had switched back to Coke Classic.

For the full year of 1985, sales from all operations rose 10 percent and profits 9 percent. In the United States, Coca-Cola soft-drink volume increased 9 percent, and internationally 10 percent. Profitability from soft drinks decreased slightly, representing heavier advertising expenses for introducing New Coke and then reintroducing old Coke.

Coca-Cola's fortunes continued to improve steadily if not spectacularly. By 1988 it was producing 5 of the 10 top-selling soft drinks in the country, and now had a total 40 percent of the domestic market to 31 percent for Pepsi.[10]

Because the soft-drink business was generating about $1 billion in cash each year, Roberto Goizueta had made a number of major acquisitions, such as Columbia Pictures and the Taylor Wine Company. However, these had not met his expectations, and the company disposed of them. Still, by 1988 there was a hoard of $5 billion in new cash and debt capacity, and the enticing problem now was how to spend it.

Table 11.2   1986 Family of Cokes

Kinds	Millions of Cases
Total of One Cola in 1980	1,310.5
1986	
Coca-Cola Classic	1,294.3
Diet Coke	490.8
Coke	185.1
Cherry Coke	115.6
Caffeine-Free Diet Coke	85.6
Caffeine-Free Coke	19.0
Diet Cherry Coke	15.0

Source: "He Put the Kick Back into Coke," *Fortune* (October 26, 1987): 48.

The most successful diversifications were in the soft-drink area. As recently as 1981 there had been only one Coke, and not too many years before, only one container—the 6½-oz glass bottle. By 1987, only one-tenth of 1 percent of all Coke was sold in that bottle.[11] Classic is the best-selling soft drink in the United States, and Diet Coke was the third largest selling.

[10] "Some Things Don't Go Better with Coke," *Forbes* (March 21, 1988): 34–35.
[11] "He Put the Kick Back into Coke," *Fortune* (October 26, 1987): 47–56.

New Coke was being outsold by Classic about seven to one. Table 11.2 shows the total sales volume, expressed as millions of cases, of the family of Coke.

The future for Coca-Cola looked bright. Per capita soft-drink consumption in the United States rose significantly in the 1980s.[12]

	Per Capita Consumption	Percent Increase
1980	34.5 gal.	—
1986	42 gal.	22

The international potential was great. The per capita consumption outside the United States was only 4 gallons. Yet 95 percent of the world's population lives outside the United States.

In a later case, we will explore Pepsi's most recent misadventures in the international arena, and Coca-Cola's great success.

CONCLUSION

Some called New Coke a misstep, others a blink. At the time there were those who called it a monumental blunder, even the mistake of the century. But it hardly turned out to be that. As sales surged, some competitors accused Coca-Cola of engineering the whole scenario, in order to get tons of free publicity. Coke executives stoutly denied this, and admitted their error in judgment. For who could foresee, as *Fortune* noted, that the episode would "reawaken deep-seated American loyalty to Coca-Cola."[13]

CONSIDER

Can you think of other learning insights arising from this case?

QUESTIONS

1. How could Coca-Cola's marketing research have been improved? Be as specific as you can.
2. When a firm is facing a negative press, as Coca-Cola was with the new Coke, what recourse does the firm have? Support your conclusions.
3. Do you think Coca-Cola would have been as successful if it had introduced the new Coke as an addition to the line, and not as a substitute for the old Coke? Why or why not?

[12] *Pepsico 1986 Annual Report*, 13.
[13] "He Put the Kick," p. 48.

4. "If it's not broken, don't fix it." Evaluate this statement.
5. Do you think Coca-Cola engineered the whole scenario with the new Coke, including fanning public protests, in order to get a bonanza of free publicity? Defend your position.
6. Would you, as a top executive at Coca-Cola, have "caved in" as quickly to the protests? Would you have "toughed it out" instead?
7. Given the inability to judge very closely the effectiveness of advertising expenditures, why do you suppose so many firms still spend millions and millions of dollars for advertising? Is it faith?

HANDS-ON EXERCISES

1. Assume that you are Robert Goizueta and that you are facing increasing pressure in early July 1985 to abandon the new Coke and bring back the old formula. However, your latest marketing research suggests that only a small group of agitators is making all the fuss about the new cola. Evaluate your options, and support your recommendations to the board.
2. You are the public relations director of Coca-Cola. It is early June 1985, and you have been ordered to "do something" to blunt the negative publicity. What ideas can you offer that might counter or replace the negatives with positive publicity?

TEAM DEBATE EXERCISE

The decision to go with the new Coke has not been made yet. One group at headquarters is dead set against any change: "If it's not broke, don't fix it." The other group firmly believes that change is not only necessary but long overdue. Debate the two positions as comprehensively and persuasively as you can. (Be sure that you confine your arguments to what was known in early 1985. You cannot use the benefit of hindsight.

INVITATION TO RESEARCH

What is the current situation with Coca-Cola? Is Coke Classic still the big winner? Is new Coke still being produced? How would you assess future possibilities?

CHAPTER 12

Elizabeth Taylor Has Distributor Trouble

Elizabeth Taylor is, of course, famous for her films and for her love life. More recently, she has become known for her perfumes. Her first signature scent, Passion, was made and launched by Elizabeth Arden, a division of Unilever, in 1987. The use of her celebrity name and promotional presence aroused good demand. White Diamonds and Fragrant Jewels followed a few years later. All these were sold in top department stores such as Dayton Hudson and Bloomingdale's, although by 1995 only White Diamonds continued to be a top seller with sales estimated at $60 million annually.

In that same year, 1995, Arden introduced another Taylor fragrance, Black Pearls. The name was chosen to reflect the prestige and quality of the rarest of pearls. With the glamorous Elizabeth Taylor sponsoring it, this brand was expected to follow her three previous perfumes into the most prestigious of retailers where its success would seem assured.

Alas, this launch did not go as planned. To its dismay, Arden found only such big retailers as J. C. Penney and Sears willing to stock it as these stores sought to upgrade their fashion images.

Abruptly, in late August, Unilever's Arden Division canceled the introduction of Black Pearls, even though the advertising campaign was already under way. With this cancellation, many in the industry doubted the product would now ever be marketed.

What torpedoed this seemingly sure thing?

SOURED DISTRIBUTOR RELATIONS

Just a few months before the September full-scale launch of Black Pearls, Arden attempted to change the playing field of the fragrance game with its major department store customers.

First, it told them that it would no longer share the costs for advertising, catalogs and window displays for any Arden product. (See the following box for a discussion of advertising allowances.) Second, Arden announced it was cutting its commissions to stores' salespeople selling Black Pearls, thus breaking a tradition in perfume marketing where manufacturers helped retailers cover salaries by directly paying salespeople 5 percent of what they sold of their brand. Arden arbitrarily cut this commission to 3 percent.

With that, these dominant retailers refused to stock Black Pearls.

The executive vice president of marketing at Arden, Ron Rolleston, expressed his disappointment at the negative reactions: "We had hoped that they would accept it, based on the strength of Elizabeth Taylor."[1]

The distribution policy changes were the brainchild of Kimberly Delsing, 42, who had been president of Calvin Klein Cosmetics before she was promoted to run Elizabeth Arden as president and chief executive. At Calvin Klein, she had had a series of blockbuster fragrances, the most notable being Obsession, and she had been able to force similar concessions from department stores.

INFORMATION BOX

ADVERTISING ALLOWANCES

Manufacturers sometimes reimburse retailers for part of the cost of ads that feature the manufacturers' goods. This is a major subsidy of advertising costs for retailers, and is commonly known as *cooperative advertising*. Typically, a manufacturer pays 50 percent of the cost of such advertising, up to a certain percentage—often 5 percent—of the retailer's total purchases from the manufacturer. Such a sharing of costs enables a store to do more advertising than would be possible otherwise.

Manufacturers benefit also because of lower local advertising rates and because retailers will show greater interest in the products so advertised. These allowances often are a win-win situation.

Given that normally both manufacturer and retailer benefit from the manufacturer's offering of advertising allowances, why do you suppose Arden would want to curb this policy?

---

[1] Teri Agins, "Elizabeth Taylor's Glamorous New Scent Will Get a Less Than Glamorous Launch," *The Wall Street Journal* (August 17, 1995): B1.

But Elizabeth Arden brands, even with Ms. Taylor, did not apparently have the market clout of Calvin Klein. And here the department stores drew a line in the sand as they feared setting a precedent that would encourage other perfume manufacturers to pressure for reduced contributions also. A further factor in retailers' intransigence may have been that sales of the last Elizabeth Taylor offering, Fragrant Jewels, had only been mediocre.

Ms. Delsing abruptly resigned, with Unilever saying this was "mutually agreed upon."

The unexpected rejections of Black Pearls by these major retail concerns forced Arden to seek secondary distributors, and it had no trouble placing the brand in Penney and Sears stores and smaller regional department stores. This brought the total number of stores slated for the initial introduction to about 2,000, but none of these were the market leaders that Arden thought it needed for a status perfume. For example, none of these outlets were in Manhattan, the traditional launching pad for new fragrances.

What had been considered to be the most prestigious offering of Elizabeth Taylor was now left with no upscale stores that had provided the setting for Ms. Taylor's other three fragrances. A letdown? An industry consultant, Alan Mottus, noted that "prestige is partly based on the stores where a fragrance is sold."[2]

Still, could not the job be done with Sears and Penney? Sears promised to introduce Black Pearls in 350 of its 801 stores and give aggressive print, broadcast, direct mail, and in-store promotions. Previously, Sears had been "given" White Diamonds a year after the perfume's initial introduction in major department stores and had been happy with the results.

A SURPRISING CANCELLATION

The cancellation of the Black Pearls introduction caught the industry by surprise. Arden had already begun a $12 million ad campaign, including 42 million scent strips and black-and-white print ads featuring Elizabeth Taylor immersed in a "Tahitian" lagoon that appeared in September issues of fashion magazines. The theme of the campaign was Elizabeth Taylor reciting copy written by her friend, pop star Michael Jackson: "The romance of the night. The ecstasy of stolen, sensual moments. Black Pearls."[3]

An industry expert estimated this distribution cancellation would cost Unilever $15 million in development, marketing, and inventory expenses.[4] But the failure of a full-scale launch would undoubtedly have been more costly.

[2] Teri Agins, "Arden Cancels Fall Launch of Liz Taylor's Fragrance," *The Wall Street Journal* (August 30, 1995): B1.

[3] Agins, "Elizabeth Taylor's New Scent," B1.

[4] Agins, "Arden Cancels Fall Launch," B1.

Other rumors about the reasons for the cancellation were not necessarily economic. Rather, they smacked of Ms. Taylor's aggravation at having a product bearing her name not being introduced in more upscale stores than Penney and Sears. Rumors were that she threatened to sue, claiming such was a violation of her contract. Whatever the validity of the rumors, the result of the misstep was that Black Pearls ads were running, but consumers were unable to buy the product.

Good marketing strategy stresses the importance of keeping initial marketing momentum in any new product introduction, lest any faltering be the death knell. In this case we see a deliberate curbing of momentum, with perhaps some justification. The industry speculated whether Black Pearls could have any chance of being a winner after such a false start.

THE PERFUME INDUSTRY

Store cosmetic counters are cluttered with more than 700 brands of scent, with more on the way. Surely a woman must have almost extraterrestrial powers of smell to be able to differentiate more than a few of these brands. Brand sponsorship, brand names, fancy containers, and descriptive adjectives such as "sheer," "light," and "subtle" have to do most of the selling job. But apparently tastes do change. In the 1980s, top names were Obsession, Poison, and Opium. Such "assertive" scents "made crowded elevators unsafe for riding," suggested one reporter. In the 1990s, "softer, subtler scents are back in vogue," and "you have to get close to notice the fragrances."[5]

The major makers of these scents are a Who's Who of the prestigious: Calvin Klein, Christian Dior, Giorgio, Estee Lauder, Chanel, Coty, Lancome. Amid such notables, Elizabeth Arden would hardly seem a heavyweight, even with Elizabeth Taylor's sponsorship.

THE REINTRODUCTION OF BLACK PEARLS

Six months after halting its distribution, on February 26th, 1996, Elizabeth Arden grandly announced the reintroduction of Black Pearls during primetime on CBS. The network publicized this as "Liz Night." Ms. Taylor appeared on four back-to-back sitcoms. The night began with "The Nanny" losing a priceless black pearl necklace. It later showed up on "Can't Stand Love," only to be stolen again. On the next show, Murphy Brown interviewed Ms. Taylor about the missing pearls, and on "High Society" the case of the missing necklace was solved. Later, TV host David Letterman took

---

[5] Lisa McKinnon, "Fragrance Breezes Through the '90s," *Cleveland Plain Dealer* (September 19, 1996): 1-E.

stabs at the star and her perfume on his show. By the time the evening was over the words "black pearls" were repeated ad nauseum.

Ms. Taylor's appearances this Monday night contributed to a 15 to 20 percent increase in viewer ratings for the shows, even though the promotion of Black Pearls was obvious.[6] Arden did not even have to pay for this exposure nor did it buy any commercial air time for the evening. Rather, for the privilege of airing Ms. Taylor, the network made a charitable contribution in her name.

In this reintroduction, Arden backed off from its autocratic cutting of retail salesperson commissions and that spring 1,800 top department store units agreed to carry and promote the brand. The inducement to do so included Ms. Taylor making appearances at department stores in seven cities. As a further concession to the powers in retailing, assurances were given that the brand would not be offered to Sears and Penney until at least a year later.

By early summer, sales results were pleasing, if not spectacular. For the peak Mother's Day selling period, many department stores reported Black Pearls in the top five or ten of their fragrances.[7] Interestingly, several old classics, such as Chanel No. 5, still accounted for 25 percent of fragrance business in some stores, this despite the fact that prices for Chanel No. 5 had risen from $45 a ounce to $240 a ounce over twenty-five years.[8] By comparison, a 1.7-ounce bottle of Black Pearls was priced at $35.

ANALYSIS

Distributor Relations

One would expect harmony and cooperation to develop naturally among the various members of a distribution channel. Sometimes the term "symbiotic relationship" is used to describe this ideal relationship. The following box discusses this in more detail.

Why is it then that we see retailers and suppliers sometimes working at cross purposes, for example, Arden unilaterally trying to reduce its commitment to its major retail customers?

The answer lies in the mistaken assumption or use of power in the channel. Who is the most important and powerful channel member? Most often today it is the large retailer with buying power and dominance in certain markets. Once in a while a large and well-known manufacturer—a Coca-Cola or Calvin Klein, for example—whose brands are widely sought by consumers,

---

[6]Chuck Ross, "Arden Whiffs Success from Liz's CBS Romp," *Advertising Age* (March 4, 1996): 34.

[7]Jenny B. Fine, "New Spring Fragrances Help Put a Twinkle in Mother's Day Sales," *Women's Wear Daily* (May 17, 1996): 1.

[8]Rose-Marie Turk, "Solid Sales in the West," *Women's Wear Daily* (June 7, 1996): S26.

INFORMATION BOX

THE SYMBIOTIC RELATIONSHIP AND CHANNEL CONFLICT

The term *symbiotic relationship* is taken from biology. It describes an environment in which different organisms live together in close association to their mutual benefit. This term aptly describes the ideal relationship between the manufacturer and the dealers and distributors who comprise the distribution channel. A symbiotic relationship should exist simply because these channel members depend on each other. They all benefit from the success of the product(s).

Unfortunately, this ideal relationship sometimes breaks down, as we saw with Elizabeth Arden and the major department stores. Then we have channel conflict. The following table lists major sources of such conflict, some emanating from the producer, others from middlemen.

Table 12.1 Sources of Producer-Distributor Conflict

Producer-created conflicts:
—Making heavy demands on middlemen, such as requiring large and varied inventories, special promotional support, extensive service facilities, and burdensome payment terms
—Refusing to protect middlemen against model changes and price changes, so that heavy markdowns are incurred
—Making similar goods available to a middleman's competitors, either similar firms or firms of a different type, such as discount stores and catalog showrooms, who may undercut other retailers' prices
—Selling to the middlemen's customers and thus competing directly with the distributors
—Promising "expert" promotional and merchandising assistance that never materializes
—Refusing to handle adjustments due to faulty products or not reimbursing dealers fully for their costs in servicing products still under warranty

Middlemen-created conflicts:
—Demanding large discounts, special promotional allowances, and more favorable pricing terms
—Demanding special shipping arrangements and quicker deliveries
—Handling competing products, especially their own private brands, and not giving adequate effort to selling the manufacturer's brand
—Giving careless servicing and disregarding product information

Discuss how a manufacturer can build loyalty among his dealers and distributors, in other words, foster a symbiotic relationship.

is the more powerful factor. Sometimes it is a toss-up between a powerful retailer and a manufacturer, with an uneasy alliance resulting.

Elizabeth Arden in retrospect blundered badly in its dealings with the major department stores. Kimberly Delsing, the top Arden executive who made these decisions, had won similar concessions in the mid-1980s when she was with Calvin Klein and its blockbuster fragrances, starting with Obsession. But Elizabeth Arden hardly had the clout of a Calvin Klein, and Black Pearls, despite the sponsorship by Ms. Taylor, was still unproven. Ms. Delsing lost her job as a consequence of her miscalculation.

The question became: Who was in the power position? Was it the prestigious department stores, or Arden? The rejection of the brand by almost all the major department stores clearly answered that: they were far more important to Arden than Black Pearls was to them.

We can project this power position in the channel of distribution beyond the perfume industry. Big retailers have become more essential, even with the biggest manufacturers. They provide entry to the market. More than this, they can "push" the brand by giving prominent displays, better inventory assortment, more suggestions by dealer salespeople, more prompt servicing, and the like. With the variety of competitive products in most industries, such gatekeepers of market entry are in the power position, able to dictate and not be dictated to. If the manufacturer is unwilling to accept this, there are far more alternatives for the retailer than for the manufacturer.

Regaining Lost Momentum

It is almost a given in marketing that once a new product loses its momentum with a false start, it can never again be a winner. The assumption is that the excitement engendered by initial promotional efforts cannot be regained. The reintroduction of Black Pearls in the spring of 1996 proves the falseness of this belief. Momentum can be regained and even increased. But it takes a blockbuster promotional effort. And this Elizabeth Taylor, Arden, and CBS achieved.

Pricing Issues

In this case we are left with an intriguing pricing question. What if Arden had priced Black Pearls higher, thus moving it closer to the great classic, Chanel No. 5? Would this have hurt or helped?

The issue is complicated by a price/quality perception: Many people perceive the highest-priced brand to be the highest quality, whether it really is or not. A further complication, however, is the elasticity of the demand: Will a high price drastically reduce overall demand for more modest prices?

WHAT CAN BE LEARNED?

Beware of jeopardizing distributor relations. As we have seen, the distributor can play a key role in the effectiveness of the manufacturer's selling efforts because the distributor may well be the only contact with the ultimate buyer. In such cases, the distributor can even deny the manufacturer entry to a particular market.

Hence, the manufacturer has a vital interest in maintaining the most harmonious and effective dealer relations. Failure to realize the importance of this, and callousness and indifference to distributor concerns, may jeopardize even a long-standing relationship. We will see an example of this in another case, Pepsi's problems in Latin America, Chapter 14.

Building a good distributor relationship. The manufacturer will benefit from aiding wholesalers and retailers by providing the following:

- Training aids and promotional material, such as advertising mats and displays
- Help with servicing problems and the handling of customer complaints
- Financial help and flexible credit arrangements to enable distributors to stock up in advance of a big selling season
- Ample warnings of model and price changes, and even protection against price changes
- Helping channel members avoid heavy markdowns on merchandise in stock

The dealer and distributor reasonably can be expected to be motivated to merchandise the product favorably and also to furnish feedback through the channel so that any difficulties can be corrected.

Most manufacturers must respect the power of large retailers. The biggest retailer of all, Wal-Mart, has led the way in using its power to wring concessions from smaller suppliers such as price ceilings, service levels, and quality standards. Such can be carried too far, as when discount and supermarket chains insist on "slotting fees" in which a supplier pays thousands of dollars for the "privilege" of having its items carried in store inventory. One slotting fee statement of a supermarket chain notes, "Just as a reminder, many times it is the 'slotting fee' that determines whether we authorize an item or not." In dealing with these large retailers, even a Coca-Cola may be "forced" to make such payments in its competition for shelf space with Pepsi.

Most manufacturers give a 2 percent discount if bills are paid within 10 days instead of 30 days when final payment is due. It has become commonplace for large retailers to routinely pay their bills closer to 30 days and take the discount anyway on the gross amount of the invoice, not on the net amount that discounts things like freight costs. Is this an abuse of power? *Forbes* magazine devoted an article to the increasingly tough policies and relationships of the big retailers with suppliers, and called it, "The Big Squeeze."[9]

Where behemoth retailers can account for up to 50 percent of some manufacturers' revenues, loss of such a customer or even a reduction of orders can be devastating. The symbiotic relationship idea seems to be eroding and suppliers may have to accept a subordinate and pressured relationship or else be content to do business only with smaller firms.

For new products, loss of marketing momentum can be overcome. Black Pearls was a new product that was taken off the market and successfully reintroduced months later with a somewhat changed strategy. Thereby, Elizabeth Taylor disproved the old platitude that marketing momentum for new products, if lost, cannot be regained. Of course, it took a glamorous star and a major TV promotional effort to do so. Lacking such heroic measures, loss of momentum for a newly introduced product may be fatal.

We should note that an older product that fades has more probability of being rejuvenated since it has developed some residual demand. A change in marketing strategy, a pricing or packaging change, or a product modification might be worth trying. Perhaps a different target market might be sought. Or a different use for the product might be promoted, such as the classic resurrection of Arm & Hammer baking soda as a deodorizer. Usually, however, a weak and fading product is not worth the effort to try to save or restart it, and should be evaluated for elimination.

CONSIDER

Can you think of other learning insights coming from this case?

QUESTIONS

1. Are advertising allowances always so desirable for retailers?
2. "Prestige is partly based on the stores where a fragrance is sold." Do you agree with that statement? Can you think of any exceptions?
3. Does the hypothesis that prestigious stores convey prestige to a fragrance have validity to other products also? To all products?
4. Do you think the big retailers have gone too far in their dictatorial relationships with suppliers?
5. Evaluate the marketability of Elizabeth Taylor today.

[9]Matthew Schifrin, "The Big Squeeze," *Forbes* (March 11, 1996): 45–46.

HANDS-ON EXERCISE

In the oak-paneled executive suite, the executives of Elizabeth Arden are pondering a pricing decision. Some strong sentiments are being expressed that Black Pearls should be priced close to Chanel No. 5, or over $200 a ounce. Others are shocked at this and maintain that it must be priced for the mainstream market, or about $30 to $40. The CEO turns to you, her trusted adviser, for your thoughts. What do you recommend, and why?

TEAM DEBATE EXERCISE

Black Pearls has just been brought on the market, but the top department stores still refuse to order it. Only Sears and Penney are willing to do so. Debate the two alternatives on the table: Go with Sears and Penney, or drop the product, at least for the time being.

INVITATION TO RESEARCH

What is the situation regarding Black Pearls today? Does it still seem to be selling, or has it been discontinued? Has Ms. Taylor promised any new fragrances bearing her name?

CHAPTER 13

Snapple: A Sorry Acquisition

In late 1994, Quaker Oats CEO William D. Smithburg bought Snapple Beverage Company for $1.7 billion. Many thought he had paid too much for this maker of noncarbonated fruit-flavored drinks and iced teas. But in a similar acquisition eleven years before, he had outbid Pillsbury to buy Stokely-Van Camp, largely for its Gatorade, then a $90 million sports drink. Despite criticisms of that purchase, Gatorade went on to become a billion-dollar brand, and Smithburg was a hero. He was not to be a hero with Snapple.

THE COMPANY, QUAKER OATS

Quaker Oats had nearly $6.4 billion in fiscal 1995 sales, of which $1.7 billion was from foreign operations. Its brands were generally strong in particular grocery products and beverage areas. In hot cereals, generations have used Quaker oatmeal, and it is still the number-three selling brand in the overall cereal category. Quaker's ready-to-eat cereals include Cap'n Crunch and Life brands. The firm is a leading competitor in the fast-growing rice cake and granola bar categories, and also in rice and pasta with its Rice-A-Roni, Pasta Roni and Near East brands. Other products include Aunt Jemima frozen products, French toast, pancake mixes, and syrups; Celeste frozen pizza; as well as grits, tortilla flour, and corn meal.

With the purchase of Snapple, sales of its beverage operation would approach $2 billion or about one-third of total corporate sales. Gatorade alone accounted for $1.3 billion worldwide in fiscal 1995 and growth continued with sales in the U.S. increasing 7 percent over the previous year, while overseas the gain was a whopping 51 percent. In order to help pay for the Snapple acquisition, several mature but still moneymaking units were divested, including pet foods and chocolates.

THE SNAPPLE ACQUISITION

The brand, Snapple, had a modest beginning in 1972 in Brooklyn, N.Y., and its beverages were initially sold to health-food stores. As the healthy lifestyle became popular among certain segments of the general public, Snapple's sales for a time increased as much as 60–70 percent a year, especially in the Northeast and West Coast. In 1992, it was purchased for $27.9 million by Boston-based Thomas H. Lee Co., which took the now-trendy brand public and built it up to almost $700 million in sales.

Unlike Gatorade, however, Snapple faced formidable competitors, including Coke's Fruitopia and Pepsi's joint venture with Lipton, which used low prices to capture 31 percent of the iced-tea market. Snapple's growth rate had turned to declines by December 1994 when, in an outpouring of supreme confidence in his own judgment, Smithburg bought Snapple for $1.7 billion. Before long, many said he had paid about $1 billion too much. Table 13.1 shows the quarterly sales results of Snapple since June 1993 before the acquisition, and after the acquisition.

William Smithburg

At the time of the purchase, Smithburg was 56 years old, but looked younger. He liked to wear suspenders stretched tightly over muscular shoulders that he had developed from years of tournament handball. He had been CEO at Quaker Oats since 1981 and had evolved from a flashy boy

Table 13.1   Snapple's Sales Growth, 1993–1996

				(millions of dollars)				
	1993 sales	% change	1994 sales	% change	1995 sales	% change	1996 sales	% change
1st quarter			$134		$112	–12%		
2nd quarter	$130		243	+87%	200	–18%	$180	–10%
3rd quarter	203		191	–6%				–20%
4th quarter	118		105	–11%				

Source: 1995 Quaker Annual Report, and various 1996 updates.
Note: While we do not have complete information for all the quarters, still the negative sales since the second quarter of 1994—before the Snapple acquisition—can be readily seen: every quarter since then has seen losses from the same quarter the preceding year.

wonder to a seasoned executive. He was also a fitness buff, and perhaps this colored his zeal for products like Gatorade and Snapple.

His interest in fitness developed as a result of a childhood bout with polio. While he recovered with no permanent damage, the experience shaped his life: "As soon as I started to walk and run again, I said, 'I have to stay healthy,' and it just became part of my life."[1] In his long tenure as CEO, that passion shaped Quaker, too. The company developed extensive fitness programs, including a heavily subsidized health club at headquarters. Quaker's product line, also, had increasingly emphasized low-fat foods compatible with the healthy lifestyle.

Indicative of Smithburg's personality, after graduating from DePaul University in 1960 with a BS in economics and marketing, he defied his father by quitting his first job only three days later. He decided to enroll in Northwestern's business school.

With an MBA in hand he joined the Leo Burnett ad agency, and later, McCann Erickson. After five years of ad agency experience, he went to Quaker as brand manager for frozen waffles in 1966. There it took him ten years to become executive vice-president of U.S. grocery products, Quaker's biggest division. Five years later in 1981 he became CEO, and was named chairman two years after that.

The same year he became chairman, he acquired Stokely-Van Camp, over-bidding Pillsbury's $62-per-share bid with a $77 offer, which carried a price tag of $238 million. His own investment banker considered this too steep, and critics in the business press abounded. But Smithburg had done his homework, and his intuition was prescient. He recognized the potential in Stokely's Gatorade, a sports drink meant to replenish lost salts and fluids of athletes. "I'd been drinking Gatorade myself, and I knew the product worked."[2] A $90 million brand in 1983, by 1996 this was a $1.3 billion brand and held 80 percent of the growing sports-drink market.

Somehow, Smithburg did not do his homework well with Snapple, despite its seeming similarity to Gatorade.

Rationale for the Snapple Purchase

Snapple was the largest acquisition in Quaker's history. The *Quaker Oats 1995 Annual Report*, discussed the rationale for this purchase and the "growth opportunity it offers to shareholders":

> Snapple appeals to all ages with its incomparable flavor variety in premium iced teas and juice drinks. Current sales are concentrated in the Northeast and

[1] Greg Burns, "Crunch Time At Quaker Oats," *Business Week* (September 23, 1996): 72.
[2] Burns, "Crunch Time," 74.

West Coast. So, the rest of the country presents fertile territory for developing the brand. Because of its excellent cold-channel distribution, the Snapple brand has taught us a great deal about reaching consumers outside our traditional grocery channels. We can apply this knowledge to Gatorade thirst quencher, thereby enhancing its availability as well.[3]

So, Smithburg saw great opportunity to expand distribution of Snapple geographically from its present regional concentration. He thought it had wide appeal and that it could enhance the sales of the already highly successful Gatorade.

Snapple beverages held good regional market positions in both the premium ready-to-drink tea and single-serve juice drink categories. It was seemingly well positioned if consumer preferences continued to shift to all-natural beverages—and away from highly carbonated, artificially flavored, and chemically preserved soft drinks.

Apparently not the least of the reasons for Smithburg's infatuation with Snapple was that it had a "sexy aura," even though problems were already emerging when he bought it. He liked to contrast it with Quaker's pet food: Pet food "was a dead, flat business with five or six big companies beating their brains out in it."[4] So, it was not surprising that the pet food business, which had been acquired less than nine years before, was sold a few months after Snapple was acquired.

Other speculations as to why Smithburg chased Snapple, besides misreading the growth potential, were that he wanted to make Quaker, which was a hotly rumored acquisition candidate, less vulnerable to a takeover. Some even speculated that Smithburg became bored with Quaker and sought the excitement of a splashy deal.[5]

PROBLEMS

One would think that Snapple's resemblance to Gatorade would bring instant compatibility and efficiencies in marketing the two brands. After all, with the proven success of Gatorade, Quaker had become the third largest beverage company, after only Coca-Cola and Pepsi. And like Gatorade, Snapple was a flavored, noncarbonated drink. Surely this was a marriage made in heaven.

But this was not the case. Only after it bought Snapple did Quaker fully realize that both Snapple's production and distribution systems were completely different from Gatorade's.

[3] *Quaker Oats 1995 Annual Report*, 6.
[4] Burns, "Crunch Time," 74.
[5] *Ibid.*

Quaker's production and distribution of Gatorade was state of the art. Its computers were closely integrated with those of its largest distributors and automatically kept these distributors well stocked, but not overstocked, with Gatorade.

The advertising of Gatorade was also markedly different. Several hundred million dollars a year were spent for Gatorade, with highly successful ads featuring Chicago Bulls star, Michael Jordan (Jordan was also a personal friend of Smithburg). Snapple's advertising, on the other hand, had run out of steam and was notably ineffective.

The production, distribution, and marketing efforts of Snapple at the time of the purchase were haphazard. Bottling was contracted to outsiders, and this resulted in expensive contracts for excess capacity when demand slowed. Snapple's 300 distributors delivered directly to stores; Gatorade's distributors delivered to warehouses. Quaker's efforts to consolidate the two distribution systems only created havoc. It tried to take the supermarket accounts away from Snapple distributors and give them to Gatorade, directing that the Snapple people concentrate on convenience stores and mom-and-pop retailers. Not surprising, Snapple distributors refused this downsizing of their operations. Eventually, Quaker backed down. But efforts at creating coordination and distribution efficiencies for 1995 were seriously delayed.

At the same time, Quaker failed to come up with a new marketing plan for Snapple in time for the peak 1995 season, which began in April. Tim Healy, president of a distributor in Chicago, noted: ". . . there was no marketing plan, no initiatives, and no one to talk to [at Quaker]."[6]

The result was that 1995 sales of Snapple fell 9 percent, and there was a $100 million loss.

CORRECTIVE EFFORTS, 1996

As the dismal results of 1995 became widely publicized, Quaker faced the urgent need to vindicate the purchase of Snapple and somehow resurrect its failing fortunes. To aid the distributors, the company streamlined operations to reduce from two weeks to three days the time it took to get orders from bottlers to distributors. To do so, it coordinated its computers with the top 50 distributors, who represented 80 percent of Snapple's sales, so that it could replenish their inventory automatically, the way it was doing with Gatorade.

The company also introduced some packaging and product changes that it hoped would be more appealing both to dealers and to customers. It brought out 32- and 64-ounce plastic bottles of Snapple for families, along with 12-

[6]Scott McMurray, "Drumming Up New Business: Quaker Marches Double Time To Put Snap Back in its Snapple Drink Line," *U.S. News & World Report* (April 22, 1996): 59.

packs and 4-packs in glass bottles. It reduced the number of flavors from 50 to 35 and made taste improvements in some of the retained flavors. At the same time seasonal products were introduced, such as cider tea for Halloween.

To develop distributor enthusiasm, a two-day meeting had been held in San Diego. Quaker brought in comedian Bill Cosby to entertain and General Norman Schwarzkopf to motivate with a stirring speech on leadership. Then distributors were told that highly visible Snapple coolers would be placed in supermarkets, convenience stores, and schools—just like Coke and Pepsi.[7]

The weakness in the 1995 advertising also received, hopefully, corrective action. Quaker enlisted the creativity of Spike Lee, who had designed hyper-kinetic TV commercials for Nike. While the campaign kept Snapple's "Made from the best stuff on earth," the new ads focused on Snapple's hope to become America's third choice in soft drinks, behind Coke and Pepsi, with such slogans as "We want to be No. 3" and "Threedom = freedom." The goal of the advertising campaign, Smithburg explained, was to maintain Snapple's "funky" image while broadening its appeal beyond the East and West Coast markets.[8]

Still, sales languished. In late July, a huge nationwide sampling campaign was undertaken. In a $40 million effort, millions of bottles of the fruit juice and iced-tea lines were given away during the height of the selling season, hopefully to spur consumer interest regardless of cost.

RESULTS OF 1996 MARKETING EFFORTS

Unfortunately, the results of the summer giveaways were dismal. Instead of gaining market share during the important summer selling months, Snapple lost ground.

Snapple tea sales fell 14 percent, and juice sales fell 15 percent. This compared poorly with industry tea sales that also dropped but only 4 percent, and industry juice sales that fell 5 percent during a particularly cool summer in the Northeast.[9]

Relentless media scrutiny even found fault with the way in which Snapple was being given away. One critic observed the sampling at a New Jersey concert in which 16-ounce cans were handed out only 20 feet from the entrance in front of signs prohibiting food or drink beyond the gate. Most people barely had time to taste the drink before throwing it away. Furthermore, "for its brand undermining efforts, Quaker gets no consumer research either. Solution: In exchange for the self-serve sample, ask a few short . . . questions."[10]

[7] Zina Moukheiber, "He Who Laughs Last," *Forbes* (January 1, 1996): 42.

[8] *Ibid*, 60.

[9] "Snapple Continues to Lose Market Share Despite Big Giveaway," *The Wall Street Journal* (October 8, 1996): B9.

[10] Gabe Lowry, "They Can't Even Give Snapple Away Right," *Brandweek* (September 30, 1996): 16.

The reputation of Smithburg was being eroded, his early success with Gatorade not enough to weather more current adversity. Online, cyber critics assailed him. In conference calls with financial analysts, he was peppered with barbed questions about this $600 million beverage for which he paid $1.7 billion. "Even my dad," Smithburg laughed. "He says, 'What are you doing with Snapple?'"[11]

Under pressure, Smithburg cast off president and chief operating officer, Philip Marineau, who he had been grooming as heir apparent for many years. This departure was widely interpreted to be the result of Snapple's failure to justify its premium pricing. Nine months later, Donald Uzzi was replaced as president of Quaker's North America beverages unit. His successor was Michael Schott, former vice president of sales of Nantucket Nectars, a small, privately held drink maker.

Some critics assumed that Smithburg's job was in jeopardy, that he could not escape personal blame for the acquisition snafu. Still, the past success of Smithburg with Gatorade continued to sustain him. The board of directors remained supportive, although they denied him any bonus for 1995. What made the continued loyalty of the board more uncertain was Quaker's stock price, which had fallen 10 percent since just before the acquisition, even as the Standard & Poor's 500-stock index had climbed to new highs.

If Snapple could not be revitalized, Smithburg had several options regarding it. All of these, of course, would be admissions of defeat and that a major mistake was made in acquiring Snapple. Any one of them might cost Smithburg his job.

One option would be to spin off the ailing Snapple to shareholders, perhaps under the wing of the booming Gatorade. Smithburg was no stranger to such maneuverings since he had divested retail, toy, and pet-food operations in his years as CEO. An outright sale could probably only be made at bargain-basement prices and would certainly underscore the billion-dollar mistake of Smithburg's purchase. A less extreme option would be to draw back from attempts to make Snapple a national brand, and keep it as a regional brand in the Northeast and West Coast where it was well entrenched.

Perseverance

By early 1997 Smithburg still had not given up on Snapple. Quaker Oats announced it was pumping $15 million into a major 4-month sweepstakes promotion for Snapple's diet drinks, this to start right after the new year when consumers might be more concerned with undoing the excesses of the holiday season and when competitors would be less likely to advertise chilled drinks

---

[11] Burns, "Crunch Time," 71.

in winter. The theme was to be, "Escape with Taste," and among other winners would be 50 grand prize trips to the refurbished Doral Resort and Spa in Miami. If the campaign developed any momentum, it should carry over to a retooled image campaign planned immediately afterwards in the spring.

This promotion was the first from new president Mike Schott, and it built on one product category that managed to grow 16 percent in convenience stores during the previous summer, even as core juices and teas slid drastically. The promotion plan was well received by distributors: "'. . . this one [promotion] is wonderfully thought out,' one distributor said. 'Diet drinks in the first quarter? It's a no-brainer.'"[12]

Since being named the brand's president late in the year, Schott had been visiting distributors to build up relations, offer greater support, and dispel rumors that Snapple was going to retrench to a regional brand.

ANALYSIS

It is difficult to see the Snapple acquisition for $1.7 billion as anything but wildly extravagant. Demand was slumping, distribution inefficiencies had surfaced, and the advertising had run out of steam. We can understand Smithburg's reasoning that he had bought Gatorade at a high price and turned it into a winner. Why shouldn't he do the same thing with Snapple? The price paid for Gatorade, $238 million for sales of $90 million at the time, was roughly comparable to the $1.7 billion for Snapple sales of almost $700 million.

But we can surely fault Smithburg for not demanding that his subordinates analyze more thoroughly the compatibility of the two operations. There should have been no surprises after the sale that the distribution systems of Gatorade and Snapple were not compatible and maybe could not be made so. Furthermore, it seems only reasonable to expect for a purchase of this magnitude that adequate research and planning would also have been done concerning the advertising and promotional efforts of Snapple, whether they were adequate for the coming year or whether changes needed to be made, and if so, what changes. Should not stockholders expect that rather solid marketing plans would be in place before the acquisition was finalized by Quaker? Without such, the decision to let go of $1.7 billion seems rather like decision making by hunch and intuition. Perhaps it was.

The spinning of wheels in 1996, after the disastrous 1995, hardly attests to the marketing prowess of Smithburg and Quaker. Sour distributor relations, ineffective advertising, a monstrous giveaway of Snapple in mid-

---

[12]Gerry Khermouch, "Snapple Diet Line Gets $15 Mil Push," *Brandweek* (November 4, 1996): 1.

summer with no positive results whatever—these are not the ingredients of effective marketing.

It could well be that the product life cycle of Snapple had peaked before the Quaker purchase, and that this accounted for the inability of Quaker management to reverse the downward trend of sales and profits. (See the following information box for a discussion of the product life cycle.) But this possibility should have been considered before the acquisition decision.

One would think that the best marketing minds in a major corporation, and any outside consultants used, should have been able to bring Snapple to

---

INFORMATION BOX

THE PRODUCT LIFE CYCLE

Just as people and animals do, products go through stages of growth and maturity—that is, life cycles. They are affected by different competitive conditions at each stage, ranging often from no competition in the early stages to intense competition later on. We can recognize four stages in a product's life cycle: introduction, growth, maturity, and decline.

Figure 13.1 depicts three different product life cycles. Number 1 is that of a standard item in which sales take some time to develop and then eventually begin a slow decline. Number 2 shows a life cycle for a product in which a modification of the product or else the uncovering of a new market rejuvenates the product so that it takes off on a new cycle of growth (the classic examples of such remarketing are Listerine, originally sold as a mild external antiseptic, and Arm & Hammer Baking Soda, which was remarketed as a deodorizer). Number 3 shows the life cycle for a fad item or one experiencing rapid technological change and intense competition. Notice its sharp rise in sales and the abrupt downturn.

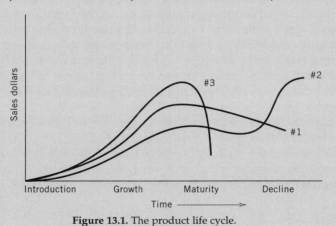

Figure 13.1. The product life cycle.

Now, which life cycle most closely represents Snapple, and where on the curve was Snapple in 1996? The second question is more easily answered: Snapple was definitely on a downward trend, which began the summer before Quaker purchased it, and this downward trend continued and even accelerated through 1995 and 1996. (See Table 13.1.) This suggests that Snapple has reached the maturity stage of its life cycle. As an admittedly trendy product, its curve in the worst scenario would resemble #3, the fad. An optimistic scenario would see a #2 curve, with strong marketing efforts in 1997 bringing a rejuvenation. Perhaps the more likely life cycle was something akin to #1, with a slow downturn continuing for a lengthy period while aggressive marketing efforts fail to stem the decline in an environment of more intense competition and less eager demand. Results in 1997 would establish the shape of the life cycle more conclusively.

Do you think Snapple is a fad item? Why or why not?

more healthy national and international sales, even if the profitability never matched previous expectations. Not the least of the evaluations needed should have been whether the premium price on Snapple products were desirable or if they made Snapple less competitive in the mass market.

Finally, it is worth emphasizing again that in the acquisition quest, extensive homework should be done. These are major, major decisions. Hundreds of millions of dollars, even billions, are at stake if an unwise acquisition has to be divested a few years later. In addition there is the management time taken up with a poorly performing product line at the expense of other responsibilities.

UPDATE

On March 27, 1997, Smithburg finally threw in the towel; he sold the ailing Snapple to Nelson Peltz, chief executive of the smallish Triarc Cos., owner of RC Cola and Arby's restaurants. The price was shockingly low, only $300 million, or just over half of Snapple's $550 million in sales. This, for a brand Smithburg had paid $1.7 billion in late 1994. The founder of Snapple, Leonard Marsh, who had previously sold his controlling interest, said that "they stole the company."[13]

Undoubtedly, Quaker was desperate to sell the money-draining Snapple, but at such a fire-sale price? As it turned out, the company had few options. Major suitors, such as PepsiCo, Coca-Cola, and Proctor & Gamble, only wanted to consider a Snapple purchase along with Gatorade, Smithburg's crown jewel and most profitable brand.

---

[13] I. Jeanne Dugan, "Will Triarc Make Snapple Crackle?" *Business Week* (April 28, 1997): 64.

On April 24, 1997, *The Wall Street Journal* reported that Quaker Oats had posted a $1.11 billion quarterly loss reflecting the final resolution of the Snapple affair, and that William Smithburg was stepping down. "Many investors have been asking for a long time why he hasn't stepped aside sooner," said one food-industry analyst.[14]

WHAT CAN BE LEARNED?

Be cautious with possible fad product life cycles. With hindsight, we can classify Snapple's popularity as a short-term phenomenon. But it was heady and contagious while it lasted. Snapple transformed iced tea into a new age product by avoiding the need for preservatives and adding fruit flavors and introducing innovative wide-mouth, 16-ounce bottles. It also used Howard Stern, with his cult following, as its spokesman.

The public offering of stock in 1993 was sensational. The original offering price was to be $14, but this was raised to $20; in the first day of trading the stock closed at $29. John Kania, a consultant, calls this "product euphoria," an unsustainable "high" that often accompanies overnight success.[15]

Two years later, Quaker paid $1.7 billion for a company whose founders paid just $500 to acquire the name. But the euphoric life cycle was turning down, and the cult following was distracted by imitators, such as Arizona Iced Tea, Mystic, and Nantucket Nectars, as well as Coke and Pepsi through alliances with Nestea and Lipton.

Perhaps what can be learned is that product life cycles are unpredictable, especially where they involve fad or cult followers who may be as fickle as the wind, and where imitation is easy. To bet one's firm on such an acquisition can be risky indeed. But in truth Smithburg had faced a similar situation with Gatorade, and won big. The moral: decision making under uncertainty can be a crap game. But prudence suggests a more cautious approach.

The illusion of compatibility. Bad acquisition decisions—in which the merger or acquisition turns out to be a mistake—often result from miscalculating the mutual compatibility of the two operations. Expectations are that consolidating various operations will result in significant cost savings. For example, instead of two headquarters' staffs, these can be reduced perhaps to a beefed-up single one. Sometimes even certain aspects of production can be combined allowing some facilities to be closed for greater cost efficiencies. Computer operations, sales forces, and distribution channels might be

---

[14]Michael J. McCarthy, "Quaker Oats Posts $1.11 Billion Quarterly Loss," *The Wall Street Journal* (April 24, 1997): A3 and A12.

[15]John Kania, "Why Snapple's Bubble Burst," *The Wall Street Journal* (December 23, 1996): A12.

combined. But for these combinations and consolidations to be feasible, the two operations essentially should be compatible.

As we saw in this case, the distribution channels of Snapple and Gatorade were not compatible, and efforts to consolidate brought serious rancor by those who would be affected. Quaker had failed to do its homework and probe deeply enough to determine the real depth of compatibility, not merely assuming compatibility because of product similarities.

Certainly we see many acquisitions and mergers of dissimilar operations: These are called diversifications. Some of these have little or no compatibility, and may not provide significant opportunities for reducing costs. Instead, they may be made because of perceived growth opportunities, to lessen dependence on mature products, to smooth out seasonality, and so on. Unfortunately, many of these dissimilar diversifications prove to be disappointing and are candidates for divestiture some years later.

The acquisition contest. Once an acquisition candidate is identified, negotiations sometimes become akin to an athletic contest: Who will win? Not infrequently, several firms may be drawn to what they see as an attractive would-be acquisition, and a bidding war commences. Sometimes management of the takeover firm strongly resists. So, the whole situation evolves into a contest, almost a game. And aggressive executives get caught up in this game and sometimes overreach themselves in their struggle to win. No matter how attractive a takeover firm might be, if you pay way too much for it, this is a bad buy.

The paradox of perseverance: when to give up? We admire people who persevere despite great odds: the student who continues with school even though family and work commitments may drag it out for ten years or more; the athlete who never gives up; the author who has a hundred rejection slips, but still keeps trying. So, how long should we persevere in what seems totally a losing cause? Isn't there such a thing as futility and unrealistic dreams, so that constructive efforts should be directed elsewhere? The enigma of futility has even been captured in classic literature with Don Quixote, the "Man from LaMancha," tilting his lance at windmills.

Was Smithburg, in his stubborn efforts to rejuvenate Snapple, exhausting the positive attributes of perseverance and entering the realm of futility, when this acquisition would better be cast off? Many Quaker Oats stockholders thought so.

So, the line is blurred between perseverance and futile stubbornness. Circumstances vary too much to formulate guidelines. Still, if a direct assault continues to fail, perhaps it is time to make an end run.

When should a weak product be axed? Weak products tend to take up too much management, sales force, and advertising attention, efforts that could better be spent making healthy products better and/or developing replacements. Publicity about such products may even cause customer misgivings and tarnish the company's image. This suggests that weak and/or unprofitable products or divisions ought to be gotten rid of, provided that the problems are enduring and not a temporary aberration.

Not all weak products should be pruned, however; rationale for keeping them may be strong. In particular, the weak products may be necessary to complete a line to benefit sales of other products. They may be desirable for customer goodwill. Some weak product may enhance the company's image or prestige. Although such weak products make no money in themselves, still their intrinsic value to the firm may be substantial. Other weak products may merely be unproven, too new in their product life cycle to have become profitable; in their growth and maturity stage they may contribute satisfactory profits. Finally, possibly a new marketing strategy will rejuvenate the weak product. That is the hope, and the proffered justification for keeping a weak product when its demise is overdue.

So, where did Snapple fit into this theoretical discussion? The only justification for procrastination would seem to be that marketing strategy alternatives to turn around the brand had not been exhausted. In the meantime, the image of Quaker Oats in the eyes of investors, and the reflection of this in stock prices, was being savaged.

Sampling caveats. Giving away free samples can be a potent, though not inexpensive, promotional strategy. The objective is to induce a sufficient number of people to want to buy the product once they have tried it. This objective rests on the assumption that the product sampled will be deemed sufficiently desirable. Or, that a person given the sample has sufficient time to do the trying out.

A cost-benefit analysis (see the Maytag case) would be helpful here, if we could reasonably estimate the probable benefits to determine whether they are worth the costs involved.

Snapple executives had no way to accurately predict the benefits of the sampling. Only afterwards, when worsening quarterly sales results were posted, did the failure of the $40 million sampling effort become evident, with not even survey information to show for it.

We can offer these guidelines for the most effective sampling efforts:

1. Do not oversample in size of product given away or in geographic coverage. This suggests that large-size containers or quantities are wasteful and may even cannibalize from regular sales. Also, regional rather than nationwide sampling might be sufficient and more cost effective.

2. Make sure the product sampled is shown in best light, that the presentation is attractive and appealing, perhaps through the packaging, display, attendants, and the information presented.
3. Use care to sample those consumers most likely to be future purchasers of the product.
4. If possible, use the sampling process to obtain marketing research information by asking a few brief questions, such as, "Have you tried this before?" "If so, how often?" "How could we make it more attractive to you?"

CONSIDER

Can you think of any other learning insights?

QUESTIONS

1. Why do you think the great Snapple giveaway was ineffective?
2. Do you think Snapple should have been sold for $300 million? Why or why not?
3. Do you think the premium retail price for Snapple was a serious impediment? Why or why not?
4. "Snapple was an albatross around Quaker's neck. The whole thing should have been written off as a lost cause at least a year earlier." Discuss.
5. "This isn't a case where a guy has gone from a genius to a dummy. Who's better at running the company?" (Investor quote in Burns, p. 74.) Discuss this statement.
6. "What's all the fuss about? Snapple is going great on our college campus. It's a success, man." Do you agree? Why or why not?
7. Do you drink Snapple? If not, why not? If so, how often and how well do you like it?

HANDS-ON EXERCISES

Before

1. A major decision is at hand. You are a vice president of the beverage operation at Quaker. William Smithburg is proposing the acquisition of Snapple for some huge sum. Before this decision is made, you have been asked to array any contrary arguments to this expensive acquisition, in other words, to be a devil's advocate (one who takes a

contrary position for the sake of argument and clarification of opposing views). What concerns would you raise, and how would you defend them?

After

2. It is late 1996. You are the assistant to Michael Schott, who has just been named president of Snapple. He asks you to formulate a strategic plan for resurrecting Snapple for 1997. What do you propose? Be as specific as you can, and be prepared to defend your recommendations.

TEAM DEBATE EXERCISE

The acquisition of Snapple by Quaker Oats is accomplished. Now begins the assimilation. A major debate has ensued regarding whether Snapple should be consolidated with Gatorade, or whether it should remain an independent entity. Debate the two positions as persuasively as possible. Be sure and identify any assumptions made.

INVITATION TO RESEARCH

What is the situation with Snapple and with Smithburg? Has Snapple been turned around by Triarc? What is Smithburg doing now? How has Quaker's stock price behaved?

CHAPTER 14

Pepsi Finds Trouble
in South America

Early in 1994, PepsiCo began an ambitious assault on the soft-drink market in Brazil. This objective was certainly a worthy one since Brazil represented the third-largest soft-drink market in the world, behind only the U.S. and Mexico. Making this invasion even more tempting was the opportunity to combat arch-rival Coca-Cola, already entrenched in Brazil. Pepsi brought new factories, trucks, and a flashy marketing campaign to the fray, and enthusiasm was high. It seemed reasonable to shoot for capturing 20 percent of Brazil's main urban markets and selling more than 250 million cases a year.

This did not happen. Things went sour. And Pepsi's problems suddenly involved more than Brazil.

THE TROUBLES IN BRAZIL

The robust soft-drink market of Brazil had attracted Pepsi before. Its hot weather and a growing teen population fueled Brazil to become one of the world's fastest-growing soft-drink markets, along with China, India, and Southeast Asia. But the potential still had barely been tapped. Brazilians consumed an average of only 264 eight-ounce servings of soft drinks a year, far below the U.S. average of about 800.[1]

Three times before over the last 25 years, Pepsi had attempted to enter this market with splashy promotional campaigns and different bottlers.

[1] Robert Frank and Jonathan Friedland, "How Pepsi's Charge Into Brazil Fell Short of Its Ambitious Goals," *The Wall Street Journal* (August 30, 1996): A1.

Each of these efforts proved disappointing and Pepsi had given up after a short time. Now it planned a much more aggressive and enduring push.

A Super Bottler, Baesa, and Charles Beach

Buenos Aires Embotelladora SA, or Baesa, was to be the key to Pepsi's rejuvenated entry into Brazil. Baesa would be Pepsi's "superbottler," one that would buy small bottlers across Latin America, expand their marketing and distribution, and be the fulcrum in the drive against Coca-Cola. Charles Beach, the CEO of Baesa, was the person Pepsi planned its strategy around.

Beach, 61, was a passionate, driven man, a veteran of the cola wars, but his was a checkered past. He had been manager for a North Carolina Coca-Cola bottler, but left to buy Pepsi's small Puerto Rican franchise in 1987. The next year he was indicted by a federal grand jury on charges of price fixing during his tenure at Coke. Beach pleaded no contest and received a $100,000 fine and a suspended prison sentence.

Then in 1989 he acquired the exclusive Pepsi franchise for Buenos Aires, Argentina, one of the most important bottling franchises outside the U.S., and by discounting and launching new products and packages, he caught Coke by surprise. In only three years he had increased Pepsi's market share in the Buenos Aires metro area from almost zero to 34 percent.[2]

With Pepsi's blessing, Beach expanded vigorously, borrowing heavily to do so. He bought major Pepsi franchises in Chile, Uruguay, and most importantly, Brazil, where he built four giant ultramodern bottling plants. Now he had a potential market of more than 100 million consumers.

Pepsi worked closely with Baesa's expansion, providing funds to facilitate it. Its production capability in the vast Brazilian market now was more than twice Pepsi's highest previous sales. The company also bought 700 new trucks, and a variety of new products and packages were introduced, including four new flavors of the Kas line of juice-based sodas developed especially for Brazil. The Brazilian operation was to be producing at full capacity within a year. PepsiCo corporate executives even saw Baesa as being the instrument for a worldwide expansion, and to emphasize the importance of this affiliate they put two of their own people on Baesa's board.

However, PepsiCo and Baesa underestimated the aggressiveness of their rival. Coca-Cola began counterattacking, especially in Brazil. It spent heavily on marketing and cold drink equipment for its choice customers. As a result Baesa was shut out of small retail outlets, and these were the most profitable for bottlers. Roberto Goizueta, CEO of Coca-Cola Company (you may remember him from the earlier case of Coca-Cola's blunder with New

[2] Patricia Sellers, "How Coke Is Kicking Pepsi's Can," *Fortune* (October 28, 1996): 78.

Coke), used his Latin American background to influence the Argentine President to reduce an onerous 24 percent tax on cola to 4 percent. This move strengthened Coke's position against Baesa, which was earning most of its profits from non-cola drinks in contrast to Coca-Cola.

By spring of 1996, Baesa's expansion plans, and Pepsi's dream bottler, were floundering. The new Brazilian plants were running at only a third of capacity. Operating problems had plagued these plants from the beginning, with bottling lines often shut down, and bent and punctured can discards were ten times what would normally be expected. Even some machinery needed for the expansion was still in crates months later. Baesa lost almost $300 million for the first half of 1996.

Management turnover exacerbated the situation. For example, the top Baesa manager in Brazil had been replaced three times since 1994. Pepsi sent a steady stream of executives from its headquarters to troubleshoot, but without positive results.

Not the least of the problems was the debt. It had grown from $15.4 million at the end of 1993 to $745 million by June 1996, nearly $100 million of this granted or guaranteed by Pepsi. In October 1996, it was announced that PepsiCo would inject another $40 million into Baesa as part of an agreement with the bottler's creditors. More than 1,500 workers had been laid off and several plants were closed.[3]

On May 9, Beach was relieved of operational responsibility, and Pepsi assigned Luis Suarez to deal with the mess. Now, other problems were emerging for Beach. Investors in his Puerto Rican operation were suing him and the company for accounting irregularities. Allegations now surfaced that Beach might have tampered with Baesa's books.[4] But PepsiCo's troubles did not end with the debacle in Brazil.

INTRIGUE IN VENEZUELA

Brazil was only symptomatic of other overseas problems. Roger Enrico, CEO of PepsiCo, had reasons to shake his head and wonder at how the gods seemed against him. But it was not gods, it was Coca-Cola. Enrico had been on Coke's black list since he had gloated a decade before about the New Coke debacle in his memoir, *The Other Guy Blinked: How Pepsi Won the Cola Wars*. Goizueta was soon to gloat, "It appears that the company that claimed to have won the cola wars is now raising the white flag."[5]

[3] Robert Frank, "PepsiCo to Inject Another $40 Million Into Latin Bottler," *The Wall Street Journal* (October 21, 1996): A6.
[4] Sellers, "How Coke Is . . ." 79.
[5] Sellers, "How Coke Is . . ." 72.

The person Enrico thought was his close friend, Oswaldo Cisneros, the head of one of Pepsi's oldest and largest foreign bottling franchises, suddenly abandoned Pepsi for Coca-Cola. Essentially, this took Pepsi out of the Venezuela market. Not a robust market this, as it only contributed about $10 million to Pepsi's net, but still, along with Baesa, it highlighted an international marketing effort gone bonkers.

Despite the close ties of the Cisneroses with the Enricos, little things led to the chasm. The closeness had developed when Enrico headed the international operations of PepsiCo. After he left this position for higher offices at corporate headquarters, Oswaldo Cisneros felt that Pepsi management paid scant attention to Venezuela: "That showed I wasn't an important player in their future," he said.[6] As Cisneros was growing older with uncertain health, he wanted to sell the bottling operation, but Pepsi was only willing to acquire 10 percent.

Coca-Cola wooed the Cisneroses with red carpet treatment and frequent meetings with its highest executives. Eventually, Coca-Cola agreed to pay an estimated $500 million to buy 50 percent of the business. The setting for this passing of the torch was company headquarters in Atlanta, with three generations of Cisneroses hosted by Coke CEO Goizueta and his wife. "It was a very family-like gathering, to symbolize that this was to be a long-term relationship," as the Goizuetas and the Cisneroses shared stories about their Cuban heritage.[7]

PROBLEMS ELSEWHERE IN THE INTERNATIONAL ARENA

Pepsi's problems in South America appeared symptomatic of its problems worldwide. It had lost its initial lead in Russia, Eastern Europe, and parts of Southeast Asia. While it had a head start in India, this was being eroded by a hard-driving Coca-Cola. Even in Mexico its main bottler reported a loss of $15 million in 1995.

The contrast with Coca-Cola was significant. Pepsi still generated more than 70 percent of its beverage profits from the U.S.; Coca-Cola got 80 percent from overseas.[8]

Table 14.1 shows the top ten markets for Coke and Pepsi. In the total world market, Coke by 1996 had a 49 percent market share while Pepsi's was only 17 percent, despite its investment of more than $2 billion since 1990 to straighten out its overseas bottling operations and improve its

[6]Sellers, "How Coke Is . . ." 75.
[7]Sellers, "How Coke Is . . ." 78.
[8]Frank and Friedland, "How Pepsi's Charge," A1.

Table 14.1 Coke and Pepsi Market Shares, Top Ten Markets

Markets	Market Shares:	Coke	Pepsi
U.S.		42%	31%
Mexico		61	21
Japan		34	5
Brazil		51	10
East-Central Europe		40	21
Germany		56	5
Canada		37	34
Middle East		23	38
China		20	10
Britain		32	12

Sources: Company annual reports, and Patricia Sellers, "How Coke is Kicking Pepsi's Can," *Fortune* (October 28, 1996): 82.

Commentary: These market share comparisons show the extent of Pepsi's ineptitude in its international markets. In only one of these top ten overseas markets is it ahead of Coke, and in some, such as Japan, Germany, and Brazil, it is practically a nonplayer.

image.[9] With its careful investment in bottlers and increased financial resources to plow into marketing, Coke continued to gain greater control of the global soft-drink industry.

If there was any consolation for PepsiCo, it was that its overseas business had always been far less important to it than to Coca-Cola, but this was slim comfort in view of the huge potential the international market represented. Most of Pepsi's revenues were in the U.S. beverage, snack food, and restaurant businesses, with such well-known brands as Frito-Lay chips and Taco Bell, Pizza Hut, and KFC (Kentucky Fried Chicken) restaurants. But as a former Pepsi CEO was fond of stating, "We're proud of the U.S. business. But 95 percent of the world doesn't live here."[10] And Pepsi seemed unable to hold its own against Coke in this world market.

In a cosmetic effort to boost its image and sales overseas against Coke, Pepsi initiated "Project Blue," described in the following box.

ANALYSIS

The Illusion of Size

In comparing firms, usually the first criterion is size: which is the bigger firm? Size seems synonymous with power and prestige. The business press

[9] Robert Frank, "Pepsi Losing Overseas Fizz to Coca-Cola," *The Wall Street Journal* (August 22, 1996): C2.

[10] Frank, "Pepsi Losing Overseas," C2.

INFORMATION BOX

A FACE LIFT: PROJECT BLUE

In spring 1996 PepsiCo launched "Project Blue" in some twenty of its markets throughout Europe and Asia. This was done with great fanfare, complete with a blue Concord jet, supermodels, and pictures from space. The $500 million project was aimed at painting over Pepsi's entire public face abroad—including cans, bottles, vending machines, and trucks—with a space-age blue logo. It also began testing the concept in two U.S. cities, Des Moines, Iowa, and New Orleans.[11]

The results of the face change in the overseas markets was spotty. Pepsi hastened to discount the mediocre sales volume and market share gains claiming that Coke had skewed the results by "heavy discounting and promotions" in these markets, and Pepsi expressed satisfaction with brand awareness scores and a boosted image among overseas consumers.[12]

Should Pepsi decide to go ahead with the face change in the U.S., costs of the conversion would be substantially higher than overseas, with thousands of trucks, vending machines, etc., having to be reworked. Many bottlers who would bear some of the costs were dismayed and urged that concrete sales gains in the two test cities instead of "fuzzy" image scores be the deciding factor in any decision to go nationwide. Meantime, Coca-Cola readied its efforts to confound the results in Des Moines and New Orleans by increased ad budgets, price promotions, and even a "Santa-Truck," a brightly lit tractor trailer, to tout its promotions.

How would you assess the need for a drastic facelift, as well as the probable effectiveness of it?

---

fans the comparisons with such yearly compilations as the *Fortune 500*, the ranking of the 500 largest U.S. firms.

In the 1996 ranking, PepsiCo was ranked the 21st largest firm with sales of $30.4 billion, while Coca-Cola was number 48, with its sales of $18 billion. However, firms can also be compared by market value, that is, the value that investors place on firms as reflected in stock market valuations. Here, Coca-Cola leaves PepsiCo in the dust, with a $124.9 billion market value, which is 6.9 times net sales, to PepsiCo's $47.5 billion, only a mere 1.6 times net sales.[13] The difference, of course, reflects investor judgment that Coca-Cola is a blue-ribbon growth stock, while PepsiCo's growth prospects are far more pedestrian.

---

[11] Robert Frank, "Pepsi To Try the Blues in Two-City Test," *The Wall Street Journal* (October 31, 1996): B12.

[12] Frank, "Pepsi to Try the Blues," B12.

[13] Sellers, "How Coke Is . . ." 72.

Hence, sheer size without corresponding profit and growth prospects is hardly the mark of the better firm, but may actually suggest a cumbersome dinosaur easy to attack.

Is PepsiCo Too Diversified?

Compared with Coca-Cola, which is mostly wedded to a single-minded emphasis on soft drinks, PepsiCo diversified extensively into restaurants and snack foods, with mixed results. But same-store sales at both Pizza Hut and Taco Bell have slumped despite efforts to restructure. Only KFC has remained a bright spot. Investors pressured CEO Roger Enrico to spin off the restaurant unit, which has few of the characteristics of Pepsi's other businesses. One manager of a fund with more than three million shares was quoted in *The Wall Street Journal:* "No one can understand why you don't just spin this thing off. It diverts management attention, it doesn't fit with the company's other business, and you're not running it well."[14] The Frito-Lay unit, maker of salty snacks, remained strong both domestically and internationally, and helped make up for weaknesses in restaurants and overseas beverages.

Concentration versus dispersion or diversification is a controversy without clear resolution. Firms are successful diversifying; indeed, most firms go this route to try to jack up growth and find promising new ventures. But other firms find that diversifying takes attention and resources away from core businesses and makes them more vulnerable to hard-driving competitors. It used to be thought that if a firm could find the right strategic fit in an acquisition, success was likely to be assured. Strategic fit refers to the mutually reinforcing effects that different business activities can have on the organization's overall effectiveness, and we will talk about this more in the Learning Insights to follow.

Was Coca-Cola's strategy of concentration better than Pepsi's of diversification? The empirical evidence suggests it was in this case. PepsiCo's restaurants, in particular, diluted attention from the main beverage operation, and were problem-ridden. But the snack food unit was a big contributor to total corporate profits. So, how do you call it—a winner or a loser, this issue of concentration versus dispersion?

The Treacherous Allure of International Operations

While international arenas often afford growth potential many times greater than a mature domestic market, still, we find anomalies in how firms fare in

---

[14] Robert Frank, "PepsiCo's Critics Worry the Glass Is Still Half Empty," *The Wall Street Journal* (September 30, 1996): B10.

these distant markets. Coca-Cola fared very well; Pepsi hardly well at all. What made the difference?

With hindsight we can identify many of the mistakes Pepsi made. It tried to expand too quickly in Argentina and Brazil, imprudently putting all its chips on a distributor with a checkered past, instead of building up relationships more slowly and carefully. It did not monitor foreign operations closely enough or soon enough to prevent rash expansion of facilities and burdensome debt accumulation by these affiliates. It did not listen closely enough to old distributors and their changing wants, and so lost Venezuela to Coca-Cola. And probably, Pepsi did not learn from its past mistakes: for example, three times before it had tried to enter the Brazilian market and had failed. Why? And why did it not use more care to prevent failure this time?

Finally, we can speculate that maybe Pepsi was not so bad, but rather, that its major competitor was so good. Coca-Cola had slowly built up close relationships with foreign bottlers over decades. It was aggressive in defending its turf. Perhaps not the least of its strengths, at least in the lucrative Latin American markets, was a CEO who was also a Latino, who could speak Spanish and share the concerns and build on the egos of its local bottlers. In selling, this is known as a dyadic relationship, and it is discussed further in the information box. After all, why can't a CEO do a selling job on a distributor and capitalize on a dyadic relationship?

INFORMATION BOX

THE DYADIC RELATIONSHIP

Sellers are now recognizing the importance of the buyer-seller interaction, *a dyadic relationship.* A transaction, negotiation, or relationship can often be helped by certain characteristics of the buyer and seller in the particular encounter. Research suggests that salespeople tend to be more successful if they have characteristics similar to their customers in age, size, and other demographic, social, and ethnic variables.

Of course, in the selling situation this suggests that selecting and hiring sales applicants most likely to be successful might require careful study of the characteristics of the firm's customers. Turning to the Pepsi/Coke confrontation in Brazil and Venezuela, the same concepts should apply and give a decided advantage to Coca-Cola and Roberto Goizueta in influencing government officials and local distributors. After all, even a CEO in interacting with customers and affiliates needs to be persuasive in presenting ideas as well as handling problems and objections.

Do you agree with the dyadic theory? Can you think of any situations where it may not work?

WHAT CAN BE LEARNED?

International growth requires tight controls. In Pepsi's problems with Baesa we have seen the risks of placing too much trust in a distributor without careful and consistent monitoring of performance and finances. It can be argued that the selection of Charles Beach to spearhead the Pepsi invasion of Coke strongholds in South America was questionable at best in view of his missteps in the past. With Beach or any other unproven major player, prudence would dictate close monitoring of plans and performance, with major changes—in expansion planning, in strategies, in financial commitments—approved by corporate headquarters. In international dealings, the tendency may be to loosen control due to the distances involved, different customs, and bureaucratic procedures, as well as cultures that may not be fully understood by headquarters. This tendency to slacken controls must be resisted.

In diversifying, a firm should seek a strategic fit. As noted before, strategic fit refers to the mutually reinforcing effects that different business activities can have on the overall performance. Sometimes this idea is graphically referred to as "2 + 2 = 5," that is, the sum of the benefits of the combined operations is more than if they had remained separate.

We recognize several forms of fit. *Product-market fit* is obtained when the different products can use the same distribution channels, sales promotion techniques, and can be sold to the same customers with the same sales force. *Operating fit* results from economies of purchasing, warehousing, overlapping of technology and engineering, production compatibility, and the like. *Management fit* occurs when existing management know-how and experience can be effectively transferred to the newly acquired activities. The common thread of strategic fit can provide a unifying focus and the company can build on joint managerial, financial, and technological strengths.

The popularity in the last several decades of conglomerate mergers involving little or no fit or similarity casts doubts on the necessity for fit. Some of these conglomerates have been successful: for example, International Telephone and Telegraph (ITT) products and subsidiary companies at one time ranged from Sheraton Hotels, Wonder Bread, and Avis Rent-a-Car to finance companies, chemicals, lawn care, and even business schools.

But other conglomerates found that trying to manage many unrelated product markets and technologies brought severe problems. In some cases, such acquisitions resulted in "2 + 2 = 3." Many conglomerates, after the initial acquisition spree, were forced to sell off subsidiaries in order to get on the profit track again.

Did Pepsi's diversifications have good strategic fits? While they all were food and drink related, one would suspect that the basic strategic fits were not good: e.g., expertise in handling soft-drink operations would seem to require a different management skill than running restaurants.

We conclude then that, although a common thread of strategic fit is not essential for all of a firm's business activities, it increases the probability of successful assimilation and synergy.

The human factor may be more important in international operations. While good judgment regarding subordinates and associates and good rapport with customers and affiliates are desirable for domestic operations, they may be more so in the international environment. The distances involved usually necessitate more decentralization and therefore more autonomy. Corporate management must have more confidence and trust in their foreign associates, and if this is misplaced, serious problems can result. Customers and affiliates may need rapport and a closer relationship with corporate management if they are not to be wooed away by other U.S. and foreign competitors. Furthermore, in some countries the political climate is such that the major people in power cannot be overlooked by the large firm wanting to do business in that country.

Beware that buildup of facilities does not exceed reasonable sales potential. Such an increase in underutilized facilities, and the consequent debt, brought Baesa to its knees. This is always a risk when a firm wildly expands without being sure that it can win a sufficient market. While the total potential in Brazil was enormous, the amount that Pepsi was likely to garner in the presence of an aggressive Coca-Cola should have been estimated conservatively. Overextension has brought many a firm to bankruptcy.

An aggressive competitor can wreak havoc on test marketing efforts. A firm uses test marketing to try out new products and/or concepts before a full-scale launching. If the results in the few test markets are positive, the decision probably will be to expand. But we have seen how an aggressive Coca-Cola "muddied the waters" in Pepsi's efforts to introduce Project Blue in overseas markets, so that at best Pepsi wound up with inconclusive results. Then Coca-Cola aggressively turned its attention to nullifying the Des Moines and New Orleans test markets.

The consequence of aggressive competitor meddling is to destroy or at least contaminate the predictability of test market results. A hapless firm such as Pepsi in this case may have to depend more on hunch than concrete results in making some costly expansion decisions. But who said competitive wars are nice and friendly. A Coca-Cola top executive has been widely quoted, "What do you do when your competitor is drowning? Get a live hose, and stick it in his mouth."[15]

---

[15]Sellers, "How Coke Is . . ." 80.

CONSIDER

Can you think of any other learning insights?

QUESTIONS

1. "While Charles Beach may have had a few indiscretions, he was by far the best man for the job. There was no one else we could have gotten who had his qualities of experience and aggressive drive." Evaluate this statement.
2. Critique Pepsi's handling of Baesa. Could it have prevented the disaster? If so, how?
3. What do you see as important differences in international and domestic markets for firms such as PepsiCo and Coca-Cola?
4. Do you think PepsiCo should divest itself of its restaurant operations? Why or why not?
5. With hindsight, how might Roger Enrico, CEO of PepsiCo, have kept Oswaldo Cisneros, his principal bottler in Venezuela, in the fold instead of defecting to Coke?
6. How might you counter a competitor who is muddying the waters in your test markets?

HANDS-ON EXERCISES

Before

1. As a market analyst for PepsiCo, you have been asked to present recommendations to Roger Enrico, CEO, and the executive board, for the invasion of Brazil's soft-drink market. The major bottler, Baesa, is already in place and waiting for Pepsi's final plans and objectives. You are to design a planning blueprint for this "invasion," complete with an estimated timetable.

After

2. The Baesa bottling operation has essentially collapsed, mired in debt, burdened with unneeded facilities, and facing monumental production and distribution snafus. Charles Beach, founder of Baesa, has been replaced. What do you do at this point? Be as specific as possible. Make any assumptions needed, but state them.

TEAM-DEBATE EXERCISES

1. Debate the controversy of whether PepsiCo should divest itself of its non–soft-drink businesses so as to concentrate all its efforts on the soft-drink core.
2. Regarding Project Blue, assume that test market results in Des Moines and New Orleans showed slight sales gains and stronger brand awareness scores, and debate the two sides of the major issue of going nationwide with the project, or scrapping it.

INVITATION TO RESEARCH

What is the situation today with PepsiCo? Has its international situation improved? How about the restaurant and snack food operations? Project Blue?

PART IV

MARKETING SUCCESSES

CHAPTER 15

Microsoft: Harnessing Innovation

In the last few months of 1992, what had been increasingly evident throughout the year finally became indisputable: the passing of the leadership of IBM in the computer industry. As *The Wall Street Journal* described it on December 21, 1992, "The generational shift in the computer industry is unfolding . . . As leadership slips away from the old behemoth . . . it is being picked up by two young juggernauts—Intel Corp. and Microsoft Corp.— which both were nurtured by IBM."[1]

This case concerns one of these "young juggernauts," Microsoft, and its cofounder and leader, William H. Gates III, who by 1992 was the richest man in America, with a net worth of over $7 billion. He was then 36 years old, and a bachelor.

BILL GATES

Bill Gates was born on October 28, 1955, in Seattle, Washington. His father was a prominent attorney, and his mother was to become a regent of the University of Washington. Growing up in an affluent and socially prominent family, it was not long before his genius intellect became clearly evident. By 11 years of age, he was far ahead of his peers in math and science, and his parents enrolled him in Lakeside, a prep school noted for its rigorous academic environment. There he was exposed to the primitive computers of the day

[1]Stephen Kreider Yoder, "How IBM's Heirs Plan to Expand Empires in Computer Industry," *The Wall Street Journal* (December 21, 1992): A1, A4.

and became immediately hooked. He spent every spare moment with computers, and he even created a computer program at age 13.

On the math achievement test Lakeside gave its students, Gates was number one. He was later to score a perfect 800 on the math SAT, and was bound for Harvard.

Bill Gates would later tell a friend that he went to Harvard University to learn from people smarter than he was . . . and left disappointed.[2] When he arrived at Cambridge, Massachusetts, in fall 1973, he had no real sense of what he wanted to do with his life; although his academic major was prelaw, he had little interest in becoming a lawyer. Computers and the entrepreneurial opportunities emerging in a rapidly changing technology engrossed his attention (as did a mean game of poker) in these undergraduate years. It came as little surprise that he dropped out of Harvard in 1975 to cofound Microsoft Corporation with a longtime friend, Paul G. Allen. Microsoft became the most successful startup company in the history of American business, and it was to become the world's largest microcomputer software company. Bill Gates was 20 years old at its founding.

What kind of person is Bill Gates? Of his intellect and overall ability there is no question. Unlike many entrepreneurs, he seems also to have the talent to run a massive and growing operation. However, criticisms of his character and his personality have flourished:

> "Gates is tenacious. That's what's scary . . . he always comes back, like Chinese water torture. His form of entertainment is tearing people to shreds."

> "A bad personality and a great intellect. In a place like Harvard, where there are a lot of bright kids, when you are better than your peers, some tend to be nice and others obnoxious. He was the latter."

> "Bill Gates wants it all. And he's on his way to getting it."[3]

HISTORICAL DEVELOPMENT OF COMPUTER TECHNOLOGY

The modern computer was first developed in the 1940s during World War II. But the concept goes back to the 1800s when a mathematical genius, Charles Babbage, unsuccessfully tried to develop an "analytical machine" to solve mathematical equations. By the end of the century, however, people used punch cards to help tabulate information from the 1890 census. The machine used was designed by Herman Hollerith, a young engineer. Soon, punch cards became widely used in all kinds of office machines, and

---

[2] James Wallace and Jim Erickson, *Hard Drive* (New York: John Wiley, 1992), 53.
[3] Wallace and Erickson, *Hard Drive*, quotes listed on backpiece.

Hollerith's company would be absorbed by a New York firm destined to dominate the computer industry for almost a century—International Business Machines (IBM).

In the 1930s IBM had financed the development of a large computing machine, the Mark I, finished in 1944. It could multiply two 23-digit numbers in about 5 seconds. But it was an electromechanical machine with thousands of noisy relays serving as switching units.

A major improvement came with the vacuum tube. The first electronic digital computer, the ENIAC, was unveiled in 1946. It weighed 30 tons and took up more space than a two-car garage. But it could handle about 5,000 additions and subtractions per second, and in its final stages of completion it helped the physicists at Los Alamos build the first atomic bomb.

In 1947 came the big breakthrough in computing technology, the transistor, which could now replace the vacuum tube. These transistors, or semiconductors as they became known, were smaller, more reliable, and cheaper to make than the old vacuum tubes. The first semiconductors were made of crystals of germanium. Later, silicon became more popular.

Another technological breakthrough came in the late 1950s. It was found that networks of transistors could be etched on a single piece of silicon with thin metallic connectors. Such integrated circuits, or chips as they became known, provided the foundation for all modern electronics, and they made possible the development of much smaller, faster, and more powerful computers.

In the 1950s IBM was so dominant that the other makers of large mainframe computers were called the seven dwarfs. They all made large mainframe computers that cost hundreds of thousands of dollars, needed many technicians to service them, and also required careful and controlled access to minimize dust, temperature, and humidity contaminants. Now, with the advances in technology and the development of the semiconductor, more practical and accessible computers—minicomputers—were possible. But in a grievous error IBM elected not to enter this new market.

Thus, it provided an unimaginable opportunity for new computer companies. Digital Equipment Corporation quickly became the leader, establishing the minicomputer market in 1965 when it introduced its PDP-8 (shorthand for Program Data Processor), which cost $18,500. It abandoned the traditional method of data input through punch cards fed into the machine; instead, the user could communicate with the computer via a keyboard.

In 1971 Intel developed the microprocessor. A microchip made it possible to encode the entire central processing unit of a computer onto a silicon chip no larger than a thumbnail. Somehow, this step was not undertaken by the large corporations, such as Digital Equipment Corporation and IBM, with their financial and technological resources. Instead, it was left to entrepreneurs, to people like Bill Gates, Steve Jobs of Apple, and similar men, usually young, with vision and a hunger for achievement.

THE MAKING OF MICROSOFT

In 1974 MITS (Micro Instrumentation and Telemetry Systems), a small company in Albuquerque, New Mexico, built Altair, the first personal computer to have any real impact on the market. Although it had serious shortcomings, its low price stimulated considerable demand from hobbyists who had dreamed of having their own personal computer, even if they had to tediously assemble it.

Bill Gates and Paul Allen, friends from high school, developed a BASIC software program for the Altair that greatly enhanced its marketability. In order to carry out negotiations with MITS, Gates and Allen formed a partnership called Micro-Soft (for microcomputer software; the hyphen was later dropped) in July 1975. Their business objective was to develop languages for the Altair and for other microcomputers that were bound to appear soon on the market. Thus, Microsoft was the first company formed for the specific purpose of producing software for such computers.

In spring 1977 Microsoft had six employees and moved into eighth floor offices in downtown Albuquerque. But for the microcomputer industry to take off it needed more reliable machines, and these began to appear in 1977—notably the TRS-80 by Tandy, the PET by Commodore, and the Apple II. Microsoft now expanded its product line beyond BASIC, with Fortran in July 1977 and later COBOL and Pascal.

By the end of 1978, Microsoft had doubled its sales over the previous year, reaching its first million, and it now had 13 employees. Allen and Gates shared the executive tasks. Since both were from Washington, it was perhaps inevitable that as Microsoft grew larger they would opt to move it to Seattle, which they did in summer 1978. Most employees moved with the company. For 1979 sales reached $2.5 million, with worldwide sales of BASIC passing 1 million copies. Microsoft was poised for its major breakthrough.

In 1980 IBM was the uncontested leader in the computer world, with sales of $28 billion. But it was not yet a player in the personal computer market. Unable to buy out a suitable firm already in this business, such as Apple, IBM decided to go ahead internally but to follow Apple's strategy of encouraging software development by independent firms.

Microsoft and IBM signed a contract November 6, 1980, for Microsoft to provide software programs. Such a collaboration was particularly significant: The industry giant was asking a small firm with a 25-year-old president to work with it in a major new developmental effort.

By mid-1981, Microsoft had 100 employees, with 35 of these involved with the IBM project. IBM accepted the operating system created by Microsoft, and MS-DOS became the official system of the IBM PC. IBM announced its first microcomputer on August 12, 1981, and it was available in stores 2 months later.

It now remained for Microsoft to make MS-DOS the standard for the industry. Less than a year after the IBM PC was announced, a number of other manufacturers also were adapting to the MS-DOS. It began to catch on even, more quickly in 1983 when Lotus released a spreadsheet program which operated only under MS-DOS. In just 3 months, Lotus 1-2-3 became the best-selling software package for spreadsheets for 16-bit machines, and this was a great boost for MS-DOS machines. By the end of 1983, 500,000 copies of MS-DOS had been sold, about 400,000 of them through IBM. Microsoft sales for the year reached $69 million, and the firm had grown to 383 employees. MS-DOS was now available for more than 60 computer systems, and other computer manufacturers were touting the "IBM compatibility" of their products—that is, their ability to run software written for the PC.

Going Public

Experts wondered why Gates waited so long to take Microsoft public. Success had continued unabated, and by 1986 its basic software was running millions of IBM personal computers and clones. By now it had myriad versions of computer languages and fast-selling applications programs such as spreadsheets and word-processing packages for IBM, Apple, and other personal computers.

Gates had stood firm in 1983 when two of his archcompetitors, Lotus and Ashton-Tate, had floated stock worth a total of $74 million. He did not budge in 1984 and 1985 when three other microcomputer software companies sold $54 million of stock. He did not budge, even though going public with a successful venture was the path to great riches.

Gates' reasons for procrastination were rather simple. Growing up in affluence, he valued control of his time and his company more than personal wealth. And unlike his competitors, Microsoft was not dominated by venture capital investors eager to harvest some of their gains. Besides, the business "gushed" cash, as *Fortune* phrased it.[4] Pretax profits were running as high as 34 percent of sales, and Microsoft needed no outside money to expand.

But by 1986 a public offering seemed necessary and desirable. Gates had been selling his managers and technical experts shares and stock options, and with over 500 people owning shares, this would be enough to

---

[4]Bro Uttal, "Inside the Deal That Made Bill Gates $350,000,000," *Fortune* (July 21, 1986): 24.

force the company to register with the Securities and Exchange Commission (SEC). At this point it seemed prudent to sell enough shares to enough investors to create a liquid market, so that trading would not be difficult.

On March 13, 1986, shares were offered at $21. By the end of the first day of trading, some 2.5 million shares had changed hands, and the price of Microsoft's stock stood at $27.75. This was soon to zoom to $35.50 before settling back to $31.25. Microsoft raised $61 million, and the public put a market value of $350 million on the 45 percent stake Bill Gates retained, making him one of the richest Americans. In subsequent years, he became the richest American of all, as the growth and value of Microsoft stock doubled and tripled.

DOMINANCE

A 1991 article in *Forbes* magazine bore the title, "Can Anyone Stop Bill Gates?"[5] The article noted that Microsoft was "massacring its competitors" and that it seemed to be heading for a near monopoly in the software industry. In the time since the article appeared, Microsoft has certainly not faltered—during this same time period, the behemoth of the computer industry, IBM itself, fared badly as described in Chapter 5, with its stock price collapsing amid layoffs of tens of thousands of employees and billion-dollar writeoffs as part of a major restructuring before its recent turnaround.

The road to market dominance for Microsoft was MS-DOS. This software system guided the inner workings of almost all of the 40 million IBM PCs and IBM-compatible personal computers in existence as of 1991. With MS-DOS standard for almost any PC, a constant stream of royalties was pouring into the company, providing high profits and furnishing ample funds for research and further developments in the forefront of technology, such as Windows.

The goal of Windows was to transform MS-DOS from a monochrome, arcane, text-based environment into a multicolor, user-friendly, graphics-based environment. Achieving this was not easy. The project began in September 1981, and after a number of embarrassing delays from announced scheduled introductions, it finally came out in November 1985. However, success was far from immediate. Few machines at that time could do justice to this new environment, either in their color monitors or in their operational capability. For example, for a PC with two disk drives, Windows was unbearably slow.

[5]Kathleen K. Wiegner and Julie Pitta, "Can Anyone Stop Bill Gates?" *Forbes* (April 1, 1991): 108–14.

Windows was to set company records for the greatest number of development hours. More than 24 developers devoted all their time to Windows for more than 3 years, and this did not include testing and documentation time. By the time it was released, Windows had had four product managers and three development directors.[6]

Just a few years later, Windows became Microsoft's best-selling software. By 1992 Microsoft was selling more than 1 million copies of its Windows program per month. This all but cemented the program's position as the standard operating system for computer users. Table 15.1 shows the great increase in Microsoft's sales and profits since it went public in 1986. Note how well the percentage growth rates in sales and profits per year have been maintained, despite the increasing size of the firm. As any firm grows larger, it has more and more difficulty holding the percentage growth rate.

As of the beginning of 1993, Microsoft planned to introduce a new operating system, called Windows NT, thereby building on the runaway success of its Windows program. The Windows NT would continue to offer everything in the Windows operating system but would add a multitude of other features, such as the ability to run many programs simultaneously, to safeguard against unauthorized use, to use vast amounts of memory, to tie many machines into networks, and to run on "multiprocessing" systems that link many chips together.[7]

Both Microsoft and Intel, the premier maker of chips, were operating under the cloud of possible antitrust rulings for building virtual monopolies with products so heavily protected by patents and copyrights that legal

Table 15.1   Microsoft's Growth in Sales and Profits, 1986–1992 (in $ thousands)

Year ended June 30	Net Revenues	Percent Increase	Net Income	Percent Increase
1986	$ 197,514	40.7%	$ 39,254	62.9%
1987	345,890	75.1	71,878	83.1
1988	590,827	70.8	123,908	54.2
1989	803,530	36.0	170,538	47.1
1990	1,183,446	47.3	279,186	63.7
1991	1,843,432	55.8	462,743	65.7
1992	2,758,725	49.7	708,060	55.9

Source: Company annual reports.

[6] Daniel Ichbiah and Susan L. Knepper, *The Making of Microsoft* (Rocklin, CA: Prima Publishing, 1991), 192.

[7] Yoder, "Heirs Plan to Expand," 1.

Table 15.2   Sales Revenues for Major PC Software Companies, 1987–1992 (in $ millions)

Company	1987	1988	1989	1990	1992
Borland	$ 38	$ 82	$ 91	$ 227	$ 474
Computer Associates	309	709	1,030	1,348	1,688
Lotus Development	396	469	557	685	903
Microsoft	346	591	831	1,183	2,759
Novell	—	—	422	498	860
Oracle	131	282	584	971	1,241

Source: *Business Week* 1000 Companies, 1990, 1991, 1992; and *Forbes* (January 4, 1993): 118.

duplication was practically impossible for competitors. With the operating system and the microprocessor being a PC's most crucial components, any PC buyer who wanted a powerful machine able to run the biggest selection of software had to go the Intel-Microsoft route. The likelihood of competitors being able to break through seemed ever more remote as Microsoft and Intel grew ever larger, were able to pour more and more funds into research, and were able to spread their costs over millions of units, making them the lowest-cost producers of the most advanced technological products. Table 15.2 shows the growth in sales revenues of Microsoft and its major competitors in the PC software industry. By 1992 the growth of Microsoft had far exceeded that of its competitors, leaving it well over a billion dollars larger than its largest competitor, Computer Associates, much larger than Lotus, and with a growth rate far outstripping these competitors.

ANALYSIS

Undoubtedly the initial success of Microsoft reflects Bill Gates's brilliant technological expertise coupled with a tenacious entrepreneurial business sense. But whereas most entrepreneurs are unable to transfer entrepreneurial talent to the organizational ability needed to manage large-scale operations, Gates seemed able to make the transference with ease. But let us go beyond the personal talents of the man and examine specific contributors to the runaway success of Microsoft.

A Distinctive and Overpowering Product

The early development of the DOS operating program gave Microsoft a major competitive edge. How durable and encompassing this edge would be was not clear, but Bill Gates was able to sell it to the mighty IBM and to persuade IBM to let him sell the program to all comers, thus allowing other manufacturers to make PC clones. The ensuing competition drove down prices, intensified innovation, and left Microsoft in the center of an $83-billion-a-year industry worldwide. While competitors struggled to match or surpass the DOS program, they were unable to make any significant inroads. Buttressed by good patent protection and ever stronger commitment to research and development, Microsoft remained unassailable. See Table 15.3 for the growth in research and development expenditures from 1986 through 1992. Note in particular the heavy commitment as a percent of sales.

Part of the durability of Microsoft's operating system is simple economics. Computer users have heavy sunk costs that act as a barrier to entry for new software. For a new operating system to be widely accepted, it would force users to throw out their old application software and buy new versions, in the process incurring sizable costs of additional software as well as substantial retraining. Consequently, Gates is the sought-after partner with hardware makers that no small firm can be.

A further competitive advantage of Microsoft today is that it is selling items that have very low marginal costs of production. For example, the first copy of a program may cost $20 million for research and development. But additional copies may cost only $20 for the disk and the manual.[8] Consequently, Microsoft projects such a major cost advantage that newcomers, no matter how much they might like to discount in order to enter the market, are hardly likely to be successful.

Table 15.3   Microsoft Growth in Expenditures for Research and Development, 1986–1992 (in $ thousands)

Year ended June 30	Research and Development Expenditures	Percentage Increase	Percent of Sales
1986	$ 20,523	—	10.4%
1987	38,076	85.5%	11.0
1988	69,776	83.3	11.8
1989	110,220	56.0	13.7
1990	180,615	63.9	15.3
1991	235,386	30.3	12.8
1992	352,153	49.6	12.8

Source: Company annual reports.

[8]Example taken from Wiegner and Pitta, "Can Anyone Stop Bill Gates," 110.

Staying in the Technological Forefront

Better than any other firm that has grown to relatively large size, Microsoft has been able to maintain its vitality and innovativeness. Perhaps reflecting the leadership of Gates, the creativity flair has flourished.

Largely credited with this has been the organizing of small, independent "business units" of programmers and marketers, each geared to specific business goals. The groups are small enough that Gates can easily interact with the key members. Each of these groups is responsible for a particular type of software. Business unit managers (BUMs) monitor how their products stack up against competitors in all aspects, from a program's technical sophistication to financial and productivity information their rivals make public. Woe to the unit that does not outperform its competitors.

Business units commonly employ brainstorming to provide ideas for new products, and Gates frequently joins programmers in such sessions. "It's very important to me and to the guys that work for us that Microsoft feel like a small company, even though it isn't one anymore," says Gates.[9] See the following box for a more detailed discussion of brainstorming.

In a rapidly growing company such as Microsoft, an esprit de corps is not surprising. Turnover is low. But Microsoft works its employees hard, with many putting in 75-hour weeks, especially during shipment deadlines for new products. Pay is not particularly high; even Gates paid himself only $190,000 a year in 1990. There are few perks, and no one has a company car. But the company is generous with stock options, and the great increases in company share prices have made dozens of programmers paper millionaires.

Does Microsoft Have Any Threats?

Defensive alliances between competitors aimed at combatting Microsoft are possible and are evolving. For example, Lotus and Novell attempted a defensive merger into a company that would have been Microsoft's size, but the deal fell through at the time. Hewlett-Packard and Sun Microsystems are united in battling Microsoft over industry standards for linking different programs.

In the past Microsoft has been notorious for rushing products to market too quickly, before all the bugs have been worked out. This happened with its original word-processing program, with Windows, and with several other software endeavors. While the problems eventually were corrected, customers may still be conditioned to skip the first version of a new product.

Added to these possible problems of unknown magnitude is the threat of antitrust action, as Microsoft gains an ever more monopolistic position.

[9] Brenton Schlender, "How Bill Gates Keeps the Magic Going," *Fortune* (June 18, 1990): 83.

INFORMATION BOX

BRAINSTORMING

Brainstorming is a technique to stimulate group creativity. A group—five to eight seems to be the best size—comes together for the sole purpose of producing ideas, and the more ideas, the better. At this point the quality and practicality of ideas is not a factor: The group simply seeks the greatest number. In a conducive environment, such as when there is no need to impress a boss and no hint of criticism, one idea tends to spark other ideas.

Only after the brainstorming session is over should any efforts be made to cull, evaluate, and select the most acceptable ideas. Alex Osborn, the father of brainstorming, and probably the foremost authority on developing creativity, lists these four rules for effective brainstorming:[10]

1. Criticism is ruled out.
2. Free-wheeling is welcomed; the wilder the idea, the better.
3. Quantity is desired; the greater the number of ideas, the more likely some useful ones will be found.
4. Combination and improvement are sought; participants are encouraged to build on or modify the ideas of others.

The problems should be as specific as possible, and ideally should be limited to one a session. One hour seems to be about the ideal length for such sessions. Brainstorming can be useful, even with participants who are not creative, in producing usable ideas. Osborn describes one typical session in which participants produced 136 ideas in 40 minutes. In addition to stimulating ideas, some of which, one hopes, will be worthy of further development, brainstorming can also be used as a training device to develop the creativity of the individual participants.

For which of the following situations would you expect brainstorming to be most effective, and why?

1. Sales in a particular territory have fallen drastically from last year.
2. Your firm is ready to introduce a new product and is planning its promotional campaign.
3. Your firm wishes to open a new retail outlet and wonders where best to locate it.

Perhaps these threats are gnat-like. But the king of the hill is always the target. Should Microsoft let its guard down on the technological forefront, not anticipate and act quickly enough in potentially promising new directions, then the king of the hill may be supplanted.

[10] Alex F. Osborn, *Applied Imagination*, 3rd ed. (New York: Scribner's, 1963).

POSTSCRIPT

Bill Gates, the most eligible of all bachelors, finally got married on January 1, 1994. Many had predicted that he eventually would marry some famous person from show business; instead he married a marketing manager.

The great growth of Microsoft continued. In August 1995, its 20th anniversary, the company introduced Windows 95, "designed to make computing more powerful, easier, faster, and more fun—every day."[11] Millions of people upgraded their systems to Windows 95. By the end of 1995, Microsoft's sales were $7.4 billion and net profits were $1.8 billion. If you refer back to Table 15.1, you can see that in three years, sales rose 164 percent and profits 157 percent. For fiscal 1995, $860 million was spent for research and development, up from $352 million in 1992. This was 14.5 percent of fiscal 1995 sales, the second highest percent-of-sales allocation and 144 percent more dollars than three years before (See Table 15.3.)—all this to try to assure that Microsoft would stay in the vanguard of computer software technology.

The *Annual Report* mentions some "uncertainties" that the company sees itself facing:

- For example, despite the huge R&D expenditures, the company still has concern about "Rapid Technological Change: The personal computer software industry is characterized by rapid technological change and uncertainty as to the impact of emerging areas such as the Internet and online services, the information highway, networked collaboration products, and electronic commerce."

- For example, litigation: "Litigation regarding intellectual property rights, patents, and copyrights is increasing in the PC software industry. In addition, there are government regulation and investigation risks along with other general corporate legal risks."[12]

In late 1993 the Justice Department took over the antitrust investigation from the Federal Trade Commission. "They're just learning about our business," said Gates. "We've only sent them like a million pieces of paper. They need a million more."[13] The indications were that it was okay for Microsoft to grow from within but not through mergers or acquisitions.

By the end of 1996, sales were $9.44 billion, up 27 percent from 1995, and profits were 2.48 billion, up 35 percent.

[11] *Microsoft Annual Report*, 5.
[12] *1995 Annual Report*, 25.
[13] G. Pascal Zachary, "Microsoft Aides To Be Deposed in U.S. Probe," *The Wall Street Journal* (June 6, 1994): A3.

WHAT CAN BE LEARNED?

Great riches can come from going public with a successful venture. We saw in this case how Bill Gates became a billionaire—and a few years later the richest American—after he took Microsoft public by issuing stock. He had founded Microsoft in 1975 and waited until 1986 to take it public. Criticism had abounded that he should have done this years earlier, but Gates was not all that interested in personal wealth. In another example of entrepreneurial success, Steven Jobs took his fledgling firm, Apple, public in 1980, only 4 years after he had started it in the family garage, and by 1983 he was worth well over $200 million.

While Gates and Jobs have extraordinary success stories, on smaller scales many small businesses can find themselves attractive to investors seeking growth companies that often offer far greater potential than the behemoths can. If the founder of the business keeps a substantial block of the company's stock, the payoff in the investing public's appraisal of the value of the enterprise can be mind boggling.

Again, beware the "king of the hill" mental trap. As we have seen with IBM and Harley Davidson in particular—firms that became dominant in their particular industry sector and felt unassailable—dominant firms tend to fall into a particular mindset that leaves them vulnerable to aggressive and innovative competitors. We have called this vulnerability the *three C's syndrome of failure:* complacency, conservatism, and conceit.

To review, *complacency* is smugness, and it typifies the self-satisfied firm content with the status quo and no longer hungry and eager for growth.

Conservatism characterizes a management that is wedded to the past, to the traditional, to the ways things have always successfully been done: "There is no need to change because nothing is different today."

Finally, *conceit* for present and potential competitors can further reinforce the myopia of the managerial perspective. A belief that "we are the best" and that "no one else can touch us" can easily permeate an organization when everything has been going well for years.

These attitudes, which originate with top management, can reduce commitment to consistency of quality, create an aloofness to customer needs and concerns, and allow a lack of innovativeness in seeking new markets and substantially improved products. Also there often is decreased emphasis on pricing for good value and more on maximizing per-unit profits. Thus, the foundation is laid for vulnerability to the aggressive competitor "foolish" enough to challenge a seemingly entrenched dominant firm.

At this time Microsoft certainly shows none of the symptoms of the three C's. But this could come if it takes for granted its mastery of the software and applications market. Remember IBM. The frontrunner must maintain constant vigilance to avoid the king-of-the-hill mental trap, with its three C's.

Be aware of the risks if you are a minor player in a high-growth arena. In a high-growth industry, the entrenched, dominant firm has the advantage (despite the eventual danger of a king-of-the-hill mindset, as just described). The dominant firm in such a situation is generating rapidly increasing sales and profits and is able to invest heavily in research and development. Where technology is rapidly changing, this is a major competitive advantage. The firm with low market share faces the need for heavy investment, not only in research and development but also in its promotion budget and its pursuit of distributors as well as other aspects of its marketing strategy. It may have to slash prices to hold or gain market share, and this cuts drastically into profits. The esteemed Boston Consulting Group Matrix, described in the following box, designates such a situation for the low-market-share firm as a question mark: that is, should it even remain in the industry against the formidable odds it faces and the major investments required to be a player?

Of course, there is the possibility that the frontrunner will stumble and become complacent and too conservative. But decades may elapse before the king-of-the-hill mindset may make this frontrunner vulnerable.

Disregard the cannibalization factor. Cannibalization refers to the situation in which one product takes sales away from other products of the firm. Generally, new products succeed to some extent at the expense of other products in the line, but hopefully there will be enough new business to increase total sales. Certainly, Microsoft's releasing of Windows 95 was bound to cannibalize sales of earlier Windows. But how do you prevent this? Eliminate new technological advances?

To be so concerned about cannibalization that needed product improvements and additions are delayed or withheld from the market can be costly. The classic example of the dangers of such delays is that of Gillette. It delayed introducing its higher quality stainless steel blade for fear that this blade, which afforded more shaves than its highly profitable super blue blade, would seriously cannibalize the other product. Only when aggressive competitors introduced their own stainless steel blades did Gillette do so. Because of this hesitance in bringing forth an innovation and improvement in shaving, Gillette's market share of the double-edge blade market fell from 90 percent to 70 percent. The loss in competitive position was never fully regained.

In high tech industries, the restraints of possible cannibalization have to be ignored if market leadership is not to be sacrificed. Technological advances are constantly in the works that promise to make obsolete existing

INFORMATION BOX

THE BOSTON CONSULTING GROUP MATRIX

The Boston Consulting Group, a leading management consulting firm, has boiled down the major strategy decisions a firm faces to only four, depending on the firm's competitive position in a particular industry and the growth of that industry. Accordingly, a firm's major business categories can be classified as stars, question marks, cash cows, and dogs. Figure 15.1 presents the matrix of this concept.

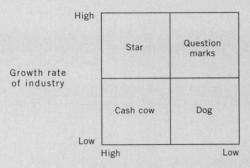

Relative market dominance compared to largest competitor
(market share)

Figure 15.1. Matrix of a firm's major business categories.
Star, dominant market position in a high-growth industry.
Question mark, weak market position in a high-growth industry.
Cash cow, dominant market position in a low-growth industry.
Dog, weak market position in a low-growth industry.

A different strategy implementation is recommended for each of these business categories, as follows:

Category	Strategy Implementation
Stars	*Build.* In a dominant market position and a rapidly growing industry, more investment and long-term profit goals are recommended, even if they come at the expense of short-term profitability.
Question Marks	*Build or Divest.* The decision whether to commit more resources to building such products into leaders or to divest and use company resources elsewhere is not easily made. It may depend on the strength of major competitors and

how well-heeled the company is: For example, a firm may decide it cannot provide sufficient financing to achieve the growth it needs, given the competition.

Cash Cows	*Harvest.* When in a dominant position in a low-growth industry, the recommended strategy is to reap the harvest of a strong cash flow. Only enough resources should be reinvested to maintain competitive position.
Dogs	*Divest.* There is no use wasting resources on poor competitive positions in low-growth industries. The recommended strategy is to sell or liquidate this business.

Microsoft is obviously in a star situation, with its dominant position in a high-growth industry. Inroads by smaller competitors thereby become very difficult as they face the question mark scenario.

Do you see any limitations to the Boston Consulting Group's model?

---

products and systems. A firm that stumbles in being in the vanguard of such technology may never recover. In such a fast-changing and evolving environment, fear of cannibalization is destructive: Hesitancy here opens the door for eager competitors.

CONSIDER

Can you identify additional learning insights that could be applicable to other firms in other situations?

QUESTIONS

1. Bill Gates has an informal management style, even in his choice of clothes, and he is emulated by the rest of the organization. Evaluate such informality in a large corporation, especially related to its marketing presence.
2. Assess the future prospects of Microsoft using a SWOT analysis (i.e., strengths, weaknesses, opportunities, and threats).
3. If Microsoft's stock price should plummet in a severe stock market decline, do you think Gates will have trouble motivating his employees, given their long working hours, few perks, and relatively low wages?
4. Many other firms in the forefront of a rapidly expanding industry have lost their competitive advantage, perhaps because they have

become less hungry, or because the three C's syndrome has crept in. Do you see any reasons why Microsoft would steer clear of the same disincentives for performance excellence?

5. We have just discussed two rather contradictory theories of market dominance: the three C's syndrome of vulnerability and the Boston Consulting Group's matrix of the invulnerability of a star. What is your position on this issue? Which is correct, and under what circumstances?

6. "The success of Microsoft is not so much a credit to Bill Gates as a flawed miscalculation by IBM." Evaluate this statement.

HANDS-ON EXERCISES

1. Lotus Corporation has been quite successful with its Lotus 1-2-3 spreadsheets. But it has been left in the dust by Microsoft with its Windows software. How would you, as chief executive of Lotus, attempt a comeback or at least attempt to maintain a competitive position? (To answer this question in depth you may need to research more specifically the products of Lotus and their uses.)

2. As Bill Gates, you are aware of the dangerous king-of-the-hill mindset. How do you combat it in your organization?

TEAM DEBATE EXERCISE

After its burgeoning success in software, Bill Gates is thinking of branching out into hardware. What particularly irks him is that, despite the great success of his firm, Intel has done better, reaching $16 billion in sales in 1995 versus Microsoft's $7.4 billion. Debate the issue of diversifying beyond software.

INVITATION TO RESEARCH

1. Compare and contrast the two highly successful young entrepreneurs, Steve Jobs and Bill Gates.

2. What is the situation with Microsoft today? Are there any threats on its horizon?

CHAPTER 16

Southwest Airlines:
"Try to Match Our Prices"

In 1992 the airlines lost a combined $2 billion, matching a dismal 1991 and bringing their three-year red ink total to a disastrous $8 billion. Three carriers—TWA, Continental, and America West—were operating under Chapter 11 bankruptcy, and others were lining up to join them. But one airline, Southwest, was profitable as well as rapidly growing—with a 25 percent sales increase in 1992 alone. Interestingly enough, this was a low-price, bare bones operation run by a flamboyant CEO, Herb Kelleher. He had found a niche, a strategic window of opportunity, and oh, how he had milked it! See the following box for further discussion of a strategic window of opportunity and its desirable accompaniment, a SWOT analysis.

HERBERT D. KELLEHER

Herb Kelleher impresses one as an eccentric. He likes to tell stories, often with himself as the butt of the story, and many involve practical jokes. He admits he sometimes is a little scatterbrained. In his cluttered office, he displays a dozen ceramic wild turkeys as a testimonial to his favorite brand of whiskey. He smokes five packs of cigarettes a day. As an example of his zaniness, he painted one of his 737s to look like a killer whale in celebration of the opening of Sea World in San Antonio. Another time, during a flight he had flight attendants dress up as reindeer and elves, while the pilot sang Christmas carols over the loudspeaker and gently rocked the plane. Kelleher is a "real

---

INFORMATION BOX

STRATEGIC WINDOW OF OPPORTUNITY AND SWOT ANALYSIS

A strategic window is an opportunity in the marketplace not presently well served by competitors that fits well with the firm's competencies. Strategic windows often last for only a short time (although Southwest's strategic window has been much more durable) before they are filled by alert competitors.

Strategic windows are usually found by systematically analyzing the environment, examining the threats and opportunities it holds. The competencies of the firm, its physical, financial, and people resources—management and employees and their strengths and weaknesses—should also be assessed. The objective is to determine what actions might or might not be appropriate for that particular enterprise and its orientation. This is commonly known as a SWOT analysis: analyzing the strengths and weaknesses of the firm and assessing the opportunities and threats in the environment. (This is also discussed in Chapter 6.)

This analysis may be a formal part of the planning process, or it may also be informal and even intuitive. We suspect that Herb Kelleher instinctively sensed a strategic window in short hauls and lowest prices. Although he must have recognized the danger that his bigger competitors would try to match his prices, he believed that with his simplicity of operation he would be able to make a profit while bigger airlines were racking up losses.

Why do you think the major airlines so badly overlooked the possibilities in short hauls at low prices?

---

maniac," said Thomas J. Volz, vice president of marketing at Braniff Airlines. "But who can argue with his success?"[1]

Kelleher grew up in Haddon Heights, New Jersey, the son of a Campbell Soup Company executive. He graduated from Wesleyan University and New York University law school, then moved to San Antonio in 1961, where his father-in-law helped him set up a law firm. In 1968 he and a group of investors put up $560,000 to found Southwest; of this amount, Kelleher contributed $20,000.

In the early years he was the general counsel and a director of the fledgling enterprise. But in 1978 he was named chairman, despite having no managerial experience, and in 1981 he became CEO. His flamboyance soon made him the most visible aspect of the airline. He starred in most of its TV commercials. A rival airline, America West, charged in ads that Southwest passengers

---

[1] Kevin Kelly, "Southwest Airlines: Flying High with 'Uncle Herb'," *Business Week* (July 3, 1989): 53.

should be embarrassed to fly such a no-frills airline, whereupon Kelleher appeared in a TV spot with a bag over his head. He offered the bag to anyone ashamed to fly Southwest, suggesting it could be used to hold "all the money you'll save flying us."[2]

He knew many of his employees by name, and they called him "Uncle Herb" or "Herbie." He held weekly parties for employees at corporate headquarters, and he encouraged such antics by his flight attendants as organizing trivia contests, delivering instructions in rap, and awarding prizes for the passengers with the largest holes in their socks. But such wackiness had a shrewd purpose: to generate a gung-ho spirit to boost productivity. "Herb's fun is infectious," said Kay Wallace, president of the Flight Attendants Union Local 556. "Everyone enjoys what they're doing and realizes they've got to make an extra effort."[3]

THE BEGINNINGS

Southwest was conceived in 1967, folklore tells us, on a napkin. Rollin King, a client of Kelleher, then a lawyer, had an idea for a low-fare, no-frills airline to fly between major Texas cities. He doodled a triangle on the napkin, labeling the points Dallas, Houston, and San Antonio.

The two tried to go ahead with their plans but were stymied for more than 3 years by litigation, battling Braniff, Texas International, and Continental over the right to fly. In 1971 Southwest won, and it went public in 1975. At that time it had four planes flying between the three cities. Lamar Muse was president and CEO from 1971 until he was fired by Southwest's board in 1978. Then the board of directors tapped Kelleher.

At first Southwest was in the throes of life-and-death low-fare skirmishes with its giant competitors. Kelleher liked to recount how he came home one day "beat, tired, and worn out. So I'm just kind of sagging around the house when my youngest daughter comes up and asks what's wrong. I tell her, 'Well, Ruthie, it's these damned fare wars.' And she cuts me right off and says, 'Oh, Daddy, stop complaining. After all, you started 'em.'"[4]

For most small firms, competing on a price basis with much larger, well-endowed competitors is tantamount to disaster. The small firm simply cannot match the resources and staying power of such competitors. Yet Southwest somehow survived. Not only did it initiate the cut-throat price competition, but it achieved cost savings in its operation that the larger airlines could not. The question then became: How long would the big carriers be content to

[2] Kelly, "Flying High," 53.
[3] Richard Woodbury, "Prince of Midair," *Time* (January 25, 1993): 55.
[4] Charles A. Jaffe, "Moving Fast by Standing Still," *Nation's Business* (October 1991): 58.

maintain their money-losing operations and match the low prices of Southwest? The big airlines eventually blinked.

In its early years, Southwest faced other legal battles. Take Dallas, and Love Field. The original airport, Love Field, is close to downtown Dallas, but it could not geographically expand at the very time when air traffic was increasing mightily. So a major new facility, Dallas/Fort Worth International, replaced it in 1974. This boasted state-of-the-art facilities and enough room for foreseeable demand, but it had one major drawback: It was 30 minutes further from downtown Dallas. Southwest was able to avoid a forced move to the new airport and to continue at Love. But in 1978 competitors pressured Congress to bar flights from Love Field to anywhere outside Texas. Southwest was able to negotiate a compromise, now known as the Wright Amendment, that allowed flights from Love Field to the four states contiguous to Texas. In retrospect the Wright Amendment forced onto Southwest a key ingredient of its later success: the strategy of short flights.[5]

GROWTH

Southwest grew steadily but not spectacularly through the 1970s. It dominated the Texas market by appealing to passengers who valued price and frequent departures. Its one-way fare between Dallas and Houston, for example, was $59 in 1987 vs. $79 for unrestricted coach flights on other airlines.

In the 1980s Southwest's annual passenger traffic count tripled. At the end of 1989, its operating costs per revenue mile—the industry's standard measure of cost-effectiveness—was just under 10 cents, which was about 5 cents per mile below the industry average.[6] Although revenues and profits were rising steadily, especially compared with the other airlines, Kelleher took a conservative approach to expansion, financing it mostly from internal funds rather than taking on debt.

Perhaps the caution stemmed from an ill-fated acquisition in 1986. Kelleher bought a failing long-haul carrier, Muse Air Corporation, for $68 million and renamed it TransStar. (This carrier had been founded by Lamar Muse after he left Southwest.) But by 1987 TransStar was losing $2 million a month, and Kelleher shut down the operation.

By 1993 Southwest had spread to 34 cities in 15 states. It had 141 planes, and these each made 11 trips a day. It used only fuel-thrifty 737s and still concentrated on flying large numbers of passengers on high-frequency, one-hour

---

[5] Bridget O'Brian, "Southwest Airlines Is a Rare Air Carrier: It Still Makes Money," *The Wall Street Journal* (October 28, 1992): A7.

[6] Jaffe, "Moving Fast," 58.

hops at bargain fares (average $58). Southwest shunned the hub-and-spoke systems of its larger rivals and took its passengers directly from city to city, often to smaller satellite airfields rather than congested major metropolitan fields. With rock-bottom prices and no amenities, it quickly dominated most new markets it entered.

As an example of Southwest's impact on a new market, it came to Cleveland, Ohio, in February 1992, and by the end of the year was offering 11 daily flights. In 1992 Cleveland Hopkins Airport posted record passenger levels, up 9.74 percent from 1991. "A lot of the gain was traffic that Southwest Airlines generated," noted John Osmond, air trade development manager.[7]

In some markets Southwest found itself growing much faster than projected, as competitors either folded or else abandoned directly competing routes. For example, America West Airlines cut back service in Phoenix in order to conserve cash after a Chapter 11 bankruptcy filing. Of course, Southwest picked up the slack, as it did in Chicago when Midway Airlines folded in November 1992. And in California, Southwest's arrival led several large competitors to abandon the Los Angeles-San Francisco route, unable to meet Southwest's $59 one-way fare. Before Southwest's arrival, fares had been as high as $186 one way.[8]

Now cities that Southwest did not serve were petitioning for service. For example, Sacramento, California, sent two county commissioners, the president of the chamber of commerce, and the airport director to Dallas to petition for service. Kelleher consented a few months later. In 1991 the airline received 51 similar requests.[9]

A unique situation was developing. On many routes, Southwest's fares were so low they competed with buses, and even with private cars. By 1991 Kelleher did not even see other airlines as his principal competitors: "We're competing with the automobile, not the airlines. We're pricing ourselves against Ford, Chrysler, GM, Toyota, and Nissan. The traffic is already there, but it's on the ground. We take it off the highway and put it on the airplane."[10]

Following are several tables and graphs that depict various aspects of Southwest's growth and increasingly favorable competitive position. See Tables 16.1, 16.2, and 16.3, and Figure 16.1. Although Southwest's total revenues were still far less than those of the four major airlines in the industry (five if we count Continental, emerging from its second bankruptcy), its growth pattern indicated a major presence, and its profitability was second to none.

[7] "Passenger Flights Set Hopkins Record," *Cleveland Plain Dealer* (January 30, 1993): 3D.

[8] O'Brian, "Rare Air Carrier," A7.

[9] O'Brian, "Rare Air Carrier," A7.

[10] Subrata N. Chakravarty, "Hit 'Em Hardest with the Mostest," *Forbes* (September 16, 1991): 49.

Table 16.1 Growth of Southwest Airlines; Various Operating Statistics, 1982–1991

Year	Operating Revenues (in $ millions)	Net Income (in $ millions)	Passengers Carried (in thousands)	Passenger Load Factor
1991	$1,314	$26.9	22,670	61.1%
1990	1,187	47.1	19,831	60.7
1989	1,015	71.6	17,958	62.7
1988	860	58.0	14,877	57.7
1987	778	20.2	13,503	58.4
1986	769	50.0	13,638	58.8
1985	680	47.3	12,651	60.4
1984	535	49.7	10,698	58.5
1983	448	40.9	9,511	61.6
1982	331	34.0	7,966	61.6

Source: Company annual reports.
Commentary: Note the steady increase in revenues and in number of passengers carried. While the net income and load factor statistics show no appreciable improvement, these statistics still are in the vanguard of an industry that has suffered badly in recent years. See Table 16.2 for a comparison of revenues and income with the major airlines.

Table 16.2 Comparison of Southwest's Growth in Revenues and Net Income with Major Competitors, 1987–1991

	1991	1990	1989	1988	1987	% 5-year Gain
Operating Revenue Comparisons (in $ millions)						
American	$9,309	$9,203	$8,670	$7,548	$6,369	46.0
Delta	8,268	7,697	7,780	6,684	5,638	46.6
United	7,850	7,946	7,463	7,006	6,500	20.8
Northwest	4,330	4,298	3,944	3,395	3,328	30.1
Southwest	1,314	1,187	1,015	860	778	68.9
Net Income Comparisons (in $ millions)						
American	(253)	(40)	412	450	225	
Delta	(216)	(119)	467	286	201	
United	(175)	73	246	426	22	
Northwest	10	(27)	116	49	64	
Southwest	27	47	72	58	20	

Source: Company annual reports.
Commentary: Southwest's revenue gains over these 5 years outstripped those of its largest competitors. While the percentage gains in profitability are hardly useful because of the erratic nature of airline profits during these years, Southwest stands out starkly as the only airline to be profitable each year.

Table 16.3 Market Share Comparison of Southwest With Its Four Major Competitors, 1987–1991

	1991	1990	1989	1988	1987
Total Revenues (millions): American, Delta, United, Northwest	$29,757	$29,144	$27,857	$24,633	$21,835
Southwest Revenues:	1,314	1,187	1,015	860	778
Percent of Big Four	4.4	4.1	3.6	3.5	3.6
Increase in Southwest's market share, 1987–1991: 22%					

Source: Company annual reports.

Tapping California

The formidable competitive power of Southwest was perhaps never better epitomized than in its 1990 invasion of populous California. By 1992 it had become the second largest player, after United, with 23 percent of intrastate traffic. Southwest achieved this position by pushing fares down as much as 60 percent on some routes. The big carriers, which had tended to surrender the short-haul niche to Southwest in other markets, suddenly faced a real

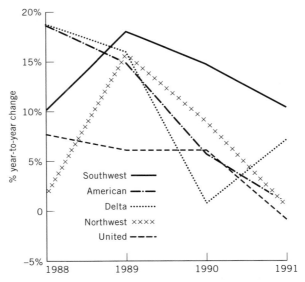

Figure 16.1. Year-to-year percentage changes in revenues, Southwest and its three major competitors, 1988–1991.

quandary in competing in this "Golden State." Now Southwest was being described as a "500 pound cockroach, too big to stamp out."[11]

The California market was indeed enticing. Some 8 million passengers each year fly between the five airports in metropolitan Los Angeles and the three in the San Francisco Bay area, making it the busiest corridor in the United States. It was also one of the pricier routes, as the low fares of AirCal and Pacific Southwest Airlines had been eliminated when these two airlines were acquired by American and USAir.

Southwest charged into this situation with its low fares and frequent flights. While airfares dropped, total air traffic soared 123 percent in the quarter Southwest entered the market. Competitors suffered: American lost nearly $80 million at its San Jose hub, and USAir still lost money even though it cut service drastically. United, the market leader, quit flying the San Diego-Sacramento and Ontario-Oakland routes where Southwest had rapidly built up service. The quandary of the major airlines was all the greater since this critical market fed traffic into the rest of their systems, especially the lucrative transcontinental and trans-Pacific routes. They could hardly abdicate California to Southwest. American, for one, considered creating its own no-frills shuttle for certain routes.[12] But the question remained: Could anyone stop Southwest, with its formula of lowest prices and lowest costs and frequent schedules? And, oh yes, good service and fun.

INGREDIENTS OF SUCCESS

Although Southwest's operation under Kelleher had a number of rather distinctive characteristics contributing to its success pattern and its seizing of a strategic window of opportunity, the key factors appear to be cost containment, employee commitment, and conservative growth.

Cost Containment

Southwest has been the lowest cost carrier in its markets. Although its larger competitors might try to match its cut-rate prices, they could not do so without incurring sizable losses. Nor did they seem able to trim their costs to match Southwest's. For example, in the first quarter of 1991, Southwest's operating costs per available seat mile (i.e., the number of seats multiplied by the distance flown) were 15 percent lower than America West's, 29 percent lower than Delta's, 32 percent lower than United's, and 39 percent lower than USAir's.[13]

[11] Wendy Zellner, "Striking Gold in the California Skies," *Business Week* (March 30, 1992): 48.

[12] Zellner, "Striking Gold," 48.

[13] Chakravarty, "Hit 'Em Hardest," 50.

Many aspects of the operation contributed to these lower costs. With a single aircraft type, Boeing 737, for all its planes, costs of training, maintenance, and inventory were low. And since a plane earns revenues only when flying, Southwest was able to achieve a faster turnaround time on the ground than any other airline. Although competitors take upwards of an hour to load and unload passengers and then clean and service the planes, some 70 percent of Southwest's flights have a turnaround time of 15 minutes, and 10 percent have even pared the turnaround time to 10 minutes.

In areas of customer service, Southwest curbed costs as well. It offered peanuts and drinks, but no meals. Boarding passes were reusable plastic cards. Boarding time was minimal because there were no assigned seats. Southwest subscribed to no centralized reservation service. It did not even transfer baggage to other carriers; that was the passengers' responsibility. Admittedly, such customer service frugalities would be less acceptable on longer flights—and this helped to account for the difficulty competing airlines had in cutting their costs to match Southwest's. Still, if the price is right, many passengers might also opt for no frills on longer flights.

Employee Commitment

Kelleher was able to achieve an esprit de corps unmatched by other airlines despite the fact that Southwest employees were unionized. But there was no adversarial relationship with unions like Frank Lorenzo had at Eastern and Continental Airlines. Southwest was able to negotiate flexible work rules, with flight attendants and even pilots helping with plane cleanup. Employee productivity remained very high, permitting the airline to be leanly staffed. Kelleher resisted the inclination to hire extravagantly when times were good, necessitating layoffs during leaner times. This contributed to employee feelings of security and loyalty. The low-key attitude and sense of fun that Kelleher engendered helped, perhaps more than anyone could have foreseen. Kelleher declared, "Fun is a stimulant to people. They enjoy their work more and work more productively."[14]

Conservative Growth Efforts

Not the least of the ingredients of success was Kelleher's conservative approach to growth. He resisted the temptation to expand vigorously—for example, to seek to fly to Europe or get into head-to-head competition with larger airlines with long-distance routes. Even in its geographical expansion, conservatism prevailed. The philosophy of expansion was to do so only when enough

14Chakravarty, "Hit 'Em Hardest," 50.

resources could be committed to go into a city with 10 to 12 flights a day, rather than just 1 or 2. Kelleher called this guerrilla warfare, concentrating efforts against stronger opponents in only a few areas, rather than dissipating strength by trying to compete everywhere.

Even with a conservative approach to expansion, the company showed vigorous but controlled growth. Its debt, at 49 percent of equity, was the lowest among U.S. carriers. Southwest also had the airline industry's highest Standard & Poor's credit rating, A minus.

LATEST INFO

In its May 2, 1994, edition, prestigious *Fortune* magazine devoted its cover and a feature article to Herb Kelleher and Southwest Airlines. It raised an intriguing question: "Is Herb Kelleher America's best CEO?" It called him a "people-wise manager who wins where others can't."[15] The operational effectiveness of Southwest continued to surpass all rivals: for example, in such productivity ratios as cost per available seat mile, passengers per employee, and employees per aircraft. Only Southwest remained consistently profitable among the big airlines, by the end of 1996 having been profitable for more than 20 years in a row. As Herb Kelleher said, "We're fit. We're trim. We're lean. We're mean."[16]

The Invasion of the Northeast

Late in October 1996, Southwest launched a carefully planned battle for East Coast passengers that would drive down air fares and pressure competitors to back away from some lucrative markets. It chose Providence, Rhode Island, just 60 miles from Boston's Logan Airport. Initially its first target was the Boston-Washington corridor, where it would provide 16 flights a day between satellite airports in Providence and Baltimore for $118 round-trip, in the process treading heavily on USAir's over-$500 fare for the same.

Southwest had previously entered Baltimore in 1993 with eight flights a day, this increasing to 42 flights a day by January 1997. In January 1996 it invaded Florida, "a very good market for them, much better than expected."[17]

The Providence airport escapes the congested New York and Boston air-traffic-control areas. From the Boston suburbs it is hardly a longer trip

---

[15]Kenneth Labich, "Is Herb Kelleher America's Best CEO," *Fortune* (May 2, 1994): 45–52.

[16]Scott McCartney, "Competitors Quake As Southwest Air Is Set to Invade Northeast," *The Wall Street Journal* (October 23, 1996): A10.

[17]Sandra Livingston, "Southwest Airlines Continues to Enjoy Success in its Field," *Cleveland Plain Dealer* (August 4, 1996): 3I.

than to Boston's Logan Airport. Southwest saturated Boston with TV and radio ads preying on travelers' anxiety over the notorious Callahan Tunnel leading to Logan from downtown Boston. And experience had shown that air travelers would drive considerable distances to fly with Southwest's cheaper fares. For example, a survey of license plates at the Baltimore airport parking lots after Southwest began service there found a huge increase in cars from the District of Columbia, Virginia, and Pennsylvania.[18]

As 1996 drew to an end, Southwest was still using only one aircraft, the Boeing 737. Now it had 106 more scheduled for delivery over five years, to add to its existing fleet of 241. It planned to pay cash for most of these new 737s.

As Southwest entered new markets, most competitors refused any longer to try to compete pricewise: They simply could not cut costs enough to compete.For example, USAir spent 12.6 cents to fly one seat one mile, compared with just 7.5 cents per seat-mile at Southwest.[19] Their alternative then was either to pull out of these short-haul markets, or be content to let Southwest have its market share while they tried to hold on to other customers by stressing first-class seating, frequent-flier programs, and other in-flight amenities.

Toward the end of April 1997, Southwest's further aggressive efforts came to the attention of the national press. It had quietly entered the transcontinental market, heretofore the domain of carriers such as United, American, and Delta. From its major connecting point of Nashville, Tennessee, it had begun nonstops both to Oakland, California and to Los Angeles, thus augmenting existing routes to Las Vegas and Phoenix. With Nashville's direct connections with Chicago, Detroit, Cleveland, Providence, and Baltimore/Washington, as well as points south, this afforded one-stop, coast-to-coast service for the first time, with fares about half as much as the other major airlines.

One airline consultant commented: "One-stop service with a 30-minute turn isn't so bad, especially if you want to get off the airplane and smoke." Herbert Kelleher modestly called the expansion "a change in emphasis, but not a change in our niche. We're just diversifying a little bit."[20]

That same month, and for the second time in a row, Southwest was ranked number one in an annual quality survey of the nine major domestic carriers. The survey rated carriers on 19 factors, including safety, on-time records, mishandled baggage, and number of bumped passengers.

---

[18]McCartney, "Competitors Quake," A10.
[19]McCartney, "Competitors Quake," A10.
[20]Scott McCartney, "Scrappy Southwest Reaches Coast in One Stop," *The Wall Street Journal* (April 22, 1997): B1, B2.

WHAT CAN BE LEARNED?

The power of low prices, and simplicity of operation. If a firm can maintain prices below those of its competitors and can do so profitably and without sacrificing quality of service, then it has a powerful advantage. Southwest was able to do this with its simplicity of operation. Competition on the basis of price is seldom used in most industries (although the airline industry has been an exception), primarily because competitors can quickly match prices with no lasting advantage to anyone. As profits are destroyed, only customers benefit, and then only in the short run. See the following issue box for a discussion of the controversy of competing on price, and the alternative.

The durability of Southwest's cost control points out the true competitive importance of low prices. Customers love the lowest price producer, if

---

ISSUE BOX

PRICE COMPETITION: SHOULD WE ATTEMPT IT?

The great limitation in using price as a competitive weapon is that competitors may retaliate and create a price war. It is not difficult to lower a price. It is not difficult to offer a stripped-down model to match a competitor's low price. Not only may no seller benefit from such a situation, but prices may even settle permanently at a lower level. As a result, most firms—except in new, rapidly growing, and technologically changing industries—find it best to compete on *nonprice* bases, rather than face a cut-throat pricing situation.

With nonprice competition, emphasis is placed instead on such factors as service, warranties, delivery, quality, and all possible efforts to obtain greater product differentiation. For example, a good reputation for quality and dependability is not easily and quickly matched by competitors.

The classic example of the impotence of price competition was the 1972 WEO, or "Where Economy Originates," campaign of A & P. Amid heavy advertising, A & P began lowering prices on 90 percent of the merchandise in its 4,200 stores. This action resulted in vicious price wars that destroyed the profits of the entire supermarket industry in 1972. But A & P suffered the most: Its net loss for the year was $51.3 million, the worst in the company's modern history. Although it had a small gain in sales and in market share, the results were not lasting.[21]

Price wars usually are anathema to sellers, but customers benefit. On balance, do you see any disadvantages of price wars from the customers' viewpoint?

---

[21]For more detail on the disastrous A & P price campaign, see Robert Hartley, *Marketing Mistakes*, 5th ed., (New York: Wiley, 1992), Chapter 11. Also relevant is Chapter 8 on the Yugo car.

quality, comfort, and service are not sacrificed too much. Although there was some sacrifice of service and amenities with Southwest, most customers found it acceptable because of the short-haul situation; and dependable and reasonable service was still maintained.

The power of a niche strategy. Directing marketing efforts toward a particular customer segment or niche can provide a powerful competitive advantage. This is especially true if no competitor is directly catering to this niche or is likely to do so with a concerted effort. Such an untapped niche then becomes a strategic window of opportunity.

Kelleher was quick to reveal the niche strategy of Southwest: When other airlines set up hub-and-spoke systems in which passengers are shunted to a few major hubs from which they are transferred to other planes going to their destination, "we wound up with a unique market niche: We are the world's only short-haul, high-frequency, low-fare, point-to-point carrier . . . we wound up with a market segment that is peculiarly ours, and everything about the airline has been adapted to serving that market segment in the most efficient and economical way possible."[22] See the following information box for a discussion of the criteria needed for a successful niche or segmentation strategy.

Southwest has been undeviating in its pursuit of its niche. Although others have tried to copy it, none have fully duplicated it. Southwest still remains the nation's only high-frequency, short-distance, low-fare airline. As an example of its strong position, Southwest accounts for more than two-thirds of the passengers flying within Texas, and Texas is the second largest market outside the West Coast. Now that Southwest has invaded California, some San Jose residents drive an hour north to board Southwest's Oakland flights, skipping the local airport where American has a hub. In Georgia, so many people were bypassing Delta's huge hub in Atlanta and driving 150 miles to Birmingham, Alabama, to fly Southwest that an entrepreneur started a van service between the two airports.[23]

Unlike many firms, Southwest has not permitted success to dilute its niche strategy. It has not attempted to fly to Europe or to get into head-to-head competition with a larger airline on longer domestic flights. And it has not sacrificed growth potential in curbing such temptations: Its strategy still has many cities to embrace.

Seek dedicated employees. Stimulating employees to move beyond their individual concerns to a higher level of performance, a truly team approach, was by no means the least of Kelleher's accomplishments. Such an esprit de corps enabled planes to be turned around in 15 minutes instead of the hour

[22] Jaffe, "Moving Fast," 58.
[23] O'Brian, "Rare Air Carrier," A7.

INFORMATION BOX

CRITERIA FOR SELECTING NICHES OR SEGMENTS

In deciding what specific niches to seek, these criteria should be considered:

1. *Identifiability.* Is the particular niche identifiable so that the persons who constitute it can be isolated and recognized? It was not difficult to identify the short-route travelers, and while their numbers may not have been readily estimated, this was soon to change as demand burgeoned for Southwest's short-haul services.

2. *Size.* The segment must be of sufficient size to be worth the efforts to tap. And again, the size factor proved to be significant: Southwest soon offered 83 flights daily between Dallas and Houston.

3. *Accessibility.* For a niche strategy to be practical, promotional media must be able to reach the segments without much wasted coverage. Southwest had little difficulty in reaching its target market through billboards and newspapers.

4. *Growth potential.* A niche is more attractive if it shows some growth characteristics. The growth potential of short-haul flyers proved to be considerably greater than for airline customers in general. Partly the growth reflected customers won from other higher cost and less convenient airlines. And some of the emerging growth reflected customers' willingness to give up their cars to take a flight that was almost as economical and certainly more comfortable.

5. *Absence of vulnerability to competition.* Competition, both present and potential, must certainly be considered in making specific niche decisions. By quickly becoming the low-cost operator in its early routes, and gradually expanding without diluting its cost advantage, Southwest became virtually unassailable in its niche. The bigger airlines with their greater overhead and less flexible operations could not match Southwest prices without going deeply into the red. And the more Southwest became entrenched in its markets, the more difficult it was to pry it loose.

Assume you are to give a lecture to your class on the desirability of a niche strategy, and you cite Southwest as a classic example. But suppose a classmate asks, "If a niche strategy is so great, why didn't the other airlines practice it?" How will you respond?

---

or more of competitors; it brought a dedication to service far beyond what could ever have been expected of a bare bones, cut-price operation; it brought a contagious excitement to the job obvious to customers and employees alike.

The nurturing of such dedicated employees was not due solely to Kelleher's extroverted, zany, and down-home personality—although this certainly helped. So did a legendary ability to remember employee names.

And company parties. And a sincere company and true interest in the employees. Flying in the face of conventional wisdom, which says an adversarial relationship between management and labor is inevitable with the presence of a union, Southwest achieved its great teamwork while being 90 percent unionized.

Whether such worker dedication can pass the test of time, and the test of increasing size, is uncertain. Kelleher himself was 62 in 1993, and his retirement looms. A successor will be a different personality. Yet there is a model for an organization growing to large size and still maintaining employee commitment.

Part of the attainment of dedicated employees is a product of the firm itself, and how it is growing. A rapidly growing firm—especially when such growth starts from humble beginnings, with the firm as an underdog—promotes a contagious excitement. Opportunities and advancements depend on growth. Where employees can acquire stock in the company and see the value of their shares rising, potential financial rewards seem almost infinite. Success tends to create a momentum that generates continued success. Yet we know that eventually, with all organizations, growth slows and adversity may come. Witness, for example, IBM and Sears before they were able to turn themselves around recently.

CONSIDER

Can you identify additional learning insights that could be applicable to other firms in other situations?

QUESTIONS

1. In what ways might airline customers be segmented? Which segments or niches would you consider to be Southwest's prime targets? Which segments probably would not be?
2. Do you think the employee dedication to Southwest will quickly fade when Kelleher leaves? Why or why not?
3. Discuss the pros and cons for expansion of Southwest beyond short hauls. Which arguments do you see as most compelling?
4. Evaluate the effectiveness of Southwest's unions.
5. On August 18, 1993, a fare war erupted. To initiate its new service between Cleveland and Baltimore, Southwest had announced a $49 fare (a sizable reduction from the then-standard rate of $300). Its rivals, Continental and USAir, retaliated. Before long the price was $19, not much more than the tank of gas it would take to drive between the

two cities—and the airlines also supplied a free soft drink. Evaluate the implications of such a price war for the three airlines.

6. A price cut is the most easily matched marketing strategy, and it usually provides no lasting advantage to any competitor. Identify the circumstances when you see it as desirable to initiate a price cut and a potential price war.

7. Do you think it is likely that Southwest's position will continue to remain unassailable by competitors? Why or why not?

HANDS-ON EXERCISES

1. Herb Kelleher has just retired, and you are his successor. Unfortunately, your personality is far different from his: You are an introvert and far from flamboyant, and your memory for names is not good. What is your course of action to try to preserve the great employee dedication of the Kelleher era? How successful do you think you will be? Did the board make a mistake in choosing you?

2. Herb Kelleher has not retired. He is going to continue until 70, or later. Somehow, his appetite for growth has increased as he has grown older. He has charged you with developing plans for expanding into longer hauls, and maybe to South and Central America and even to Europe. Be as specific as you can in developing such expansion plans.

TEAM DEBATE EXERCISE

Debate the issue of whether Southwest should have expanded with a transcontinental strategy. Does this expansion pose serious dangers to a previously short-haul carrier?

INVITATION TO RESEARCH

What is the current situation with Southwest? What is its market share in the airline industry? Is it still maintaining a high growth rate? Has its stock continued to climb? How has the long-haul strategy worked out?

CHAPTER 17

GM's Saturn:
A New Auto Strategy

In many ways General Motors' Saturn subsidiary has been a sales and marketing success. It represents the first really effective effort by a U.S. automaker to emulate and even surpass Japanese cars, offering low prices, good looks, and surprising reliability. In addition, the Saturn has been the vanguard of enlightened customer service. Sales have exceeded expectations, as well as production capability, with customers waiting up to 2 months for their Saturns. In an advertising campaign in late 1992, Saturn pleaded with customers not to be discouraged and buy another brand—that a Saturn was worth the wait.

However, by early 1993, the Saturn was only a dubious success. Although the car was not expected to make money for several years after production started in November 1990, losses had been far higher than anticipated: more than $700 million in 1991.

How can any product possibly be considered a success with such a profit drain, despite the encouraging customer satisfaction and sales and the major challenge it presents to Japanese cars? Yet, potentially, Saturn could be the U.S. car industry's greatest success—if GM doesn't muff this window of opportunity.

PRELUDE

The beginnings of Saturn, its conception, go back to 1982. Originally, it represented an ambitious effort by General Motors to make small cars in the United States as cheaply and well as they could be made overseas. Roger

Smith, the CEO of GM at the time, called the $5 billion undertaking "the key to GM's long-term competitiveness."[1]

The project represented GM's attempt to rethink every aspect of auto making. It was hoped that production innovations could save $2,000 from the cost of building a subcompact car. Initial plans called for selling 400,000 units yearly.

So important was the project deemed to be in the total GM scheme of things that by 1985 Saturn had become a new GM subsidiary. A new factory was to be built from scratch, and in the search for a new site, bids flooded in from dozens of states. GM finally chose a site near Spring Hill, Tennessee.

Hardly had work begun on the new factory in early 1986 than some company goals began changing. As new models of low-price imports began coming in from Korea and Yugoslavia, GM executives abandoned the idea of being cost-competitive with these. Now they began targeting the car for the middle of the import pack, where prices were several thousand dollars higher. As a result the car had grown larger, now positioned between cars like the Chevy Cavalier and the company's midsize cars such as the Oldsmobile Ciera. And sales estimates were downsized. A "first-phase" plant was opened with a capacity for 250,000 cars, with a second factory to be added only if sales were strong enough.

By early 1987 pessimists were predicting that the Saturn was doomed. Although production was at least several years away, already demand seemed to be slackening for small cars, and GM was experiencing difficulty with high-tech factories. The more optimistic rumors were that GM might try to save face by folding the separate Saturn subsidiary into the Chevrolet or Pontiac division.

INTRODUCTION

As the 1980s were drawing to a close, GM's share of the U.S. passenger-car market slumped to 33 percent, a loss of 11 points in only 5 years. At the same time, Japanese carmakers had a 7-point gain in market share, to 26 percent. Consumer surveys were even bleaker: A study by J. D. Power & Associates found that 42 percent of all new-car shoppers would not even consider a GM car.[2] Now Saturn began to assume a position of greater importance to GM. Its new fundamental goal was to sell 80 percent of its cars to drivers who otherwise would not have bought a GM car.

---

[1] William J. Hampton, "Will Saturn Ever Leave the Launchpad?" *Business Week* (March 16, 1987): 107.

[2] James B. Treece, "Here Comes GM's Saturn," *Business Week* (April 9, 1990): 57.

Saturn's ascendancy on the eve of its production inauguration had the full support of GM chairman Roger Smith, although his term of office was soon to end. Smith saw the Saturn as having a bigger role than simply appealing to import buyers. He saw it as an example for the rest of GM as to how to reform its own ponderous and tradition-ridden culture. Indeed, Saturn had created an innovative blend of enlightened labor relations, participatory management, and new technology for the latest manufacturing operations. GM was especially interested in the manufacturing and labor breakthroughs that Saturn had initiated. Just as much so, but not to be recognized until a year or so later, was the great innovation in traditional passenger-car marketing and customer relations and servicing.

The company was now becoming so optimistic of Saturn's competitiveness that one marketing strategy under consideration was to have dealers place a Honda Civic, Toyota Corolla, and Accura Integra in the same showroom with a Saturn, and let customers make their own direct comparisons.

Admittedly, the final version of the Saturn was not the 60-mile-per-gallon, $6,000 subcompact as originally envisioned, but it was a gem nevertheless. Dealers were allowed to drive prototypes at GM's Mesa, Arizona proving grounds, and they were enthusiastic about the car's power train and handling: "We went 100 miles per hour, and it was still going strong," said a Saturn dealer from St. Louis. "It was going through curves at 75 to 80 that imports couldn't."[3] Another dealer who also sold Hondas remarked that Saturn, besides having the quickness and nimbleness of a Honda, "doesn't have the vibrations that the current domestic models have."[4]

The first Saturns were ready for sale in November 1990. In that first month, 641 were sold. Sales more than doubled by January 1992, to 1,520. And the rush was on, limited only by the production capabilities of the single factory. Table 17.1 shows the growth in units sold from the beginning through July 1992. Table 17.2 shows comparative figures of the sales and market share of Saturn to other GM units and also to major Japanese competitors and the total car market for 1991 and 1992. Saturn's surge was awesome.

AFTER TWO YEARS

As demand outstripped supply, dealers were staring at empty lots. In July 1992, Saturn dealers sold 22,305 cars—an average of 115 apiece, twice the rate per dealer for the nearest competitor, Toyota.[5] Foreign rivals continued to flood the market with new models, but Saturn was meeting them head on.

---

[3] Treece, "Here Comes GM's Saturn," 58.
[4] Treece, "Here Comes GM's Saturn," 58.
[5] David Woodruff, "Saturn," *Business Week* (August 17, 1992): 86.

Table 17.1   Selected Monthly Sales, Saturn, November 1990–July 1992

Month	Units	Percent Increase
November 1990	641	
January 1991	1,520	137.1%
March 1991	3,302	117.7
May 1991	6,832	106.9
July 1991	8,538	25.0
November 1991	8,355	(2.1)
January 1992	10,757	28.7
March 1992	16,757	55.8
May 1992	18,031	7.6
July 1992	22,305	23.7

Source: David Woodruff, "Saturn: GM Finally Has a Real Winner, But Success Is Bringing a Fresh Batch of Problems," *Business Week* (August 17, 1992): 86–87.
Commentary: Note the steady increase in monthly sales during this time period. Table 17.2 shows further statistics on Saturn's growth. A winner of major proportions for a U.S. automaker seemed to be emerging.

Table 17.2   Saturn Sales and Market Share Comparisons

	August		Year to Date	
	1991	1992	1991	1992
Retail Sales (units):				
Saturn	7,000	12,039	40,858	129,753
All GM Subcompacts	33,387	36,322	224,127	306,952
All Subcompacts	171,089	153,936	1,152,287	1,212,509
Total GM	221,547	198,172	2,012,599	1,992,835
Total Industry	690,442	644,808	5,601,704	5,584,494
Market Share:				
Saturn	1.0%	1.9%	0.7%	2.3%
All GM Subcompacts	4.8	5.6	4.0	5.5
Total Detroit Subcompacts	10.0	10.6	8.8	10.0
Total Toyota	5.0	4.3	4.0	4.2
Total Nissan	1.9	2.8	1.9	2.2
Total Honda	4.1	3.5	2.8	2.6
Total Japanese Nameplates	13.0	12.3	10.3	10.8
Total Subcompacts	24.8	23.9	20.6	21.7

Sources: Industry statistics.
Commentary: Note the substantial Saturn gains, both in sales and market share, from 1991 to 1992 against all other makes, domestic and foreign. Note in particular the market share gains against Japanese competitors: Toyota, Nissan, and Honda. The GM charge for Saturn to take away business from the Japanese imports appeared to be fully realized as 1992 drew to a close. And Saturn had yet to make a profit.

It had become the highest quality American-made brand, with as few defects as Hondas and Nissans. In customer satisfaction ratings, according to a survey by J. D. Power & Associates, buyers rated the Saturn ahead of all American-made cars and most imports. Only Lexus and Infiniti—much higher priced cars—were ranked higher. (See Table 17.3.)

The success of Saturn, however, was causing some problems at GM headquarters. To bring plant capacities in line with the demand, GM would have to pump in more money at a time when the auto giant was facing serious financial problems. In 1991 its North American operations had a devastating $7.5 billion loss. Every dollar spent on Saturn meant that struggling divisions such as Chevrolet, which badly needed to update its outmoded models, would receive less. And at a time when GM was closing assembly plants to the anguished consternation of union workers and local governments, the arena was politically not conducive for a still money-losing Saturn to receive funds to fully capitalize on its burgeoning customer demand.

A GM decision to delay any new investment would seriously jeopardize Saturn. At the end of July 1992, Saturn dealers had only a 10-day supply of cars on hand. This was one-sixth the normal stock. Dealers worried that customers would switch to competing brands because of unacceptable delays in servicing their orders, which could devastate Saturn's momentum and make it easy for the great GM bureaucracy to downplay an innovative but unprofitable new division.

Table 17.3   1992 Customer Satisfaction Ratings
(Score on J. D. Power's Survey of New-Car Buyers)

Lexus	179
Infiniti	167
Saturn	160
Acura	148
Mercedes-Benz	145
Toyota	140
Industry Average	129

Source: J. D. Power's Survey of New-Car Buyers, 1992, as reported by David Woodruff, "Saturn," *Business Week* (August 17, 1992): 86-87; and Raymond Serafin and Cleveland Horton, "Automakers Focus on Service," *Advertising Age* (July 6, 1992): 3, 33.

Commentary: Nissan's Infiniti and Toyota's Lexus have established new industry benchmarks for coddling luxury-car buyers. Into that elite group, Saturn has surprisingly placed a close third, by redefining the standard for treatment of buyers of lower-priced mass-volume cars. This high rating is credited to Saturn's elimination of price haggling, a high commitment to quality control, and the trailblazing example of replacing 1,800 cars after a coolant mix-up. Saturn's customer-satisfaction commitment is not lost on Chrysler: All Chrysler brands finished below industry averages, and Chrysler announced a $30 million massive training effort to improve the way its dealerships handle shoppers and owners.

Several options short of massive new plant investments were possible. GM chair Robert C. Stempel, who replaced Roger B. Smith, thought it possible to up the productivity at the single Spring Hill plant. Saturn President Richard G. LeFauve was rightly concerned about the dangers of pushing too hard for production at the expense of quality. During a visit by Stempel, after production goals had been increased along with the number of defects, line workers staged a slowdown, resulting in an easing of production goals. LeFauve saw a temporary solution in adding a third shift, which could boost capacity by 44 percent.[6]

Rather than add another plant, LeFauve proposed an additional $1 billion investment in Spring Hill, which would bring its capacity to 500,000 and enable the division to meet demand for new models. Increased production would permit expansion beyond the 195 original Saturn dealers so that all states could be covered.

Saturn executives worried how to keep their value-conscious buyers as the buyers grew older and wanted to upgrade to bigger cars with more comfort and features. Plans for larger cars and new models depended on further GM investment.

Stempel argued that present Saturn buyers should easily move up to existing GM brands that traditionally cater to older buyers, such as Oldsmobile, Buick, and Cadillac. Still, it was doubtful that Saturn buyers would readily fall into such a trade-up mode, given that most of them were former import buyers who would not have purchased a GM product other than a Saturn.

If GM top management could be convinced to expand Saturn, it was more likely that an older plant would be retooled, rather than a new one built from scratch, regardless of the technological advantages a new facility would offer. Rejuvenating an older plant would save several hundred million dollars and would be more palatable to unions and communities that had experienced the trauma of plant shutdowns. The following issue box discusses the decision problems in allocating scarce resources among competing claims.

The unique relations of Saturn with its auto workers will be described more fully in the next section. All workers were given a voice in management decisions, and 20 percent of their pay was linked to quality, productivity, and profitability. In late 1992, dissident union workers forced a vote on the teamwork-oriented labor contract that had been approved in November 1991 by a 72 percent margin. They claimed that this innovative contract ignored some seniority rights earned at other GM plants. On January 13, 1993, workers voted 2-to-1 to keep their teamwork-oriented labor

---

[6]Woodruff, "Saturn," 88.

ISSUE BOX

HOW SHOULD WE PARCEL OUT INVESTMENT FUNDS?

By mid-1992, the GM executive suite was facing a dilemma of mean consequences. Record multi-billion-dollar losses had strapped the company financially. Yet perhaps never before had the demands for additional investment been so compelling. Saturn, although yet to turn a profit, was a bright star that needed substantial additional production facilities to fully tap its potential. But other divisions, ones dating to the beginnings of GM, needed substantial expenditures to either keep them competitive, or to bring them back from the brink. Chevrolet in particular needed funds:

> This flagship division of GM two decades ago was selling one-fifth of all cars in the United States. Now its market share had fallen to only 12.1 percent. Accentuating the seriousness of Chevrolet's decline, it had long served as GM's entry-level division, the one whose customers often "graduated" to bigger, more expensive GM cars. Chevy dealers were convinced that the aging, hard-to-sell cars in their showrooms were the direct result of GM's generosity to Saturn.[7]

How should problems like this be resolved? Should the nascent star receive whatever it takes to fulfill its promise? Should scarce dollars be committed to resurrecting and sustaining deprived divisions? Should some sort of compromise be worked out, satisfying no one but creating the most equitable solution? Stake-holders in such allocation decisions are more than employees and managers; dealers, communities where plants are located, suppliers, even customers, have a stake.

How would you resolve this dilemma? Explain your rationale, and support it as persuasively as you can.

---

contract, with the vote "reflecting strong endorsement of the partnership between union and management, which works hand in hand with Saturn's mission, philosophy, and values."[8]

INGREDIENTS OF SUCCESS

A New Labor-Management Climate

A large part of Saturn's success has been an enlightened labor-management relationship, one unique among U.S. carmakers in its sharing of responsibility, although a similar approach has been used by Japanese firms.

[7]Kathleen Kerwin, "Meanwhile, Chevy Is Sulking in the Garage," *Business Week* (August 17, 1992): 90–91.

[8]"Saturn Workers Keep Contract," *Cleveland Plain Dealer* (January 15, 1993): E1.

At first the Saturn plant was conceived as a high-tech operation with robots and automated guided vehicles. But GM's experiences in a joint venture with Toyota Motor Corporation in Fremont, California, suggested that a change in labor-management relations could be more important for productivity and quality.

LeFauve, the president of the new subsidiary, was convinced that factory-floor workers could make a difference, and he led the way for GM management and the United Auto Workers (UAW) to work closely together almost from the beginning. Saturn employees and managers ate in the same cafeterias. Under a "team concept," workers were split into groups of six to 15 and headed by a supervisor chosen jointly by workers and managers. Each team was responsible for meeting its own training and production goals. Workers started at a base pay equal to about 90 percent of the average pay at GM and other major U.S. automaker plants. Then they earned bonuses if specific production levels and quality targets were met.

In 1988, Saturn managers began visiting GM plants and UAW halls in search of workers. Recruiters sought current and laid-off workers willing to shed old habits and work as a team. The choice was not easy for some: They would have to quit their union locals and give up all seniority rights. And there would be no going back. Those who accepted the challenge developed a cultlike commitment.

Training was rigorous. New arrivals faced five days of "awareness training" to teach them how to work in teams and build consensus. Beyond that, workers received 100 to 750 hours of training that even included learning to read a balance sheet, since Saturn opened its books internally and wanted employees to know how much their operations were adding to the cost of a car.

Integration of Production

In contrast to other GM assembly plants, Spring Hill went beyond the usual paint shop and body and assembly plant. Its highly integrated facility includes a power-train factory that casts, machines, and assembles engines and transmissions. A plastic-molding plant and a shop for assembling the instrument panel and dash into a single unit are also on site. Saturn consequently does not have to rely on key components supplied by factories hundreds of miles away, thus saving on freight costs and shipping delays. Still, some glitches could occur, and a minor delay could shut down the whole operation, but these delays have become increasingly rare.[9]

---

[9] Woodruff, "Saturn," 89.

Quality Control

From the beginning, Saturn sought to emphasize quality and freedom from defects. If it was ever to have a chance with its target customers, buyers of imports, this was essential. The customer satisfaction ratings (see Table 17.3) confirmed that Saturn had indeed achieved this objective. And while many buyers of imports were skeptical of any American car at first, the durability of Saturn's reputation for quality was converting more and more of them back to an American car.

Buyers' complaints had been quite limited, but Saturn strove to correct those received. Early on there were two recalls: one for defective seats and another for corrosive engine coolant. Some early complaints were of insufficient headroom and noisy, vibrating engines. The company addressed these complaints quickly, lowering rear seats half an inch below the initial design, redesigning engine mounts, and adding more insulation under the hood. However, the company's handling of the necessary recalls epitomized a unique approach to customer relations and to the commitment to quality. The following information box details an almost unbelievable innovation in the treatment of recalls.

Most often credited for the high quality ratings was the revolutionary labor agreement. This agreement made partners of Saturn's blue-collar and white-collar workers and gave everyone the authority to solve quality problems, from phoning suppliers for corrective action to rearranging machinery to improve quality and productivity. Motivation was spurred by bonuses for meeting specific production levels and quality targets.

Worker comfort was considered in design of the final assembly line, the theory being that less strain on workers translates into fewer mistakes. Consequently, the whole facility was air conditioned. The floor of the assembly line was wood instead of concrete—a first in North America—thus making standing all day less tiresome. And the line itself was designed with the worker in mind: Car bodies moved on pallets that could be raised or lowered for the worker's ease, and workers rode with the body they were working on rather than walking to keep up with the body, as on other assembly lines.

Dealer Strategy

While the success of Saturn left many dealers with insufficient cars to even come close to meeting demand, still dealers had to be pleased when their monthly sales of 115 apiece in July 1992 were twice the rate per dealer of their nearest competitor, Toyota. Saturn had been slow in opening new dealerships, especially with demand outstripping production capability. With only 195 dealers by late 1992, these were virtually assured of no close

---

INFORMATION BOX

RECALL MAGIC IN FOSTERING QUALITY CREDIBILITY

Only a few months after production commenced for the Saturn, the company was forced to send out 1,836 letters to customers, telling them that the car's radiator had been supplied with a faulty coolant and that the cars must be recalled. Such recalls are rather common in the industry, and car owners grudgingly put up with the inconvenience. But Saturn's recall was different. It offered to replace the cars, not just repair them. Consequently, regardless of odometer readings, each customer was supplied with a brand new Saturn, at no cost. One couple, unwilling to wait 3 weeks for Saturn to deliver a replica of their old car, chose a red model from the lot. It had a sunroof, unlike their old car, but they were given this $530 option for free. Saturn also paid for a rental car for the delay and even drove the couple to the rental company's lot.[10] Not surprising, Saturn's actions converted the recall into a major coup in customer relations and initiated the image—as no words alone could ever have—of an overwhelming commitment to quality and customer satisfaction.

In the process of handling the recall, Saturn broke other new ground. It publicly named Texaco as the supplier of the bad coolant. When Texaco learned that it would be identified in the Saturn recall, it rushed its explanation to customers: a freak accident, in which a special order of coolant contained too much sodium hydroxide, making it caustic and corrosive, especially for Saturn's aluminum engines. In light of the unfavorable publicity focused on the supplier, Texaco prepared to bear the costs associated with this mistake.

Thus, Saturn placed new responsibilities on its suppliers, that they provide parts meeting specifications without requiring Saturn inspectors to ensure quality. At risk was severe damage to a supplier's reputation.

Assess the pros and cons of such drastic handling of recalls in other situations and with other firms. On balance, can we as consumers expect such liberalization in any other recalls of the auto industry?

---

competition from other Saturn dealers. This strategy of maintaining fewer dealers flies in the face of traditional practice of having many dealerships in each market.

Initially most dealerships were on the east and west coasts, the heart of import demand. For example, in California's Santa Clara County, imports had more than 65 percent of the market. Many of the chosen dealers had also sold imports, because Saturn management believed they would know best how to appeal to such buyers.

[10]"Offers New Cars to Customers Whose Cars Were Recalled," *Business Week* (May 27, 1991): 38.

The decision to concentrate initially on the coasts left some states without any dealerships. It also left the populous Midwest undercovered. The Midwest was the heart of the "Buy American" sentiments, however, and the area where GM was already strongest. It was believed that aggressive Saturn efforts here could cannibalize sales from other GM makes instead of stealing sales from foreign automakers.

Advertising

The company turned to San Francisco's Hal Riney & Partners for folksy, offbeat advertising. The target customer was similar to a target Honda Civic buyer: median age, 33; 68 percent female; 52 percent married; 60 percent with college degrees; 46 percent holding managerial or professional jobs; and with median household income over $40,000.[11] Ads focused on buyers' lifestyles, playing up product themes that baby boomers could easily relate to, such as safety, utility, and value. The approach did much to create an image for Saturn as an unusual car company. The pricing practices further advanced this theme.

Innovation in Pricing and the Selling Process

Saturn initiated a new approach to pricing and the car-selling process that was a revolution in the auto industry. A variable price policy had long been traditional in this industry: A customer would attempt to drive the best bargain possible and in the process be in an adversarial contest with the car salesperson and his or her sales manager. Since the consumer lacked sufficient knowledge about costs and markups, and often was uncomfortable and inexperienced with haggling, many car buyers disliked having to negotiate and were never sure if they were getting a reasonable deal.

Saturn cars carried no rebates, and they were priced at a set bottom price, with no haggling or negotiating needed or accepted. In late 1992 prices started at $9,195, even after an average 8 percent hike for 1993 models. Customers loved the change in automobile retailing. And they knew they were not paying more than a neighbor for the same car.

Other automakers began to emulate Saturn. Ford started selling its subcompact Escort models at one low price. Chrysler was testing the concept. Even Japanese companies were closely watching the acceptance of the innovation. Somehow, GM appeared slow to embrace the one-price policy elsewhere in the organization.

---

[11] Larry Armstrong, "If It's Not Japanese, They Wouldn't Bother Kicking the Tires," *Business Week* (April 9, 1990): 61.

Ruling out haggling was only one part of the Saturn innovation in retailing. In formal courses in Spring Hill, managers and salespeople were instructed in low-pressure selling techniques. (The following box discusses the issue of high pressure versus soft sell.) The theme of the training was that pampering customers could create word-of-mouth advertising that

---

ISSUE BOX

HIGH PRESSURE VERSUS SOFT SELL: WHICH IS MORE EFFECTIVE?

We can recognize a wide range of selling techniques, ranging from a laissez-faire approach, which we sometimes encounter in retail stores with bored clerks almost having to be forced to ring up the purchase, to such high-pressure techniques that unethical and illegal practices result. The continuum below reflects this range.

High Pressure	Medium Pressure		No Pressure
deceptive tactics and false statements	strong selling efforts	soft sell	laissez-faire

What degree of pressure or lack of pressure is the most effective? To a considerable extent this depends on the audience of the sales presentation. If the prospect is a sophisticated and professional purchasing agent or buyer, obvious efforts to high pressure would be anathema. On the other hand, effective selling requires some pressure, even though this may be kept very subtle: the salesperson should be persuasive and at least ask for the order and encourage the prospect to make a decision. With a naive consumer, high pressure can be very effective, and there is the temptation to misuse it. Selling practices in the ghetto have often involved high pressure and dishonest tactics. With educated and sophisticated consumers, it is doubtful that strong high pressure makes for very effective selling.

Mayer and Greenberg, after seven years of field research, concluded that ego drive and empathy were the key ingredients in the most effective selling.[12] Ego drive makes the salesperson want and need to make the sale—it becomes a conquest and a powerful means of enhancing the ego. But empathy—the ability to feel as the other person does—must complement this. Otherwise, the salesperson will tend to bulldoze the way through to close a sale and thereby drive off many prospects. So we can conclude that some middle ground between no pressure and high pressure is best for most selling situations and with most prospects.

As a customer, have you experienced high pressure? What was your reaction? What conclusions can you draw about the effectiveness of high pressure?

---

[12] David Mayer and Herbert M. Greenberg, "What Makes a Good Salesman," *Harvard Business Review* (July-August 1964): 119–25.

would be particularly effective in such high-priced and even traumatic purchases as cars.

Combining a good product and top-notch service was bound to lead to happy Saturn customers. But good customer relations went even further. Both dealerships and Saturn headquarters followed up with customers to ascertain their satisfaction. Such follow-up even went so far as special Saturn newsletters, Saturn clubs, and famous homecoming weekends in Spring Hill, Tennessee. In spring 1995, 44,000 people were drawn to this small town and its Saturn plant for such a "homecoming" and tour of the plant, which included meeting many of the people involved with making their Saturns.

GM'S DILEMMA

Saturn's apparent success was not a particular cause for rejoicing at corporate headquarters in late 1992. Undoubtedly it would have been if the new venture were proving profitable, but several years and billions of dollars of new investment were expected to be necessary before Saturn turned the corner. Meanwhile, General Motors faced a serious cash crunch, all the more serious after a $7.5 billion loss from North American operations in 1991. At issue was how limited investment dollars should be allocated. (Refer back to the box on page 256 for more discussion of this management dilemma.)

Once former chair Roger B. Smith, who conceived the Saturn project as a laboratory in which to reinvent his company, retired from GM, the firm's commitment may have cooled. Saturn has initiated some notable innovations in American carmaking, including labor relations changes such as intensive training programs, rewards for high customer satisfaction ratings, and joint responsibility with management. Its no-dicker, one-price policy was being emulated by other carmakers, but not by GM elsewhere in its organization. Its commitment to customer satisfaction became an actuality and not merely talk. And most of all, Saturn achieved—whether permanently or temporarily—quality levels deemed impossible by U.S. firms still bedeviled by defects and by an uncomplimentary image compared with foreign imports. So Saturn had much to offer its parent. It remains to be seen whether the ponderous-moving behemoth with its host of entrenched interests will be able to embrace enough of the Saturn innovations for a significant turnaround. It also remains to be seen at the time of this writing whether a myopic devotion to profits might doom the Saturn as a great experiment that failed.

POSTSCRIPT

Saturn announced on June 17, 1994, that its operations would be profitable for the year. U.S. sales were expected to reach 270,000 units, up from just under 230,000 the year before. Donald Hudler, then head of Saturn sales and marketing, estimated eventual sales of about 500,000 cars a year, with about 100,000 coming from overseas. To achieve this would require substantial investment in production and engineering as well as additional dealers.

Some analysts were skeptical of such projections without major product redesign: the basic sedan, for example, had not changed appreciably since first introduced in 1990. But Saturn's small size and money-losing history hardly gave it the resources to finance significant model changes without major additional investment by GM. Saturn also faced increasing competition, even from GM with its new Chevrolet Cavalier.

Still, Saturn had the great customer appeal of superior dealer service and rigorous quality control; it continued to have the highest customer satisfaction ratings of any U.S. cars. But could it maintain such standards?

In 1995 it launched a new 1996 sedan, and did so with minimal product-line losses for the changeover. In early July 1996, Saturn launched a new 1997 coupe, and did so with no interruption at all to plant output, this being the U.S. auto industry's best launch of all. Indicative of what an accomplishment this was, in 1995 it took Chrysler 75 days to reach full production line speed, and Ford 50 days. GM's new vans still had not achieved full line speed after six months.[13]

In its sixth year of sales, 1996, Saturn was the second bestselling retail car in the U.S., behind only Honda Accord. It had a 60 percent customer loyalty rating—meaning that 60 percent of its car buyers bought their next car from Saturn, too. And it still routinely outperformed all other manufacturers except the many times more expensive Lexus and Infiniti on the J.D. Power & Associates Customer Satisfaction Index.[14]

Saturn began introducing its innovative marketing to used cars. For used Saturns as well as other "extensively checked-out makes," it offered limited warranties, a 30-day/1,500 miles trade-in policy, as well as a 3-day money-back guarantee. And a hassle-free, high-pressure–free selling environment.

In September 1996, Don Hudler, now president of Saturn Corporation, sent a letter to "Dear Members of the Saturn Family." In it he announced a new midsize car in the works. It would be built in another plant at Wilmington, Delaware, would be designed and engineered by many of the original Saturn team, would have a totally unique design but with all the Saturn "cues you have come to expect—body construction, driving character, and features—in a new size and shape." It "will help extend the Saturn culture and philosophy to other parts of the nation."[15] What was perhaps most noteworthy was that the announced launch date was several years in the future. Presumption, or the kind of family atmosphere Saturn owners have come to cherish?

[13] Jim Harbour, "Another First At Saturn," *Automotive Industries* (August 1996): 17.

[14] "Masters of Marketing," *Builder* (September 1996): 82.

[15] Per letter from Don Hudler to "Dear Members of the Saturn Family," September 1996.

WHAT CAN BE LEARNED?

A good reputation lingers, but it must be zealously safeguarded. Saturn gained a notable reputation for quality, unique among U.S. cars and one of the best among all cars. Such a reputation for being defect-free was an invaluable asset, both in keeping present customers who were likely to rebuy a Saturn (provided that appealing new models were forthcoming) and in attracting new customers by word-of-mouth publicity.

However, one of the ironies of a good reputation or public image is that it can quickly be destroyed. In the case of Saturn, if the company lapses a bit on its quality control—especially in pursuit of the profit demands of the parent—then the good reputation will be jeopardized. Then Saturn will reside with the other U.S. cars: just another domestic car unable to compete with the imports in workmanship and quality.

In large firms, politics and profit potential are not always compatible, perhaps to the detriment of the firm. Saturn, with its untapped and growing consumer demand, would seem worthy of substantial additional investment by GM. This may not fully come to pass, and corporate pressures may intensify to do more with less. GM now finds itself with limited financial resources and consequent allocation problems. Long entrenched divisions such as Chevrolet and Oldsmobile are competing with Saturn for needed funds. This intrafirm rivalry has not escaped the attention of the national business press, as noted in the information box on page 256.

In the presence of long-established corporate power relations, Saturn, the upstart, may find itself thwarted by internal jealousies and entrenched interests.

Is there a moral here? Perhaps it is that huge organizations have profound difficulty in breaking from their traditional patterns (might we even call these ruts?). For some it may be impossible; for others, great adversity may sweep a new climate of change into a moribund organization.

Imitation is not a dirty word. Many organizations shun imitation; nothing else will do but to be innovators. Executive pride is often at stake. *Innovation* suggests leadership; *imitation* denotes a follower.

However, imitation has much to recommend it. Successful practices deserve to be imitated. Adopting such practices lessens risks from striking out on your own and often can hasten profitability.

Saturn represented innovation with General Motors. But most of the Saturn ideas were borrowed liberally from Japan. For example, just-in-time parts shipments were holding manufacturing costs down, but not without some danger of slowing the assembly line. Saturn workers were trying to eliminate bottlenecks and reduce costs, just as workers do at factories run by

Toyota and Honda. Likewise, management and union relations were Japanese in style. The result became a commitment to quality unique among U.S. carmakers but imitative of Japanese imports.

Customer service is so much more than lip service. To most firms an expressed commitment to customer service falls in the same realm as apple pie, motherhood, and the flag—that is, it conveys a pious statement that no one could disagree with. But a solid commitment to customer service, as in the Saturn example, has immediate short-term profit consequences. To pamper customers, especially to the extraordinary extent of replacing the product—in the case of Saturn, another new car—smacks of an unbelievable disavowal of profits. If defective products are out of control, such a practice can become an albatross. But the publicity of correcting company or supplier faults by going far beyond the expected or reasonable can pay dividends. It gives concrete evidence of the wholehearted commitment of the firm to providing defect-free products, thus often garnering publicity that millions of dollars of advertising never could. It makes a major statement to employees and suppliers alike that deviations from quality standards cannot be tolerated. It shows that the company is willing to sacrifice its profitability in the quest for absolute quality standards. Nothing else could engender such a spirit of pride and responsibility.

When possible, build a cadre or family of supporters. This is difficult, and even impossible, to do for many products. Yet, perhaps it is more possible than many firms realize. Several things are necessary for such to be accomplished. First, the product or brand must be conspicuous, easily identified to all. A Samuel Adams beer, a Harley, and a Saturn certainly fit this requirement. Then the firm must involve its supporters into a very closely knit group. Harley Davidson and Saturn have certainly carried this concept to the furthest with clubs, outings, and communications—for example, the homecoming weekends at Spring Hill that bring in tens of thousands of Saturn owners. The power of such family identification brought a phenomenal 60 percent retention rate of repeat buyers for Saturn, with many of those who did not repeat only doing so because there was no adequate trade-up model, a deficiency that will be addressed in a few more years. This building of a family identification is a great challenge. But it offers wonderful rewards for those few innovative and committed enough to see it for their customers.

CONSIDER

What additional learning insights do you see as emerging from the Saturn case?

QUESTIONS

1. Do you see GM management facing any problems if it tries to transplant the Saturn concepts to other divisions?
2. Do you fault top management for pressuring Saturn to turn a profit at this critical juncture of its growth? Why or why not?
3. What problems do you see for Saturn in maintaining its quality and customer relations? Is it likely that these can be resolved?
4. Evaluate the Saturn policy of relatively few dealers, each having a wide sales territory. What pros and cons do you see?
5. How do you personally feel about the haggling that is involved in most car purchases? Do you prefer a one-price policy?
6. "Saturn is experimenting with a 'pie in the sky' marketing strategy. It is an abdication of reality." Evaluate this statement.
7. Do you know any persons who own Saturns? If so, what are their attitudes toward the car? Any complaints? Would they recommend Saturns to others?
8. You probably have seen some of the Saturn commercials. Unlike other automobile ads, they rarely discuss the car itself and its features. Do you think this is effective advertising? Why or why not?

HANDS-ON EXERCISES

1. You are a staff assistant to GM CEO Roger Smith in the early 1980s. He has asked you to give a briefing to the executive committee on whether Saturn should be set up as a separate division or should be made part of Chevrolet. Prepare the briefing, listing as many pros and cons as you can for such a separate division, how you evaluate their importance, and finally, what your recommendation would be.
2. You are one of the biggest and most successful Chevy dealers, but now you are incensed at the investment dollars given Saturn at the expense of Chevrolet. What do you do? How effective do you think this action will be?

TEAM DEBATE EXERCISE

It is early 1995. Despite Saturn's first venture into profitability in 1994, GM corporate management is considering whether to draw in Saturn's autonomy and bring it more under the corporate umbrella. This would mean building larger-size Saturns at other GM factories, using more standardized GM parts, and in general giving Saturn management less control over styles and pricing and forced into more conformity. Debate the issue of continued autonomy versus creeping uniformity.

INVITATION TO RESEARCH

What is the present situation of Saturn, with regard to production and sales, consumer attitudes regarding satisfaction and quality, the labor force, and profitability? Does the make still appear to have a faithful cadre?

PART V

QUESTION MARKS

CHAPTER 18

McDonald's: Could There Be Storm Clouds on the Horizon?

Few business firms anywhere in the world can match the sustained growth of McDonald's. Initially, it grew with one simple product—a hamburger— and although McDonald's today has broadened its product mix somewhat, it still remains uniquely undiversified.

Now, some skeptics are wondering about McDonald's. Is it nearing the end of its phenomenal growth? Are there chinks in its armor that were not there before, and are these likely to widen?

THE MCDONALD'S GROWTH MACHINE

In its *1995 Annual Report*, McDonald's management was justifiably proud. Sales and profits had continued the long trend upward, and even seemed to be accelerating. (See Table 18.1.) Far from reaching a saturation point, the firm was opening more restaurants than ever, some 2,400 around the world in 1995, up from 1,800 the year before. "We plan to add between 2,500 and 3,200 restaurants in both 1996 and 1997, with about two-thirds outside of the U.S. In other words, we opened more than six restaurants per day in 1995; over the next two years, we plan to open eight a day."[1] And, "Our growth opportunities remain significant: on any given day, 99 percent of the world's population does not eat at McDonald's . . . yet."[2]

Company management extolled the power of the McDonald's brand overseas, and how on opening days lines were sometimes "miles" long.

[1] *McDonald's 1995 Annual Report*, 8.
[2] *McDonald's 1995 Annual Report*, 7.

Table 18.1   Growth in Sales and Profits, 1985–1995

	Sales (millions)	Percent Gain	Income (millions)	Percent Gain
1985	$11,011		$ 433	
1986	12,432	12.9%	480	12.2%
1987	14,330	15.3	549	14.4
1988	16,064	12.1	646	17.7
1989	17,333	7.9	727	12.5
1990	18,759	8.2	802	10.3
1991	19,928	6.2	860	7.2
1992	21,885	9.8	959	11.5
1993	23,587	7.8	1,083	12.9
1994	25,987	10.2	1,224	13.0
1995	29,914	15.1	1,427	16.6

Source: McDonald's 1995 Annual Report
Commentary: Of particular interest is how the new expansion policies have brought a burst of revenues and profits in the mid-1990s. How audacious we are to even question these growth policies. But we have.

"Often our challenge is to keep up with demand. In China, for example, there are only 62 McDonald's to serve a population of 1.2 billion."[3] By the end of 1995, the company had 7,012 outlets in 89 countries of the world, with Japan alone having 1,482. Table 18.2 shows the top ten countries in number of McDonald's units.

Sometimes in marketing its products in different cultures, some adjustments have to be made. The following box describes the changes McDonald's made for its first store in India, which opened October 13, 1996.

Table 18.2   Top Ten Foreign Markets in Number of Units at year end, 1995

Japan	1,482 restaurants
Canada	902
Germany	649
England	577
Australia	530
France	429
Brazil	243
Mexico	132
Netherlands	128
Taiwan	111

Source: McDonald's 1995 Annual Report
Commentary: Is the popularity in Japan a surprise?

[3] *McDonald's 1995 Annual Report,* 7.

INFORMATION BOX

McMUTTON BURGERS FOR INDIA

No all-beef patties are to be found in McDonald's packed restaurant in Delhi, India. Ground lamb has been substituted in the "Maharaja Mac" and other 100 percent pure mutton burgers in deference to the Hindu majority's reverence for the cow. The first no-beef McDonald's in the world also serves no pork, since this would offend India's Muslim minority.

Vegetarians can choose between veggie burgers and "Vegetable McNuggets," all cooked by a separate staff who do not handle meat products, conforming to another taboo. Such "Indianizing" has brought heavy crowds—from families to turbaned Sikhs to young Western wannabes—to jam the three-floor restaurant. Yet, there are militant critics: "I am against McDonald's because they are the chief killers of cows in the world," said Maneka Gandhi, an animal-rights activist and daughter-in-law of assassinated prime minister Indira Gandhi. "We don't need cow killers in India."[4] But most customers were not concerned about this, and said their only complaint was that the burgers were too small and bland for hearty, spice-loving Indian palates.

A second McDonald's opened in Bombay a week after the Delhi opening. It drew more than 12,000 customers on its first day.

Should the militant activists become more violent about McDonald's "conducting a global conspiracy against cattle," do you think McDonald's should abandon the India market? Why or why not?

Growth Prospects in the U.S.

With 11,368 of its restaurants in the U.S., isn't McDonald's rapidly reaching a point of saturation in its domestic market, if not overseas? Top management vehemently disputes this conclusion. Rather, it offers a startling statistical phenomenon to support accelerating expansion. Called Greenberg's law, after newly appointed McDonald's U.S. chairman Jack Greenberg, it maintains that the more stores McDonald's puts in a city, the more per capita transactions will result. Thus, with two stores in a city there might be 16 transactions per capita per year. Add two or four more stores and the transactions will not only double, or quadruple, but may even do better than that. The hypothesized explanation for this amazing phenomenon seemingly rests on two factors: convenience and market share. With more outlets, McDonald's increases its convenience to consumers, and adds to its market share at the expense of competitors. Hence, the justification for the expansion binge.

[4]"Delhi Delights in McMutton Burgers," *Cleveland Plain Dealer* (November 6, 1996): 3D.

In the quest for this domestic expansion, the company over the last five years had been able to reduce the cost of building a new U.S. traditional restaurant by 26 percent through standardizing building materials and equipment and global sourcing, as well as improving construction methods and building designs. But it had also found abundant market opportunities in satellite restaurants. These were smaller, had lower sales volume, and served simplified menus. This format proved cost efficient in such nontraditional places as zoos, hospitals, airports, museums, and military bases as well as in retail stores such as Wal-Mart, The Home Depot, and some other major stores. For example, such satellite restaurants were in some 800 Wal-Mart stores by the end of 1995, with more planned. In October 1996, a McDonald's Express opened in a 1,200-square-foot space in an office building in Lansing, Michigan, perhaps a harbinger of more such sites to come.

In its eager search for ever more outlets, McDonald's did something it had never done before. It took over stores from weak competitors. In late summer 1996 it bought 184 company-owned Roy Rogers outlets. "Here was an opportunity that was maybe once in a lifetime," Greenberg stated.[5] Earlier the same year, it acquired Burghy's, an 80-store fast-food chain in Italy. And in New Zealand, it added 17 restaurants from the Georgie Pie chain.

The new stores being opened were seldom like the old ones. The popularity of drive-thru windows generated 55 percent of U.S. sales, and in the process fewer seats were needed inside. This left more space available for gas stations or for indoor playgrounds—Ronald's Playplaces—to attract families. McDonald's made joint ventures with Chevron and Amoco to co-develop properties. And it signed an exclusive marketing deal with Disney for promoting each other's brands.

McDonald's had always been a big spender for advertising, and this has been effective. Even back in the 1970s, a survey of school children found 96 percent identifying Ronald McDonald, ranking him second only to Santa Claus.[6] In 1995, advertising and promotional expenditures totaled approximately $1.8 billion, or 6 percent of sales.[7]

Factors in the Invincibility of McDonald's

Through the third quarter of 1996, McDonald's could proudly claim 126 consecutive quarters of record earnings. Since its earliest days, the ingredients of success were simple, but few competitors were able to effectively emulate them. The basic aspects were:

---

[5]Gary Samuels, "Golden Arches Galore," *Forbes* (November 4, 1996): 48.
[6]"The Burger That Conquered the Country," *Time* (September 17, 1973): 84–92.
[7]*McDonald's 1995 Annual Report*, 9.

- A brief menu, but having consistent quality over thousands of outlets.
- Strictly enforced and rigorous operational standards controlling service, cleanliness, and all other aspects of the operation.
- Friendly employees, despite a high turnover of personnel because of the monotony of automated food handling.
- Heavy mass media advertising directed mostly at families and children.
- Identification of a fertile target market—the family—and directing the marketing strategy to satisfying it with product, price, promotional efforts, and site locations (at least in the early years, the suburban locations with their high density of families).

However, by the end of 1996, international operations were the real vehicle of growth, providing 47 percent of the company's $30 billion sales and 54 percent of profits. Of no small concern, the domestic operation had not blossomed accordingly.

STORM CLOUDS FOR THE DOMESTIC OPERATION?

Souring Franchisee Relations

In the market-share game, in which McDonald's is leading the way among all its competitors, corporate management concluded that the firm with the most outlets in a given community wins. But as McDonald's unprecedented expansion continued, many franchisees were skeptical of headquarters' claim that no one loses when the company opens more outlets in a community, since market share rises proportionately. Still, the franchise holder had to wonder how much his sales would diminish when another McDonald's opened down the street.

The 7,000-member American Franchisee Association, an organization formed to look after franchisees' rights, claimed that McDonald's operators were joining in record numbers.[8] Other franchisees formed a clandestine group called the Consortium, representing dissidents who felt present management was unresponsive to their concerns. They remembered a kinder and gentler company. See the following box for contrasting franchisee views on the high-growth market share policy.

Other concerns of franchisees were a new set of business practices developed by corporate headquarters, known as Franchising 2000. The company claimed it instituted this as a way to improve standards for quality, service, cleanliness, and value by giving franchisees better "tools." But some

---

[8]Richard Gibson, "Some Franchisees Say Moves by McDonald's Hurt their Operations," *The Wall Street Journal* (April 17, 1996): A1 and A8.

INFORMATION BOX

THE CONTENTMENT OF TWO MCDONALD'S FRANCHISEES

In 1980, Wayne Kilburn and his wife, Mary Jane, took over the only McDonald's in Ridgecrest, California, a town of 26,000. The Kilburns prospered in the years to come. Then McDonald's instituted its "market-share plan" for Ridgecrest. Late in 1995 it put a company-owned restaurant inside the Wal-Mart. A few months later it built another outlet inside the China Lake Naval Weapons Center. A third new company-owned store went up just outside the naval base. "Basically, they killed me," *Forbes* reports Kilburn saying. And he claimed his volume dropped 30 percent.[9]

In its *1995 Annual Report,* corporate headquarters offers another view concerning franchisee contentment. Tom Wolf is a McDonald's franchisee with 15 restaurants in the Huntington, West Virginia, and Ashland, Kentucky, markets. He opened his first McDonald's in 1974, had eight by the end of 1993, and opened seven more in the last two years, including two McDonald's in Wal-Mart stores and another in an alliance with an oil company; in addition he added indoor Playplaces to two existing restaurants.

Has all this investment in growth made a difference? The *Annual Report* quotes Tom: "I wouldn't change a thing. Sales are up. I'm serving more customers, my market share is up and I'm confident about the future. Customers say that the Playplaces and Wal-Mart units are 'a great idea.' The business is out there. We've got to take these opportunities now, or leave them for someone else to take."[10]

"The high growth, market share policy should not bother any franchisee. It simply creates opportunities to invest in more restaurants." Evaluate this statement.

---

saw this as a blatant attempt to gain more power over the franchised operations. One provision revived a controversial A, B, C, and F grading system, with only franchisees that receive As and Bs eligible for more restaurants. Furthermore, McDonald's began using Franchising 2000 to enforce a single pricing strategy throughout the chain, so that a Big Mac, for example, would cost the same everywhere. The corporation maintained that such uniformity was necessary for the discounting needed to build market share. Those not complying risked losing their franchise.

Franchise relations should not be a matter of small concern to McDonald's. Table 18.3 shows the ratio of franchised restaurants to total restaurants both in the U.S. and outside the U.S. As can be seen, franchises constitute by far the largest proportion of restaurants.

[9]Samuels, "Golden Arches Galore," 48.
[10]*McDonald's 1995 Annual Report,* 32.

Table 18.3 Percent of Franchised to Total Traditional Restaurants, Selected Years, 1985–1995

	1985	1988	1992	1995
Traditional restaurants				
Total	8,901	10,513	13,093	16,809
Operated by franchisees	6,150	7,110	9,237	11,240
Percent franchised to total	69.1%	67.6%	70.5%	66.9%

Source: Calculated from McDonald's 1995 Annual Report
Commentary: While by 1995, the ratio of franchised to total restaurants had dropped slightly, still more than two-thirds are operated by franchisees. Perhaps this suggests that franchisee concerns ought to receive more consideration by corporate headquarters.

Menu Problems

Since 1993, domestic per-store sales slumped from a positive 4 percent to a negative 3 percent by the third quarter of 1996, this being the fifth quarter in a row of negative sales gains. In part this decline was thought attributable to older customers drifting away: "Huge numbers of baby-boomers . . . want less of the cheap, fattening foods at places like McDonald's. As soon as their kids are old enough, they go elsewhere."[11]

In an attempt to garner more business from this customer segment, McDonald's with a $200 million promotional blitz launched its first "grownup taste" sandwich, the Arch Deluxe line of beef, fish, and chicken burgers. It forecast that this would become a $1 billion brand in only its first year. But before long, some were calling this a McFlop. In September 1996, Edward Rensi, head of U.S. operations, tried to minimize the stake in the new sandwich, and sent a memo to 2,700 concerned franchisees, "The Arch Deluxe was never intended to be a silver bullet."[12] On October 8, Rensi was replaced by Jack Greenberg.

McDonald's domestic troubles were not entirely new. As far back as the late 1980s, competitors, including Pizza Hut and Taco Bell, were nibbling at McDonald's market share, and Burger King was more than holding its own. Even the great traditional strength of McDonald's of unsurpassed controlled standards over food, service, and cleanliness seemed to be waning: A 1995 Restaurants and Institutions Choice in Chains survey of 2,849 adults gave McDonald's low marks on food quality, value, service, and cleanliness. Top honors instead went to Wendy's.[13]

In 1991, McDonald's reluctantly tried discounting, with "Extra Value Meals," largely to keep up with Taco Bell's value pricing. But by 1995, price

[11] Shelly Branch, "McDonald's Strikes Out With Grownups," Fortune (November 11, 1996): 158.
[12] Ibid.
[13] Ibid.

promotions were no longer attracting customers, and per-store sales began slumping. The new, adult-oriented Deluxe line was not only aimed at older adults, but with its price 20 percent more than regular items, the hope was to parry the discounting.

The company had had previous problems in expanding its line. The McDLT was notably unsuccessful despite heavy promotion. And more recently, the low-fat McLean, an effort to attract weight-conscious adults, was a complete disaster. In fact this beef and seaweed concoction sold so badly that some operators kept only a few frozen patties on hand, while others, as revealed in an embarrassing TV exposé, sold fully fatted burgers in McLean boxes to the few customers asking for them.

Some years before, the company had tried but failed to develop an acceptable pizza product. It also was unable to create a dinner menu that would attract evening-hour traffic. Two other experiments were also abandoned: a 1950s-style cafe and a family-type concept called Hearth Express that served chicken, ham, and meatloaf.

ANALYSIS

Despite the many years of uninterrupted growth in sales and profits, and in number of stores opened, we have placed McDonald's in this "Question Mark" category. The company may be approaching a crossroads in which the enduring growth trend could be endangered. In the stock market frenzy of 1996, perhaps the stock market was anticipating this. In an investor climate that loved growth companies, McDonald's share price languished, almost as if it belonged to a mediocre public utility.

The international market still offered tremendous growth possibilities, despite the more than 8,000 outlets McDonald's already had. But domestically things were not going as well, even though operating statistics looked better than ever. Most of the gains in revenues and income reflected a sharp increase in number of new stores. For example, in 1996 McDonald's opened 2,500 new stores, and that was four times the number of stores opened just four years before. Same-store sales dropped 2.5 percent on average from 1994 to 1995 for U.S. restaurants—all this despite vigorous discounting and promotional efforts.

Relations with franchisees, formerly the best in the industry, deteriorated as corporate management pursued policies more dictatorial and selfish than ever before, and signalled the end of the kinder and gentler company that franchisees remembered.

In particular, the new policy of major expansion in the quest for increased market share without regard to how this would affect established franchisees portended worsening relations with franchisees, and the start of an adversarial instead of cooperative climate.

Of course, the cost/benefit consequences of an aggressive expansion policy might seemingly be in the company's best interest, especially with the greater cost efficiencies of recent development. If total market share can be substantially increased, even if same-store sales go down, the accounting analyses may support a more-and-more-stores policy. But the effect on individual franchisees could be negative indeed. How much is the franchisee to be considered in this aggressive new strategy of McDonald's outlets competing not so much with Wendy's, Burger King, and Taco Bell, as with other McDonald's outlets?

A major domestic challenge for a growth-oriented McDonald's perhaps should have been the menu: how to appeal to adults and expand the market potential. While corporate executives concluded that the best way to continue growth was to open ever more restaurants in the quest for greater total market share, another growth alternative would be to rejuvenate or diversify the menu offerings and thus appeal to more than families and children. But McDonald's had not been able to do this in the past, except for introducing the breakfast menu many years ago.

What direction could such menu changes involve? In view of past failures, we have little confidence in predicting or recommending. Yet, McDonald's, as well as any chain organization whether fast food or otherwise, can test different prices and strategies—or in McDonald's case, different menus and different atmospheres—in just a few outlets and expand further only if results are favorable.

To summarize, is McDonald's in jeopardy? And the answer is a resounding No. Is it likely to continue its great growth in sales and profits into the foreseeable future? Here, some are beginning to have doubts. If the market share strategy proves problematic over the coming years, and without success in widening the appeal of domestic restaurants, the main engine of growth in future years would be the international operation. Table 18.4 shows the trend in number of restaurants outside the U.S. with those in the U.S. for selected years since 1985. Table 18.5 compares sales and operating income for U.S. and outside U.S. operations since 1991. Note in particular that income from outside the U.S. surpassed domestic by 1995.

Table 18.4 Percent of Non-U.S. to Total Traditional Restaurants, Selected Years, 1985–1995

	1985	1988	1992	1995
Traditional restaurants				
Total U.S. and non-U.S.	8,901	10,513	13,093	16,809
Non-U.S.	1,929	2,606	4,134	6,468
Percent of Total	28.3%	24.8%	31.6%	38.5%

Source: Computed from *McDonald's 1995 Annual Report*
Commentary: Here we can see the increasing importance of non-U.S. operations in the decade of the 1990s.

Table 18.5   Comparison of U.S. and Non-U.S. Revenue and Income, 1991–1995

	1991	1992	1993	1994	1995
Systemwide sales (billions of dollars)	$19.9	21.9	23.6	26.0	29.9
U.S.	$12.5	13.2	14.2	14.9	15.9
Non-U.S.	7.4	8.6	9.4	11.0	14.0
Operating income (billions of dollars)	1.7	1.9	2.0	2.2	2.6
U.S.	1.0	1.1	1.1	1.1	1.2
Non-U.S.	0.7	0.8	0.9	1.1	1.4

Source: Compiled from *McDonald's 1995 Annual Report*
Commentary: The growing importance of non-U.S. operations to McDonald's total sales and income is readily apparent.

Still, the U.S. is a huge market, and no growth-minded firm would want to see its luster tarnished here. Whether thousands of new restaurants in the coming years, without some diversification in menus and motifs, will fuel the growth needed to continue the trend may be questioned. After all, how many military bases, hospitals, museums, zoos, and the like remain untapped? As to outlets in major retail stores, is there likely to be a limit to the potential here?

LATEST INFO

As 1996 drew to a close, spurred by its own customer surveys that found McDonald's lagging behind both Wendy's and Burger King in taste, corporate executives were scrambling to put more flavor in their burgers and trying to implement these changes for the capstone month of December. In the crash program, the company was even forgoing its traditional lengthy testing that had always accompanied proposed product changes.

Perhaps this reflected the importance of December's sales to a heretofore disappointing year. While McDonald's did not release same-store sales figures, analysts believed these had been flat or down for most of the year. The new "Deluxe" line of sandwiches was still getting only mixed reviews. One securities analyst told his clients, "Relative to what Wendy's and Burger King offer consumers, Arch Deluxe and its kin are magnificently mediocre."[14]

By spring 1997, McDonald's domestic fortunes temporarily improved. On April 11, in a coup of a promotion, stores began giving away miniature versions of the hottest toy in the country, Beanie Babies, with the purchase of a child's $1.99 Happy Meal. Demand became so great that most outlets could not keep them in stock; some people bought Happy Meals and threw out the food just to collect the Beanie Babies. Customers drove great distances to find

[14]Richard Gibson, "Can New Spices Warm Up Sales at McDonald's?" *The Wall Street Journal* (December 23, 1996): B1 and B2.

any restaurant that still had some. While such shortages might disappoint, they hardly surprised customers who had experienced even more difficulty finding the regular-sized stuffed toys. McDonald's executives gloated: "By our guesstimates, conservatively, one in every three Americans will have a Teenie Beanie Baby in their house by mid-May."[15]

The short-term phenomenon of Teenie Beanie Babies did not end McDonald's domestic problems, however. In one of the most dramatic price cuts in the history of the fast-food industry, the price of the Big Mac, McDonald's flagship hamburger, was reduced from about $1.99 to 55 cents when customers also bought french fries and a soft drink. (The 55 cents price was chosen as a throwback to 1955, the year McDonald's was founded.) Some franchisees were shocked, and quietly raised the prices of fries and soft drinks.

In the *1996 Annual Report*, mailed to shareholders in April 1997, the company said that 1997 "will be a year of transition" for U.S. business, and that it would add fewer restaurants than in 1996. It disclosed that average annual sales of U.S. restaurants open for more than a year declined 6.4 percent. Growth was even faltering in international operations with 1996 sales and profits in most countries having increased substantially less than the year before.[16]

WHAT CAN BE LEARNED?

It is possible to have strong and enduring growth without diversification. For more than four decades, since 1955, McDonald's has grown continuously and substantially. In all this time, the product was essentially the hamburger in its various trappings and accompaniments. Almost all other firms in their quest for growth have diversified, sometimes wisely and synergistically, and other times imprudently and even recklessly. McDonald's has remained undeviatingly focused.

With such a commitment, the product should be something with universal appeal, frequently consumed, and having almost unlimited potential. The hamburger probably meets these criteria better than practically any other product, along with beer, soft drinks, and tobacco. Soft drinks, of course, are a natural accompaniment of the hamburger.

But eventually, even the hamburger may not be enough as the international market becomes saturated and the domestic market oversaturated.

---

[15] Richard Gibson and Calmetta Y. Coleman, "Teenie Beanie Babies Generate Great Big Buzz," *The Wall Street Journal* (April 11, 1997): B1, B3.

[16] Reported in Richard Gibson, "McDonald's, After Stumbling Last Year in U.S., to Add Fewer Restaurants in '97," *The Wall Street Journal* (April 14, 1997): B8.

Then McDonald's may be forced to seek complimentary diversifications or lose the growth mode.

The insight to be gained, however, is that firms in pursuit of growth often jump into acquisitions far too hastily when the better course of action would be to more fully develop market penetration of their existing products.

Beware the reckless drive for market share. A firm can usually "buy" market share, if it is willing to sacrifice profits in so doing. It can step up its advertising and sales promotion. It can lower its prices, assuming that lower prices would bring more demand. It can increase its sales staff and motivate them to be more aggressive. As a consequence, sales and competitive position will usually rise. But costs may rise disproportionately. In other words, the benefits to be gained may not be worth the costs.

McDonald's, as we have seen in its domestic operation, has struck a strategy of aggressively seeking market share by opening thousands of new units. As long as the development costs can be kept sufficiently low to permit these new units good profits and not cannibalize or take too much business away from other McDonald's restaurants, then the strategy is defensible. Still, the costs of damaged franchisee relations, the intangibles of lowered morale, cooperation, and festering resentments are difficult to calculate but can be real indeed.

Maintaining the highest standards requires constant monitoring. McDonald's heritage and its competitive advantage has long been associated with the highest standards and controls in the industry for cleanliness, fast service, dependable quality of food, and friendly and well-groomed employees. The following box discusses strategy countering by competitors and the great difficulty in matching nonprice strengths.

Alas, in the last few years even McDonald's has apparently let its control of operational standards slip. As mentioned earlier, a 1995 survey of adults gave McDonald's low marks on food quality, value, service, and cleanliness. Wendy's won top honors instead. Why this lapse? Perhaps because the burgeoning international operation became the focus of attention. But maintaining high standards among thousands of units, company-owned as well as franchised, requires constant monitoring and exhortation. With great numbers of stores, this becomes increasingly difficult.

Can controls be too stringent? In a belated attempt to improve standards and tighten up corporate control, McDonald's instituted the controversial Franchising 2000. Among other things, this called for grading franchisees, with those receiving the lower grades being penalized. McDonald's also wanted to take away any pricing flexibility for its franchisees: all restaurants must now charge the same prices, or risk losing their franchise. Not surprisingly, some franchisees were concerned about this new "get tough" management.

INFORMATION BOX

MATCHING A COMPETITOR'S STRATEGY

Some strategies are easily countered or duplicated by competitors. Price-cutting is the most easily countered. A price cut can often be matched within minutes. Similarly, a different package or a warranty is easily imitated by competitors.

But some strategies are not so easily duplicated. Most of these involve service, a strong and positive company image, or both. A reputation for quality and dependability is not easily countered, at least in the short run. A good company or brand image is hard to match because it usually results from years of good service and satisfied customers. The great controls of McDonald's—the high standards of product quality, service, and cleanliness—would seem to be easily imitated, but they proved not to be, as no other firm fully matched the enforced standards of McDonald's, at least until recently.

Somehow it seems that the strategies and operations that are the most difficult to imitate are not the wildly innovative ones, not the ones that are complex and well researched. Surprisingly—and even difficult to accept—the most difficult to imitate are the very simple ones: simply doing a better job in servicing and satisfying customers and in performing even mundane operations cheerfully and efficiently.

What explanation can you give for competitors' inability to match the standards of McDonald's?

Can controls be too stringent? As with most things, extremes are seldom desirable. All firms need tight controls over far-flung outlets to keep them sufficiently informed of emerging problems and opportunities and maintain a desired image and standard of performance. In a franchise operation this is all the more necessary since we are dealing with independent entrepreneurs rather than hired managers. However, controls can be too harsh and rigid to give any room for special circumstances and opportunities. If the enforcement is too punitive, the climate becomes more that of a police state than a teamwork relationship with both parties cooperating to their mutual advantages.

And this brings us to the next insight for discussion.

Is there room for a kinder, gentler firm in today's hotly competitive environment? Many long-time McDonald's franchisees remembered with sadness a kinder, gentler company. This was an atmosphere nurtured by founder Ray Kroc. To be sure, Kroc insisted that customers be assured of a clean, family atmosphere with quick and cheerful service. To Kroc, this meant strict standards, not only in food preparation but also in care and maintenance of facilities, including toilets. Company auditors closely checked that the standards were adhered to, under Kroc's belief that a weakness in one restaurant could have a detrimental effect on other units in the system. Still, the atmosphere was helpful—the inspectors were "consultants"—rather than adversarial. Kroc could boast in his autobiography that the company was responsible for making more than 1,000 millionaires, the franchise holders.[17]

Many franchisees traced the deterioration of franchiser–franchisee relations to the 1992 death of Gerald Newman, McDonald's chief accounting officer. He spent much of his time interacting with franchisees, sometimes encouraging—he had a reputation for a sympathetic ear—sometimes even giving them a financial break.[18]

So, is it possible and desirable to be a kind and gentle company? With franchisees? Employees? Suppliers? Customers? Of course it is! Organizations, and the people who run them, often forget this in the arrogance of power. They excuse this "get tough" mindset on the exigencies of competition and the need to be faithful to their stockholders.

Kind and gentle—is this an anachronism, a throwback to a quieter time, a nostalgia long past its usefulness? Let us hope not!

CONSIDER

Can you add other learning insights?

QUESTIONS

1. How do you account for the reluctance of competitors to imitate the successful efforts of another firm in their industry? Under what circumstances is imitation likely to be embraced?
2. To date McDonald's has shunned diversification into other related and unrelated food retailing operations. Discuss the desirability of such diversification efforts.
3. "Eventually—and this may come sooner than most think—there will no longer be any choice locations anywhere in the world for new hamburger outlets. As a McDonald's stockholder, I am getting worried." Discuss.
4. Contrast McDonald's with the earlier case involving Maytag's England operation. What insights can be developed from these two cases?

---

[17]Ray Kroc and Robert Anderson, *Grinding It Out: The Making of McDonald's* (New York: Berkley Publishing, 1977), 200.
[18]Gibson, "Can New Spices Warm Up Sales," A8.

5. Do you think we were right to place McDonald's in the "Question Mark" category? Why or why not?
6. Is it likely that McDonald's will ever find a saturated market potential for its hamburgers?
7. If you ran McDonald's, what changes, if any, would you institute? Please give your rationale for your recommendations.

HANDS-ON EXERCISES

1. You have been given the assignment by Edward Rensi in 1993 to instill a recommitment to improved customer service in all domestic operations. Discuss in as much detail as you can how you would go about fostering this among the 10,000 domestic outlets.
2. As a McDonald's senior executive, what long-term expansion mode would you recommend for your company?

TEAM DEBATE EXERCISE

1. Debate this issue: McDonald's is reaching the limits of its growth without drastic change. (Note: the side that espouses drastic change should give some attention to the most likely directions for such, and be prepared to defend these expansion possibilities.)
2. Debate the issue of a "get-tough" attitude of corporate management toward franchisees even if it riles some, versus involving them more in future directions of the company. In particular, be prepared to address the controversy of unlimited market-share expansion.

INVITATION TO RESEARCH

Is McDonald's becoming more vulnerable to competitors today? Does it have any emerging problems? Has it attempted any major diversifications? Is the international operation still overshadowing the domestic?

CHAPTER 19

Tobacco: An Industry Beleaguered

Cigarettes are among the world's most profitable consumer products. A cigarette "costs a penny to make, sell it for a dollar, it's addictive, and there's fantastic brand loyalty." So said master investor Warren Buffett as he unsuccessfully sought to take over RJR Nabisco, the tobacco conglomerate.[1] Perhaps because of its profitability the morality of the business has long been suspect.

Criticisms have accelerated in recent years and bans widely imposed. Stubbornly, the tobacco industry and its executives, even before Congress, refused to admit that anything was wrong or unhealthy about cigarettes, and some of the major firms in the industry even aggressively struck back at their critics. But a comeuppance for the industry appears at hand.

CONTROVERSIAL STRATEGIES IN TODAY'S SHRINKING MARKET

Faced with a steadily declining market in the United States, the tobacco industry has responded with a proliferation of brands: More than 300 brands were created, boasting such features as being longer, slimmer, cheaper, flavored, microfiltered, pastel colored, and even striped. One of these was an R. J. Reynolds brand called Uptown.

---

[1]"The Tobacco Trade: The Search for El Dorado," *Economist* (May 16, 1992): 21.

The Controversy over Uptown

Uptown was packaged in a showy black-and-gold box and was a menthol blend. R. J. Reynolds designed the product to appeal to a particular market segment, much as the other new brands had been designed.

Because cigarette consumption had fallen in the United States, tobacco companies were increasingly directing their efforts to specific groups, such as women, Hispanics, and blacks. Blacks in particular seemed a fruitful target market: 39 percent of black males smoke, while 30.5 percent of white males do.[2] Using careful research and design, everything about Uptown—even the name—was tailored to the tastes of black consumers. It was, indeed, the first cigarette aimed specifically at African-American smokers. Alas, this was the rub.

A storm of protests quickly ensued. Critics maintained that the marketing of Uptown represented a cold-blooded targeting of blacks, who already suffered a lung cancer rate 58 percent higher than whites. The protests even reached the office of Louis Sullivan, the Secretary of Health and Human Services. He quickly sided with the critics: "Uptown's message is more disease, more suffering and more death for a group already bearing more than its share of smoking-related illness and mortality."[3] He called for an "all-out effort to resist the attempts of tobacco merchants to earn profits at the expense of the health and well-being of our poor and minority citizens."[4]

Given the virulence of the protests, R. J. Reynolds abandoned its plans to test market the cigarettes in Philadelphia. It decried the negative attention being focused on the brand by a few zealots and angrily compared the acceptability of a retailer designing a line of clothing for blacks with the outcry accompanying the same marketing strategy for a cigarette.

On March 16, 1990, the *Chicago Tribune* announced that R. J. Reynolds Tobacco Company had stated it was not likely to pursue the controversial marketing of Uptown. But the company defended its marketing efforts.[5] The critics had won.

A Similar Controversy: Dakota

Another new cigarette brand, also targeted to a specific group, found itself beset with controversy. This was Dakota, aimed at "virile females."[6] Critics

---

[2] Michael Quinn, "Don't Aim That Pack at Us," *Time* (January 29, 1990): 60.

[3] Quinn, "Don't Aim That Pack," 60.

[4] Ben Wildavsky, "Tilting at Billboards," *New Republic* (August 20, 1990): 19.

[5] Janet Cawley, "Target Marketing Lights Smoky Fire," *Chicago Tribune* (March 16, 1990): 1.

[6] Paul Cotton, "Tobacco Foes Attack Ads that Target Women, Minorities, Teens and the Poor," *Journal of the American Medical Association* (September 26, 1990): 1505.

of tobacco's relationship with lung cancer and heart disease were quick to attack this as a blatant appeal to women.

Another group was especially upset. In some American Indian native languages, *Dakota* means friend. Yet, to a group that already had high rates of smoking addiction, such a brand name seemed a betrayal.

Controversies over Tobacco Company Sponsorships

As a result of the 1971 ban on the use of TV and radio cigarette commercials, the tobacco companies desperately sought other media in which to place their hundreds of millions of advertising dollars. They were fairly successful in doing so, but by the early 1990s serious questions were being raised about their use of certain of these media.

Great criticisms and aggressive actions taken against billboards promoting cigarettes and alcohol in black communities already have been seen. Advertising support of black media by tobacco companies was also coming under fire. Yet, such support for many years existed in a vacuum, with few other major firms and industries supporting advertising in black media.

Now, tobacco company support for minority organizations also began to be questioned. The National Association of Black Journalists turned down a $40,000 Philip Morris donation: "We couldn't take money from an organization deliberately targeting minority populations with a substance that clearly causes cancer," said the group's president, Thomas Morgan. "We simply became more aggressive in our fund-raising so we could do without it."[7] But for many small minority publications, such resistance was not an option: They would have simply folded without the advertising dollars furnished by tobacco companies.

Women's organizations also are beholden to support from the tobacco industry, which has liberally provided money to such groups at a time when other sources were virtually nonexistent. As a major example of such support, Virginia Slims brought women's tennis into prominence at a time when no one else would. And this raises another major controversy, discussed in the following box.

The Old Joe Camel Controversy

In 1988 R. J. Reynolds Tobacco Company stumbled upon a promotional theme for its slumping Camel brand. Using a sunglass-clad, bulbous-nosed cartoon camel that it called Joe, a $75-million-a-year advertising campaign

---

[7]Cotton, "Tobacco Foes Attack Ads," 1506.

ISSUE BOX

TOBACCO COMPANY SPONSORSHIP OF ATHLETIC EVENTS

Is it right to allow tobacco companies to sponsor certain athletic events? What seems like a simple and uncontroversial question becomes far more complex when we consider the sponsorship of tennis tournaments such as Virginia Slims. There is no longer any doubt that cigarette smoking causes serious damage to heart and lungs. Yet, tennis requires top physical fitness and aerobic capacity.

Although the sponsorship of such athletic events came about as the industry sought alternative media after being banned from TV and radio, their sponsorship has particular advantages from the industry's perspective. It creates the false association of cigarette smoking with vitality and good health, and it directly targets women. Essentially, the company is taking advantage of the inadequate funding of women's sports by making itself a strong presence in this sector.

So we have an unhealthy product—as even the tobacco industry is now reluctantly conceding—sponsoring a prestigious athletic event for women that would probably never be able to exist without such funding. Do we refuse to accept this sponsorship? Do we ban all cigarette promotions that appear to have some tie-in with health and fitness? Does the evil outweigh the good?

You are a militant feminist leader with strong convictions that women's athletic events should be promoted more strongly. The major source of funding for tennis and golf tournaments has been the tobacco industry, with no alternative sponsors likely in the near future. Discuss your position regarding the acceptability of tobacco company sponsorships. What is your position on this controversy? Present your rationale as persuasively as you can.

---

was instituted. The company featured Joe in an array of macho gear, and it targeted the campaign to appeal to younger male smokers who had been deserting the Camel brand in droves.

The campaign was an outstanding success. In only 3 years, Camel's share of sales among the 18- to 24-year age group almost doubled, from 4.4 percent to 7.9 percent.

But the appeal of Old Joe went far beyond the target age group. It was too potent. It was found to be highly effective in reaching young people, especially children under 13. Children were enamored with the camel character. Six-year-olds in the United States even recognized Joe Camel at a rate nearly equal to their recognition of Mickey Mouse.[8]

---

[8] Judann Dagnoli, "JAMA Lights New Fire Under Camel's Ads," *Advertising Age* (December 16, 1991): 3, 32.

According to a study published in the *Journal of the American Medical Association*, teenagers are far better able than adults to identify the Camel logo. Children as young as three could even identify the cartoon character with cigarettes. Of even more concern, Camel's share of the market of under-age children who smoke is nearly 33 percent, up from less than a percentage point before the Old Joe campaign. See Table 19.1 for the results of the survey.

THE PROTESTS EXPAND

Uptown

Critics of Uptown initially focused attention on its billboard advertising in ghetto neighborhoods. They soon expanded their protests beyond a single cigarette brand to cigarettes in general and to alcohol as well and began whitewashing offending billboards. Their only recourse, they argued, was to use civil disobedience to attract attention to their cause. Although maintaining that they had nothing against billboards in general, protestors demanded more educational themes as well as such wholesome products as orange juice for these billboards in ghetto neighborhoods.

Dr. Harold Freeman, director of surgery at Harlem Hospital, is coauthor of a study that found that men in Harlem have a lower life expectancy than men in Bangladesh, at least partly because of alcohol and tobacco use. Speaking to an audience at Harlem's Abyssinian Baptist Church, Dr. Freeman asked, "Is it ethical, is it moral, to sell cigarettes and alcohol specifically to a community that is dying at a much higher rate than others?"[9] And with this, the church's pastor, Rev. Calvin O. Butts III, led his flock out of the church and throughout the city, painting signs with black paint to denote their Afrocentric perspective.

Table 19.1   Survey Results of Knowledge and Attitudes Regarding Camel's Old Joe Advertisements

	Students	*Adults*
Have seen Old Joe	97.7%	72.2%
Know the product	97.5	67.0
Think ads look cool	58.0	39.9
Like Joe as friend	35.0	14.4
Smokers who identify Camel as favorite brand	33.0	8.7

Source: Data from the *Journal of the American Medical Assn.,* as presented in Walecia Konrad, "I'd Toddle a Mile for a Camel," *Business Week* (December 23, 1991): 34. The results are based on a survey of 1055 students, ages 12 to 19 years, and 345 adults, aged 21 to 87 years.

[9] Dagnoli, "JAMA Lights New Fire," 3, 32.

The agitation against billboards was by no means limited to Harlem. For example, in Dallas, County Commissioner John Wiley Price led a group that whitewashed 25 billboards, resulting in arrests and misdemeanor charges. Chicago priest Michael Pfleger was also arrested for allegedly painting billboards and throwing paint at a billboard company employee.

Antismoking and antibillboard activists were having a field day. California launched a $28.6 million antismoking campaign using money from cigarette taxes. Similarly, the Office of Substance Abuse Policy began a nationwide 7,000-billboard campaign targeting drug and alcohol abuse.

Business began heeding the mounting pressure. In June 1990 the Outdoor Advertising Association of America, representing 80 percent of billboard companies, announced a new policy encouraging its members to keep billboard ads for products that are illegal for minors at least 500 feet from schools, as well as from places of worship and hospitals. The association also recommended voluntary limits on the number of billboards that advertise cigarettes and alcohol in any given area, such as minority neighborhoods. Gannet Outdoor, the largest billboard company in North America, began putting decals on billboards near schools and churches indicating that no alcohol or tobacco ads were to be posted there.

Assessment of the Controversy of Targeting Minorities. Was R. J. Reynolds Company the ogre that some critics depicted it as? Or were the critics self-seeking extremists more interested in publicity and crying wolf when the wolf was really rather toothless?

Without question, inner-city blacks have shown higher rates of tobacco and alcohol use than their suburban contemporaries; along with this, they have higher incidences of the accompanying health problems. And despite a few weak company disclaimers, there can be little doubt that tobacco firms thought they had developed a new and effective market targeting strategy. The dispute hinges on this:

> Are certain minority groups—such as blacks and women—particularly susceptible to marketing blandishments so that they need to be protected from potentially unsafe products?

While the proponents of controls argue that certain groups, such as young blacks, need such protection, others see that as indicative of paternalism. Even some black leaders decry the billboard whitewashing and the contentious preachings of certain ministers. To Adolph Hauntz, president of the Dallas Merchants and Concessionaires Association, whitewashing signs "treats blacks as if we are a stupid bunch of people that are overly influenced by billboards." And former NAACP Executive Director Benjamin Hooks made the same point, condemning billboard whitewashing for "saying that white people have enough sense to read the signs and disregard them and black people don't."[10] Certainly, tempting people is hardly the same as oppressing them. After all, no one has to buy cigarettes and alcohol.

Butts, Sullivan, and others countered that comments such as those of Hooks simply reflected the tobacco and alcohol industries' success in muting criticisms of their minority targeting policies by their large donations to such groups as the NAACP, the United Negro College Fund, and the National Urban League.

Regardless of the pro and con arguments concerning the susceptibility of inner-city youth to advertisements for unhealthy products, there is more validity to the contentions of susceptibility when we consider the vulnerability of children to the attractive and sophisticated models found in most of these commercials.

Finally, if local, state, or federal legislation is enacted to ban certain products from being promoted on billboards, as was done with radio and TV advertising two decades ago, where should the line be drawn? Should promotions in ghetto neighborhoods be banned for products that are economically extravagant, such as expensive athletic shoes? Or should promotions be banned for high-cholesterol foods that might cause high blood pressure? Or for high-powered "muscle" cars?

Joe Camel

Not surprisingly, a storm of criticism ensued after the American Medical Association's disclosure of the study that found that Joe Camel appealed far more to children than to adults. Health advocates demanded that the Federal Trade Commission ban the ads. Surgeon General Antonia Novella took the unprecedented step of asking RJR to cancel its campaign voluntarily. Even *Advertising Age* published an editorial entitled "Old Joe Must Go."[11] The basis for the concern, of course, was that the popular ads might encourage underage children to start smoking.

RJR refused to yield. It denied that the ads are effective with children: "Just because children can identify our logo doesn't mean they will use the product."[12] Defensively, Reynolds moved to counter the bad press. It distributed pamphlets and bumper stickers and put up billboards discouraging kids from smoking. And it stoutly maintained its right to freedom of speech.

---

[10] Wildavasky, "Tilting at Billboards," 20.
[11] "Old Joe Must Go," *Advertising Age* (January 13, 1992).
[12] *Ibid.*

Assessment of the Old Joe Controversy. Some advertising people believed RJR's stubbornness was badly misguided: "RJR . . . is taking a huge chance. By placing Old Joe as a freedom-of-speech issue instead of an unintentional marketing overshoot, the conglomerate risks goading Congress into bans and restrictions on all tobacco advertising. Lawmakers might, for instance, look more favorably on legislation just introduced . . . which would shift responsibility for tobacco products to the Food and Drug Administration [which] could regulate the tobacco industry into oblivion."[13]

Old Joe was a marketing success beyond all management expectation. But in a time of increasingly critical attention by society, should any firm in a sensitive industry hold itself aloof from a groundswell of denunciations? Are some bumper stickers and billboards with messages to discourage kids from smoking likely to be more than token and impotent efforts, given the popularity of a cartoon character that commands virtually as much recognition and affection as Mickey Mouse?

Then this thought may be raised: Could it be that targeting the young is a long-range strategy for gaining future smokers? See the following box for identification of more cigarette issues.

ISSUE BOX

CIGARETTES AND SMOKING

The controversies concerning cigarettes go beyond those detailed in this chapter.

- Should smoking be restricted in the workplace? In restaurants? In airplanes?
- What about some firms' decision to bar employees from smoking even when they are not at work?
- Should the tobacco industry pay for employee suits concerning their "right to smoke"?
- Should nonsmokers be protected against passive smoke?
- In general, are the rights of smokers being violated?

Discuss, and even debate, these questions and any other smoking issues you come up with.

TARGETING FOREIGN MARKETS

With increasing restraints on cigarette advertising in the United States and the steadily diminishing per capita consumption of cigarettes, it is not sur-

---

[13]Craig Stoltz, "RJR Appears Intent on Sticking with Old Joe to the Bitter End," *Adweek Eastern Edition* (March 23, 1992): 18.

prising that the industry began focusing greater attention on foreign markets. Unfortunately for cigarette makers, criticisms and restraints did not long remain subdued in these markets, either.

At least as early as 1984, the Royal College of Physicians in the United Kingdom harshly denounced tobacco usage, stating that smoking killed 100,000 people a year in the United Kingdom and resulted in 50 million lost working days a year.[14] But the Royal College particularly condemned the lack of availability of low-tar cigarettes, "which are practically unknown in the Third World. The incidence of lung cancer among men in the Natal Bantustan in South Africa has increased 600 percent in the last 11 years. Developed countries bear a heavy responsibility for the worldwide epidemic of smoking."[15]

By 1990 *The New York Times* was reporting strong criticisms by women's groups and health organizations in India over attempts to promote Ms, a new cigarette brand aimed at upwardly mobile Indian women. Billboards and print ads for the products showed strong, happy Indian women in Western-style clothes and affluent settings. Opposition groups condemned the "evil message that cigarette smoking is part of a healthy and logical way of feminine life."[16]

Despite intense lobbying by the tobacco industry, two European community (EC) directives on tobacco advertising were proposed by the European Commission in 1989. The first, barring television advertisements, was readily accepted by EC governments and went into effect in October 1991. The second directive would ban press and poster advertising, and was backed by the European Parliament. The second measure awaiting passage would ban tobacco advertising in "any form of communication, printed, written, oral, by radio and television broadcast and cinema." Even logos on cigarette lighters and matches would be forbidden. The tobacco industry, which claimed there was no link between tobacco publicity and the 430,000 deaths a year in Europe from smoking-related diseases, not surprisingly was frantic at this possible outcome.[17] But John Major, prime minister of Great Britain, opposed the measure, and a minority of countries were likely to block it temporarily. (However, bans on print ads for tobacco are already in force in such EC countries as France, Italy, and Portugal.)

With Western Europe's mounting inhospitality to the industry, U.S. tobacco firms today are eagerly pushing into Asia, Africa, Eastern Europe and the former Soviet Union. These markets are big—$90 billion a year—

---

[14] "Developing Countries: Governments Should Take Action Against Cigarettes Before Too Many People Acquire the Potentially Lethal Habit," *New Scientist* (December 1, 1983): 42.

[15] "Developing Countries," 42.

[16] "Women in Delhi Angered by Smoking Pitch," *The New York Times* (National Edition), (March 18, 1990): 11.

[17] "EP Backs Ban on Tobacco Advertising," *Europe 2000* (March 1992): R41.

and the local cigarette makers appear highly vulnerable to the slick and aggressive efforts of U.S. firms. For example, Marlboro's cowboy is even more widely known in most of Asia than in the United States. As a result, Philip Morris can get its message across simply by playing the brand's theme song or flashing a single image of the cowboy.[18]

For years, Western companies were kept out of these lucrative markets by governments eager to preserve state tobacco monopolies or anticapitalist ideologies. But these barriers have crumbled, especially in Eastern Europe. Tobacco companies have been invited into enormous new markets such as the former Soviet Union, where "cigarette famines" have long existed. Now Philip Morris is shipping billions of cigarettes to Russia.

Countries in the expanding sales area had few marketing or health-labeling controls. In Hungary, for example, Marlboro cigarettes were even handed out to young fans at pop music concerts.[19]

In Asia protectionist tariffs and import bans had to be cracked before these markets could be entered by foreign tobacco firms. The United States was successful in using Section 301 of its 1974 Trade Act to threaten retaliatory tariffs on the exports of such countries as Japan, South Korea, Taiwan, and Thailand if their markets were not opened to U.S. tobacco firms. Tobacco-state representatives in Congress have been strong influences in such pressures, and they were successful in opening up these markets. By 1992 cigarette advertising on television in Japan—it is not allowed in the United States—had soared from fortieth to second place in air time since 1987 and even appeared during children's shows. Smoking has greatly increased among women, who had been largely ignored before the Western firms arrived but were now prime targets. Tobacco companies found good market potential among women in such Asian areas as Hong Kong, where fewer than 5 percent of women smoked. Philip Morris tapped this market with its Virginia Slims, a feminine brand famous for its slogan, "You've come a long way, baby."[20]

Assessment of the Overseas Push by U.S. Tobacco Firms. A firm seems entitled to make all the profit it can make. If certain markets are drying up or are being severely constrained, should not a firm have the right to seek other markets aggressively? This is what the tobacco companies are doing.

The issue is clouded because cigarette smoking is generally conceded to be hazardous to health. But it is not immediately so, and by no means certainly so. As long as many people are willing to take the risk, one might

---

[18] Mike Levin, "U.S. Tobacco Firms Push Eagerly into Asian Market," *Marketing News* (January 21, 1991): 2.

[19] "The Tobacco Trade," 23.

[20] "The Tobacco Trade," 24.

ask how can the tobacco makers and growers and advertisers and retailers be so negatively judged?

When sophisticated and aggressive promotional efforts are directed at developing countries, where consumers are more easily swayed and far more vulnerable to promotional blandishments, does our perception of what is ethical and what is undesirable conduct change? Should it?

THE SIEGE INTENSIFIES

Allegations of Rigging Nicotine Levels

A new threat to the serenity of the tobacco industry was charges of long-time rigging of nicotine levels to assure that smokers stayed hooked. Adding fuel to such allegations were Brown & Williamson Tobacco Corp. internal documents, including a 54-page handbook, obtained by *The Wall Street Journal,* that indicated the tobacco companies were adding ammonia-based compounds to their cigarettes. Such compounds essentially increase the potency of the nicotine a smoker actually inhales. The B & W documents asserted that Philip Morris's Marlboro, the top brand with a 30 percent share of the U.S. market, may have been the first to use such ammonia technology. Regardless of who was the trailblazer, the practice seemingly had been widely emulated within the tobacco industry.[21]

Nicotine was viewed by most scientists as the active ingredient that causes cigarettes to be addictive. Anything that enhances the delivery of this into the bloodstream, then, would increase the addictive potential. The industry would not admit this. It maintained that nicotine simply provided better flavor: "The primary purpose for using DAP [an ammonia additive] is to increase taste and flavor, reduce irritation, and to improve body." While admitting that this also increased nicotine delivery, a B & W spokesperson called this "an incidental effect."[22] Of course, tobacco companies still doggedly denied any links between cigarette smoking and heart disease, cancer, or other ailments.

But in 1996, newly disclosed documents suggested that Philip Morris, the nation's foremost tobacco company, had in place as far back as the 1970s a system to hide and destroy potentially damaging data about smoking and health because of liability suits: "These documents appear to be further evidence of the industry's extraordinary effort to keep information secret. These are just the tip of the iceberg of evidence of document destruction."[23]

[21] Alix M. Freedman, "Tobacco Firm Shows How Ammonia Spurs Delivery of Nicotine," *The Wall Street Journal* (October 18, 1995): A1 and A6.

[22] Freedman, "How Ammonia Spurs Delivery of Nicotine," A6.

[23] Alix M. Freedman and Milo Geyelin, "Philip Morris Allegedly Hid Tobacco Data," *The Wall Street Journal* (September 18, 1996): B11.

Repercussions

The industry was already under heavy fire before the latest revelations. The increasing pressure, spearheaded by David Kessler, the Food and Drug Administration's (FDA) commissioner, showed a sharp contrast to the situation when he assumed office in 1990. Then, a few health coalitions were complaining about smoking, but this had been going on for decades. Few people in government paid any attention mostly because the tobacco industry seemed invulnerable: it had the support of powerful southern congressmen and it also had great monetary resources to provide for the finest legal arsenal and lobbying efforts.

Though perhaps not immediately obvious to tobacco executives, the climate was subtly changing. In 1985, both Aspen and Vail in Colorado banned smoking in restaurants. Other scattered bans followed. The slow trend abruptly accelerated in 1993 when the Environmental Protection Agency declared smoke a carcinogen. By the end of that year, 436 cities had smoking restrictions. Smoking came to be banned from all domestic air flights regardless of length.

Even the courts were now joining the act. In addition to criminal investigations by the Justice Department in New York and Washington, thirteen other states were seeking reimbursement from the industry for the costs of treating smoking-related illnesses. And the industry was facing eight class-action suits, filed by smokers claiming they became hooked while the industry concealed the addictive nature of its product. Dr. Kessler also added the resources of the FDA to take up the struggle against cigarettes.

Previous defense strategies of the industry had always been that it was a smoker's free choice to smoke despite an "unproven" risk of lung cancer, so how dare the government interfere. Now Dr. Kessler, given the newest revelations about the ability of the industry to control nicotine with a powerful addictive hold, had a new strategy to present to Capitol Hill. Former Surgeon General C. Everett Koop exhorted him, "Do anything you can" to regulate tobacco. "The country is going to be behind you."[24]

On August 10, 1995, in the White House, President Clinton with Dr. Kessler standing nearby, unveiled tough proposed regulations on cigarette marketing and sales. This marked the new FDA role against tobacco and one of the most aggressive federal moves ever against the industry.

Even the seemingly fertile overseas markets were rising against the industry. An aggressive European ad campaign by Philip Morris backfired and had to be abandoned amid a barrage of lawsuits, complaints to regulators, and government criticism. The campaign cited scientific studies to claim that

[24] Laurie McGinley and Timothy Nash, "Long FDA Campaign and Bit of Serendipity Led to Tobacco Move," *The Wall Street Journal* (August 22, 1995): A4.

second-hand smoke wasn't a meaningful health risk to nonsmokers. It even suggested that inhaling secondary smoke was less dangerous than eating cookies or drinking milk: "Life is full of risks," declared one headline above a picture of three cookies. "But they're not all equal."[25]

The stakes were high, with Philip Morris having tobacco sales of $11.4 billion in Europe in 1995. But resentment against the tobacco industry was rising by governments struggling to contain burgeoning health-care costs.

Joe Camel was doing somewhat better in Argentina, despite intense criticism by antismoking activists. The first such campaign in Latin America saw sales of the formerly marginal Camel brand shooting up 50 percent, a gain perhaps reflecting that Argentina has no national cigarette age limit.[26]

The Industry Fights Back

The fight was on. Tobacco firms, as well as the advertising industry, attacked with lawsuits against the FDA while tobacco-state legislators desperately worked to replace the proposed regulations with friendlier laws. In the first half of 1996, more than $15 million was spent for lobbying, according to governmental reports. More millions went to campaign donations to influence lawmakers, and additional millions to defend against lawsuits.[27]

The tobacco industry has been notorious for defending its position aggressively and not being reluctant to embrace confrontation. For example, the professor in Georgia whose study found that Joe Camel was more recognized than Disney or Sesame Street characters, thereby calling into question the tobacco industry's claims that their ads were not targeting children, became a target himself. The industry pressured the school administration to fire him. "The only protection he really had was tenure."[28] This saved his job.

Philip Morris has been the most aggressive player in attacking critics. In 1994 it sued the city of San Francisco, trying to overturn one of the nation's toughest antismoking ordinances. The ordinance had banned smoking in offices and would shortly also ban it in restaurants. Philip Morris sought to have the court declare the ordinance invalid and unenforceable.

Geoffrey Bible, chairman of Philip Morris, declared an all-out war on tobacco's enemies, with legal attacks and newspaper ads. "We are not going to be anybody's punching bag," he said. "When you are right and you fight, you

[25] Martin Du Dois and Tara Parker-Pope, "Philip Morris Campaign Stirs Uproar in Europe," *The Wall Street Journal* (July 1, 1996): B1.

[26] Jonathan Friedland, "Under Siege in the U.S., Joe Camel Pops Up Alive, Well in Argentina," *The Wall Street Journal* (September 10, 1996): B1.

[27] "Tobacco Lobbyists Spend Millions," *Cleveland Plain Dealer* (September 9, 1996): 8A.

[28] Example cited in Maureen Smith, "Tenure," *University of Minnesota Update* (November 1995): 4.

win."[29] Bible has spent his career pushing Philip Morris around the world, and he practices what he preaches: smoking cigarettes and attacking all critics.

Those struggling to preserve the tobacco industry and its efforts to avoid any regulation are by no means limited to cigarette producers. Tobacco is so ingrained in many sectors of our economy that many would suffer were it curbed—for example, local distributors, truckers, people who own and/or replenish vending machines, those involved with billboard ads for cigarettes, and the hundreds of vendors who see cigarette sales as a major part of their total business. And of course there are those tobacco growers in the southern states who cannot countenance switching their crops to lower yielding alternatives. Against the arguments that alternative employment would replace cigarette dependence, many look back over decades of such dependence and cringe at the thought of losing it.

LATE-BREAKING NEWS

In spring 1997, new developments portended monumental changes for the tobacco industry. In late March, the solidarity of the industry was shaken as Liggett Group settled a lawsuit with 22 states, and in the process, finally admitted that smoking is addictive and caused cancer. Further information from Liggett showed that children were targeted for tobacco sales.

The middle of April, the two biggest tobacco companies, Philip Morris and RJR Nabisco, began talks with attorneys general for 25 states suing to recover billions of dollars in public health-care costs for sick smokers. The industry sought protection from all current and future litigation and was willing to contribute $300 billion over a 25-year period to a settlement fund and make other concessions such as disclosing the industry's research into smoking and health, as well as accepting restrictions on the marketing of cigarettes. Despite the huge sum offered to settle, opponents calculated that this amount would not exact a harsh enough toll on this highly profitable industry, and that it could easily cover it simply by raising prices 25 cents a pack. "Anything that gets (the liability) off the map, no matter what it costs, would cause tobacco stocks to rise," one said.[30] And rise the tobacco stocks did, with news of such a settlement. As we go into printing, negotiations are still underway, with nothing certain at this time.

Undoubtedly the tobacco industry's position in such negotiations would be bolstered by a major victory that Reynolds scored in a Florida state court

---

[29]Suein L. Hwang, "Philip Morris's Passion to Market Cigarettes Helps It Outsell RJR," *The Wall Street Journal* (October 30, 1995): A1.

[30]Alix M. Freedman, Suein L. Hwang and Milo Geyelin, "Tobacco Firms Offer to Disclose Research," *The Wall Street Journal* (April 17, 1997): A2, A4.

on May 5, 1997 where a jury found that the firm wasn't responsible for the death of a three-pack-a-day smoker who died of lung cancer at age 49. The trial had been closely watched as a bellwether for future litigation against the industry.

Despite the threats to the industry, Philip Morris reported its first-quarter net income rose 13 percent. International business was particularly strong, despite some countries' efforts to curb it: PM reported that it sold more cigarettes in almost all overseas markets; Marlboro, the world's most popular brand, had strong gains in Europe, the Middle East, Japan and the growth markets of the Philippines and Indonesia.[31]

WHAT CAN BE LEARNED?

Is it ethically right to vigorously promote a product seen by many as unsafe and even deadly? This issue gets to the heart of the whole matter of tobacco production and marketing. Considered by practically all health experts as dangerous and, in the long term, life-threatening, tobacco had been protected by powerful governmental interests, even if such support is eroding.

The industry stubbornly refused to admit the health charges, citing its own research to the contrary. And the industry is huge, with many stakeholders: tobacco growers, processors, retailers, tax collectors, influential people in the halls of government, even the paster of billboard ads.

Not the least of the proponents for the industry are the users themselves—even though this is a declining number every year in this country. They discount the health dangers as being both far in the future and affecting only a minority of users. "And never me."

The morality? It is easy for stakeholders to rationalize that any bad consequences are uncertain at best, that the good outweighs any bad possibilities. Still, one wonders if the profit motive is not the overriding consideration, far ahead of possible health risks.

Too many times, what is ethical lies in the eyes of the beholder.

Does a militant minority represent acceptable behavior in promoting its own self-interest? In a pluralistic society, minorities are encouraged to press for their positions. The issue becomes one of degree. What level of critical behavior—no matter how justified many might see such criticisms—is acceptable? Is whitewashing billboards acceptable behavior? Destroying offending billboards? Firebombing the stores of opportunistic shop owners? Where do we draw the line? Furthermore, who is to be the judge of what is

[31] Rebecca Quick, "Philip Morris 1st-Quarter Net Rose 13% on Strong Growth in Tobacco Overseas," *The Wall Street Journal* (April 17, 1994): A4.

acceptable and nonacceptable: a firebrand preacher, a government agency, the police department, the courts?

Is it not perfectly right for any firm, or industry, to pursue its own best interests, as long as it stays within the current law? Ah, this is the rationale that supports tobacco efforts, whether Joe Camel, targeting naive consumers, foreign markets, or nicotine enhancement in pursuit of addiction: These actions were considered entirely legal. Do not laws reflect the majority views on what is moral and ethical? There are many who would say that laws often do not reflect prevailing majority views, that they rather reflect the positions of powerful minority interests. Many would see tobacco regulations—or lack of—as such.

Perhaps the real issue is whether a firm's best interests should take precedence over those of its customers and of society. Either position can be argued. On the one hand, should not a firm seek to foster a better corporate image and benefit both society and itself? On the other, should not a firm seek to maximize its profitability to the benefit of stockholders, creditors, suppliers, employees, and the like, regardless of outside critics?

Effective marketing strategies may need to be reconsidered in today's changing social milieu. Strategies honed in the past may no longer be appropriate; they may be vulnerable to public protests, boycotts, negative publicity, even governmental pressure and regulation. How is a firm to cope with this changing environment?

The answer would seem to lie in increased sensitivity, especially concerning relations with minorities, whether of race, sex, or age. A new brand or a new marketing strategy should be carefully assessed for its acceptability and freedom from potential criticism, before widespread introduction. Even then, surprises may come. Stoutly maintaining a strategy in the face of mounting opposition may not be the best course of action, for the firm or its industry. Sometimes this assessment may necessitate scrapping a successful product or brand or advertising campaign.

Unacceptable actions in one environment may no longer be transferred to another without risk. Cigarette firms, finding the U.S. market hostile to aggressive promotions, naturally turned their efforts to more hospitable market segments and countries. Not many years ago, such efforts would have been not only effective but would have activated very little critical attention or publicity. Now, a firm may find only a short-term advantage in targeting another market for products and practices criticized at home. Criticism tends to become contagious, even though oceans may separate markets. A firm may no longer be insulated from adverse publicity and possible punitive regulations when it attempts to move aggressively into minority segments and foreign markets. Yet, the great inroads of Philip Morris and its Marlboro brand in foreign markets seems almost impossible to stem by governments.

Is a firm's public image of little consequence as long as it has a loyal body of customers who support it? This is the position taken by the tobacco industry: Defiant of an increasing number of critics; secure in the loyalty of a sizable group of addicted customers; aided and abetted by powerful political interests whose constituents have an economic stake in the viability of the industry. For decades this mindset of disregard for the public image has successfully prevailed, despite the cries of critics, including most of the medical profession.

Now, finally, could it be that the cigarette makers—and especially Geoffrey Bible of Philip Morris, the industry's most ardent defender—have made a monumental miscalculation? That they are mistakenly assuming that the past will ever dictate the future? That attitudes and power positions will remain unchanging? The current offer of a $300 billion settlement suggests that the industry is at last running scared despite its brave posturing.

In today's litigious environment, callousness regarding society's growing concerns may be courting disaster. The tobacco industry proudly boasted that it had never lost a lawsuit accusing it of responsibility for lung cancer and other physical ills and deaths. The industry had always successfully defended itself on the grounds of unproven charges of cigarette smoking contributing to such health hazards, and also on the grounds of individual choice and individual freedom. Now this defense may be crumbling despite some reversals. Lawsuits are on the rise, powerful lawyers are gathering new ammunition, and the industry still faces the threat of multimillion dollar judgments. Our litigious environment appears on the threshold of doing what lawmakers in a pluralistic society with many diverse agendas have been unable to do: Bring the tobacco industry to heel.

In these learning insights, we have raised more questions than answers or caveats. But the questions raised ought to be of concern to tobacco executives—and executives of other firms whose products and ways of doing business may not be viewed as in the best interests of the general public. A reckoning may be lurking in the wings.

CONSIDER

Can you think of other learning insights or ethical issues?

QUESTIONS

1. Do you have any problems with the idea of militant ministers leading their followers to whitewash offensive billboards? If not, is tearing down such billboards acceptable? Please discuss as objectivity as possible.

2. Do you consider the proof adequate that cigarettes pose a substantial health threat and should be banned or tightly constrained? If you accept this position, should tobacco growers be allowed to continue growing such "unsafe" harvests?

3. Is there really any difference in the targeting of minority markets by brewers and the liquor industry and the obvious targeting by certain tobacco brands?

4. Playing the devil's advocate (one who argues an opposing point for the sake of argument), what arguments would you put forth that the cigarette manufacturers should be permitted complete freedom in targeting developing countries?

5. How do you assess the relative merits of the tangible financial contributions that the tobacco industry has made to various minority groups and media, and the negative health consequences of smoking?

6. What is the ethical difference between promoting cigarettes and promoting fatty, cholesterol-laden foods?

7. Are the rights of nonsmokers being too highly emphasized? Do smokers have any rights?

8. Do you actually think Joe Camel leads youngsters to become smokers when they become older? Why or why not?

HANDS-ON EXERCISES

1. You are the public relations spokesperson for Philip Morris. You have been ordered by Geoffrey Bible to plan a public relations campaign to overturn some of the banning of cigarettes. Be as specific and creative as you can. How successful do you think such efforts would be?

2. You are an articulate young African-American woman who smokes Uptown cigarettes and likes them. At a church outing, your minister denounces Uptown and the company that makes them. Describe how you might respond to such a tirade against your favorite brand.

TEAM DEBATE EXERCISES

1. A great controversy is brewing in the executive offices of Philip Morris: One group, led by CEO Bible, is strongly in favor of aggressively attacking all critics and defending cigarettes with no holds barred. Another group, supported by some prominent board members, believes the company and the industry should soften its stance and even be conciliatory. Debate the two strategic alternatives.

2. Debate the issue: The rights of nonsmokers are being emphasized too much. Smokers have rights, too.

INVITATION TO RESEARCH

1. Is the popularity of Joe Camel waning today?
2. What is the current situation regarding overseas incursions by U.S. tobacco companies?
3. Has the tobacco industry encountered any new criticisms?
4. What is the status of the $300 billion settlement for the industry?
5. Has Congress enacted any anti-tobacco legislation?

PART VI

ENTREPRENEURIAL ADVENTURES

CHAPTER 20

Parma Pierogies: Latent Promise

Mary Poldruhi may well be the best-known entrepreneur in Cleveland, Ohio. Even President Clinton knows her. While on the campaign trail in Cleveland in August 1992, he, his wife Hillary, and the Gores stopped in to have lunch at her year-old restaurant. This, of course, brought national exposure by the press. It also led to Mary's invitation to Washington for an inaugural luncheon, "Faces of Hope," a unique celebration of ordinary citizens who faced and conquered hardships. Clinton had drawn the guest list from thousands of persons he met during his cross-country campaign. Those invited for the inauguration had stories that touched him in a more personal way: "There are people here today who've succeeded against all odds," Clinton told his guests. "There's a young woman here today who opened a restaurant, when no bank would give her money. She just got on the telephone and called everybody with a Polish surname, said she wanted to open a Polish restaurant. Finally, she found enough people to bankroll her."

MARY POLDRUHI

Born into a big, traditional, ethnic family in Cleveland, Ohio, Poldruhi is the oldest of eight children. Because of her father's opinion that "girls don't have to go to college, just be secretaries, get married, and have babies," she worked as a secretary at Ohio Bell Telephone Company. She was promoted to customer service official and then advertising consultant for the Yellow Pages. Finding no challenge in these jobs, she left Ohio Bell to acquire a real estate license. But she dreamed of being an entrepreneur, and a Polish restaurant seemed a natural business opportunity. Working in real estate gave her the flexible hours she needed to pursue her dream.

"Everybody has that American dream to start their own company. You start from nothing with a lot of energy. I feel if you are committed to it and do a lot of hard work, you can succeed." At 33 years old, Poldruhi was a dynamo. "I am thinking global. The sky's the limit. Every city in the country has ethnics. I think we will be the next hottest fast food chain in the country." Well, perhaps it is a little soon to think about beating up on McDonald's, but Central European food could fill a unique marketing niche.

Articles about Poldruhi and her restaurant have appeared in *Time*, *Cleveland Magazine*, *Restaurant Hospitality*, and *Tempo* and in such newspapers as *The Wall Street Journal*, the *Cleveland Plain Dealer*, and a number of smaller suburban newspapers. Poldruhi was honored as "Woman-of-Achievement of 1993" by the National Association for Women in Careers.

Poldruhi's ingenuity was hardly better evidenced than in her initial fund-raising, which the president referred to. At first she had tried to get seed money from banks, but those she contacted either refused or made unacceptable demands as loan conditions. Showing a nascent flair for promotion and media relations, she wrote to two local TV celebrities, explaining her project and her plight and soliciting their interest and, hopefully, their public support. She must have been very compelling and persuasive, for they joined her endeavor. Next, she began looking in the Yellow Pages for people who might have money to invest, such as doctors, dentists, and lawyers. Since her business idea was for an ethnic restaurant, Poldruhi thought the best way to segment the market for investors would be to seek out only those who might have an ethnic heritage, as evidenced by names ending in "*-ski.*" She made cold calls mostly by telephone and raised $240,000 from 80 investors. In a quote that appeared in *Time* magazine, Poldruhi said, "I would have called every '-ski' in the United States and Poland if I had to."[1] Her persistence, confidence, and focus raise an interesting question: Is there an entrepreneurial personality? See the following box.

THE RESTAURANT

Poldruhi named her restaurant Parma Pierogies—Parma being the name of the Cleveland suburb—and she gave it the motif of a pink flamingo in white socks. (Pink flamingos still grace some yards in Parma.) The menu is for the most part ethnic and, naturally, features pierogies. These pierogies are offered boiled or deep-fried and come stuffed with such traditional fillings as potato and cheddar as well as innovative ones like spinach and mozzarella, all topped

---

[1] Thomas McCarroll, "Starting Over," *Time* (January 6, 1992): 63.

ISSUE BOX

IS THERE AN ENTREPRENEURIAL PERSONALITY?

The issue of whether certain persons have the right personality traits for self-employment and others do not and should not even consider it is akin to the enduring controversy of the leadership personality and even the sales personality: Are certain persons, because of their innate personality traits, bound to be leaders or to be great salespeople?

Most experts today disagree with the idea that leaders, and great salespeople, are born, not made. Diverse personalities have found success in leadership and in sales. But still the belief persists among some that the great ones were naturals.

How about entrepreneurship? Psychologists have designed tests to determine if a person has the right aptitude, but the tests' validity is suspect. Still, we can identify certain traits that may make some persons more successful in working for themselves. Most of this identification comes from the beliefs and actions of already successful entrepreneurs.

The true entrepreneur is a doer, not a dreamer. A lot of people have ideas, but few are determined to do something about them now, and few have the courage to give up the security of a regular paycheck to do it. Persistence, great self-confidence, an ability to disregard disappointments and rejections and keep trying—these are often mentioned by entrepreneurs. And some people just cannot stand working for someone else.

Mary Poldruhi most likely would have been successful outside of entrepreneurship. The qualities that make for successful entrepreneurs should work well in other endeavors. But her dream of entrepreneurship was irrepressible.

Do you think you have what it takes to be an entrepreneur? Why or why not?

---

with butter and onions. Some call them Polish ravioli. The moderately priced menu is rounded out with other ethnic specialties such as potato pancakes and a selection of fruit-filled dessert pierogies. Poldruhi has also reluctantly offered the popular kielbasa, although this violates her conception of healthy food.

Mary Poldruhi likes to emphasize the healthiness of pierogies. They are high in carbohydrates, and each contains only one gram of fat. They have considerably fewer calories than most other fast foods, as the menu prominently notes:

PIEROGIES ARE GOOD FOR YOU!

½ Dozen even with 1 oz. real butter and 1 oz. real sour cream is only about 500 calories! A "big burger" and fries is 1200 calories!

Prices are modest. A half-dozen pierogies with the toppings and salad cost only $4.99, and there is no tipping.

A VISIT

The first Parma Pierogies was located in a one-story building on the corner of a street with heavy local traffic. It shared the building with a bakery. The parking lot was small, having a capacity for about 10 cars. Her neighbors were mostly small commercial establishments, and all other fast food restaurants were at least a quarter-mile away.

Upon entering the premises, one is conscious of a predominance of pink and green colors and of soft music. The menu is on the wall and easily visible as you enter. Along another wall are articles and photographs highlighting the history of this enterprise, including pictures of celebrities. The eating area of the original restaurant was small, accommodating 16 tables, with a maximum capacity of 64 people. The feeling is one of casual comfort.

Customers give the cashier their order and receive a drink, straw, napkin, and a disposable fork and knife on a tray with the number of the order. They pay, take the tray, and find a seat, and employees bring the order to the table in a few minutes. Those who order coffee can expect free refills from an attentive waitress.

The restaurant is open seven days a week. During weekdays and Sundays, Mary Poldruhi has three to four servers; on the busy weekends she needs a few more employees. Overall, she has about 20 employees. Some 60 percent of the business comes from people dining in the restaurant: the rest comes from carry-out. Customers come from all over metropolitan Cleveland, and some even from as far away as Columbus, Ohio, 150 miles distant. In her first establishment, Mary sold 12,000 pierogies a week.

One of her concerns—one shared by most fast-food restaurants—is the turnover of employees. Most are part-time; the few full-time employees are housewives whose hours are limited to daytime. Students are the major source of part-time employees, but many prospectives would rather babysit on weekends, because it is easier work. Consequently, Poldruhi has to rely more than she would like on unskilled workers, and she has problems finding sufficient time to fully train them. She has also employed handicapped workers.

THE FUTURE

Mary Poldruhi is eager to expand. The 12,000-pierogies-a-week business convinces her that there is good potential for more restaurants with the same format. Are such growth ideas merely idle dreams, or do they represent a realistic probability? Several factors need to be considered.

First, does the ethnic food idea have staying power? Are pierogies a menu item that customers will order time after time? After two years of successful operation, the answer is *yes*: Repeat business has been strong.

Second, does the menu have broad appeal, or is it limited to a narrow consumer sector? The restaurant features Central European ethnic food, and many large cities in the north and northeast have sizable ethnic populations. These groups should be as attracted to the Parma Pierogies concept as the people of Cleveland.

Third, can the customer base be expanded? That is, are non-ethnics likely to be attracted to such a menu? Mary Poldruhi believes this is very much the case, and she notes that her restaurant is already appealing to many different consumers. Furthermore, she sees the health food idea as having great potential in a nation becoming more and more concerned about healthy living and health foods.

Fourth, is she likely to acquire the capital to expand fairly rapidly, or is this such a limiting factor that competitors may easily wedge into the market as they see the food concept becoming popularized? Financing may not be all that big a problem, for several reasons, as we will discuss next. The possibilities for obtaining venture capital and growth money outside of normal banking channels should be encouraging for many other small entrepreneurs. But some banks are more receptive to new entrepreneurial ideas and well-thought-out business plans than others.

Mary is already thinking about going public—that is, selling stock to investors. Once a business achieves fair success, with a good track record and a promising future, a public offering of stock is likely to be eagerly subscribed to by investors wanting in on the ground floor. This is even more likely when the business is somewhat unique from existing businesses, as Mary Poldruhi's is. Given her talent for gaining publicity, Poldruhi should be as successful in selling stock as she was in initially getting celebrities and 80 investors to back her.

The use of franchising offers the possibility for rapid expansion. See the following box for a discussion of franchising.

Mary Poldruhi already has a list of 2,000 potential franchisees from coast to coast, and she faces the possibility of a real business breakthrough. Additional expansion in metropolitan Cleveland is the first step, a sort of "testing of the waters." The ethnic compositions of Chicago, Detroit, and Pittsburgh are very similar to Cleveland's, making those cities reasonable expansion candidates. Interestingly, Mary Poldruhi sees great potential in non–Central European markets such as Los Angeles, "where we can play up the health aspect. Healthy food and good service are the wave of the future, and this concept fits right in there."[2]

[2]"Five for the Future," *Restaurant Hospitality* (December 1993): 80.

INFORMATION BOX

FRANCHISING

Franchising is a contractual arrangement in which the franchisor extends to independent franchisees the right to conduct a certain kind of business according to a particular format. While the franchising arrangement may involve a product, a more common type of franchise today provides a service rather than a product. The major contribution of the franchisor is a carefully developed, promoted, and controlled operation. Franchise operations depend on similar physical facilities and external signs to identify their far-flung outlets. Important to a franchise are prescribed standards and procedures to ensure uniform offerings and service.

A firm realizes two major advantages in expanding through franchised outlets rather than company-owned units. First, expansion can be very rapid, since the franchisees put up some or most of the money. Almost the only limit to growth is the need to screen applicants, to find suitable sites for new outlets, and to develop the managerial controls necessary to ensure consistency of performance. Second, people normally operate their own outlets more conscientiously because they are entrepreneurs with a personal stake, not hired managers.

The potential franchisee or licensee finds that the major advantage over other means of self-employment lies in the lower risk of business failure or, to say it positively, a greater chance of success. By going with an established franchisor, an entrepreneur will have a business that has proven customer acceptance and recognition. The franchisee can also benefit from well-developed managerial and promotional techniques and from the group buying power that is afforded.

One of the controversies between franchisors and franchisees is how rigid should be the controls and standards of operation. These range from the very strict policies of McDonald's to the much looser ones of many of the small franchise operations. As a prospective franchisee, which would you favor, and why?

UPDATE

By February 1997, Parma Pierogies (PP) was six years old. Mary took comfort in the fact that most new entrepreneurial ventures fail within the first two years, and hers had far exceeded that. Rather than expanding rapidly before the concept and her operating skills were completely proven, she had been conservative during these years. She moved her first restaurant to a larger site about a half mile away in 1994. She opened one new unit, on the east side of Cleveland in a non-ethnic neighborhood, also in 1994.

But with 1996 drawing to an end, Mary was poised to begin her expansion mode. First, she planned to saturate metropolitan Cleveland with five more restaurants in the next year, and then more gradually expand to other metro areas. Long-term goals were for 100 restaurants in the next five years.

The franchise package was in its final preparation. Three options would be available:

1. Regular large restaurants, of about 3,000 square feet with 80 seats. These would require an investment of about $500,000, but PP would help in the financing.
2. A smaller version, with about 30 seats and a drive-through window. The investment would be about $300,000.
3. A food court in a mall, requiring an investment of about $200,000.

Franchise fees would be in line with other competitive opportunities: $35,000 fee, one-time charge; 8 percent of gross sales; 2 percent of gross sales for national advertising.

Word of mouth, but more importantly, an aggressive use of free publicity, had propelled PP initially. The great publicity of President Clinton's two visits, and Mary's Washington visit, was worth tens of thousands of dollars of advertising. She used other creative publicity efforts. For example, Mary offered a pierogie with corned beef and cabbage for St. Patrick's Day and sent samples out to every radio station. For the successful and highly popular Cleveland Indians baseball team (playing to a sold-out ballpark), she concocted "Go Tribe" pierogies. She regularly sent press releases to the media every month.

However, Mary saw the need for TV advertising as she began her big Cleveland expansion drive. A 30-second TV blitz was planned for January–February 1997 to the tune of $50,000. The theme was to be "Tired of burgers, try Parma Pierogies."

Other growth possibilities seemed intriguing. With a production facility that produced 14,000 pierogies a week, and could be easily expanded, wholesaling into supermarkets, restaurants such as Marriott, and local bars and taverns seemed natural, and businesses were approaching Mary with this in mind. Another growth avenue showing promise was catering. A number of church outings and weddings had brought individual orders for 100 dozen pierogies. The highlight of catering efforts was the Cleveland Rock and Roll Hall of Fame inauguration in which PP was asked to supply the food for 500 media people. Finally, mail order remained a practical potential. Frozen pierogies ship well.

Mary saw competition as practically zero in early 1997. She knew of one pierogie start-up in Baltimore, but nothing consequential elsewhere.

Is this the nascent start of a major and unique fast-food operation? Maybe. Mary's favorite quote is: "If all obstacles had to be overcome first, nothing would ever be attempted."

WHAT CAN BE LEARNED?

Mary Poldruhi's accomplishments lead us to several rather significant insights for entrepreneurs. While individuals and situations differ, the latent promise of Parma Pierogies has considerable transferability to other persons and situations.

If at all possible, seek to differentiate. Such an admonition applies to all businesses, not merely to entrepreneurs. But it is more important to the latter simply because they are trying to wrest a place in the market with a new enterprise. If resources are limited—as they are with most small businesses—an attractive difference from existing competitors may be the crucial ingredient.

The pierogi, with its Central European flair and its healthy food connotation, offers an interesting change from the hamburger, chicken, taco, and pizza menus of the major fast-food restaurants. The market for pierogies is many times less than that for hamburgers, but this fact is offset by the absence of competition. The existence of a niche suggests that aggressive growth efforts, even in such a limited market, could bring great success. And Mary Poldruhi does not even accept the idea that the market may be limited: "Healthy foods . . . are the wave of the future."

Good publicity can jet-start an entrepreneurial effort. Poldruhi excelled in gaining publicity for her nascent enterprise, even to the unbelievable extent of gaining the patronage of the President of the United States and being singled out as an outstanding example of entrepreneurship. She zealously cultivated all efforts at publicity, spending little for advertising as a result. Early on she was able to enlist the interest and support of local television celebrities, and the ingenuity of her fundraising was a natural for media attention. But Mary Poldruhi enhanced her media exposure, not by blatantly seeking it out, but rather by being cooperative and appreciative of any reporters or researchers who had an interest.

Publicity can be a powerful tool for any business if it is carefully crafted, being neither too overt and self-seeking nor too secretive and proprietary. In particular, the media are attracted to a good story.

The franchising format offers great opportunities, but also lurking dangers. Franchising is significantly different from other types of business operations. Rapid growth is possible through franchising—far more rapid than the growth a firm can achieve on its own, even with substantial resources. Because somebody else is putting up most or all of the capital for an outlet, the major requirements for expansion are finding and wooing sufficient investors/licensees and locating attractive sites for additional units. Both requirements can be met carelessly in the quest for wild expansion or carefully for controlled expansion.

In franchising, a few poor operations can hurt the other outlets because all operate under the same format and logo. This is similar to the situation of any chain operation (a few stores can hurt the image of the rest of the chain), but a franchise system is composed of independent entrepreneurs who tend to be less controllable than the hired managers of a chain.

The rapid growth made possible through a franchise system can be its downfall. Because growth in the number of units can occur easily and quickly, it is tempting to rush headlong into opening more units to meet the demand of prospective licensees and receive the up-front licensing fee. Emphasis on growth often means that existing operations are ignored. As a consequence, they are undercontrolled, and emerging problems do not receive adequate attention. Screening of people and locations tends to become superficial. Eventually, the bubble may burst, and the franchisor may be faced with the realization that many outlets are marginal and need to be closed. It remains to be seen whether Mary Poldruhi will be prudent in her quest for expansion or succumb to the very real temptation to be reckless.

Tight controls are particularly needed in franchise operations. All firms, but especially franchise chains, need to maintain tight controls over widespread outlets in order to be sufficiently informed about emerging problems and opportunities, to optimize use of resources, and to protect a desired image and standard of performance.

Establishing a control process requires three basic steps:

1. Standards of performance must be set and communicated to those persons involved.
2. Performance should be checked against these standards.
3. Deviations from expected performance usually require corrective action.

As a franchise enterprise grows, such controls become all the more important. For Mary Poldruhi, formal controls will be less important with a handful of outlets than with 20 or more.

When standards are specifically designated and communicated to those responsible for adhering to them, the next step of the control process can be imposed: measuring performance against the standards. Performance is best measured when outside auditors, inspectors, or district and home-office executives visit the premises unannounced, perhaps with a checklist in hand, and grade actual against expected performance. All aspects of the operation should be checked—from the grease content of the french fries to the soap supply in the restrooms.

After deviations from the standards are identified and their importance assessed, measures should be taken to correct the situation. Although franchise operations involve independent owners, the franchisor still has authority to impose sanctions on unacceptable performance. Such sanctions typically consist of warnings, probation, and finally, if performance still does not meet standards, removal of the franchise. Will Mary Poldruhi be tough enough to do this? In expanding a new enterprise, owners may be tempted to be soft in order to avoid alienating desired franchisees. In the long run, this can be most unwise.

CONSIDER

Do you see any other learning insights coming from this adventure in entrepreneurship?

QUESTIONS

1. Do you think Mary Poldruhi's expansion dreams are realistic? Why or why not?
2. What do you think of Parma Pierogies's motif of a pink flamingo with white socks?
3. The high turnover of employees makes for uneven service. Do you have any constructive ideas for improving this?
4. Does the menu of Parma Pierogies appeal to you? What, if anything, would you like to see added?
5. Mary Poldruhi is actively involved in the day-to-day operation of her business. Do you see any potential problems as she expands geographically?
6. President Clinton did not stop at Parma Pierogies on his campaign trip to Cleveland just before the 1996 election, despite Mary Poldruhi's ardent hope that he would. Do you think people will see this as somewhat of a repudiation of her pierogies?

HANDS-ON EXERCISES

1. Mary Poldruhi has hired you as a marketing expert to guide her growth beyond metropolitan Cleveland. What marketing strategy plans can you offer? Be as specific as possible and defend your ideas.
2. You have been hired by Mary to be the sales manager for non-restaurant diversifications, such as catering, selling to groceries, and mail order. Design a marketing strategy for tapping these potential segments.

TEAM DEBATE EXERCISE

It is the end of the third year of PP's operation, and sales are satisfactory although profits are fairly modest. A major controversy is brewing between Mary and some of her major investors. Mary advocates a go-slow strategy, at least for a few more years, but these investors think expansion should be far more vigorous. Debate the issue of slow growth versus vigorous growth

INVITATION TO RESEARCH

Investigate the current situation with Parma Pierogies. Has expansion taken place? Has the business been taken public? How successful does it appear to be?

CHAPTER 21

Boston Beer: Bearding the Big Boys

The brewing industry seems in turmoil. Major old brands are seeing their sales diminish spectacularly. For example, original Coors sales volume in 1995 was less than one-third what it was in the 1980s. Budweiser's sales fell 9 percent from 1990 to 1994. And Miller's major player, Lite, experienced a gut-wrenching 18 percent decline in these four years.

But little breweries, microbrewers, were in the ascendancy, even though their total share of industry sales by 1995 was only 1 percent. Still, this was $1.3 billion, with a growth percentage rate in the double-digits each year.

After decades in which the number of independent breweries dwindled before the seemingly unbeatable onslaught of the major brewers, today this industry provides great entrepreneurial opportunities. A host of new beers, called craft beers, offers more than 2,600 brands: fruity beers, honey beers, fiery chili beers, spiced beers and ice beers. And this does not count the lagers. In 1995, new breweries were opening at the rate of five a week in the United States.[1] Boston Beer led the charge of the little players. Now the big brewers were desperate, and even seeking to join the ranks of the micro-brewers. A staid industry was fermenting.

THE ASCENDANCY OF BOSTON BEER—SEIZING AN OPPORTUNITY

Jim Koch (pronounced cook) founded Boston Beer after being a consultant for Boston Consulting Group for six and a half years. Entrepreneurship

---

[1]"Fast Track," *Entrepreneur* (December 1995): 112.

obsessed him, and he wondered if the brewing industry might not be ripe for a new type of product and a new approach.

Years before, his great-great-grandfather, Louis Koch, had concocted a recipe at his St. Louis brewery that was a heavier, more full-bodied beer than such as Budweiser or Miller. However, it was much more expensive to produce than the mass-market beers. It involved a lengthy brewing and fermentation process, as well as such premium ingredients as Bavarian hops that cost many times more than those regularly used by other brewers.

Koch thought he saw a strategic window of opportunity in a particular consumer segment: men in their mid-20s and older who were beer aficionados and would be willing to pay a premium for a good-tasting beer. What was far from certain was how large a segment this would be. Were there enough such sophisticated drinkers to support the new company he envisioned?

In 1984, he detected a clue that this might indeed be the case: sales were surging for import beers such as Heineken and Beck's with their different tastes. He saw this as portending that enough Americans would be willing to pay substantially more for a full-bodied flavor.

Koch also believed these imports were very vulnerable to well-made domestic brews. They faced a major problem in maintaining freshness with a product that goes sour rather quickly. He knew that the foreign brewers, in trying to minimize the destructive influence of the time lag between production and consumption, were adding preservatives and even using cheaper ingredients for the American market.

Some small local brewers were offering stronger tastes. But they were having great difficulty producing a lager with consistent quality. And he sensed they were squandering their opportunity. Although they could produce small batches of well-crafted beer, albeit of erratic quality, what they mainly lacked was ability and resources to aggressively market their products.

He decided to take the plunge and gave up his lucrative job with the prestigious Boston Consulting Group. Amassing sufficient capital to start a new venture is the common problem with almost all entrepreneurs, and so it was with Koch. Still, he was better off than most. He had saved $100,000 from his years with Boston Consulting, and he persuaded family and friends to chip in another $140,000. But while this might be enough to start a new retail or service venture, it was far less than the estimated $10 million or more needed to build a state-of-the-art brewery.

Koch got around this major obstacle. Instead of building or buying he contracted an existing firm, Pittsburgh Brewing Company, to brew his beer. It had good facilities, but more than this, its people had the brewing skills coming from more than 30 years in operation. He called his new beer Samuel Adams, after a Revolutionary War patriot who was also a brewer.

But a mighty problem still existed, and the success of the venture hinged on this. Koch would have to sell his great-tasting beer at $20 a case to break even and make a reasonable profit. This was 15 percent more than even the premium imports like Heineken. Would anyone buy such an expensive beer, and one that did not even have the cachet of an import? See the following information box about the merits of a high-price strategy.

It fell to Koch as the fledgling firm's only salesperson to try to acquaint retailers and consumers with his new beer, this unknown brand with the very high price. "I went from bar to bar," he said. "Sometimes I had to call 15 times before someone would agree to carry it."[2]

He somehow conjured up enough funds for a $100,000 ad campaign in the local market. Shunning the advertising theme of the big brewers that stressed the sociability of the people drinking their brand, Koch's ads attacked the imports: "Declare your independence from foreign beer," he urged. The name Samuel Adams was compatible with this cry for independence. Foreign brews were singled out as not having the premium ingredi-

---

INFORMATION BOX

COMPETING ON PRICE, REVISITED: THE PRICE/QUALITY PERCEPTION

In the Southwest Air case, we examined the potent strategy of offering the lowest prices—if this could be done profitably due to a lower expense and overhead structure than competitors.

Here, Boston Beer is attempting to compete while having some of the highest prices in the industry. Is this crazy? Why would anyone pay prices higher than even the expensive imported beers, just for a different taste?

The highest price can convey an image of the very highest quality. We as consumers have long been conditioned to think this. With cars, we may not be able to afford this highest quality, such as an Infiniti, Lexus, or Mercedes convertible. But with beer, almost anyone can afford to buy the highest price brew sometimes, maybe to influence guests or to simply enjoy a different taste that we are led to think is better.

Sometimes such a price/quality perception sets us up. It might be valid, or might not be. Especially is this true where quality is difficult to ascertain, such as with beer and liquor, with bottled water, with perfume, as well as other products with hidden ingredients and complex characteristics.

Do you think you have ever fallen victim to the price/quality misperception? How does one determine quality for an alcoholic beverage such as vodka, gin, and scotch, as well as beer? By the taste? The advertising claims? Anything else?

---

[2]Jenny McCune, "Brewing Up Profits," *Management Review* (April 1994): 18.

ents and quality brewing of Samuel Adams. Koch appeared on most of his commercials, saying such things as: "Hi, I'm Jim Koch. It takes me all year to brew what the largest import makes in just three hours because I take the time to brew Samuel Adams right. I use my great-great-grandfather's century-old recipe, all malt brewing and rare hops that cost 10 times what they use in the mass-produced imports."[3]

Gradually his persistence in calling on retailers and his anti-import ads, some of which garnered national attention in such periodicals as *Newsweek* and *USA Today*, induced more and more bartenders and beer drinkers to at least try Samuel Adams. Many liked it, despite the high price. (Or, perhaps, because of it?)

Now his problem became finding distributors, and this proved particularly troubling for a new firm in an industry where major brands often had a lock on existing wholesalers. The situation was so bad in Boston—no wholesaler would carry Samuel Adams, even though it was a local brand— that Boston Beer bought a truck and delivered the cases itself.

He slowly expanded his distribution one geographical area at a time, from Boston into Washington, D.C., then to New York, Chicago, and California, taking care that production could match the steady expansion without sacrificing quality. He brought in his secretary at Boston Consulting, Rhonda Kaliman, to assist him in building a sales organization. This grew from less than a dozen sales reps in 1989 to 70 nationwide by 1994, more than any other microbrewer and about the same number as Anheuser-Busch, the giant of the industry. Now Samuel Adams salespeople could give more personalized and expert attention to customers than competitors whose sales reps often sold many beverage lines.

Sales soared 63 percent in 1992 when the company went national and achieved distribution in bars and restaurants in 48 states. In a continual search for new beer ideas, Boston Beer added a stout, a wheat beer, and even a cranberry lambic, a type of beer flavored with fruit. Adding to the growing popularity were numerous industry awards and citations Samuel Adams had received since 1984. Not only was it voted the Best Beer in America four times at the annual Great American Beer Festival, but it received six gold medals in blind tastings.

Jim Koch and two of his brewmasters were testing their entry into the Great American Beer Festival—"Triple Bock." They had not yet tried to market this creation, although their expectations were high. But this was so different. It boasted a 17 percent alcoholic content with no carbonation and they planned to package it in a cobalt blue bottle with a cork. It was meant to be sipped as a fine brandy. "It's a taste that nobody has ever put into a

[3]McCune, "Brewing Up Profits," 19.

beer," Koch said.[4] Too innovative? Jim and his colleagues pondered this as they sipped on this beautiful day in April, 1994.

THE BREWING INDUSTRY IN THE 1990s

In 10 years, the company had forged ahead to become a major contender in its industry and the largest U.S. specialty brewer. But a significant change in consumer preferences was confronting the industry in the 90s. The big brands that had been so dominant, to the extent that smaller brewers could not compete against their production efficiencies, now were seeing their market shares decline. The brand images they had spent millions trying to establish were in trouble. Many were cutting prices in desperate attempts to keep and lure consumers. For example, special price promotions in some markets were offering 12-packs of Budweiser, Coors, and Miller for just $1.99.

The shifting consumer preferences, and the severe price competition with their regular brands, were compelling the big brewers to seek the types of beers that would command higher prices. Imports were still strengthening, growing at an 11 percent rate between 1993 and 1994. But microbrews seemed the wave of the future, with prices and profit margins that were mouth watering to the big barons of the industry.

Consequently, the major breweries came up with their own craft brands. For example, Icehouse, a name that conveys a microbrewery image, was actually produced in megabreweries by Miller Brewing. So too, Killian's Irish Red, a pseudo-import, was made by Coors in Golden, Colorado. Killian's, stocked in retailer's import cases and commanding a high price, muscled its way abreast of Samuel Adams as the largest specialty beer in the United States.

The brewing industry was desperately trying to innovate. But no one saw anything revolutionary on the horizon, not like the 1970s, when light beer made a significant breakthrough in the staid industry. Now, "ice" beers became the gimmick. First developed in Canada, these are beers produced at temperatures a little colder than ordinary beer. This gives them a slightly higher alcohol content. Whether because of this, or the magic of the name *ice*, these products captured almost 6 percent of total industry sales in 1994, more than all the imports combined. But, still, the potential seems limited.

Anheuser-Busch, with a still dominant 44 percent of U.S. beer sales despite its 9 percent sales volume slide in the early 1990s, asserted its reluctance to change: "The breweries that we have are designed to produce big brands. Our competition can't compete with big brands. That's why they've

[4]McCune, "Brewing Up Profits," 20.

had to introduce lots of little brands."[5] But even Anheuser, despite its words, was sneaking into microbrewing by buying into Redhook Ale Brewery, a Seattle microbrewery that sold 76,000 barrels of beer in 1993, versus Anheuser's 90 million. Anheuser's distributors applauded this move as a badly needed step in giving them higher-profit, prestige brands. When Anheuser tiptoed into this market, other giants began to look for microbreweries to invest in.

This troubled Jim Koch: "I'm afraid of the big guys. They have the power to dominate any segment they want." Then he expressed his confidence: "Still my faith is that better beer will win out."[6]

THE CONTINUING SAGA OF BOSTON BEER

In August 1995, Boston Beer announced an initial public stock offering (IPO) of 5.3 million shares, of which 990,000 shares would be made available directly to the public through a coupon offer. The selling of shares to the general public was unlike any other IPO, and as such caught the fancy of the national press.

The company put clip-and-mail coupons on Samuel Adams six-packs and other beer packages. These offered customers a chance to buy 33 shares of stock at a maximum price of $15, or $495 total. Only one subscription was allowed per customer, and these were honored on a first-come, first-served basis. The success was overwhelming. First distributed in October, by the first of November the offering was oversubscribed. The company expected that the total funds generated from the IPO would be $75 million.[7] But when the new stock offering finally came out on November 20, 1995, heavy demand led it to being priced at $20 a share. Two days later it was selling on the New York Stock Exchange for $30. Interestingly, its stock symbol is SAM.

Boston Beer was riding high. It reported an impressive 50 percent growth in 1994 over 1993, brewing 700,000 barrels and becoming the largest microbrewery in the country. The entire microbrewing industry was producing more than double the volume in 1990. By now Boston Beer had 12 different beers, including 6 seasonals, and was distributing in all 50 states through 300 wholesalers. Its newest beer, the 17-percent alcohol content Triple Bock, had been introduced to the market.[8]

Most of Boston Beer's production continued to be contract brewed. In early 1995, it did encounter difficulties with Pittsburgh Brewing, the first of

[5] Patricia Sellers, "A Whole New Ballgame for Beer," *Fortune* (September 19, 1994): 86.

[6] *Ibid.*

[7] "Boston Beer's Plan for Offering Stock," *The New York Times—National Edition* (August 26, 1995): 20.

[8] "Little Giants," *Beverage-World* (December 1994): 26.

the three contract breweries it was now using. Because of an alleged over-draft of $31 million by its owner, Michael Carlow, who was accused of fraud, the brewery was to be auctioned off. Jim Koch stoutly professed having no interest in buying the brewery and that any problems of Pittsburgh Brewery would have no effect on Boston Beer.[9] See the following information box for a discussion of contracting out rather than building production facilities.

By 1996, the term "microbrew" evolved into "craft beer." As Jim Koch put it, "A microbrewery is a brewer that makes less than 15,000 barrels a year. Today, that means someone who's just starting up or somebody who has never been successful."[10] Such craft beers now accounted for 2 percent of U.S. beer sales and were the higher-priced end of the market.

As the leader in this "craft" beer sector, Boston Beer produced more than 900,000 barrels in 1995, up from 700,000 the year before. For 1996 this increased 40 percent. *Brandweek* magazine marveled at this: "In a craft-beer

---

INFORMATION BOX

THE MERITS OF KEEPING FIXED COSTS TO A MINIMUM

There is much to be said for any enterprise, new or older, to keep its fixed overhead to a minimum. If it can escape having to commit large sums to physical plant and production facilities, its breakeven point is far less, which means that less sales are needed to cover expenses and interest payments, leaving more to go into profits. In the event of adversity, such a firm can retrench much more nimbly than if burdened with heavy overhead. In every such decision of renting or buying, the economics of the particular situation needs to be carefully analyzed.

Arguments against such contracting out usually maintain that efficiency will be sacrificed, since direct control is lacking. So, this argument would maintain that Pittsburgh Brewing could not do as good a job as Boston Beer could have done itself. Yet, the empircal evidence is that Boston's contract brewers were giving it the high standards it wanted. It set the standards and insisted on them being met, or it would find another contract brewery.

Still, the "edifice complex" tantalizes most top executives, as well as hospital and school administrators, who see the stone and mortar of their buildings and factories as conveying tangible evidence of their own importance and accomplishments. They will claim that such is important to the public image of their organization.

Given the approximately $100 million that Boston Beer receives from its IPO, would you predict some of this will go for "stones and mortar"?

---

[9]"Sam Adams Brewer May Be On Block," *Boston-Business-Journal* (February 24, 1995): 3.
[10]Bob Bauer, "Bubbling Ahead," *Supermarket News* (September 23, 1996): 50.

world populated by the likes of Pete's Wicked Ale, Rogue, Ruffian and Rhino Chasers, it can come as a shock to recognize that the outstanding success story continues to be a brand with a portrait of a politically incorrect two-centuries-dead white Anglo male on the package.[11]

As brands proliferated—the new craft-beer segment now comprised over 1,000 brands—Koch continued an aggressive strategy of line extension for the Samuel Adams brand with eight year-round flavors and seven seasonal ones. To make the brand more approachable, he advertised it as Sam Adams rather than Samuel Adams. A number of other brands were also introduced, such as Oregon Ale that used American hops rather than the European ones of Samuel Adams. In an effort to hedge his bets, Koch took an option to acquire Cincinnati's Hudepohl-Schoenling brewery should consumers show resistance to contract-only beers. He also explored an alliance with Britain's Whitbread to develop new brews for the British market.

Anheuser-Busch now viewed Boston Beer as a significant rival and in fall 1996 launched an advertising campaign challenging Boston Beer to reveal itself as a mass-produced brand rather than a small regional craft brewery. One of the ads used a Halloween theme showing a Boston Beer executive being haunted by the ghost of Samuel Adams; the "ghost" urged him to be honest with consumers and tell them that the beer was actually produced somewhere else than Boston.[12]

ANALYSIS

Entrepreneurial Character

Although many entrepreneurial opportunities come in the retail and service industries, mostly because these typically require less start-up investment, Jim Koch saw the possibility in beer, even without a huge wallet. He started with $100,000 of his own money and $140,000 from friends and relatives. He had the beer recipe and determination. By contracting out the production to an existing brewery with unused production capacity, the bulk of the start-up money could be spent on nonproduction concerns, such as advertising.

His determination to gain acceptance of his beer, despite its high price and nonforeign origin, is characteristic of most successful entrepreneurs. They press on, despite obstacles in gaining acceptance. They have confidence that their product or concept is viable. They are not easily discouraged.

At the same time, Koch believed he had something unique, a flavor and quality that neither domestic nor imported brews could deliver. He had the

---

[11] Barry Kermouch, "Samuel Adams," *Brandweek* (September 9, 1996): 42.

[12] Bill McDowell, "A-B Campaign Chastises Boston Beer Marketing," *Advertising Age*, (October 28, 1996): 4.

audacity to further make his product unique by charging even higher prices than the imports, thus conveying an image of highest quality.

His search for uniqueness did not end with the product. He developed an advertising theme far different than that of other beers by stressing quality and aggressively attacking the imports: "Declare your independence from foreign beer." And he was the spokesman on TV and radio commercials, giving them a personal and charismatic touch.

As Boston Beer moved out of regional into national distribution, he developed a sales force as large as Anheuser-Busch, the giant of the industry. His grasping of uniqueness even went to Boston Beer's initial public stock offering, in which customers were invited to buy into the company through coupons on six-packs, and it was oversubscribed in only a few weeks.

Controlled Growth

The temptation for any firm, but especially for newer, smaller firms, when demand seems to be growing insatiably is to expand aggressively: "We must not miss this opportunity." Such optimism can sow the seeds of disaster, when demand suddenly lessens because of a saturated market and/or new competition. And a firm is left with too much plant and other fixed assets, and a burdensome overhead.

Controlled growth—we might also call this "aggressive moderation"—is usually far better. Now a firm is not shunning growth, even vigorous growth, but is controlling it within its current resources and not overextending itself. Boston Beer showed this restraint by expanding within its production capability, adding several more contract brewers as needed. It expanded market by market at the beginning, only moving to a new geographical area when it could supply it. First was Boston, then Washington, D.C., then New York, Chicago, California, and finally all 50 states.

Besides husbanding resources, both material and personnel, aggressive moderation is compatible with the tightness of controls needed to assure high-quality product and service standards. Even more than this, moderation allows a firm to build the accounting and financial standards and controls needed to prevent the dangerous buildup of inventories and expenses.

WHAT CAN BE LEARNED?

The "price-quality perception." We have a curious phenomenon today regarding price. More consumers than ever are shopping at discount stores because they supposedly offer better prices than other retailers. Airlines competing with lowest prices, such as Southwest and Continental, are greatly increasing airline traffic. Yet for many products, especially those that are complex and have hidden ingredients, a higher price than competitors is the major indicator of higher quality. Boston Beer certainly confirms that higher price can successfully differentiate a firm, especially if the taste is robustly different, and if the theme of highest quality is constantly stressed in advertising.

Perhaps the moral is that both low prices and high prices can be successful. A strategy of lowest prices, however, tends to be more vulnerable, since competitors can easily and quickly match these low prices (not always profitably, of course), while a high-price strategy stressing quality tends to attract fewer competitors. But it will also attract fewer customers, as with higher-priced goods such as office furniture. The high-price strategy should be more generally successful with products that are relatively inexpensive to begin with, such as beer, and ones where the image of prestige and good taste is attractive.

The challenge of the right approach to growth. In the analysis section we discussed the desirability of controlled growth or aggressive moderation and noted that Boston Beer practiced this well. There are some who would challenge such a slowness in grabbing opportunities. Exuberant expansion instead is advocated, when and if the golden opportunity is presented (some would call this "running with the ball"). Operations should be expanded as fast as possible in such a situation, some would say. But there are times when caution is advised.

Risks lie on all sides as we reach for these opportunities. When a market begins to boom and a firm is unable to keep up with demand without greatly increasing capacity and resources, it faces a dilemma: stay conservative in the expectation that the burgeoning potential will be short-lived, and thereby abdicate some of the growing market to competitors, or expand vigorously and take full advantage of the opportunity. If the euphoria is short-lived, and demand slows drastically, the firm is then left with expanded capacity, more resource commitment than needed, high interest and carrying costs, and perhaps even jeopardized viability because of overextension. Above all, however, a firm should not expand beyond its ability to maintain organizational and accounting control over the operation. Wild expansion is tantamount to letting a sailing ship brave the uncertainties of a storm under full canvas.

Keep the breakeven point as low as possible, especially for new ventures. Fixed investments in plant and equipment raise the breakeven point of sales needed to cover overhead costs and make a profit. Boston Beer kept its breakeven point low by using contract breweries. Now this would have been a mistake if the quality of production at these breweries was erractic or not up to Boston Beer expectations. These were indeed vital requirements if it were to succeed in selling its high-priced beer. But by working closely with experienced brewers, quality control apparently was no problem.

Certainly the lower breakeven point makes for less risk. Despite research and careful planning, the environment is constantly changing as to customer attitudes and preferences, and particularly in actions of competitors.

When a decision involves high stakes and an uncertain future—which translates into high risks—is it not wiser to approach the venture somewhat conservatively, not spurning the opportunity, but also not committing major resources and efforts until success appears more certain?

The importance of maintaining quality. For a high-priced product, a brief letdown in quality control can be disastrous to the image. The story is told of Jim Koch ordering a draft of his own Samuel Adams at a restaurant across from Lincoln Center in New York City. He was horrified at the taste. He called the manager and they went to the basement and looked at the keg. "It was two-and-a-half months past its pull date." The manager quickly changed the past-its-prime keg, which the distributor, intentionally or not, had sold the restaurant.[13] Sometimes a lapse in quality is not the fault of the manufacturer, but of a distributor or dealer. Whoever is at fault, the brand image is tarnished. And it is difficult to resurrect a reputation of poor or uncertain quality.

CONSIDER

Can you think of any other learning insights?

QUESTIONS

1. Have you ever tried one of the Boston Beer brews? If so, how did you like the taste? Did you think it was worth the higher price?
2. The investment community evidently thinks Boston Beer has great growth probabilities to have bid up the initial issue price so quickly. Do you agree? Why or why not?
3. "This myriad of specialty beers is but a fad. People will quickly grow tired of expensive, strong-flavored beer. Much of it is just a gimmick." Discuss.
4. What problems do you see retailers facing with the burgeoning number of different beers today? What might be the implications of this?
5. Playing the devil's advocate (one who takes an opposing view for the sake of argument and deeper analysis), critique the strategy of charging some of the highest prices in the world for your beer.

---

[13] McCune, "Brewing Up Profits," 16.

6. We saw in one of the last sections of the chapter the detection of a problem with the freshness of a beer at a restaurant by Jim Koch himself. How can Boston Beer prevent such incidents from happening again? Can such distributor negligence or shortsighted actions be totally prevented by Boston Beer?

7. Do you think Boston Beer can continue to compete effectively against the giant brewers who are now moving with their infinitely greater resources into the specialty-beer market with their own microbrews? Why or why not?

HANDS-ON EXERCISES

1. You are Jim Koch. You have just learned that Michael Feuer, founder of OfficeMax, has grown his entreprenurial endeavor to a $1.8 billion enterprise in just seven years. It has taken you ten years to grow Boston Beer to a $50 million firm. You are depressed at this, but determined to greatly increase your company's growth. How would you go about setting Boston Beer on a great growth path? Be as specific as you can. What dangers do you see ahead?

2. It is 1986 and Boston Beer is beginning its growth after hiring Pittsburgh Brewery to produce its beer. Jim Koch has charged you with coordinating the efforts at Pittsburgh Brewery, paying particular attention to assuring that your quality standards are rigidly maintained. How would you go about doing this?

TEAM DEBATE EXERCISE

Debate how Boston Beer should commit the $100 million it received in late 1995 from the public stock offering. In particular, debate whether the bulk of the proceeds should go to building its own state-of-the-art brewery, or something else.

INVITATION TO RESEARCH

How is Boston Beer faring? Is it encountering any problems in its expansion? Has the stock price continued to rise?

PART VII

ETHICAL AND SOCIAL PRESSURES

CHAPTER 22

ADM: Price Fixing and Political Cronyism

In June 1995, a whistleblower informed federal investigators of the scheme of a giant multinational conglomerate, Archer-Daniels-Midland, to control sales of a widely demanded food additive and thus keep prices high worldwide. For three years, he had been secretly recording meetings of the firm's senior executives with Asian and European competitors. The whistleblower, Mark E. Whitacre, was revealed by an attorney who was supposedly conferring with him as a possible client.

Repercussions quickly followed. The company charged him with stealing from the firm and fired him. The plot became more complicated. But overhanging all was the role of the corporation and its 77-year-old top executive: Did they truly act unethically and illegally, or were the allegations ballooned out of all proportions?

THE WHISTLEBLOWER, MARK E. WHITACRE

Mark Whitacre joined Archer-Daniels in 1989, and spent about half his career there helping antitrust investigators. He was a rising star, recruited to head the fledgling BioProducts division, where he rose to become a corporate vice-president and a leading candidate to become the company's next president while still in his thirties.

He had been recruited from Degussa AG, a German chemical company where he was manager in organic chemicals and feed additives. However, his resume inflated his credentials with the title executive vice-president; he was only a vice-president.

While at ADM, he earned a business degree from a home-study school in California, Later ADM issued biographical material crediting him with an MBA from Northwestern University and the prestigious J.L. Kellogg School of Management. In an interview, Whitacre admitted the claims about his MBA were inflated to impress Wall Street analysts, but he blamed ADM: "I feel bad about it. I, along with other executives that speak at analysts' meetings, cooperated . . . it's a common practice."[1]

His ambition was to become president of ADM, which he claimed was promised him repeatedly.[2] How becoming a governmental informer would help him with this ambition seems murky.

Over three years he secretly helped investigators obtain videotapes revealing two senior executives meeting with Asian and European competitors in various places around the world. The executives were vice-chairman Michael D. Andreas, son and heir apparent of the 77-year-old Dwayne Andreas, chairman and chief executive; and vice-president Terrence Wilson, head of the corn-processing division. Sometimes Whitacre would wear a hidden microphone to obtain the incriminating evidence of price fixing. The following box discusses whistleblowing in general, but the travails of Whitacre graphically portray a worse scenario.

FBI agents on the night of June 27 entered the headquarters of the huge grain-processing company in Decatur, Illinois. They carted off files and delivered grand jury subpoenas seeking evidence of price collusion of ADM and competitors. Whitacre was one of the executives subpoenaed, and met with an attorney recommended by the company's general counsel office, a common practice when companies face governmental inquiries.

Shortly after this meeting, the attorney disclosed to ADM that Whitacre was the federal informant in their midst, thus imperiling Whitacre's position in the company. This seemed a clear ethical violation of the confidentiality of lawyer/client relations. But the attorney, John M. Dowd of a prominent law firm doing business with ADM, claimed that Whitacre authorized him to do so. Whitacre and his new attorney angrily denied any such authorization.

In any case, now the company had the knowledge to retaliate. They fired him, accused him of stealing $2.5 million, and reported these findings to the Justice Department. Later, the company increased the amount it claimed Whitacre had stolen to $9 million. They charged that he had been embezzling money by submitting phony invoices for capital expenditures, then channeling the payments into offshore bank accounts.

---

[1] "ADM Informant Faces Widening Allegations; He Attempts Suicide," *The Wall Street Journal* (August 14, 1995): A4.
[2] *Ibid.*

INFORMATION BOX

WHISTLEBLOWING

A whistleblower is an insider in an organization who publicizes alleged corporate misconduct. Such misconduct may involve unethical practices of all kinds, such as fraud, restraint of trade, price fixing, bribes, coercion, unsafe products and facilities, and violations of other laws and regulations. Presumably, the whistleblower has exhausted the possibilities for changing the questionable practices within the normal organizational channels and, as a last resort, has taken the matter to government officials and/or the press.

Since whistleblowing may result in contract cancellations, corporate fines, and lost jobs, those who become whistleblowers may be vilified by their fellow workers and fired and even framed by their firms. This makes whistleblowing a course of action only for the truly courageous, whose concern for societal best interest outweighs their concern for themselves.

However, there is somtimes a thin line between an employee who truly believes the public interest is jeoparidzed and the individual who has a gripe or is a fanatic. There are some who believe management is condoning misconduct when in fact such misconduct is isolated and without management awareness or acceptance. And some see whistleblowing as a means of furthering their own interests, such as gaining fame or even advancing their careers.

Ralph Nader, in a 1972 book on whistleblowing, suggested that corporate employees have a primary duty to protect society that exists over and above secondary obligations to the corporation. He gives examples of whistleblowing heroes, as well as a course of action for other would-be whistleblowers.[3]

Do you think you could ever be a whistleblower? Under what circumstances?

The Justice Department saw the credibility of their key witness being weakened by such allegations, especially since Whitacre acknowledged that he had indeed participated in the bogus invoice schemes, although he said the payments were made with the full knowledge and encouragement of company higher-ups. Nevertheless, he and as many as 12 other ADM executives came under criminal investigation for evading taxes. The Justice Department's criminal fraud section further examined allegations that the off-the-books payments were approved by top management.[4]

A few days later, Whitacre tried to kill himself. At dawn, he drove his car into the garage of his new home, closed the door, and left the engine run-

---

[3] Ralph Nader, Peter Petkas, and Nate Blackwell, *Whistleblowing* (New York: Bantam Books) 1972.

[4] Ronald Henkoff, "Checks, Lies and Videotape," *Fortune* (October 30, 1995): 110.

ning. On this morning he was supposed to fly to Washington to meet with federal authorities. He had arranged for the gardener to come to work late that morning, but the gardener arrived shortly after seven and found Whitacre unconscious in his car.

Shortly before the suicide attempt, Whitacre had written a letter to *The Wall Street Journal*, acknowledging that he had received money from ADM through unusual means: "Regarding overseas accounts and kickbacks; and overseas payments to some employees, Dig Deep. It's there! They give it; then use it against you when you are their enemy."[5]

On September 13, 1995, F. Ross Johnson, an ADM board member, in a talk at Emory University's Goizueta Business School commented on Whitacre's suicide attempt: "You know, he tried to commit suicide. But he did it in a six-car garage, which, I think, if you're going to do it, that's the place to do it. [The audience laughed.] And the gardener just happened to come by. So now he is bouncing around."[6]

Whether the suicide attempt was genuine or contrived, Whitacre apparently faced a traumatic period in his life. He wound up in a suburban Chicago hospital with no job and no place to live. He had money problems, being unable to touch any of the funds in his overseas accounts. He and his wife had moved out of their $1.25 million estate near Decatur, Illinois, after contracting to buy a house near Nashville for $925,000. After the suicide attempt, they attempted to back out of the deal, only to be sued for breach of contract.

With all this, somehow Whitacre seemed to have landed on his feet by early October. True, he and his family were living in a rented house in the Chicago area, but he had become chief executive of Future Health Technologies, a startup biotechnology firm, at a six-figure salary comparable to what he earned legally at ADM.

THE ALLEGATIONS AGAINST THE COMPANY

By fall 1995, three grand juries were investigating whether ADM and some of its competitors conspired to fix prices. Three major product lines of ADM were allegedly involved: lysine, high-fructose corn syrup, and citric acid. Lysine is an amino-acid mixed with feed for hogs and chickens to hasten the growth of lean muscles in the animals. High-fructose corn syrup is a caloric sweetener used in soft drinks. Citric acid, like lysine, is a corn-derived product used in the detergent, food, and beverage industries.

The importance of these products in the total product mix of ADM is indisputable. For example, while lysine is virtually unknown to the public,

---

[5]"ADM Informant Faces . . . ": A1.
[6]"ADM and the FBI 'Scumbags'," *Fortune* (October 30, 1995: 116.

it is a key ingredient in the feed industry. About 500 million pounds are produced annually. Prices since 1961 have been averaging more than $1 a pound. So millions of dollars are at stake to manufacturers. With modern facilities at its sprawling complex in Decatur, Illinois, ADM can produce about half the world's purchases of lysine annually. And this is one of the company's highest profit products.

The sweetener, high-fructose corn syrup, is a major product for ADM, with a $3 billion-a-year market worldwide. Soft drinks account for more than 75 percent of annual production.

ADM entered the citric-acid business in 1991 when it acquired a unit of Pfizer. Today it is the primary U.S. maker of this additive. One of the largest customers is Procter & Gamble, which uses it for detergents.

As one example of the seemingly incriminating evidence of price fixing uncovered in videotapes, Michael Andreas is shown during a meeting he attended with lysine competitors at the Hyatt Regency Hotel at Los Angeles International Airport. There the participants discussed sales targets for each company as a means of limiting supply. This would destroy the free supply/demand machinations of the market and would permit prices to be kept artificially high, thus increasing the profits of the participants.[7]

With the charges and countercharges of Whitacre and the company, investigations went beyond price fixing to tax evasion for high-level executives sanctioned by top management. Whitacre was the tip of the iceberg. The criminal-fraud division of the Justice Department began investigating whether the company illegally paid millions of dollars in off-the-books compensation to an array of company executives through foreign bank accounts.

It is worth noting the severity of the penalties if suits successfully come to pass. Fines for price fixing can range into the hundreds of millions of dollars, and some executives could even be given jail sentences. Furthermore, class-action suits by shareholders and customers can result in heavy damage awards. See the following information box for a discussion of the famous price-fixing conspiracy of 1959 that set the precedent for jail sentences for executives involved.

ADM AND DWAYNE ANDREAS

The story of Archer-Daniels-Midland Co. is really the story of its chairman, Dwayne O. Andreas. In 1947, ADM chairman, Shreve Archer, died after choking on a chicken bone. Dwayne Andreas was a vice-president at Cargill, a rival firm. For the next 18 years he advanced steadily in the industry and

[7] Reported in "Investigators Suspect a Global Conspiracy In Archer-Daniels Case," *The Wall Street Journal* (July 28, 1995): A1 and A5.

INFORMATION BOX

THE FAMOUS PRICE-FIXING CONSPIRACY OF 1959

In 1959, the biggest conspiracy of its kind in U.S. business history impacted the nation's thinking regarding business ethics.

Twenty-nine companies, including such giants as General Electric, Westinghouse, and Allis-Chalmers, were found guilty of conspiring to fix prices in deals involving about $7 billion of electrical equipment. The products involved in the conspiracy included power transformers, power switchgear assemblies, turbine generators, industrial control equipment, and circuit breakers. The companies were fined $1,924,500. Of particular note in this case, 52 executives (none of these top executives) were prosecuted and fined about $140,000. Even more startling, seven of the defendants received jail sentences. This was a first under federal antitrust laws.

On top of all that, almost 2,000 private-action, treble-damage cases were brought as a result of the court findings. In one of these alone, damages of $28,800,000 were awarded.

Incentives for the illegal actions stemmed from several sources. Without doubt, top management was exerting strong pressure on lower executives to improve their performance. Collusion with executives in other firms seemed to be a practical way to do this, especially in an environment rather blasé toward antitrust collusion. This attitude changed with the harsh penalties imposed by Judge J. Cullen Ganey.

Those executives who lost their jobs and went to jail were readily offered equivalent jobs in other corporations. The business community accepted them with open arms. Do you think they deserved such acceptance?

---

became wealthy, while Archer-Daniels showed little growth. In 1966, at age 47, Andreas was asked to become a director at ADM. The founding families sold him a sizable amount of stock and proposed to groom him for the top spot. Four years later, he was named chief executive officer.

In 1995, Andreas was still firmly in command and running the publicly traded company almost as a personal dynasty. In 25 years he had built up the firm into the nation's biggest farm-commodity processor, with $12.7 billion in annual revenue. Table 22.1 shows the steady growth of revenues since 1986, while Table 22.2 shows the growth of earnings, not quite as steady but still almost two and a half times greater than in 1986.

POLITICAL MANUEVERING

Although company headquarters were at Decatur, Illinois, Andreas's influence in Washington was probably unparalleled by any other business leader.

Table 22.1   ADM Revenues, 1986–1995

Year Ending June 30	Sales (Millions)	Year-to-Year Percent Increase
1986	$5,336	
1987	5,775	10.8%
1988	6,798	11.8
1989	7,929	11.6
1990	7,751	(2.2)
1991	8,468	9.3
1992	9,232	9.0
1993	9,811	6.5
1994	11,374	15.9
1995	12,672	11.4
Gain since 1986		137.5%

Source: Adapted from *1995 ADM Annual Report.*

ADM led corporate America in political contributions; it contributed hundreds of thousands of dollars to both parties. Furthermore, Andreas supported Jimmy Carter's campaign—ADM even bought his struggling peanut farm in 1981. But Andreas also contributed generously to Ronald Reagan and George Bush. During the Reagan years, when U.S. firms were entering the Soviet market, ADM was in the vanguard. Andreas became close to then-Soviet president, Mikhail Gorbachev. But as a hedge, he also courted Boris Yeltsin, Gorbachev's emerging rival.

Perhaps his greatest political supporter became Senator Robert Dole, who is from the farm state of Kansas. When Dole's wife, Elizabeth, took over administration of the American Red Cross, Andreas donated $1 million to the cause. Dole also was given use of an ADM corporate plane, for which he paid the equivalent of a first-class ticket. An added factor in the friendship

Table 22.2   ADM Net Earnings 1986–1995

Year Ending June 30	Earnings (Millions)	Year-to-Year Percent Increase
1986	$230	
1987	265	15.2%
1988	353	33.2
1989	425	20.3
1990	484	13.9
1991	467	(3.5)
1992	504	7.9
1993	568	12.7
1994	484	(14.8)
1995	796	64.5
Gain since 1986		246.1%

Source: Adapted from *1995 ADM Annual Report.*

and rapport was the proximity of their vacation homes: Dole and his wife own a unit in Sea View, Florida, as do David Brinkley, a renowned TV newsman, and Robert Strauss, an ADM board member, and, of course, Dwayne Andreas.[8] Interestingly, President Clinton also regards Andreas as an ally.

Such political presence has brought great rewards to the company. ADM is a major beneficiary of federal price supports for sugar. Because such supports have kept sugar prices artificially high, ADM's sweetener, high-fructose corn syrup, has been attractive for giant companies such as Coca-Cola. Estimates are that fructose generates about 40 percent of ADM's earnings.[9]

Archer-Daniels also benefits from the 54-cent-a-gallon excise-tax break on ethanol, being the major producer of this corn-based fuel additive. Indeed, it is doubtful if the ethanol industry would exist without this tax break, and Bob Dole has been its most ardent congressional supporter.

Despite all the campaign contributions and personal rapport with the seats of power in Washington, Andreas and ADM have done little direct lobbying. Rather, such efforts have been done indirectly through various commodity and trade associations. For example, the American Peanut Sellers Association, with ADM support, handles the lobbying on peanut price supports.[10]

The Board of Directors

The investigations and the charges and countercharges drew fire from some of the major institutional holders of ADM stock. For example, the California Public Employees Retirement System—Calpers, as it is known, and owner of 3.6 million shares of Archer-Daniels—complained, charging that the board was too closely tied to Chairman and CEO Dwayne Andreas. "The ADM board is dominated by insiders, many of whom happen to be related to the CEO," Calpers complained. Calpers also criticized the ADM board for approving a 14 percent pay raise for Andreas, "rather than demand the CEO's resignation."[11] Other institutional investors also joined the criticisms: for example, the United Brotherhood of Carpenters, the Teamsters Union, and New York's major pension funds.

Shareholders had several other major criticisms of the board. It was supposed to authorize all capital expenditures above $250,000. The alleged claims for offshore pay were disguised as requests for spending on plant

---

[8] Reported in "How Dwayne Andreas Rules Archer-Daniels By Hedging His Bets," *The Wall Street Journal* (October 27, 1995): A8.

[9] *Ibid.*

[10] *Ibid.*

[11] Joann S. Lublin, "Archer-Daniels-Midland Is Drawing Fire From Some Institutional Holders," *The Wall Street Journal* (October 11, 1995): A8.

and equipment, and these the board passed with no hesitation. As to the charges of price-fixing and the allegations against major executives, the board was conspicuously uncritical, and finally made some token efforts to look further into the charges.

Brian Mulroney, former prime minister of Canada, co-chaired the special committee charged with coordinating the company's response to the federal investigations. One would think that part of his job was to safeguard the interests of shareholders. But major institutional shareholders doubted his objectivity, and noted his very close relations to Dwayne Andreas. Critics contended that what was needed was not a rubber-stamp special committee but "a team of experts to lead a full-blown, independent investigation."[12]

Regarding the composition of the board, critics seemed to have a case: The board was hardly objective and unbiased toward company top management; rather, it was highly supportive and dominated by insiders, many of whom were related to the CEO. For example, four of Archer-Daniels 17 directors were members of the Andreas family. An additional six directors were retired executives or relatives of senior managers. The outside directors also had close connections to Andreas, such as Robert S. Strauss, the Washington lawyer whose firm represented ADM, and Mulroney, who was also with a law firm used by the company. Even Harvard University Professor Ray Goldberg, a member of the board, had strong ties with Andreas, dating back to his dissertation.

While close bonds of boards with management are not unusual with many companies, such cozy relations can be detrimental to shareholders' best interests.

ANALYSIS

ADM's Conduct

ADM was found guilty of unethical conduct, and even illegalities regarding price fixing. Certain other activities of this giant company also posed ethical controversies even if they were not illegal—for example, packing the board with cronies dedicated to preserving the establishment at the expense of stockholders; the great quest for preferential treatment in the highest corridors of power; and just perhaps, the setting up of Whitacre. Let us examine these ethical issues.

Packing the board so that it is exceptionally supportive of the entrenched management may be condemned as not truly representing the rights of stockholders. But with Andreas at the helm, ADM's stock value rose at an

---

[12] Henkoff, "Checks, Lies, . . ." 110.

annual average rate of 17 percent over the last decade. Few stockholders could dispute Andreas's contribution to the firm, even though they might fume at his riding roughshod over his critics—especially institutions holding large amounts of stock.

Some would maintain that the courting of favoritism and special treatment from high-level Washington politicians may have gone too far. But should not any organization have the right to do its best to push for beneficial legislation and regulation? Of course, some will be more effective than others in doing so. Is this so much different than competition in the marketplace?

Whitacre's Role

Why did Whitacre choose to be a government mole? As of this writing, nothing has been written about this. Still in his thirties, Whitacre had advanced to high position in the company, with corresponding substantial compensation (enough to afford an estate valued at more than a million dollars), and who was at least one of the top candidates for the presidency of the firm. Yet he had been secretly taping supposedly illegal discussions. Why? What did he have to gain? There was so much to lose.

Added to this, he must have been a very capable executive, yet he was naive enough to leave himself vulnerable by accepting, and maybe even initiating, illegal scams through false invoices and overseas bank accounts. Then he apparently naively confessed to a company lawyer his involvement as an informant for the FBI, not just recently but for three years. It doesn't make much sense, does it?

Latest Info

In October 1996, ADM pleaded guilty to criminal price-fixing charges and paid a record $100 million fine. But ADM's troubles were not ended.

Early in December, a federal grand jury charged Michael Andreas, former executive vice president and heir apparent to his father to run the company, and Terrance Wilson, former head of ADM's corn-processing division, with conspiring with Asian makers of lysine to rig the price of the livestock feed additive. Andreas had taken a leave of absence and Wilson retired in October. It was thought that any conviction or guilty plea by Michael Andreas would destroy his chances of continuing his family's three-decade-long reign over ADM. However, Dwayne Andreas may yet preserve the patrimony: His nephew, G. Allen Andreas, a 53-year-old lawyer, was one of three executives named to share Dwayne Andreas's responsibilities in a newly formed office of chief excecutive.

In a surprising twist to the case, Mark Whitacre, the whistleblower, was also indicted.[13]

On April 11, 1997, a federal judge approved a $30 million settlement for ADM shareholders who had seen their portfolios plunge when the federal price-fixing investigation hit the headlines. The class-action lawsuit accused ADM of inflating its stock price by not revealing that a large part of its profits came from price-fixing. This settlement raised to $190 million the amount ADM has agreed to pay to settle lawsuits and criminal price-fixing charges.

WHAT CAN BE LEARNED?

Price fixing is one of the easiest cases to prosecute. Conspiracies to fix prices are direct violations of the Sherman Act. The government does not need to prove that competition was injured or that trade was restrained. All that needs to be proven is that a meeting took place with agreements to fix prices, bids, or allocate market share.

The penalties for price conspiracies have greatly increased since the celebrated electrical equipment industry conspiracy of 1959. Given the ease of prosecution, one would think that no prudent executive would ever take such a risk. Yet, there have been sporadic instances of price-fixing since then, and we have it here with Michael Andreas, the son of Dwayne. Is there no learning experience?

Is political patronage necessary? We know that ADM sought political patronage and preferential treatment to an extraordinary degree—perhaps more than any other firm. Is this so bad?

Purists argue that this distorts the objectivity of our governmental institutions. Others say it is part of the democratic process in a pluralistic society. It might be so vital to our type of government that it cannot be eliminated— at best, can only be curbed.

On the other hand, it simply adds one more dimension to the competitive environment. Other firms can be encouraged to flex their muscles in the halls of government.

But when it comes to violations of the law, which supposedly reflects the wishes of society, then no firm is immune to the consequences. Even if its political patronage has been assiduously cultivated, it cannot escape the consequences of its illegal actions. The press, and the legal establishment, see to that.

Beware the "shareholder be damned" attitude. Some shaeholders of ADM suspect that ADM had this attitude. As a consequence, the company faced

---

[13] "Former ADM Aides Indicted," *Cleveland Plain Dealer* (December 4, 1996): C1; and Scott Kilman and Thomas M. Burton, "Three Ex-ADM Executives, Including Informant, Indicted in Antitrust Case," *The Wall Street Journal* (December 4, 1996): A3.

at least two dozen shareholder lawsuits. As it approached the 1995 October annual meeting, nine big institutional investors announced plans to vote against reelecting ADM directors. But the move was largely symbolic, since their combined shares represented only 4.9 percent of the 505 million outstanding shares.[14] And their views received little attention in the meeting. Nor, apparently did those of other shareholders. *The Wall Street Journal* reported that at the meeting Andreas squelched criticisms of the issue of the antitrust probe and other allegations as he "summarily cut off a critic by turning off his microphone: 'I'm chairman. I'll make the rules as I go along,' Mr. Andreas said."[15]

A cozy relationship with the board encourages such attitudes. And when operating performance is continually improving, such shareholder criticisms may be seen as merely gnats striving for attention, and thus worthy of being ignored. If the top executive is inclined to be autocratic, then the environment is supportive.

But is this wise? Should adversity set in, sometime in the future, then such attitudes toward investors can be self-destructive, even with a supportive board. If performance deteriorates, no board can maintain its sheeplike support for incumbent management, not in the face of vehement shareholders (especially large institutional investors) or major creditors.

But does adversity have to come? Only the profoundest optimist can think that success is forever. In ADM'S case, adversity is here and now.

An organization's ethical tone is set by top management. If top management is unconcerned about ethical conduct, or if it is an active participant in less than desirable practices, this sets the tone throughout the organization. It promotes erosion of acceptable moral conduct in many areas of the operation. It becomes contagious as even those inclined to be more morally scrupulous join their colleagues. Then we have the "follow-the-leader" mindset.

In such an unhealthy environment, a few whistleblowers may arise and attempt to right the situation, often unsuccessfuly and at great personal risk. Others who cannot tolerate the decline in moral standards, but don't have the courage to be whistleblowers, will leave the company. Almost inevitably, the misconduct will come to light, and repercussions of the severest kind result. Perhaps top management can escape the blame, though lower-level executives will be sacrificed. Occasionally, top management also comes under fire, and is forced to resign. Unfortunately, too often with healthy retirement benefits.

---

[14]"Probe Tears Veil of Secrecy at Archer-Daniels-Midland," *Cleveland Plain Dealer* (October 18, 1995): 3C.

[15]"How Dwayne Andreas Rules," A1.

CONSIDER

Can you think of other learning insights?

QUESTIONS

1. What is your position regarding top management's culpability for the misdeeds of their subordinates?
2. Do you think ADM's efforts at gaining political favoritism went too far? Why or why not?
3. "If Dwayne's son is found guilty of price-fixing, there's no way that the big man himself cannot be found guilty." Evaluate this statement.
4. "With all the false invoices and persons involved in these millions of dollars of payouts off-the-books, there's no way the company could not have known what was going on." Evaluate.
5. Speculate on what would lead Whitacre to "betray" his company. If a number of possibilities are mentioned, which do you think is most compelling?
6. With the severe penalties and ease of prosecution of price-fixing cases, why would any firm or any executive attempt it today?
7. Why do you suppose, with all its efforts to gain preferential treatment through courting the mighty in government, ADM has not resorted to direct lobbying? Has it missed a golden opportunity to further its causes?

HANDS-ON EXERCISES

Before

1. Assume that Dwayne Andreas wants to maintain high ethical standards in his organization. Describe how he should go about this.

After

2. Assume that several key executives have been found guilty of price-fixing; assume further that there are also indictments of illegal payments to certain executives. Further, the Senate ethics committee is investigating whether there have been improprieties in dealings with some members of Congress. How would you as CEO attempt damage control?

TEAM DEBATE EXERCISE

Debate the ethics of aggressively courting prominent politicians and government administrators. The two extreme positions would be: (1) going as far as you can short of being charged with outright bribery; (2) limiting relationship building to a few token contributions to trade association lobbying efforts.

INVITATION TO RESEARCH

What has happened regarding the allegations of price-fixing? Was ADM's public image badly tarnished? Is Dwayne Andreas still active as chairman and CEO? What has happened to Whitacre?

CHAPTER 23

Met Life: Deceptive Sales Tactics

In August 1993, the State of Florida blew the whistle on giant Metropolitan Life, a company dating back to 1868, and the country's second largest insurance firm. Met Life agents based in Tampa, Florida, were alleged to have duped customers out of some $11 million. Thousands of these customers were nurses, lured by the sales pitch to learn more about "something new, one of the most widely discussed retirement plans in the investment world today."[1] In reality, this was a life-insurance policy in disguise, and what clients were led to think were savings deposits were actually insurance premiums.

As we will see, the growing scandal rocked Met Life, and brought it millions of dollars in fines and restitutions. What was not clear was the full culpability of the company: Was it guilty only of not monitoring agent performance sufficiently to detect unethical and illegal activities, or was it the great encourager of such practices?

RICK URSO: THE VILLAIN?

The first premonitory rumble that something bad was about to happen came to Rick Urso on Christmas Eve 1993. Home with his family, he received an unexpected call from his boss, the regional sales manager. In disbelief he heard there was a rumor going around the executive suites that he was about to be fired. Now, Urso had known that the State of Florida had been

---

[1] Suzanne Woolley and Gail DeGeorge, "Policies of Deception?" *Business Week* (January 17, 1994): 24.

investigating, and that company auditors had also been looking into sales practices. And on September 17, two corporate vice-presidents had even shown up to conduct the fourth audit that year, but on leaving they had given him the impression that he was complying with company guidelines.

Urso often reveled in his good fortune and attributed it to his sheer dedication to his work and the company. He had grown up in a working-class neighborhood, the son of an electrician. He had started college, but dropped out before graduating.

His sales career started at a John Hancock agency in Tampa, in 1978. Four years later, he was promoted to manager. He was credited with building up the agency to number two in the whole company.

He left John Hancock in 1983 for Met Life's Tampa agency. His first job was as trainer. Only three months later he was promoted to branch manager. Now his long hours and overwhelming commitment were beginning to pay off. In a success story truly inspiring, his dedication and his talent as a motivator of people swept the branch from a one-rep office to one of Met Life's largest and most profitable. In 1990 and 1991, Urso's office won the company's Sales Office of the Year award. By 1993 the agency employed 120 reps, seven sales managers, and 30 administrative employees. And Urso had risen to become Met Life's third-highest-paid employee, earning $1.1 million as manager of the branch. With such a performance history, the stuff of legends, he became the company's star, a person to look up to and to inspire trainees and other employees.

His was the passion of a TV evangelist: "Most people go through life being told why they can't accomplish something. If they would just believe, then they would be halfway there. That's the way I dream and that's what I expect from my people.[2] He soon became known as the "Master Motivator," and increasingly was the guest speaker at Met Life conferences.

On the Monday after that Christmas, the dire prediction came to pass. He was summoned to the office of William Groggans, the head of Met Life's Southeast territory, and was handed a letter by the sober-faced Groggans. With trembling hands he opened it and read that he was fired for engaging in improper conduct.

The Route to Stardom

Unfortunately, the growth of his Tampa office could not be credited to simple motivation of employees. Urso found his vehicle for great growth to be the whole-life insurance policy. This was part life insurance and part savings. As such, it required high premiums, but only part earned interest and

---

[2] Weld F. Royal, "Scapegoat or Scoundrel," *Sales & Marketing Management* (January 1995): 64.

compounded on a tax-deferred basis; the rest went to pay for the life insurance policy. What made this so attractive to company sales reps was the commission: A Met whole-life policy paid a 55 percent first-year commission. In contrast, an annuity paid only a 2 percent first-year commission.

Urso found the nurses' market to be particularly attractive. Perhaps because of their constant exposure to death, nurses were easily convinced of the need for economic security. He had his salespeople call themselves "nursing representatives." His Tampa salespeople carried their fake retirement plan beyond Florida, eventually reaching 37 states. A New York client, for example, thought she had bought a retirement annuity. But it turned out to be life insurance even though she didn't want such coverage because she had no beneficiaries.[3]

As the growth of the Tampa agency became phenomenal, his budget for mailing brochures was upped to nearly $1 million in 1992, ten times that of any other Met Life office. This gave him national reach.

Urso's own finances increased proportionately because he earned a commission on each policy his reps sold. In 1989, he was paid $270,000. In 1993, as compensation exceeded $1 million, he moved his family to Bay Shore Boulevard, the most expensive area of Tampa.

End of the Bonanza

A few complaints began surfacing. In 1990, the Texas insurance commissioner warned Met Life to stop its nursing ploy. The company made a token compliance by sending out two rounds of admonitory letters. But nothing apparently changed. See the following information box about the great deficiency of token compliance without follow-up.

An internal Met Life audit in 1991 raised some questions about Urso's pre-approach letters. The term *nursing representative* was called a "made-up" title. The auditors also questioned the term *retirement savings policy* as not appropriate for the product. However, the report concluded by congratulating the Tampa office for its contribution to the company. Not surprisingly, such mixed signals did not end the use of misleading language at that time.

In the summer of 1993, Florida state regulators began a more in-depth examination of the sales practices of the Urso agency. As a result of this investigation, Florida Insurance Commissioner Tom Gallagher charged Met Life with several violations. Now Met Life began more serious investigations.

The crux of the investigations concerned promotional material Urso's office was sending to nurses nationwide. From 1989 to 1993, millions of direct-mail pieces had been sent out. Charges finally were leveled that this material

---

[3]Jane Bryant Quinn, "Yes, They're Out to Get You," *Newsweek* (January 24, 1994): 51.

INFORMATION BOX

THE VULNERABILITY OF COMPLIANCE, IF IT IS ONLY TOKEN

A token effort at compliance to a regulatory complaint or charge tends to have two consequences, neither good in the long run for the company involved:

1. Such tokenism gives a clear message to the organization: "Despite what outsiders say, this is acceptable conduct in this firm." Thus is set the climate for less than desirable practices.
2. Vulnerability to future harsher measures. With the malpractice continuing, regulators, convinced that the company is stalling and refusing to cooperate, will eventually take more drastic action.

Actually, the firm may not have intended to stall, but that is the impression conveyed. If the cause of the seemingly token effort is really faulty controls, one wonders how many other aspects of the operation are also ineptly controlled so that company policies are ignored.

Discuss what kinds of controls Met Life could have imposed in 1990 that would have made compliance actual and not token.

---

disguised the products agents were selling. For example, one brochure coming from Urso's office depicted the Peanuts character Lucy in a nurse's uniform. The headline described the product as "retirement savings and security for the future a nurse deserves." Nowhere was insurance even mentioned, and allegations were that nurses across the country unknowingly purchased life insurance when they thought they were buying retirement savings plans.

As the investigation deepened, a former Urso agent, turned whistle-blower, claimed he had been instructed to place his hands over the words "life insurance" on applications during presentations.

MET LIFE CORRECTIVE ACTIONS

With Florida regulators now investigating, the company's attitudes changed. At first, Met Life denied wrongdoing. But eventually it acknowledged problems. Under mounting public pressure, it agreed to pay $20 million in fines to more than 40 states as a result of unethical sales practices of its agents. It further agreed to refund premiums to nearly 92,000 policyholders who bought insurance based on misleading sales information between 1989 and 1993. These refunds were expected to reach $76 millon.

Met Life fired or demoted five high-level executives as a result of the scandal. Urso's office was closed, and all seven of his managers and several reps were also discharged. Life insurance sales to individuals were down 25 percent through September 1994 over the same nine-month period in 1993. Standard & Poor's downgraded Met's bond rating based on these alleged improprieties.

Shortly after the fines were announced, the Florida Department of Insurance filed charges against Urso and 86 other Met Life insurance agents, accusing them of fraudulent sales practices. The insurance commissioner said, "This was not a situation where a few agents decided to take advantage of their customers, but a concerted effort by many individuals to dupe customers into buying a life insurance policy disguised as a retirement savings plan."[4]

The corporation, in attempting to improve its public image, instituted a broad overhaul of its compliance procedures. It established a corporate ethics and compliance department to monitor behavior throughout the company and audit personal insurance sales offices. The department was also charged to report any compliance deficiencies to senior management and to follow up to ensure the implementation of corrective actions.

In Met Life's *1994 Annual Report*, Harry Kamen, CEO, and Ted Athanassiades, president, commented on their corrective actions regarding the scandal:

> We created what we think is the most effective compliance system in the industry. Not just for personal insurance, but for all components of the company. We installed systems to coordinate and track the quality and integrity of our sales activities, and we created a new system of sales office auditing.
>
> Also, there were organizational charges. And, for the first time in 22 years, we assembled all of our agency and district managers—about a thousand people—to discuss what we have done and need to do about the problems and where we were going.[5]

Meantime, Rick Urso started a suit against Met Life for defamation of character and for reneging on a $1 million severance agreement. He alleged that Met Life made him the fall guy in the nationwide sales scandal.

The personal consequences on Urso's life were not inconsequential. More than a year later he was still unemployed. He had looked for another insurance job, but no one would even see him. "There are nights he can't sleep. He lies awake worrying about the impact this will have on his two teenagers." And he laments that his wife cannot go out without people gossiping.[6]

[4]Sean Armstrong, "The Good, The Bad and the Industry," *Best's Review*, P/C (June 1994): 36.

[5]*Met Life 1994 Annual Report*, 16.

[6]Royal, "Scapegoat," 65.

WHERE DOES THE BLAME LIE?

Is Urso really the unscrupulous monster who rose to a million-dollar-a-year man on the foundations of deceit? Or is Met Life mainly to blame for encouraging, and then ignoring for too long, practices aimed at misleading and even deceiving?

The Case Against Met Life

Undeniably Urso did things that smacked of the illegal and unethical. But did the corporation knowingly provide the climate? Was his training such as to promote deceptive practices? Was Met Life completely unaware of his distortions and deceptions in promotional material and sales pitches? There seems to be substantial evidence that the company played a part; it was no innocent and unsuspecting bystander.

At best, Met Life top executives may not have been aware of the full extent of the hard selling efforts emanating at first from Tampa and then spreading further in the organization. Perhaps they chose to ignore any inkling that things were not completely on the up and up, in the quest for exceptional bottom-line performance. "Don't argue with success" might have become the corporate mindset.

At the worst, the company encouraged and even demanded hard selling and tried to pretend that such could still be accomplished with the highest ethical standards of performance. If such ethical standards were not met, then, company top executives could argue, they were not aware of such wrongdoings.

There is evidence of company culpability. Take the training program for new agents. Much of it was designed to help new employees overcome the difficulties of selling life insurance. In so doing, they were taught to downplay the life insurance aspects of the product. Rather, the savings and tax-deferred growth benefits were to be stressed.

In training new agents to sell insurance over the phone, they were told that people prefer dealing with specialists. It seemed only a small temptation to use the title *nursing representative* rather than *insurance agent*.

After the scandal, Met Life admitted that the training might be faulty. Training had been decentralized into five regional centers, and the company believed that this may have led to a less standardized and less controlled curricula. Met Life has since reorganized so that many functions, including training and legal matters, are now done at one central location.[7]

The company's control or monitoring was certainly deficient and uncoordinated during the years of misconduct. For example, the marketing

---

[7]"Trained to Mislead," *Sales & Marketing Management* (January 1995): 66.

department promoted deceptive sales practices while the legal department warned of possible illegality but took no further action to eliminate it.

An Industry Problem?

The Met Life revelations focused public and regulatory attention on the entire insurance industry. The Insurance Commissioner of Florida also turned attention to the sales and marketing practices of New York Life and Prudential. The industry itself seems vulnerable to questionable practices. With millions of transactions, intense competition, and a widespread and rather autonomous sales force, opportunity exists for misrepresentation and other unethical dealings.

For example, just a few months after the Tampa office publicity, Met Life settled an unrelated scandal. Regulators in Pennsylvania fined the company $1.5 million for "churning." This is a practice of agents replacing old policies with new ones, in which additional commissions are charged and policyholders are disadvantaged. Class-action suits alleging churning have also been filed in Pennsylvania against Prudential, New York Life, and John Hancock.

But problems go beyond sales practices. Claims adjusters may attempt to withhold or reduce payments. General agents may place business with bogus or insolvent companies. Even actuaries may create unrealistic policy structures.

With a deteriorating public image, the industry faces further governmental regulation, both by states and by the federal government. But cynics, both within and outside the industry, wonder whether deception and fraud are so much a part of the business that nothing can be done about them.[8]

ANALYSIS

Here we have a lapse in complete feedback to top executives. But maybe they did not want to know. After all, nothing was life-threatening here, no product safety features were being ignored or disguised, nobody was in physical danger.

This raises a key management issue. Can top executives hide from less than ethical practices—and even illegal ones—under the guise that they did not know? The answer should be *No!* See the following information box for a discussion of management accountability.

So, we are left with top management of Met Life grappling with the temptation to tacitly approve the aggressive selling practices of a sales executive so successful as to be the model for the whole organization, even

---

[8] Armstrong, "The Good, the Bad," 35.

INFORMATION BOX

THE ULTIMATE RESPONSIBILITY

In the Maytag case in Chapter 9 we examine a costly snafu brought about by giving executives of a foreign subsidiary too much rein. With Met Life the problem was gradually eroding ethical practices. In both instances, top management still had ultimate responsibility and cannot escape blame for whatever goes wrong in the organization. Decades ago, President Truman coined the phrase, "The buck stops here," meaning that in this highest position rests the ultimate seat of responsibility.

Any manager who delegates to someone else the authority to do something will undoubtedly hold them responsible to do the job properly. Still, the manager must be aware that his or her own responsibility to higher management or to stockholders cannot be delegated away. If the subordinate does the job improperly, the manager is still responsible.

Going back to Met Life, or to any corporation involved with ethical and illegal practices, top executives can try to escape blame by denying that they knew anything about the misdeeds. This should not exonerate them. Even if they knew nothing directly, they still set the climate.

In Japan, the chief executive of an organization involved in a public scandal usually resigns in disgrace. In the United States, top executives often escape full retribution by blaming their subordinates and maintaining that they themselves knew nothing of the misdeed. Is it truly fair to hold a top executive culpable for

---

though faint cries from the legal staff suggested that such might be subject to regulatory scrutiny and disapproval.

The harsh appraisal of this situation is that top management cannot be exonerated for the deficiencies of subordinates. If controls and monitoring processes are defective, top management is still accountable. The pious platitudes of Met Life management that they have now corrected the situation hardly excuse them for permitting this to have developed in the first place.

Ah, but embracing the temptation is so easy to rationalize. Management can always maintain that there was no good, solid proof of misdeeds. After all, where do aggressive sales efforts cross the line? Where do they become more than simply puffing, and become outright deceptive? See the following information box regarding puffing, and this admittedly gray area of the acceptable. Lacking indisputable evidence of misdeeds, why should these executives suspect the worst? Especially since their legal departments, not centralized as they were to be later, were timid in their denunciations?

Turning to controls, a major caveat should be posed for all firms: In the presence of strong management demands for performance—with the often

---

INFORMATION BOX

WHERE DO WE DRAW THE LINE ON PUFFING?

Puffing is generally thought of as mild exaggeration in selling or advertising. It is generally accepted as simply the mark of exuberance toward what is being promoted. As such, it is acceptable business conduct. Most people have come to regard promotional communications with some skepticism—"It's New! The Greatest! A Super Value! Gives Whiter Teeth! Whiter Laundry! . . ." and so on. We have become conditioned to viewing such blandishments as suspicious. But dishonest, or deceptive? Probably not. As long as the exaggeration stays mild.

But it can be a short step from mild exaggeration to outright falsehoods and deceptive claims. Did Met Life's "nursing representatives," "retirement plans," and hiding the reality of life insurance cross the line? Enough people seemed to think so, including state insurance commissioners and the victims themselves. This short step can tempt more bad practices than if the line between good and bad were more definitive.

Do you think all exaggerated claims, even the mild and vague ones known as puffing, should be banned? Why or why not?

---

implicit or imagined pressure to produce at all costs, or else—the ground is laid for less than desirable practices by subordinates. After all, their career paths and even job longevity depend on meeting these demands.

In an organizational climate of decentralization and laissez faire, such abuses are more likely to occur. Such a results-oriented structure suggests that it's not how you achieve the desired results, but that you meet them. So, while decentralization is, on balance, usually desirable, it can, in the right environment of top management laxity of high moral standards, lead to undesirable—and worse—practices.

At the least, it leads to opportunistic temptation by lower- and middle-level executives. Perhaps this is the final indictment of Met Life and Rick Urso. The climate was conducive to his ambitious opportunism. For a while it was wonderful. But the clinks and the abuses of accepted practices could not be disguised indefinitely.

And wherever possible, top management will repudiate its accountability responsibilities.

LATEST INFO

Will we ever learn? A similar scandal showed up in late 1996, this time involving Prudential Insurance Company, the nation's largest life insurance company. The Florida insurance commissioner charged on December 9 that it had deceived thousands of elderly Floridians into buying additional life insurance that cheated them out of their retirement nest eggs. Insurance Commissioner Bill Nelson ordered the company to show why it should not be stripped of its license to sell life insurance in Florida and pay "the stiffest of fines."[9]

The allegations were that Prudential and its agents "churned" or "twisted" life insurance sales by deceptively manipulating more than 100,000 consumers. Among other things, Florida charged that Prudential managers were told not to report customer complaints, that Prudential training films glorified deceptive sales tactics, and that critical records were destroyed. ABC's Prime Time Live ran a segment on December 11, 1996, based on its six-month investigation of Prudential's life insurance sales operation.

WHAT CAN BE LEARNED?

Unethical and illegal actions do not go undetected forever. It may take months, it may take years, but a firm's dark side will eventually be uncovered. Its reputation may then be besmirched, it may face loss of customers and competitive position, it may face heavy fines and increased regulation.

The eventual disclosure may come from a disgruntled employee (a whistleblower). It may originate from a regulatory body or an investigative reporter. Or it may come from revelations emanating from a lawsuit. Eventually, the deviation is uncovered, and retribution follows. Such a scenario should be—but is not always—enough to constrain those individuals tempted to commit unethical and illegal actions.

What made the Met Life deceptive practices particularly troubling is that they were so visible, and yet were so long tolerated. A clear definition of what was acceptable and what was not seemed lacking by much of the sales organization. Something was clearly amiss, both in the training and in the controlling of agent personnel.

The control function is best centralized in any organization. Where the department or entity that monitors performance is decentralized, tolerance of bad practices is more likely than when centralized. The reason is rather simple. Where legal or accounting controls are decentralized, the people conducting them are more easily influenced and are likely to be neither as objective nor as critical as when they are more at an arm's length. So, reviewers and evaluators should not be close to the people they are examining. And they should only report to top management.

---

[9]"Prudential Accused of Deception," *Cleveland Plain Dealer* (December 10, 1996): 3C; and Leslie Scism, "Florida Threatens to Pull Sales License From Prudential for Deceptive Dealings," *The Wall Street Journal* (December 10, 1996): A17.

A strong sales incentive program invites bad practices. The lucrative commission incentive for the whole-life policies—55 percent first-year commission—was almost bound to stimulate abusive sales practices, especially when the rewards for this type of policy were so much greater than for any other. Firms often use various incentive programs and contests to motivate their employees to seek greater efforts. But if some are tempted to cross the line, the end result of public scrutiny and condemnation may not be worth whatever increases in sales might be gained.

Large corporations are particularly vulnerable to public scrutiny. Large firms, especially ones dealing with consumer products, are very visible. This visibility makes them attractive targets for critical scrutinty by activists, politicians, the media, regulatory bodies, and the legal establishment. Such firms ought to be particularly careful in any dealings that might be questioned, even if short-term profits have to be restrained. In Met Life's case, the fines and refunds approached $100 million. Although the firm in its 1994 annual report maintained that all the bad publicity was behind, that there were no ill effects, still we can wonder how quickly a besmirched reputation can truly be restored, especially when competitors are eager to grab the opportunity.

CONSIDER

What additional learning insights do you see?

QUESTIONS

1. Do you think Rick Urso should have been fired? Why or why not?
2. Do you think the Met Life CEO and president should have been fired? Why or why not?
3. Why was the term life insurance seemingly so desirable to avoid? What is wrong with life insurance?
4. Given the widespread publicity about the Met Life scandal, do you think the firm can regain consumer trust in a short time?
5. "This whole critical publicity has been blown way out of proportion. After all, nobody was injured. Not even in their pocketbook. They were sold something they really needed. For their own good." Evaluate.
6. "You have to admire that guy, Urso. He was a real genius. No one else could motivate a sales organization as he did. They should have made him president of the company. Or else he should become an evangelist." Evaluate.
7. Do you think the arguments are compelling that the control function should be centralized rather than decentralized? Why or why not?

HANDS-ON EXERCISES

Before

1. It is early 1990. You are the assistant to the CEO of Met Life. Rumors have been surfacing that life insurance sales efforts are becoming not only too high-pressure but also misleading. The CEO has ordered you to investigate. You find that the legal department in the Southeast Territory has some concerns about the efforts coming out of the highly successful Tampa office of Urso. Be as specific as you can about how you would investigate these unproven allegations, and how you would report this to your boss, assuming that some questionable practices seem apparent.

2. It is 1992. Internal investigations have confirmed that Urso and his "magnificent" Tampa office are using deceptive selling techniques in disguising the life insurance aspects of the policies they are selling. As the executive in charge in the Southeast, describe your actions and rationale at this point. (You have to assume that the later consequences are completely unknown at this point.)

After

3. The * * * * has hit the fan. The scandal has become well-publicized, especially with such TV programs as "Dateline" and "20/20." What would you do as top executive of Met Life at this point? How would you attempt to save the public image of the company?

TEAM DEBATE EXERCISE

The publicity is widespread about the "misdeeds" of Met Life. Debate how you would react. One position is to defend your company and rationalize what happened and downplay any ill-effects. The other position is to meekly bow to the allegations and admit wrongdoing and be as contrite as possible.

INVITATION TO RESEARCH

How is Met Life faring after this extremely bad publicity? Do sales seem to be rebounding? Can you find any information on whether the image has improved, whether the situation has virtually been forgotten by the general public? Can you find out whether Rick Urso has found another job? Are Kamen and Athanassiades still the top executives of Met Life? What conclusions can you draw from your research?

CHAPTER 24

Conclusions: What Can Be Learned?

In considering mistakes, three things are worth noting:

1. Even the most successful organizations make mistakes but survive as long as they maintain a good "batting average."
2. Mistakes should be effective teaching tools for avoiding similar errors in the future.
3. Firms can bounce back from adversity, and turn around.

We can make a number of generalizations from these mistakes and successes. Of course we recognize that marketing is a discipline that does not lend itself to laws or axioms. Examples of exceptions to every principle or generalization can be found. However, the decision maker does well to heed the following insights. For the most part they are based on specific corporate and entrepreneurial experiences and should be transferable to other situations and other times.

INSIGHTS REGARDING OVERALL ENTERPRISE PERSPECTIVES

Importance of Public Image

The impact, for good or bad, of an organization's public image was a common thread through a number of cases. In particular, the cases in Part I: Nike, Food Lion, and United Way. But public image certainly played a big role, positively or negatively, in other cases such as Harley Davidson, Southwest Airlines, Saturn, Parma Pierogies, Boston Beer, and the tobacco industry among these.

Nike presents an example of the power of an image that is compatible with the product and attractive to much of the target market. The carefully nurtured association with some of the most esteemed athletes in the world, men and women whom many of its customers were eager to emulate, if only in their dreams, propelled Nike and its "swoosh" logo to dominance in the athletic apparel industry.

Food Lion showed how bad publicity can destroy, at least temporarily and maybe for much longer, the growth of a company. Coupled with a militant and hostile union that would not let the publicity die, the fallacy of cutting corners to enhance profitability turned out to be misguided indeed.

The non-profit, United Way, was brought to its knees by revelations about the excesses of its long-time chief executive, William Aramony. Donations dwindled and local chapters withheld funds from the national organization as the reputation of the largest charitable organization was sullied.

As for the tobacco industry, it seems to be forever putting its foot in its mouth in its undeviating quest to maximize profits at any cost.

Harley Davidson, the cycle maker, shows an image turnaround of monumental proportions. For decades the image of the black-jacketed motorcyclist was in the pits; but in the 1980s this turned around to become even a status symbol. Harley executives helped develop the new mystique, and then exploited it.

We saw some other successes in enhancing an image and capitalizing on a positive image. For example, Saturn, Boston Beer, and Southwest Airlines were able to nurture positive public images that enhanced their growth. And Mary Poldruhi of Parma Pierogies, showed an innate talent in building a public image, even catching the attention and support of President Clinton.

The importance of a firm's public image is undeniable, yet some continue to disregard this and either act in ways detrimental to image or else ignore the constraints and opportunities that a reputation affords.

Power of the Media. We have seen or suspected the power of the media in a number of cases. Coca-Cola, Food Lion, United Way, IBM, the tobacco industry, and Parma Pierogies are obvious examples. This power is often used critically—to hurt a firm's public image. The media can fan a problem or exacerbate an embarrassing or imprudent action. In particular, this media focus can trigger the herd instinct, in which increasing numbers of people join in protests and public criticism. And the media in their zeal can sometimes cross the line, as the newest information on Food Lion's lawsuit suggests.

We can make five key generalizations regarding image and its relationship with the media:

1. It is important to maintain a stable, clear-cut image and undeviating objectives.
2. It is very difficult and time-consuming to upgrade an image.
3. An episode of poor quality has a lasting stigma.
4. A good image can be quickly lost if a firm relaxes in an environment of aggressive competition.
5. Well-known firms, and particularly not-for-profit firms dependent on voluntary contributions, are especially vulnerable to critical public scrutiny and must be overly prudent in safeguarding their reputations.

Need for Growth Orientation—But Not Reckless Growth

The opposite of a growth commitment is a status quo mindset, uninterested in expansion and the problems and work involved. Harley Davidson's downfall in the 1950s was its contentment with the status quo. Yet even now with the favorable attitudes toward its big motorcycles, the company is choosing a slow growth production policy and only partially satisfying demand. One wonders whether the mystique of the "Harley" will sufficiently protect it from major competitive inroads in a period of growing demand for big bikes.

In general, how tenable is a low-growth or no-growth philosophy? Although at first glance it seems workable, it usually sows the seeds of its own destruction. Almost four decades ago the following caution was made:

> Vitality is required even for survival; but vitality is difficult to maintain without growth, at least in the American business climate. The vitality of a firm depends on the vigor and ambition of its members. The prospect of growth is one of the principal means by which a firm can attract able and vigorous recruits.[1]

Consequently, if a firm is obviously not growth-minded, its ability to attract able people diminishes. Customers see a growing firm as reliable, eager to please, and constantly improving. Suppliers and creditors tend to give preferential treatment to a growing firm because they hope to retain it as a customer when it reaches large size.

In other cases firms had strong growth commitments, but somehow their growth in bureaucratic overhead let competitiveness slip and they fell back, sometimes after decades of market dominance. IBM and Sears readily come to mind here, before their great turnarounds. So does Borden as it now reaps the consequences of reckless growth and unwise diversifications. IBM

---

[1]Wroe Anderson, *Marketing Behavior and Executive Action* (Homewood, IL.: Irwin, 1957) 59.

and Sears have downsized, selling off some of their businesses to concentrate on the core. Borden faces a similar choice but with uncertain results.

Therefore, an emphasis on growth can be carried too far. Somehow the growth must be kept within the abilities of the firm to handle it. Several examples, such as Microsoft, Southwest Airlines, and McDonald's, showed how firms can grow rapidly without losing control. But we have the bungled growth efforts of Maytag's Hoover Division in the United Kingdom, Pepsi in South America, the Snapple acquisition by Quaker Oats, and Borden again. Good financial judgment must not be sacrificed to the siren call of growth.

We can make several generalizations about the most desirable growth perspectives:

1. Growth targets should not exceed the abilities of the organization to assimilate, control, and provide sufficient managerial and financial resources. Growth at any cost—especially at the expense of profits and financial stability, and prudent acquisitions—must be shunned. In particular, tight controls over inventories and expenses should be established, and performance should be monitored promptly and completely.

2. The most prudent approach to growth is to keep the organization and operation as simple and uniform as possible, to be flexible in case sales do not meet expectations, and to keep the breakeven point as low as possible, especially for new and untried ventures.

3. Concentrating maximum efforts on the expansion opportunity is like an army exploiting a breakthrough. The concentration strategy—such as that of Southwest Airlines and McDonald's—usually wins out over more timid competitors who diffuse efforts and resources. But such concentration is more risky than spreading efforts.

4. Rapidly expanding markets pose dangers from both too conservative and overly optimistic sales forecasts. The latter may overextend resources and jeopardize viability should demand contract; the former opens the door to more aggressive competitors. There is no definite answer to this dilemma, but the firm should be aware of the risks and the rewards of both extremes.

5. A strategy emphasizing rapid growth should not neglect other aspects of the operation. For example, in retailing, older stores should not be ignored in the quest to open new outlets. Basic merchandising principles, such as inventory control and new merchandise planning, should not be violated. Otherwise, the sales coming from expansion are built on a shaky foundation, growth is not assimilated, and the seeming strength and success is only an illusion.

6. Decentralized management is more compatible with rapid growth than a centralized organization since it puts less strain on home office executives. However, delegation of decision making to field executives must be accompanied by well-defined standards and controls and executed by high-caliber field personnel. Otherwise, the Maytag Hoover fiasco may be repeated.
7. In the quest for rapid growth, the integrity of the product and the reputation of the firm must not be sacrificed. This should be heeded particularly when customers' health and safety may be jeopardized. Today the risk of providing poor quality or unsafe products and services/handling may threaten the very viability of the firm, as we saw with Food Lion. And, is it possible that the tobacco industry may yet find its comeuppance?

Strategic Windows of Opportunity. Several of the great successes we examined resulted from finding and exploiting strategic windows of opportunity. Microsoft's software breakthroughs and its continuing innovative aggressiveness led to bearding once mighty IBM in stock market valuation and profits. Southwest Airlines found its opportunity by being so cost effective that it could offer cut-rate fares with highly dependable short-haul service no other airline could match.

We can make these generalizations regarding finding opportunities and strategic windows:

1. Opportunities often exist when a traditional way of doing business has prevailed in the industry for a long time—maybe the climate is ripe for a change.
2. Opportunities often exist when existing firms are not entirely satisfying customers' needs.
3. Innovations are not limited to products but can involve services as well, in such things as methods of distribution.
4. For industries with rapidly changing technologies—usually new industries—heavy research and development expenditures are usually required if a firm is to avoid falling behind its competitors. But heavy R & D expenditures do not guarantee being in the vanguard, as shown by the tribulations of IBM despite its huge expenditures.

Power of Judicious Imitation. Some firms are reluctant to copy successful practices of their competitors; they want to be leaders, not followers. But successful practices or innovations may need to be copied if a firm is not to be left behind. And sometimes the imitator outdoes the innovator. Success can lie in doing the ordinary better than competitors.

GM's Saturn achieved its initial success by imitating many of the successful practices of its Japanese competitors. And Nike outdid Adidas, with the same marketing strategy. We can make this generalization:

> It makes sense for a company to identify the characteristics of successful competitors (and even similar but noncompeting firms) that contributed to their success, and then adopt these characteristics if they are compatible with the imitator's resources. Let someone else do the experimenting and risk taking. The imitator faces some risk in waiting too long, but this usually is far less than the risk of being an innovator.

The Need for Prudent Crisis Management

Crises are unexpected happenings that pose threats, ranging from moderate to catastrophic, to the organization's well-being. A number of cases involved crises: for example, Food Lion, United Way, Maytag, Euro Disney, Coca-Cola, Elizabeth Taylor, Pepsi, ADM, and Met Life. Some handled their crisis reasonably well, such as Food Lion, United Way, Euro Disney, and Elizabeth Taylor, although we can question how such crises were allowed to happen in the first place. However, Maytag, ADM, Pepsi, and Met Life either overreacted or else failed badly in salvaging the situation.

Most crises can be minimized if a company takes precautions, is alert to changing conditions, has contingency plans, and practices risk avoidance. For example, it is prudent to prohibit key executives from traveling on the same air flight; it is prudent to insure key executives so that their incapacity will not endanger the organization; and it is prudent to set up contingency plans for a strike, an equipment failure or plant shutdown, the loss of a major distributor, unexpected economic conditions, or a serious lawsuit. Some risks, of course, can be covered by insurance, but others probably not. The mettle of any organization may be severely tested by an unexpected crisis. Such crises need not cause the demise of the company, however, if alternatives are weighed and actions taken only after calm deliberation.

Crises may necessitate some changes in the organization and the way of doing business. Firms should avoid making hasty or disruptive changes or, on the other extreme, making too few changes too late. The middle ground is usually best. Advanced planning can help a company minimize trauma and enact effective solutions.

Vulnerability to Competition and the Three C's

Competitive advantage can be short-lived, success does not guarantee continued success, and innovators as well as long-dominant firms can be overtaken and surpassed. With Harley Davidson, IBM, Sears, and even United Way, we saw the three C's syndrome of complacency, conservatism, and conceit that often blankets the mindset of leading organizations in their industries. We suggest that a constructive attitude of never underestimating competitors can be fostered by:

- Bringing fresh blood into the organization for new ideas and different perspectives.
- Establishing a strong and continuing commitment to customer service and satisfaction.
- Periodically conducting a corporate self-analysis designed to detect weaknesses as well as opportunities in their early stages.
- Continually monitoring the environment and being alert to any changes.

We will discuss environmental monitoring, or sensors, in the next section. For now let us recognize that the environment is dynamic, more often with subtle and hardly recognizable changes, but these may eventually have profound impact in ways of doing business. To operate in this environment, an established firm must constantly be on guard to protect its position as well as seize opportunities.

Environmental Monitoring. A firm must be alert to changes in the business environment; changes in customer preferences and needs, in competition, in the economy, and even in international events such as nationalism in Canada, NAFTA, OPEC machinations, changes in Eastern Europe and South Africa, and advances in Pacific Rim countries in productivity and quality control. IBM, Sears, and Harley Davidson failed to detect and act upon significant changes in their industries. Borden misjudged the dynamics of its industry. And Pepsi in South America failed to realize the intricacies of penetrating and protecting its several markets there.

How can a firm remain alert to subtle and insidious or more obvious changes? It must have sensors constantly monitoring the environment. The sensor may be a marketing or economic research department, but in many instances such a formal organizational entity is not really necessary to provide primary monitoring. Executive alertness is essential. Most changes do not occur suddenly and without warning. Feedback from customers, sales representatives, and suppliers; news of the latest relevant material and projections in business journals; and even simple observations of what is happening in stores, advertising, prices, and new technologies can provide information about the environment and how it is changing. Unfortunately, in the urgency of dealing with current operating problems, it is easy to overlook or disregard changing environmental factors that may affect present and future business.

Following are generalizations regarding vulnerability to competition:

1. Initial market advantage tends to be rather quickly countered by competitors.
2. Countering by competitors is more likely to occur when an innovation is involved than when the advantage involves more commonplace effective management and marketing techniques, such as superb customer service.
3. An easy-entry industry is particularly vulnerable to new and aggressive competition, especially if the market is expanding. In new industries, severe price competition usually will weed out the marginal firms.
4. Long-dominant firms tend to be vulnerable to upstart competitors because of their complacency, conservatism, and even conceit. They frequently are resistant to change and myopic about the environment.
5. Careful monitoring of performance at strategic control points and comparing similar operating units and their trends in various performance categories can detect weakening positions needing corrective action before situations become serious. (This will be discussed further in the next section.)
6. In expanding markets it is a delusion to judge performance by increases in sales rather than by market share; an increase in sales may hide a deteriorating competitive situation.
7. A no-growth policy, or a temporary absence from the marketplace, even if fully justified by extraordinary circumstances, invites competitive inroads.

Effective Organization

From our cases we can identify several organizational attributes that can help or hinder effectiveness:

Management by Exception. With diverse and far-flung operations, it becomes difficult to closely supervise all aspects. Successful managers therefore focus their attention on performances that deviate significantly from the expected at *strategic control points*. Subordinates can handle ordinary operations and less significant deviations. Thereby the manager is not overburdened with details.

Management by exception failed, however, with Maytag and its overseas Hoover division. The flaw lay in failing to monitor faulty promotional plans. By the time results were coming in, it was too late.

The Deadly Parallel. As an enterprise becomes larger, a particularly effective organizational structure is to establish operating units of comparable characteristics. Sales, expenses, and profits can then be readily compared, with both strong and weak performances identified so that appropriate action can be taken. Besides providing control and performance evaluation, this *deadly parallel* fosters intrafirm competition, and this can stimulate best efforts. For the deadly parallel to be used effectively, the operating units must be as equal as possible in sales potential. This is not difficult to achieve with retail units, since departments and stores can be divided into various sales volume categories—often designated as A, B, and C units—and operating results within the same volume category can be compared. While the deadly parallel is particularly effective for chain-store organizations, it can also be used with sales territories and certain other operating units where sales and applicable expenses and ratios can be directly measured and compared with similar units.

Lean and Mean. A new climate is sweeping our country's major corporations. In one sense it is good: It enhances their competitiveness. But it can be destructive. Microsoft and Southwest Airlines have been in the forefront of the lean-and-mean movement; IBM and Sears have moved to it, but with trauma to employees as downsizing had to be extreme and disruptive. Lean and mean firms develop flat organizations with few management layers, thus keeping overhead low, improving communication, involving employees in greater self-management, and fostering innovative-mindedness.

In contrast, we saw the organizational bloat of Borden and such behemoths as IBM and Sears before their turnarounds, with their many management levels, entrenched bureaucracies, and massive overhead. A virtual cause-and-effect relationship exists between the proportion of total overhead committed to administration/staff and the ability to cope with change and innovate. It is like trying to maneuver a huge ship: Bureaucratic weight slows the response time.

The problem with the lemming-like pursuit of the lean-and-mean structure is knowing how far to downsize without cutting into bone and muscle. As thousands of managers and staff specialists and college graduates can attest, questionable productivity gains have not always been worth the loss of jobs and the destruction of career paths.

Resistance to Change. People as well as organizations are naturally reluctant to embrace change. Change is disruptive; it destroys accepted ways of doing things and muddles familiar authority and responsibility patterns. It makes people uneasy because their routines are disrupted and their interpersonal relationships with subordinates, coworkers, and superiors are modified. Previously important positions may be downgraded or even eliminated, and people who view themselves as highly competent in a particular job may be forced to assume unfamiliar duties amid the fear that they cannot master the new assignments. When the change involves wholesale terminations in a major downsizing, as with IBM, Sears, Borden, and Euro Disney, the resistance and fear of change can become so great that personnel efficiency is seriously jeopardized.

Normal resistance to change can be combatted by good communication with participants about forthcoming changes. Without such communication, rumors and fears fester. Acceptance of change is facilitated if employees are involved as fully as possible in planning the changes, if their participation is solicited and welcomed, and if assurance can be given that positions will not be impaired, only changed. Gradual rather than abrupt changes also make a transition smoother.

In the final analysis, however, making needed changes and embracing different opportunities should not be delayed or canceled because of possible negative repercussions on the organization. If change is desirable, as it often is with long-established bureaucratic organizations, then it should be initiated in order to be competitive. Individuals and organizations can adapt to change—it just takes some time.

SPECIFIC MARKETING STRATEGY INSIGHTS

Strengths and Limitations of Advertising

We can gain several insights regarding the power and effectiveness of advertising, but we face some unanswered questions and contradictions. At the time of Coca-Cola's blunder with its New Coke, it was spending $100 million more for advertising than Pepsi, and all the while was losing market share. Advertising could not prevent the slow erosion of sales for Snapple. Such ineffectual outcomes cast doubts about the power of advertising.

However, the right theme can bring success, as witness Nike's great success with celebrity endorsements in creating an image irresistible to many of its customers. And the low-key, homey nonproduct advertising of Saturn succeeded in nurturing "the Saturn family." Maytag Hoover's promotional campaign certainly created great attention and interest, misguided though the plan was. The advertising blitz of Elizabeth Taylor brought Black Pearls back again. And how can we forget the success of the Joe Camel theme, despite public protests?

Thus we can see the great challenge of advertising. One never knows for sure how much should be spent to get the job done, to reach the planned objectives of perhaps increasing sales by a certain percentage or possibly gaining market share. However, despite the inability to measure directly the effectiveness of advertising, it is the brave—or foolhardy—executive who decides to stand pat in the face of aggressive increased promotions by competitors. We draw these conclusions:

> There is no assured correlation between expenditures for advertising and sales success. But the right theme or message can be powerful. In most cases, advertising can generate initial trial. But if the other elements of the marketing strategy are relatively unattractive, customers will not be won or retained.

Limitations of Marketing Research

Marketing research is usually touted as the key to better decision making and the mark of sophisticated professional management. It is commonly thought that the more money spent for marketing research, the less chance for a bad decision. But heavy use of marketing research does not guarantee the best decision, as we saw with Coca-Cola.

At best, marketing research increases the "batting average" of correct decisions—maybe only by a little, sometimes by quite a bit. To be effective, research must be current and unbiased. Marketplace attitudes can change radically if months elapse between the research and the product introduction. And the several million dollars in taste-test research for Coca-Cola hardly reassure us about the validity of even current marketing research. Admittedly, results of taste tests are difficult to rely on, simply because of the subjective nature of taste preferences. Still, the Coca-Cola research did not even uncover the latent and powerful loyalty toward tradition, and it gave a false "go" signal for the new flavor.

We do not imply that marketing research has little value. Most flawed studies would have been invaluable with better design and planning. One wonders whether better market research would not have enabled Disney to structure its pricing and other strategies more realistically to the market conditions facing its Euro Disney project.

Surprisingly, we see that many successful new ventures initially used little formal research. Microsoft, Southwest Airlines, Parma Pierogies, and Boston Beer apparently relied on entrepreneurial hunch rather than sophisticated research. Why have we not seen more extensive use of marketing research for new ventures? Consider the following major reasons:

1. Most of the founding entrepreneurs did not have marketing backgrounds and therefore were not familiar and confident with such research.
2. Available tools and techniques are not always appropriate to handle some problems and opportunities. There may be too many variables

to ascertain their full impact, and some of these will be intangible and incapable of precise measurement. Much research consists of collecting past and present data that, although helpful in predicting a stable future, are of little help in charting revolutionary new ventures. If the risks are higher without marketing research, these are often offset by the potential for great rewards.

The Importance of Price as an Offensive Weapon

We generally think of price promotions as the most aggressive marketing strategy and the one most desirable from the point of view of society. We have seen one notable marketing success that geared its major strategy on lower prices than competitors: Southwest Airlines. We saw another case where high prices were a real detriment in meeting performance goals: Euro Disney. And we saw low-price competition cutting into the profits of McDonald's. Still, in another case, Boston Beer, a highest price strategy was a key factor in its marketing success.

The major disadvantage of low prices as an offensive weapon is that other firms in the industry are almost forced to meet the price-cutter's prices—in other words, such a marketing strategy is easy to match. Consequently, when prices for an entire industry fall, no firm may have any particular advantage, and all suffer the effects in diminished profits. Thus, in many situations, competitive advantage is seldom won by price-cutting. But then there is Southwest Airlines, and an example not in this edition, Wal-Mart. Because of their greater operating efficiencies and lower overhead cost structures, such firms can realize good profits while most competitors do not even attempt to meet their prices.

In general, other marketing strategies are more successful for most firms—strategies such as better quality, better product and brand image, better service, and improved warranties. All are aspects of nonprice rather than price competition.

At the same time, we have to recognize that in new industries, which are characterized by rapid technological changes and production efficiencies, severe price competition can be expected—and is even necessary to weed out the host of marginal operations that hoped to cash in on a rapidly growing market. Even a substantial position in such an industry may not insulate a firm from price competition that can jeopardize its viability.

Analytical Tools for Marketing

We identified several of the most useful analytical tools for marketing decision-making. In Euro Disney we discussed breakeven analysis, a highly useful tool for making go/no go decisions about new ventures and alternative business strategies. In Maytag, the cost-benefit analysis was described that might have prevented the bungled promotion in England. And we encountered the SWOT analysis in the Sears and Southwest Airlines cases. While these analyses do not assure the best decisions, they do bring order and systematic thinking into the art of marketing decision-making.

Franchising

An important mode for great growth in expansion through more outlets is franchising. This was discussed more fully in the McDonald's and Parma Pierogies cases. The great growth comes from the release of the financial burden of company-owned outlets; rather, independent franchisees put up the money for new outlets. However, franchisee relations can present problems, as McDonald's is recently finding. And as Mary Poldruhi turns to franchising her Parma Pierogies concept, much depends on how selective she can be in finding competent and enthusiastic franchisees.

A Kinder, Gentler Stance?

In at least two cases, we could identify an arrogant mindset as leading to difficulties. The French did not appreciate this arrogance by Disney, and such arrogance eventually caught up with Aramony of United Way.

At the other extreme, is there room in today's competitive environment for a kinder, gentler stance by a business firm? While a firm normally comes into contact with a number of different parties, let us consider this question with regard to three: suppliers, distributors, and customers. (Relations with employees and the great controversy of downsizing are beyond the scope of this discussion.)

Relations with Suppliers and Distributors. With the movement toward just-in-time deliveries in the search for more efficiency and cost containment, manufacturers are placing greater demands on suppliers. Those who cannot meet these demands will usually lose out to competitors willing to do so. The big manufacturer or retailer can demand ever more from smaller suppliers, since it is in the power position and the loss of its business could be overwhelming. Most of the big retailers, particularly discounters such as Wal-Mart and Kmart as well as supermarket chains, are imposing "slotting fees" on some of their suppliers. A slotting fee is essentially a toll charged by the retailer for the use of its space; suppliers pay this up-front if they wish to be represented in the retailer's stores. Other demands include driving cost prices down to rock bottom even if this destroys the supplier's profits, and insisting that the supplier take responsibility for inventory control, provide special promotional support, and the like.

While the Wal-Marts and others argue that such use of clout leads to greater marketing efficiencies and lower consumer prices, it can be carried too far. The term *symbiotic relationship* is used to describe the relationship between the various channel of distribution members: all benefit from the success of the product and it should be to their mutual advantage to work together. The manufacturer and the distributor thus should represent a valued partnership.

The same idea should hold for the dealers or distributors of a powerful manufacturer. They are on the same side, they are not in competition with one another. Yet, we have seen four cases where a manufacturer created soured distributor relations. Elizabeth Arden tried to coerce, in this case, powerful department stores, and found them shunning Liz Taylor's Black Pearls. Pepsi was not closely attuned to its long-time Venezuela bottler and lost distribution in that entire country. Quaker Oats found an incompatibility with its acquired distributors for Snapple. And McDonald's callously disregarded concerns of its domestic franchisees in its eager quest to open more and more outlets.

Would not a kinder, gentler approach to the other members of the channel of distribution team have prevented or resolved these problems?

Relations with Customers. Most firms pay lip service to customer satisfaction. Some go much further in this regard than others. Few have gone as far as Saturn in creating a loyal and enthusiastic body of customers. A symbiotic relationship can also be seen as applying to manufacturer/customer relations: They both stand to win from highly satisfied customers. And again, isn't a kinder, gentler relationship a positive?

ETHICAL CONSIDERATIONS

We have examined more than a few cases dealing with ethical controversies. For example, ADM's indictment for price fixing and its more subtle efforts to gain special influence in the halls of government. Then there was Met Life's indictment for deceptive sales practices, the increasing public criticisms toward the tobacco industry, and the exposés of undesirable practices by Food Lion and United Way. While we cannot delve very deeply into social and ethical issues (for more depth of coverage, see R. F. Hartley, *Business Ethics* [New York: John Wiley & Sons], 1993), several insights are worth noting:

1. A firm can no longer disavow itself from the possibility of critical ethical appraisal. Activist groups may well publicize alleged misdeeds long before governmental regulators will. Legal actions may follow.

2. Public protests may take a colorful path, with marches, picketing, billboard whitewashing, and the like, and may enlist public and media support for their criticisms.

Should a firm attempt to resist or to defend itself? The overwhelming evidence is to the contrary. The bad press, the adversarial relations, and the effect on public image are hardly worth such a confrontation. The better course of action may be to back down as quietly as possible, repugnant though such an action may be to management convinced of the reasonableness of its position.

GENERAL INSIGHTS

Impact of One Person

In many of the cases, one person had a powerful impact on the organization. Phil Knight of Nike is an outstanding example. Less well-known is Jim Koch of Boston Beer. For turnaround accomplishments, Lou Gerstner of IBM stands tall, with Vaughn Beals of Harley Davidson no slouch. Bill Gates, the youthful founder of Microsoft and America's richest man, is perhaps the most well-known. The cover and feature article of *Fortune* magazine, May 2, 1994, highlighted Herb Kelleher, the CEO of Southwest Airlines: "Is Herb Kelleher America's Best CEO?"[2] Less well-known, but a small entrepreneur to be admired, is Mary Poldruhi of Parma Pierogies.

One person can also have a negative impact on an organization. William Aramony almost destroyed United Way by his high living and arrogance. Less well-known is Dwayne Andreas, the long-time CEO of ADM, who set the climate for illegalities both embarrassing and reprehensible. The impact of one person, for good or ill, is one of the recurring marvels of history, whether business history or world history.

Prevalence of Opportunities for Entrepreneurship Today

Despite the maturing of our economy and the growing size and power of many firms in many industries, abundant opportunity for entrepreneurship still exists today. Such opportunity is present not only for the change-maker or innovator, but also for the person who only seeks to do things a little better than existing, and complacent, competition.

Thousands of entrepreneurial successes are unheralded, although dozens have been widely publicized. While we dealt specifically with new business ventures in Part VI, other cases are not so many years away from their births: for example, Microsoft and Southwest Airlines. Opportunities are there for

---

[2]Kenneth Labich, "Is Herb Kelleher America's Best CEO?" *Fortune* (May 2, 1994): 44–52.

the dedicated. Venture capital to support promising new businesses has increased to well over $1 billion a year. New stock issues and new company formations are booming. But, as we saw with Mary Poldruhi and her Parma Pierogies, some entrepreneurs have successfully bypassed traditional sources of financing.

But entrepreneurship is not for everyone. The great venture capitalists look at the person, not the idea. Typically they distribute their seed money to resourceful people who are courageous enough to give up security for the unknown consequences of their embryonic ventures, who have great self-confidence, and who demonstrate a tremendous will to win.

CONCLUSION

We learn from mistakes and from successes, although every marketing problem seems cast in a unique setting. One author has likened marketing strategy to military strategy:

> Strategies which are flexible rather than static embrace optimum use and offer the greatest number of alternative objectives. A good commander knows that he cannot control his environment to suit a prescribed strategy. Natural phenomena pose their own restraints to strategic planning, whether physical, geographic, regional, or psychological and sociological.[3]

He later adds:

> Planning leadership recognizes the unpleasant fact that, despite every effort, the war may be lost. Therefore, the aim is to retain the maximum number of facilities and the basic organization. Indicators of a deteriorating and unsalvageable total situation are, therefore, mandatory. . . . No possible combination of strategies and tactics, no mobilization of resources . . . can supply a magic formula which guarantees victory; it is possible only to increase the probability of victory.[4]

Thus, we can pull two concepts from military strategy to help guide marketing strategy: the desirability of flexibility in an unknown or changing environment and the idea that a basic core should be maintained in crisis. The first suggests that the firm should be prepared for adjustments in strategy as conditions warrant. The second suggests that there is a basic core of a firm's business that should be unchanging; it should be the final bastion to

[3]Myron S. Heidingsfield, *Changing Patterns in Marketing* (Boston: Allyn & Bacon, 1968): 11.
[4]Heidingsfield, *Changing Patterns in Marketing*, 11.

fall back on for regrouping if necessary. Harley Davidson stolidly maintained its core position, even though it let expansion opportunities slither away. Sears and IBM had solid cores that they were able to maintain and from which they could mount new attacks.

In regard to the basic core of a firm, every viable firm has some distinctive function or "ecological niche" in the business environment:

> Every business firm occupies a position which is in some respects unique. Its location, the product it sells, its operating methods, or the customers it serves tend to set it off in some degree from every other firm. Each firm competes by making the most of its individuality and its special character.[5]

Woe to the firm that loses its ecological niche.

QUESTIONS

1. Design a program aimed at mistake avoidance. Be as specific, as creative, and as complete as possible.
2. Would you advise a firm to be an imitator or an innovator? Why?
3. "There is no such thing as a sustainable competitive advantage." Discuss.
4. How would you build controls into an organization to ensure that similar mistakes do not happen in the future?
5. Array as many pros and cons of entrepreneurship as you can. Which do you see as most compelling?
6. Do you agree with the thought expressed in this chapter that a firm confronted with strong criticism should abandon the product or the way of doing business? Why or why not?
7. We have suggested that the learning insights discussed in this chapter and elsewhere in the book are transferable to other firms and other times. Do you completely agree with this? Why or why not?
8. Do you agree or disagree with the author's contention that a kinder, gentler stance toward channel members would be desirable and profitable? Why or why not?

HANDS-ON EXERCISE

Your firm has had a history of reacting rather than anticipating changes in the industry. As the staff assistant to the CEO, you have been assigned

[5]Alderson, *Marketing Behavior*, 101.

the responsibility of developing adequate sensors of the marketplace. How will you go about developing such sensors?

TEAM DEBATE EXERCISE

Debate the extremes of forecasting for an innovative new product: conservative versus aggressive.